The 100 Greatest Cricketers

Author's Note

I am very grateful to New Holland Publishers, first for asking me to be involved in the original project in 2006 and then for backing this updated edition. My thanks also go to Bruce Kennedy for the faith he showed in me, to Steve Waugh, for his unwavering support over the years and for writing the foreword to this book, to Getty Images, who provided all the photographs and as always were extremely helpful, and to a group of perceptive sports-minded people — Mike Coward, Ian Heads, Phil Jennings, Neil Marks, James Nicholls and Ian Russell — who were always willing to offer comment, friendship, argument and guidance as I tried to finalise my list of the top 100 cricketers.

Each chapter includes a brief statistical summary of the relevant player's career. For cricketers who played little or no one-day international cricket, records in Test and first-class matches are included. For more 'modern' players, records are for Tests and one-day internationals. These statistics are correct as at June 30, 2009.

Geoff Armstrong

First published in Australia in 2006 by
New Holland Publishers (Australia) Pty Ltd
Revised and updated 2009.
Sydney • Auckland • London • Cape Town
1/66 Gibbes Street Chatswood NSW 2067 Australia
218 Lake Road Northcote Auckland New Zealand
86 Edgware Road London W2 2EA United Kingdom
80 McKenzie Street Cape Town 8001 South Africa
Copyright © 2009 in text: Geoff Armstrong
Copyright © 2009 New Holland Publishers (Australia) Pty Ltd
All rights reserved. No part of this publication may be reproduced,
stored in a retrieval system or transmitted, in any form or by any means,
electronic, mechanical, photocopying, recording or otherwise, without the
prior written permission of the publishers and copyright holders.
10 9 8 7 6 5 4 3 2 1
National Library of Australia Cataloguing-in-Publication entry

    Armstrong, Geoff.
    100 greatest cricketers / Geoff Armstrong.
    Rev. ed.

ISBN: 9781741109436 (hbk.)

    Bibliography.
    Cricket players–Biography.
    Cricket–History.
    796.3580922
Publisher: Fiona Schultz
Managing Editor: Martin Ford
Designer: Stew O'Brien
Printer: SNP/Leefung Printing Co. Ltd (China)
All photos courtesy of Getty Images.

The 100 Greatest Cricketers

Revised and Updated

Geoff Armstrong

Foreword by Steve Waugh

If ever there was a book that required a cricket tragic to pen it, this is it. How could anyone possibly digest reams of statistics, analyse the technical and mental aspects of each player, compare cricketers from varying eras, and make sense of match and media reports to finally arrive at the top 100 players of all time, and then assemble them into nine teams?

Luckily, such a creature exists. I've been fortunate to have worked closely with this man on all of my 12 books. Geoff Armstrong is a walking cricket encyclopedia capable of churning out views, opinions and 'gee whiz' information on just about every cricketer ever to lace on a boot, and back that material up with figures that few others would know about. I like the fact that he hasn't played the game at the top level, nor mixed exclusively with the cricket fraternity, as it allows him to be unbiased in his judgments and detached from the hype that surrounds certain players.

In surveying Geoff's selections it is hard to argue that he hasn't put a lot of thought into each and every position, and he seems to believe he is pretty correct in his assertions. However, the beauty of this book is that your opinion counts, too. You don't have to agree with his selections; instead, you can read his thoughts and then in your mind counter his line-ups with your own. I'm sure there will be heated debate about many of Geoff's choices.

I find it hard to believe, for example, that there is not room for Gordon Greenidge, Courtney Walsh, Anil Kumble, Shaun Pollock, Stuart MacGill or Jack Russell in the final 100. Jack, to me, was a victim of some misguided selection policies during his career, which meant he didn't play as much Test cricket as he should have. He was blessed with phenomenal hands and intuition that made him the equal of Ian Healy in my era. Stuart was simply unlucky, having to compete against the genius of Shane Warne for a position in Australia's Test line-up — if he had been allowed to fully showcase his skills more regularly at the highest level, he would have surely got a guernsey somewhere in this list.

How could you leave Jacques Kallis, statistically Test cricket's greatest ever all-rounder, in the Eighth XI? I do think that the Fifth XI would be very pleased to accommodate a dynamic duo such as Ricky Ponting and Barry Richards in their batting order, and that the Seventh XI would be very happy to have a couple of fair quicks named Andy Roberts and Michael Holding to open the bowling. Would the Second XI beat the First XI?

What is certain is that while it is near impossible to judge one era against another, suffice to say that a great player from the 20th century would be great in the 21st century, and so on. Having said this, there is no doubt that through its history, the game has changed dramatically. Just before the first edition of this book was published, I was watching a Test match from 1984-85, Australia versus the West Indies at the Adelaide Oval, and Gordon Greenidge was caught hooking on the deep fine-leg fence for 95. Today, that same shot would be a six by 20 metres because of the roped boundary and the batsman would be saluting a standing ovation for his hundred.

I congratulate Geoff on the dedication and professionalism he has applied to this task, and hope you, the reader, enjoy the challenge of selecting your own teams as you debate his selections with your friends.

Steve Waugh

Contents

Introduction 10

The First XI
- No. 1 Don Bradman 16
- No. 2 WG Grace 19
- No. 3 Garry Sobers 22
- No. 4 Shane Warne 25
- No. 5 Imran Khan 28
- No. 6 Jack Hobbs 31
- No. 7 Malcolm Marshall 34
- No. 8 Sachin Tendulkar 37
- No. 9 Sydney Barnes 40
- No. 10 Adam Gilchrist 42
- No. 11 Graeme Pollock 45

The Second XI
- No. 12 Dennis Lillee 50
- No. 13 Viv Richards 53
- No. 14 Richard Hadlee 56
- No. 15 Wally Hammond 59
- No. 16 Fred Spofforth 62
- No. 17 Len Hutton 65
- No. 18 Ian Botham 68
- No. 19 Victor Trumper 71
- No. 20 Alan Knott 74
- No. 21 Brian Lara 77
- No. 22 Muttiah Muralitharan 80

The Third XI
- No. 23 Sunil Gavaskar 84
- No. 24 Greg Chappell 87
- No. 25 Bill O'Reilly 90
- No. 26 Frank Worrell 93
- No. 27 Wasim Akram 96
- No. 28 Kapil Dev 99
- No. 29 George Headley 102
- No. 30 George Lohmann 105
- No. 31 Jack Blackham 107
- No. 32 Glenn McGrath 110
- No. 33 Herbert Sutcliffe 113

The Fourth XI
- No. 34 Keith Miller 118
- No. 35 & 36 Everton Weekes and Clyde Walcott 121
- No. 37 Allan Border 125
- No. 38 Alan Davidson 128
- No. 39 Godfrey Evans 131
- No. 40 Steve Waugh 134
- No. 41 Wilfred Rhodes 137
- No. 42 Curtly Ambrose 139
- No. 43 Jim Laker 142
- No. 44 Archie MacLaren 145

The Fifth XI
- No. 45 Frank Woolley 150
- No. 46 Ricky Ponting 153
- No. 47 Denis Compton 156
- No. 48 Ray Lindwall 159
- No. 49 Kumar Shri Ranjitsinhji 162
- No. 50 Richie Benaud 165
- No. 51 Fred Trueman 168

No. 52 Barry Richards	171
No. 53 Arthur Shrewsbury	174
No. 54 Alec Bedser	176
No. 55 Syed Kirmani	179

The Sixth XI
No. 56 Javed Miandad	184
No. 57 Harold Larwood	187
No. 58 Mike Procter	190
No. 59 Rahul Dravid	193
No. 60 Charlie Macartney	196
No. 61 Joel Garner	199
No. 62 Geoff Boycott	202
No. 63 & 64 Bishan Bedi and Bhagwat Chandrasekhar	205
No. 65 Les Ames	209
No. 66 Virender Sehwag	211

The Seventh XI
No. 67 Neil Harvey	216
No. 68 Charlie Turner	219
No. 69 Ken Barrington	222
No. 70 Monty Noble	225
No. 71 & 72 Andy Roberts and Michael Holding	228
No. 73 Bob Simpson	232
No. 74 Johnny Briggs	235
No. 75 Rohan Kanhai	237
No. 76 Wasim Bari	240
No. 77 Matthew Hayden	243

The Eighth XI
No. 78 John Snow	248
No. 79 Clem Hill	251
No. 80 Ian Healy	254
No. 81 Waqar Younis	257
No. 82 Dudley Nourse	260
No. 83 Graham Gooch	263
No. 84 Hugh Trumble	266
No. 85 Peter May	268
No. 86 Billy Murdoch	271
No. 87 Fazal Mahmood	274
No. 88 Jacques Kallis	277

The Ninth XI
No. 89 Stan McCabe	282
No. 90 Clive Lloyd	285
No. 91 & 92 Bill Lockwood and Tom Richardson	288
No. 93 Vijay Hazare	292
No. 94 Jeff Thomson	295
No. 95 Andrew Flintoff	298
No. 96 Graeme Smith	301
No. 97 Andy Flower	304
No. 98 Kumar Sangakkara	307
No. 99 Arthur Mailey	310

The Hundreth Man
| No. 100 Doug Walters | 313 |

| Further Reading | 316 |
| Index | 322 |

Introduction

From the moment I started writing this book I found myself bouncing ideas and opinions off cricket people I know and respect. Everyone I approached was very helpful, but none more so than the former Sheffield Shield cricketer, writer and all-round fine bloke, Neil Marks.

One day, as I was explaining why I'd preferred Arthur Mailey to Clarrie Grimmett — and after Neil had supported my decision to leave Bill Ponsford out by recalling a story his father Alec, a former New South Wales Shield batsman, had once told him about Ponsford throwing his wicket away on a wet MCG pitch rather than stand up to Sam Everett and Alan Fairfax — he suddenly said, 'Run that first team of yours by me again.'

'Grace and Hobbs to open the batting,' I replied confidently. It had taken a while to settle on my top XI, but now I truly felt that I'd nailed it. 'Bradman, Tendulkar, Pollock, Sobers, Gilchrist, Imran, Marshall, Warne and Barnes.'

'No Miller, eh?' was my good friend's immediate reaction. 'And what's your second side?'

'Hutton and Trumper — I don't care how good Gavaskar was against the West Indies, I've got to go for Victor — Viv Richards, Hammond, Lara, Botham, Knott, Hadlee, DK Lillee, Spofforth and Murali.'

There was silence for a moment, and then Neil said bluntly, 'That side would beat your first team.'

He seemed very keen on the idea of Dennis Lillee bowling to Dr Grace. (Neil seemed even more excited about the thought of Jeff Thomson charging in at WG, but that confrontation will have to wait for another game!) My team has Bradman and Sobers and Gilchrist and Warne. I loved the thought of 'Gilly' striding out to join Sobers in the middle after The Don had scored his hundred ... and then the world's greatest ever leg-spinner could go to work on the final day. I was happy to stick with my first XI, though Neil had certainly made me think. Constantly revising my opinions of the game's most famous players, and learning about just how accomplished (and, in rare cases, how overrated) they were or are, was the real joy of this project.

When the publishers, New Holland, approached me about coming up with a book of the top 100 cricketers of all time my initial reaction was to decline, on the basis that it is impossible to produce such a definitive line-up. I had been involved with a TV documentary series and book, ESPN's *Legends of Cricket*, in 2002, but I had not been part of the selection process that led to ESPN nominating their 25 greatest players (Bradman, Sobers, Viv Richards, Warne and Hobbs were their top five). But then I thought about how much fun the process would be — not just the debates I would have in my own mind but also the arguments I'd have with critics who would quickly say, 'You can't leave that player out!' or, 'This player has to be ranked higher than that!' Of course, there is no perfect measure on which to base selections — those who say you cannot compare eras do have a point — but there is also no yardstick to 'prove' you wrong, which means as a means of generating a debate among friends the subject is fantastic.

The concept I came up with for this Top 100 was to pick nine teams, and then make my favourite all-time player the '100th man'. Each team includes two openers, three middle-order batsmen, an all-rounder, a wicketkeeper and four bowlers, at least one of whom was a spinner. Previous studies of all-time greats have tended to ignore wicketkeepers, so this system sets that mistake straight. Only those men who have played Test cricket were considered, on the basis that this elite form of the game has always been the ultimate measure of a player's quality. This meant that acclaimed players from the 18th century, such as Edward 'Lumpy' Stevens, the bowler so accurate he forced the introduction of a third (middle) stump, were not considered. Neither were Fuller Pilch and Alfred Mynn, greats from the 'round-arm' era of the early to middle 1800s, or the remarkable 'Johnny' Mullagh, star of the Aboriginal tour of England in 1868. Also sadly precluded by this embargo were the South Africans, Vintcent van der Bijl, Garth Le Roux and Clive Rice, whose international careers were stifled by the 'apartheid' boycott that ran from 1971 to 1992.

The teams selected for the first edition of this book, published in 2006, in proposed batting order, were:

First XI: WG Grace, Jack Hobbs, Don Bradman, Sachin Tendulkar, Graeme Pollock, Garry Sobers, Adam Gilchrist, Imran Khan, Malcolm Marshall, Shane Warne, Sydney Barnes

Second XI: Len Hutton, Victor Trumper, Viv Richards, Wally Hammond, Brian Lara, Ian Botham, Alan Knott, Richard Hadlee, Dennis Lillee, Fred Spofforth, Muttiah Muralitharan

Third XI: Sunil Gavaskar, Herbert Sutcliffe, George Headley, Greg Chappell, Frank Worrell, Kapil Dev, Wasim Akram, Jack Blackham, George Lohmann, Bill O'Reilly, Glenn McGrath

Fourth XI: Archie MacLaren, Clyde Walcott, Everton Weekes, Allan Border, Steve Waugh, Keith Miller, Wilfred Rhodes, Alan Davidson, Jim Laker, Godfrey Evans, Curtly Ambrose

Fifth XI: Barry Richards, Arthur Shrewsbury, Ricky Ponting, KS Ranjitsinhji, Denis Compton, Frank Woolley, Richie Benaud, Syed Kirmani, Ray Lindwall, Fred Trueman, Alec Bedser

Sixth XI: Virender Sehwag, Geoff Boycott, Rahul Dravid, Charlie Macartney, Javed Miandad, Mike Procter, Les Ames, Harold Larwood, Joel Garner, Bishan Bedi, Bhagwat Chandrasekhar

Seventh XI: Bob Simpson, Matthew Hayden, Rohan Kanhai, Neil Harvey, Ken Barrington, Monty Noble, Johnny Briggs, Wasim Bari, Andy Roberts, Michael Holding, Charlie Turner

Eighth XI: Graham Gooch, Billy Murdoch, Clem Hill, Peter May, Dudley Nourse, Jacques Kallis, Ian Healy, Hugh Trumble, Fazal Mahmood, John Snow, Waqar Younis

Ninth XI: Stan McCabe, Herbie Taylor, Vijay Hazare, Clive Lloyd, Inzamam-ul-Haq, Andy Flower, Andrew Flintoff, Bill Lockwood, Jeff Thomson, Tom Richardson, Arthur Mailey

100th Man: Doug Walters

For this edition, I have 'dropped' just two players — Herbie Taylor and Inzamam-ul-Haq — and replaced them with South Africa's Graeme Smith and Sri Lanka's Kumar Sangakkara. Smith opens the batting for the Ninth XI instead of Taylor, and Sangakkara will bat at No. 3, with Hazare and Lloyd each moving down one place in the batting order. I thought about relegating Flintoff, on the basis that his form since the 2005 Ashes series no longer entitles him to a place in such elite company, but the truth is no alternative all-rounder has emerged in the last three years to take his position.

Performances in limited-over cricket were considered when comparing players who appeared after 1979, but great skill in the shorter game was not in itself enough for a player to make the grade. Thus, Michael Bevan, who averaged 29.07 in Test cricket but 53.53 in one-day internationals, was omitted, but at the same time Sachin Tendulkar, Wasim Akram, Steve Waugh and Joel Garner improved their rankings because of their performances in ODIs. It is, in my view, too early for the moment to use Twenty20 matches as a guide to a cricketer's status, no matter how explosive a batsman such as India's Yuvraj Singh or Pakistan's Shahid Afridi might be in the most abbreviated form of the game.

In the main, the players selected built career records that compare most favourably with their contemporaries. Further, the assumption was made that players who were great in their era would be similarly special in any other. Sure, a bowler such as Sydney Barnes, a batsman such as Arthur Shrewsbury, or a keeper such as Jack Blackham would have to adapt to succeed in the 21st century, but it seems a fair bet that with their talent, dedication and toughness they'd go all right. The men in this Top 100 all developed a habit of producing fantastic performances for extended periods during their careers (as distinct from in just one series or year). This is one of the reasons why WG Grace, who stood out among his teammates and opponents as distinctly as did Don Bradman two generations later, is ranked as high as No. 2. In contrast, players who saved their best work for Tests against inferior opposition or when conditions were kind were marked harshly; hence the absence of Zaheer Abbas. Also, just because a modern-day player has accumulated a lot of runs or wickets or completed a record number of wicketkeeping dismissals does not automatically win him a place. Mark Boucher's achievement in completing more than 400 dismissals in both Tests and ODIs is considerable, and he has shown many times that he is a very good keeper and he has also averaged nearly 30 with the bat in Tests. However, I have never thought he was as good or as combative a gloveman as Rod Marsh, and there is no place for Marsh in this Top 100. Anil Kumble took 619 Test wickets, but as with Boucher I believe this is proof of his enormous tenacity and durability, rather than greatness. In my view, Kumble is not entitled to be ranked ahead of bowlers such as Bhagwat Chandrasekhar, Hugh Trumble, Johnny Briggs and Arthur Mailey, who all make this Top 100, or even Abdul Qadir and Derek Underwood, who did not.

Similarly, Courtney Walsh is not among the fast bowlers selected. (Neither are any of Chaminda Vaas, Makhaya Ntini, Allan Donald, Shaun Pollock, Bob Willis or Brett Lee, even though each of them has taken more than 300 Test wickets.) In fact, though, the West Indian fast man I had most trouble omitting was Wes Hall, such a key figure in the Windies' rise to the top of world cricket in the 1960s. But I also wanted to recognise two champion English bowlers from before World War I, Tom Richardson and Bill Lockwood, and also Jeff Thomson and Waqar Younis. So Hall misses out, as do a number of other outstanding opening bowlers — such as Walsh, Jack Gregory, Brian Statham and Graeme McKenzie. This situation reflects how difficult it is to confine a list of the game's finest players to just a century. Before you complain that your favourite is ranked too low, ponder who is classed above him.

It was important in developing this Top 100 not to fall into the trap of picking players just because it has become fashionable to rate them highly. It is actually astonishing how some men's reputations have grown as the memories of their playing days recede, while other more accomplished or important cricketers have been all but forgotten. Don Tallon, the much acclaimed Australian wicketkeeper in Bradman's 'Invincibles' of 1948, is a classic example of this. From the day Sir Donald first said that Tallon was the greatest wicketkeeper he ever saw, the Queenslander became everyone's choice as Australia's No. 1. But, in reality, to rank Tallon ahead of Blackham, cricket's first great keeper (who played his last Test 14 years before Bradman was born), is absurd. Similarly, as it became almost a habit to talk up the virtues of Clarrie Grimmett (a campaign led for the best part of 50 years by Grimmett's old spin-bowling partner Bill O'Reilly), everyone forgot that no less than Sir Jack Hobbs thought Arthur Mailey was Grimmett's superior. I also had to be careful not to discard a player such as Graham Gooch just because they had not been overly successful against my home country, Australia. This said, had England's Ted Dexter scored more than two centuries in 19 Tests against Australia he might have won a place in the Ninth XI's middle-order.

With some players — most notably Trumper, Frank Woolley and KS Ranjitsinhji — it is impossible to ignore the universal admiration their cricket generated when they were at their peak. Trumper's batting average hardly entitles him to a place among the 20 greatest cricketers of all time, but the way teammates and opponents revered him makes him a certainty. The glamour and excitement a cricketer can bring to the game was also a factor in the rankings, which means that the dynamic Virender Sehwag is rated higher than most might expect, while Charlie Macartney, who liked to aim a drive back at the bowler's head just to let him know who was boss, is put before Neil Harvey and Clem Hill, even though on statistics alone a case can be made that either or both of these two great Australian left-handers was superior.

Sehwag, born on October 20, 1978, was the youngest man in my original Top 100. That honour is now passed on to Graeme Smith, who was born on February 1, 1981, which in a way is appropriate, given all that Smith has achieved as a young South African captain. His effort in being named his country's captain at just 22, and then holdng the job with a fair measure of success for six years and more, is unprecedented in the history of the game and as an achievement should not be underrated. Still, 21st-century cricketers such as Sehwag and Smith, Flintoff and Sangakkara (and other modern stars such as Ricky Ponting, Kevin Pietersen, Mitchell Johnson, Mahela Jayawardene and Dale Steyn), create a dilemma for a study such as this, because their careers are most likely far from over. Will the years ahead add to these players' reputations, as they did with men such as Richard Hadlee and Jim Laker, who were so effective late in their careers, or will their records fall away, in the manner of, say, Arthur Morris or Lawrence Rowe? During the past three years, Sehwag's Test batting average has dropped and jumped from 53 to 49 back to 53 down to 50, but for all his inconsistency I have left him in the Sixth XI. It still seems that all he needs is confidence to play like a champion, but as India's selectors lost some faith in him so, it seemed, he lost a little faith in himself.

Of course, confidence comes in many forms, from Denis Compton's panache and Keith Miller's devil-may-care, to Viv Richards' remarkable aura and Steve Waugh's incessant insistence that he and his teammates back themselves, whatever the cost. I know I can't be as confident as a great Test cricketer that my selections are 100 per cent correct, but in every instance I am more than prepared to argue my case. For it is not the intention of this book to settle friendly arguments so much as to start them…'I mean, Neil, do you really think that Lillee was a better bowler than Marshall? That Hadlee was better than Imran? That Miller was a better all-rounder than Botham and Kapil Dev?'

Geoff Armstrong

The 100 Greatest Cricketers

Don Bradman

WG Grace

The First

Graeme Pollock

Adam Gilchrist

The First XI

Garry Sobers

Shane Warne

Imran Khan

XI

Jack Hobbs

Sydney Barnes

Sachin Tendulkar

Malcolm Marshall

The 100 Greatest Cricketers

No. 1 Don Bradman

What is most compelling about Don Bradman's Test batting record is not that he stands out from his contemporaries and those that came before him, but that he also overwhelms all who followed in his wake. It was not a benchmark he established, more a dream. His batting average, built over 20 years from the Australian summer of 1928–29, is 99.94 runs per innings. Only five others from between the wars played 40 or more Test innings and averaged over 50: England's Herbert Sutcliffe (60.73), Wally Hammond (58.46), Jack Hobbs (56.95), the West Indies' George Headley (60.83) and South Africa's Dudley Nourse (53.82). The next best Australians were Bill Ponsford (48.23) and Stan McCabe (48.21). It couldn't have been that the pitches were dead flat for Bradman, but not for everyone else.

As at June 30, 2009, the closest to Bradman of all those to play even 20 Test innings was South Africa's Graeme Pollock, at 60.97. Three batsmen — Pollock, Headley and Sutcliffe — averaged between 60 and 61; another nine — only one of whom, Ricky Ponting, is Australian — averaged between 56 and 60. Of the 61 batsmen who had made 15 or more Test centuries, only the West Indies' Clyde Walcott (15 centuries in 74 innings) played fewer than Bradman's 80 Test innings. Yet only Sachin Tendulkar (42 in 261), Ricky Ponting (37 in 221), Sunil Gavaskar (34 in 214), Brian Lara (34 in 232), Steve Waugh (32 in 260), Jacques Kallis (31 in 221) and Matthew Hayden (30 in 184) had scored more hundreds than The Don's 29. Bradman averaged a century every 2.76 Test innings, a double century every 6.67 Test innings. Only 16 other players with 50 innings in Test history have averaged better than a single century every 6.67 Test innings. He scored 12 double centuries in Test matches; next best is nine by Lara and seven by Wally Hammond, who played 140 innings. Only twice did Bradman score a century in a Test that Australia lost, and these were his first and third Test hundreds. To say he was worth two players a side is to do him a disservice.

Bradman was 20 years old when he made his first two Test centuries, the fifth youngest Test centurion to come out of Australia (after the teenagers Archie Jackson, Neil Harvey and Doug Walters, and Phillip Hughes). By that stage, cricket sages could see that he would become one of Australia's finest players, but no one then could have foreseen that he would be recognised, at the time of his death in 2001, as the most famous and distinguished Australian of them all. He had become cricket's greatest batsman with a nerveless, aggressive and entertaining style. His coaching classic, *The Art Of Cricket* (published in 1958) confirms that he understood the game as well as anyone, a fact reflected in his batting after World War II when he actually averaged slightly more in Tests than he had pre-war. Whether hooking, cutting or driving, he kept the ball on the ground, and he never seemed to get caught going back when he should have been forward, or vice versa.

The classic Bradman pull shot which became one of his trademarks.

The First XI

However, the secret to what really set him apart may have been revealed in *Remembering Bradman*, edited by Margaret Geddes in 2002. As Wisden Australia noted in its review of that book, Bradman is quoted as saying, 'I didn't realise I was a freak until after I retired. You know, I've never run around an oval in my life, but I never once got out batting because I was tired.' It is true that if you go right though his cricket career, innings by innings, it is very rare to find an instance where he threw his innings away, rarer still to find a suggestion that he 'lost concentration'. The great cricket writer Neville Cardus once asked him to explain his success, and he replied, 'I treat every ball as though it was the first ball, whether I've just broken my duck or whether I've just passed the double century. And I never consider the possibility that anyone can get me out.' If you marry that single-minded attitude, an excellent technique, a superior understanding of the game, a love of the sport, flash reflexes, great ambition, an unflappable temperament and sufficient courage to a supreme level of natural fitness, maybe then you have a batsman with a century average.

A rare photograph of Bradman the bowler, at the nets in 1938 during his first Ashes tour as Australian captain.

You do need a lot to explain why The Don was always phenomenal. From 1930 on, he almost invariably batted at No. 3, or occasionally at No. 4, the prime position in the batting order. Perhaps you could knock him for only playing Test cricket in Australia and England — unlike the well-travelled warriors of today — but that was hardly his fault, for his country didn't play Test matches in the Caribbean or on the sub-continent until the 1950s. Illness stopped him going to South Africa with the Australian team in 1935-36. No other batsman in cricket history has ever had a provocative strategy such as bodyline devised for his benefit — and there is no doubt the English bowlers targeted him — yet even during that acrimonious season, Bradman topped the Test batting averages for either side.

It wasn't until he made 232 at The Oval in 1930, his ninth Test, that he first pushed his Test batting average over three figures, and it stayed there for just one innings, because he was dismissed for four in the first Test of the 1930-31 home series against the West Indies. A season later, when the South Africans toured Australia, Bradman's 299 not out in the fourth Test in Adelaide forced his average from 99.83 to 112.29, the highest it would ever reach. The average remained over 100 for 10 innings, but then didn't get that high again until the second Ashes Test after World War II, in Sydney when he scored 234. Had Bradman retired after the 1938 England tour, his career average would have been 97.94. Following the war, the average always hovered around the 100 mark, never much over or under. His 173 not out at Leeds in the fourth Test of 1948 pushed it up to 101.39, with just The Oval Test to go. After England were bowled out for 52 and the first Australian wicket didn't fall until 117, the likelihood was that Bradman would bat only once, so he went needing just that boundary to preserve the century average. Unfortunately, a googly from Eric Hollies — and many argue the emotion of his farewell innings — got the better of him.

Being from the bush (he was raised in Bowral, 100km south-west of Sydney) and working class, he played out the dreams of thousands of Australians. At just 173cm, slim but wiry, first impressions might have suggested he was fragile, but then his athleticism in the field and the fours careering from his bat revealed he was indeed a tough and surprisingly powerful competitor. Most cricket fans love an underdog who wins through, and Bradman won through time and again. He was unique, almost infallible. When he was out second ball in his final Test innings, he finally proved he was human. That duck completed the legend.

Three cheers before his final Test innings. Sadly, he was out second ball for a duck.

What is often forgotten about Bradman is that he was also a brilliant outfielder. If he'd bowled as well, it just wouldn't have been fair. Victor Trumper, Frank Woolley, Barry Richards, Greg Chappell and Brian Lara may have been more stylish batsmen than Don Bradman, but batting is much more about scoring runs than it is impressing judges as gymnasts and divers try to do. Bradman averaged substantially more than half as much again per Test innings than any other batsman in the sport's history, a statistic beyond argument when it comes to who might have been the world's best batsman. Whether that makes him more valuable than the supreme allrounder, or even the greatest bowler, is another matter, but it would be a very brave selection panel who would pick someone else first, if that meant the other team's selectors could then take him from you.

DON BRADMAN (AUSTRALIA)
Test Cricket

Tests	Inn	NO	Runs	HS	Ave	100	50	Ct	Balls	Runs	Wkts	Ave	Best	5/	10/
52	80	10	6996	334	99.94	29	13	32	160	72	2	36.00	1-8	—	—

First-Class Cricket

Mat	Inn	NO	Runs	HS	Ave	100	50	Ct	Balls	Runs	Wkts	Ave	Best	5/	10/
234	338	43	28067	452*	95.14	117	69	131	2114	1367	36	37.97	3-35	—	

The First XI

WG Grace

No. 2

It's possible to mount the case for Dr William Gilbert Grace as cricket's greatest player on two fronts. First, there is the plain fact that he *made* cricket, or least the 'modern' version of it; his runs, wickets and reputation attracted athletes to the sport, fans to the ground, countrymen and women to the culture. Secondly, there are his records — all of them — that put him as far above his contemporaries as Sir Donald Bradman's batting statistics stand alone today. 'WG' was not known as 'The Champion' for nothing.

The reason this study puts Bradman in first place is that while many of the Englishman's stats were eventually matched and then bettered by champions of future eras, no batsman in the nearly 60 years since The Don's retirement has got even close to his remarkable level of consistent and colossal run-getting. Even so, for many years in England some considered it almost heresy to suggest that WG had been usurped as No. 1. As late as 1997, the long-time correspondent for *The Times*, John Woodcock, picked his top 100 cricketers and put Grace on top. Elsewhere, many modern experts will argue that Garry Sobers was the greater allrounder — but as well as scoring more than 54,000 first-class runs, 126 hundreds and 254 fifties, WG also took more than 2800 first-class wickets, captured five wickets in an innings 246 times, 10 wickets in a match 66 times. He was also a fine cover field in his youth, moved mainly to point later on, and a sure catch. He is reputed to have once thrown a cricket ball 122 yards, and definitely threw it 116, 117 and 118 yards in an exhibition at the Oval in 1868 that also involved the Australian Aboriginal touring side.

In the 1860s, when Grace began his first-class career, cricket was more a pastime for the upper classes and prepared batting wickets were very much a thing of the future. Later, largely on the back of WG's influence, it would become a truly national sport. Cricket might not have been as competitive then as it is today, but in its own way, it was just as awkward. Uneven pitches should have brought the champion batsman back to the field, but for WG it seems to have had the opposite effect — he played first-class cricket for 43 years and was clearly the dominant player and personality in the game for more than 30 of them. In 1871 he scored 10 centuries and 2739 first-class runs at 78.25. No one else scored more than one century or averaged more than 45. Between 1868 and 1880 (the year of his Test debut), he topped the first-class averages 10 times, including seven years straight to 1874. Between 1868 and 1876 he scored 54 first-class hundreds in England. No one else scored even 10. In the decade 1871 to 1880, Grace averaged more than 49 in first-class cricket when no one else could do better than 26, or total even a third of Grace's runs. He also took a little matter of 1174 wickets in those 10 years, second highest across the country behind Alfred Shaw.

'The Champion'.

Nowhere throughout his career did Grace dominate the sport more than in the time-honoured Gentlemen v Players matches. In the years before Test cricket, this was the English game's premier fixture. In the 35 years before his first appearance in these matches, the amateur Gentlemen had won just seven times; of their next 50 games they won 31 and lost seven to their professional rivals. Over 41 years he made 15 hundreds for the Gentlemen, and took 271 wickets. Of all his hundreds in these matches, perhaps his first was his finest — 134 out of 201 in 1868, in an innings in which none of his comrades was able to reach double figures.

Grace's influence on the art of batting was considerable, as he stuck to principles of batsmanship that we now take for granted but at the time had hardly been thought of. 'I have always believed in footwork,' he explained to disciples. His game was built around a well-constructed, well-rehearsed technique, an ability to see the ball early and a common sense that allowed him to always choose the correct shot. Like all the great batsmen, he was always balanced whatever was bowled at him. No batsman at the time or since played with the bat closer to the pad, and when he went back, which he mostly did, he went right back, and across, his head over the line.

Grace stood tall at the crease, strong and athletic in his youth, more burly as he approached middle age, and though he had a high backlift he could get the bat down on shooters quicker than anyone. The willow always looked tiny in his massive hands. He knew where the gaps in the field were (which was handy when playing against opposing teams of 15, 18 or even 22) and, if you believe the legend, the quicker the bowling, the more he liked it. He certainly preferred the solid drive to a defensive push or a

The England team that toured Australia in 1891-82. Grace, as always, is the most prominent figure. George Lohmann is third from left in the back row. Another great bowler, the left-armer Johnny Briggs, is seated two places to WG's right.

Grace in playful mood with two other gentleman cricketers from the 1890s, Lord Hawke (left) and JR Mason.

mere deflection. 'Games aren't won by leaving the ball alone,' he once said, 'I hate defensive strokes, you can only get three off 'em'. His timing was such that one opponent glumly suggested that he used 'a bat that seemed all middle'.

Charles Fry, an England cricket captain, football international and once holder of the world long jump record, recognised Grace's enormous influence on the game. 'He revolutionised batting,' Fry wrote. 'He turned it from an accomplishment into a science ... the theory of modern batting is, in all essentials, the result of WG's thinking and working on the game.'

Grace's Test record is 22 matches, 1098 runs at 32.29 with two centuries. Excellent for his day, it is hardly mighty in the Bradman mould. However, he did not play a Test match until he was 32, when he scored 152 at The Oval in 1880, England's first Test at home. As captain, he led England in 13 Tests, all against Australia, for eight victories and two losses (despite winning only four tosses). At 50 years and 320 days, he remains the oldest man to captain his country in a Test, in his farewell match — the first Test at Trent Bridge in 1899.

Grace at the wicket, a man ahead of his time.

Grace died on 23 October 1915, just four months after Victor Trumper, of a heart attack after an air raid during the Great War. Back in 1873, WG had become the first man to achieve the 'double' in an English first-class season — 1000 runs and 100 wickets — by scoring 2139 runs and taking 106 wickets. He promptly did it again the following year, and every year until 1878, then twice more in the 1880s. No other player managed the feat until 1882, and no one else scored 2000 runs and took 100 wickets in a season until 1899, the year WG celebrated his 51st birthday.

These types of figures reflect an extraordinary supremacy. A Test batting average of 99.94 is probably more amazing. Probably.

WG GRACE (ENGLAND)

Test Cricket

Tests	Inn	NO	Runs	HS	Ave	100	50	Ct	Balls	Runs	Wkts	Ave	Best	5/	10/
22	36	2	1098	170	32.29	2	5	39	666	236	9	26.22	2-12	–	–

First-Class Cricket

Mat	Inn	NO	Runs	HS	Ave	100	50	Ct	Balls	Runs	Wkts	Ave	Best	5/	10/
872	1493	105	54896	344	39.55	126	254	887	126157	51545	2876	17.92	10-92	246	66

Note: Grace took his 10-92 in a 12-a-side match

No. 3 Garry Sobers

Those who like to argue that Garry Sobers is the game's No. 1 player do so on the basis that the greatest cricketer must be an allrounder, someone great in all facets of the game. Maybe this is impossible, for in reality no one has yet achieved this, though Sobers has gone closest. He was a cricketer good enough to average over 57 with the bat, win Test matches whether bowling left-arm fast-medium, finger spin or wrist spin, and a fieldsman of the absolute highest quality in any position. If Bradman's supreme quality was that he was all but guaranteed to score more runs than anyone else, and WG Grace's greatest achievement was that he made the game, Sobers' unique appeal was that he was going to have an influence on any game he was involved in at some stage, in some way.

Sobers' career Test bowling average is 34.03. His strengths as a bowler were his versatility and his ability to often rise to the occasion. Inevitably, the time and energy he devoted to being the West Indies' best batsman reduced his impact as a bowler, though it is also true that his role as a bowler often became an alibi for him to bat in the middle order. He averaged 72 as a No. 3 batsman and nearly 64 as a No. 4, but 107 of his 160 innings in Test cricket were played from Nos. 5, 6 or 7. One of the reasons his bowling average was inflated was that throughout the 1960s, when he was at his best, he was a member of a champion side, one that featured two imposing fast bowlers in Wes Hall and Charlie Griffith and an accomplished off-spinner in Lance Gibbs. Thus, he rarely bowled downwind with his quicks or into the breeze with his slows. Then, after Hall and Griffith faded from the scene, he was obliged to bowl long, defensive spells. Despite all this, he finished with 235 Test wickets, which at the time of his final Test in 1974 ranked him seventh of all time, and the leading left-hander. Perhaps the cost per wicket is not a true guide to his value, but the great bowlers average significantly less and it is the reason he is ranked third in this study, rather than No. 1.

Sobers first announced himself as a cricketer of high quality when he went on a scoring spree that netted him 2250 runs at 93.75 in 18 Tests from 1958 to 1960. Early in this sequence he hit Test cricket's then highest score — 365 not out — against Pakistan in Kingston, during a series in which he smashed 824 runs in five Tests. In a run of 10 innings, against Pakistan and India, he made six centuries. Against England at home in 1959-60, he hit three more tons, while scoring 709 runs in five Tests. In Australia in 1960-61, expectations were huge, and Sobers played one or two majestic innings, chief among them his famous 132 in Brisbane on the first day of what became cricket's first Tied Test. But as the series went on, he also frustrated his fans by sometimes attempting shots that were overly ambitious at best, irresponsible at worst. In his book of the 1960-61

Sobers bowling his 'Chinaman' spinners, just one of three distinct bowling styles he used successfully in Test matches.

The First XI

tour, the famous Australian writer and commentator AG 'Johnnie' Moyes wrote of Sobers: 'So often he touched greatness shared by few of the present generation. His finest innings bore comparison with anything we have seen for many years and yet somehow he did not inspire the same confidence as (Rohan) Kanhai, who reached Australia with a lesser reputation but increased it immeasurably by so many grand innings.'

Away from the batting crease, Moyes called Sobers' fielding 'simply magnificent', while his bowling was 'more than useful', especially his spinners. This description of his bowling reflected the fact that at this point in his career, Sobers was not a prolific wicket-taker. In the '60-61 series he took 15 wickets, his main quality being his versatility, which gave captain Frank Worrell the opportunity to play an extra batsman in the final three Tests. He had taken four wickets in the first Test innings he ever bowled in, back in March 1954, but by the end of the Australia series he had only 55 Test wickets, at an average of more than 43.

Sobers with the Wisden Trophy after dominating the 1966 series in England.

As good as Kanhai was, from 1963 Sobers was usually rated the better batsman, as well as being the greatest all-round cricketer of the 20th century. He was, in Richie Benaud's words, 'delightfully orthodox in his batting and yet, at the same time, a wonderful improviser against the ball that, for a fraction of a second, looks as though it will beat him'. Fred Trueman described his thought process when batting as being 'lightning quick'. While playing for South Australia in the Sheffield Shield, Sobers originally went back but then leaned forward into an Alan Davidson slower ball and smashed it so hard over wide mid-on that it flew an

Sobers aims a cover drive during the series against England in the Caribbean in 1967-68.

estimated 150 metres. In 1968, he hit Glamorgan's Malcolm Nash for six sixes in an over without ever having to slog. Sir Clyde Walcott thought he was the 'best all-rounder, best left-hander and best swing bowler'.

Sir Donald Bradman called him the 'five-in-one cricketer' (batsman, fieldsman and three-in-one bowler), but in England in 1966 Sobers was all that and captain, too. He led the West Indies superbly to a 3-1 series victory, scored 722 runs including three centuries, a 94 and an 81, at an average of 103.14, took 20 wickets at 27.25 and 10 catches, and won all five tosses! At Lord's he hit 163 not out in the West Indies second innings, after he and his cousin, David Holford (105 not out in his second Test), came together with their side effectively 5-9 and added an unbeaten 274. Sobers always rated this his greatest Test innings, because of the state of the game, the fact he had to guide his inexperienced partner and because he prevailed in a tactical battle with his opposing number, Colin Cowdrey. At first the England captain crowded both batsmen, and Sobers counter-attacked. Cowdrey then chose to defend against Sobers and attack Holford, so Sobers kept attacking, but also took the easy singles, making no attempt to monopolise the strike. Holford's confidence grew, to the point that in the end he was batting as vibrantly as his much more illustrious relative. At Trent Bridge, he opened the bowling and trapped Geoff Boycott lbw with a big inswinger that Boycott later called 'the best delivery I ever faced in cricket'. At Headingley, Sobers hit 174, including 103 between lunch and tea on the second day, and then — bowling fast and slow — took 5-41 and 3-39 as the Windies won by an innings and 55 runs.

The full flow of the bat was always a feature of Sobers' batting.

It's unlikely even Grace could have done all that Sobers did in that amazing English summer. Perhaps no other batsman could have made the famous 254 he scored as captain of the 'World XI' against Australia at the MCG in 1971-72, runs spectacularly scored against an attack led by a rampaging Dennis Lillee. Bradman called that knock the 'greatest exhibition of batting ever seen in Australia'. Very few other slips fieldsman could have dived sideways and forward to take the catch that dismissed Neil Harvey during the final day of the Tied Test of 1960-61, especially when fielding to a bowler of Wes Hall's lightning speed. If a better all-round cricketer than Sobers ever emerges, that man will be the greatest cricketer the game has ever seen.

GARRY SOBERS (WEST INDIES)
Test Cricket

Tests	Inn	NO	Runs	HS	Ave	100	50	Ct	Balls	Runs	Wkts	Ave	Best	5/	10/
93	160	21	8032	365*	57.78	36	30	109	21599	7999	235	34.04	6-73	6	–

First-Class Cricket

Mat	Inn	NO	Runs	HS	Ave	100	50	Ct	Balls	Runs	Wkts	Ave	Best	5/	10/
383	609	93	28315	365*	54.87	86	121	407	70789	28941	1043	27.75	9-49	36	1

The First XI

Shane Warne

No. 4

There have been many, many changes in cricket over the past 150 years, but few things have been more startling that the re-emergence of spin bowling in the 1990s. No less than Bill 'Tiger' O'Reilly, the legendary Australian leg-spinner of the 1930s, wrote in 1985 that 'the art of leg-spinning is in danger of disappearing from the game'. Imagine the last 15 years of international cricket without Muttiah Muralitharan, Saqlain Mushtaq, Stuart MacGill, Daniel Vettori, Mushtaq Ahmed, Harbhajan Singh, Anil Kumble, Danesh Kaneria? Imagine it without Shane Warne?

The 1980s was the decade of speed. The West Indies had an army of firebrands, other teams had their fair share of quicks as well. Pakistan's Abdul Qadir was really the only spin bowler to have a sustained impact. 'I know that cricket has suffered a great deal because of the discrimination against leg-spin, in favour of fast bowling, and I will go on saying it for as long as I live,' bemoaned O'Reilly. The cricket world believed it was simply being pragmatic. Fast bowling was much more likely to get batsmen out. Spinners equalled runs, so captains were reluctant to bowl them.

In the calendar year 1990, the leading wicket-takers in Test cricket were Waqar Younis, Wasim Akram, Devon Malcolm, Ian Bishop, Angus Fraser, Danny Morrison, Richard Hadlee and Curtly Ambrose. In 1991, it was Craig McDermott, Curtly Ambrose, Malcolm Marshall, Phillip DeFreitas, Merv Hughes, Courtney Walsh and Patrick Patterson. All pacemen. Eleven bowlers took 20 or more wickets in Tests in 1992, but only one of them — New Zealand off-spinner Dipak Patel — was a slow bowler. Bill O'Reilly died in 1992, 10 months after Shane Warne's Test debut, just 85 days before Warne's first outstanding bowling performance in international cricket. Not even Tiger could have believed all that he was going to miss.

The greatest leg-spinner in full cry at The Oval in 2005.

Warne had played in only seven first-class matches and taken just 26 first-class wickets before his debut Test. At the end of his first Test series, his bowling average was 228. By the start of the final day of the second Test of Australia's home series against the West Indies in 1992-93, Warne's fifth Test, that average had been reduced to a fraction more than 90. But then Warne bowled a fabulous 'flipper' — a short-pitched delivery that could fizz off the pitch and stun batsmen looking to pull or cut — to Richie Richardson ... the ball shattered the Windies

25

captain's stumps, broke a crucial partnership, and set up Australia's first defeat of their fierce rivals in a 'live' Test (one that might decide a series) since 1981. The young leggie finished with 7-52. Suddenly a hero, especially in Melbourne, Warne had little success in the rest of that series, but was brilliant in three Tests in New Zealand straight after. Then he was off to England, where his Ashes experience began with a viciously turning leg break that made one of the best players of spin in the game, former England captain Mike Gatting, look miserably out of his depth.

From then until he retired from Test cricket at the end of the 2006–07 Ashes series, with quicks such as Merv Hughes, Craig McDermott, Glenn McGrath, Jason Gillespie and Brett Lee opening the bowling, Australia was competitive on seaming wickets, while Warne gave them an advantage over everyone on the turners. His presence also meant that the Australian attack was beautifully balanced. On a flat wicket he could bowl nice and tight, always at the stumps, and as the wicket deteriorated you could see the opposition starting to sweat, because they knew they'd be facing him on his terms before the match was out. Never was this better shown than at Adelaide in December 2006, when an England side that had made 6–551 declared in their first innings simply froze on the final day, as if the great leg-spinner had cast a spell on them. He finished with 4-49 from 32 overs, and then the Aussies scored at a run-a-ball to win a match most people believed had been destined for a draw.

Warne in Pakistan in 1994, his third year of Test-match cricket

Three things set Warne apart from the spinners who came before him. First, he rarely bowled a bad ball. Secondly, Warne was as perceptive a bowler as has ever played the game. For the previous 30 years, most spinners had believed they had to work out batsman by being relentless rather than innovative. Warne brought surprise into vogue. Thirdly, he was adaptable (still is, when you consider the way he has inspired the Rajasthan Royals in the Indian Premier League). The Warne of 2006 was a different bowler to that of 1993, or 1997, or 2001. He bowled the flipper less often, possibly because his surgically repaired shoulder didn't want him to. Instead, he developed a straighter ball that drifted onto the line of the stumps and three or four times a Test snared batsmen lbw, despite the fact they were playing well forward. His wrong 'un had also improved. The one constant was that his leg break turned a mile, especially if it pitched outside the line of the leg stump. Pitches seemed to spin more on the first day whenever Warne was playing, a point he demonstrated for the last time in Test cricket on Boxing Day 2006, when he took his 700th wicket, Andrew Strauss bowled, while taking 5-39 before an adoring MCG crowd. He was always able to change plans effectively in the middle of a game, a spell, even an over. Having to bowl differently to two batsmen never worried him, so a single didn't upset his rhythm. He was also a tough aggressive cricketer, with extraordinarily strong hands and fingers, who could bowl all day.

The First XI

His method was technically magnificent. Back-leg drive was the key to him achieving energy on the ball, and the perfect timing of the shoulder rotation ensured a magnificent follow-through and curvaceous flight. The ball came out of the hand with a mighty flick, which meant it drifted and dropped, often savagely. The key role played by that shoulder was amply demonstrated when he hurt it in 1998; without the joint in perfect working order, Sachin Tendulkar took to him. The thing that makes Warne unique in legspinning history is that he was so great so young. Something else that sets him apart is his impact on one-day cricket. The conventional wisdom before 1993 was that spinners were too easily hit to be a factor in a 50-over game, but Warne turned that idea on its head when he was given a chance in the one-dayers during the 1993-94 Australian season. In his first four matches he took nine wickets for 87 runs; for the season he took 22 wickets at 13.68 while conceding only 3.34 runs per over. Later, he would play crucial roles in two World Cups, using a cricket brain as alert and clever as any in the game. Few teams now go into a one-day game without at least one slow bowler.

Of course, Warne's career was not all smooth sailing, with not just injury proving a hurdle. His resilience, though, was extraordinary. Having been suspended for 12 months after failing a drugs test in early 2003, first Test back he took 10 wickets against Sri Lanka at Galle, including his 500th Test wicket. Later in the year, he passed Muralitharan to become the game's leading Test wicket-taker, a status he still enjoyed upon his retirement (though Murali has since overtaken him again). In 2005, his starring role in the Ashes series in England was probably the most exceptional of his life, and settled the argument as to whether he or Dennis Lillee was the greatest of all Australian bowlers. At year's end he was named the BBC's overseas sporting personality of the year — his 40 Test wickets being judged more worthy even than Roger Federer's three Wimbledon crowns and Lance Armstrong's seven Tour de France cycling triumphs. Never has a bowler, fast or slow, been more entitled to mix in such exalted company.

A remarkable comeback: Warne was man of the match in both the semi-final and final of the 1999 World Cup.

SHANE WARNE (AUSTRALIA)

Test Cricket

Tests	Inn	NO	Runs	HS	Ave	100	50	Ct	Balls	Runs	Wkts	Ave	Best	5/	10/
145	199	17	3154	99	17.33	–	12	125	40705	17995	708	25.42	8-71	37	10

One-Day International Cricket

ODIs	Inn	NO	Runs	HS	Ave	100	50	Ct	Balls	Runs	Wkts	Ave	Best	4/
194	107	29	1018	55	13.05	–	1	80	10642	7541	293	25.74	5-33	13

No. 5 Imran Khan

No Pakistani cricketer has enjoyed the same level of fame and esteem as has Imran Khan. A superb allrounder and incisive captain, Imran changed the way Pakistani cricket was perceived around the world, bringing a new respect for his national team in the same way Frank Worrell boosted the status of the West Indies in the 1960s. Almost certainly, whatever occurs in the future, Imran will remain the most important figure in the history of the game in Pakistan.

The 'Lion of Pakistan'

He first came to prominence as a cricketer in the mid 1970s, in a side that contained fine players such as Mushtaq Mohammad, Asif Iqbal, Majid Khan and Zaheer Abbas but which rarely won. Their batting was stylish, but frail. The bowling was mediocre. Into this mix, Imran brought brilliant, shrewd pace bowling, genuine batting skill, supreme self-confidence and an ability to sustain excellence under pressure. His bowling run-up started slowly, leaning forward, gathering momentum, until he leapt at the bowling crease. At his peak, Imran could swing the ball both ways and possessed a lethal bouncer, which he was never afraid to use. Most significantly, he pioneered the concept of 'reverse' swing, the ability to get the old ball to bend, sometimes prodigiously. As a batsman, he delighted in improvising and smashing bowlers in the latter overs of a one-day innings, but his runmaking was based on a sound and orthodox defensive technique. Perhaps Imran's most important innings was his 72 in the 1992 World Cup final, when he and Javed Miandad overcame a poor start to the innings by batting slowly at first and then accelerating, in the process setting up his nation's most memorable day in cricket. His Test career average of 37.69 (3807 runs from 126 innings in 88 Tests), coming as it did on top of all his overs and all his wickets, is testimony to his batting skill.

Imran first became captain of Pakistan for the tour of England in 1982 and, but for periods when he was recovering from injuries, was unequivocally the team's commander-in-chief for the next decade. He provided runs, wickets, calm, example and inspiration. In time, he became a shrewd tactician as well, and took full responsibility for the development of Pakistan's next generation of stars, including Wasim Akram, Waqar Younis, Salim Malik, Inzamam-ul-Haq and Saeed Anwar. Five of Imran's six Test hundreds and 14 of his 18 fifties came during 48 Tests in charge, when his batting average was 52.35. As a bowling captain, he averaged 20.27 and took four of his six 10-wicket hauls. He was so influential and skilful, which is why Imran is the highest ranked Asian cricketer in this study, and why he is rated more valuable even than the two great fast bowlers, Malcolm Marshall and Dennis Lillee.

The First XI

Imran first played for Pakistan in England in 1971, at age 18, but it was not until the start of 1977, in Australia, that he announced himself as a genuine Test-match cricketer. In the third Test, at the SCG, he took 12-165 (6-102 and 6-63), the best figures ever by a Pakistani bowler in Australia. Then it was to the Caribbean, where Imran's battles with Andy Roberts, Colin Croft and Joel Garner were a feature of the series. He bounced them and they bounced him back; by retaliating first, he demonstrated that he would not be backing down against anyone. He was a major star in World Series Cricket, and then, after 'peace' was restored to international cricket, he celebrated his 28th birthday in 1980 by scoring his first Test century and becoming the second Pakistani (after Intikhab Alam) to complete the 1000 runs/100 wickets Test double. The hundred — 123 against Marshall, Garner, Croft and Sylvester Clarke — was made after coming to the wicket at 5-95. During a three-Test series in Australia in 1981-82, he became Pakistan's leading wicket-taker in Tests. And then, against Sri Lanka, he took 14-116 (8-58 and 6-58) in the final Test, in Lahore, which remains the best match analysis by a Pakistan bowler in Test history.

The huge leap before the delivery stride that became Imran's calling card.

In England in 1982 he was a revelation. Imran was not afraid to acknowledge that he was one of his team's best bowlers, and accordingly gave himself long spells. Occasionally, he impressed with his willingness to go against the norm, such as at Lord's, when he introduced opening bat and part-time medium pacer Mudassar Nazar to bowl a match-winning spell and refused to take the second new ball just because it was available. In his first Test innings as a bowling captain, Imran took seven English wickets and finished with 21 for the three-match series. The series was lost narrowly, but there were strong indicators that his Pakistani team now had steel in its spine.

This view was confirmed in home series against Australia (a 3-0 cleansweep) and India (3-0 in six Tests). Imran took 53 wickets in the nine Tests, including 40 against the Indians, in an astonishing display of fast-bowling excellence. That he did so on wickets that traditionally offer little to pacemen, while leading his team and scoring runs too, it can be argued that this was the greatest fast-bowling performance over a season in cricket history. He took his 200th Test wicket during a match performance of 11-79 against India in Karachi, including a spell of 5-3 from 25 balls. A Test later, in Faisalabad, a known graveyard for quick bowlers, he took 11 wickets again, as well as scoring a century which included 21 runs from one Kapil Dev over. In the fourth Test, on a pitch so docile that he was able to declare at 3-581 (Kapil Dev 0-111), he then took 6-35 and 2-45 as Pakistan won by an innings and 119 runs.

The 100 Greatest Cricketers

A grand farewell — World Cup final, Melbourne, 1992.

Astonishingly, Imran had performed heroically despite a deteriorating leg complaint that was eventually diagnosed as a severe stress fracture in the shin. He missed nearly two years of Test cricket, but returned to lead his nation to its first series victory in England. Imran claimed his 300th wicket in the third Test of that series, in which he took 10-77 in the match (3-37 and 7-40), and then scored a century at The Oval, as Pakistan ran up a first innings total of 708.

Having initially decided to retire after the 1987 World Cup, when Pakistan was stunned by Australia in the semi-final, Imran was convinced to resume his career the following year, and promptly took Pakistan to the Caribbean in early 1988 for what developed into one of the great Test series. His men won the first Test by nine wickets and were in front in the second until Viv Richards and Jeffrey Dujon scored second-innings hundreds. Pakistan, set 372, made a brave attempt at the target, but the game ended with No. 11 Abdul Qadir keeping out the last over from Richards. In the third Test, the Windies snuck home by two wickets after Winston Benjamin and Dujon added an unbeaten 61 for the ninth wicket on the final day.

Imran was 38 years old when he won the 'International Cricketer of the Year' award in Australia in 1989-90, underlining the fact that he was a great Test and one-day player, and two years later he came back to the country of his first major Test performance to lead Pakistan to the World Cup. No cricket legend has enjoyed a more fantastic finale, or been more entitled to it.

IMRAN KHAN (PAKISTAN)

Test Cricket

Tests	Inn	NO	Runs	HS	Ave	100	50	Ct	Balls	Runs	Wkts	Ave	Best	5/	10/
88	126	25	3807	136	37.69	6	18	28	19458	8258	362	22.81	8-58	23	6

One-Day International Cricket

ODIs	Inn	NO	Runs	HS	Ave	100	50	Ct	Balls	Runs	Wkts	Ave	Best	4/
175	151	40	3709	102*	33.41	1	19	37	7461	4845	182	26.62	6-14	4

The First XI

Jack Hobbs

No. 6

If WG Grace, the pioneer who made batting a matter of technique, and Don Bradman, the ultimate run-maker, were cricket's two greatest batsmen, then Jack Hobbs was the bridge in between, literally and figuratively. He made his first-class debut in 1905, for a Surrey XI against a Gentlemen of England side captained by Grace, and played his last Test in the Ashes battle of 1930, Bradman's first great series. Grace was the first batsman with a sustainable technique, Hobbs' technique was as perfect as there has ever been and Bradman used a great technique to the most devastating effect.

There was no arrogance, wild gestures or hint of rebellion about Jack Hobbs. He came from a battling background, and never forgot it, even after he became Sir John Berry Hobbs in 1953, after hitting 197 first-class centuries (15 in Tests), 98 of them after his 40th birthday. He was of medium build, athletic, safe, quick and very certain rather than flash in the field. Most importantly, he was the bloke you wanted to bat for your life, determined, shrewd, decent, sure. Everyone from the young lads selling the scorecards to the wise old members in the pavilion loved him and respected him, and in different ways identified with him. That was Hobbs' strength, the source of his great appeal. He never let you down.

No one has scored more first-class hundreds or more first-class runs. Yet Hobbs' career first-class batting average is only 50.65, below dozens of batsmen in the game's history and a number of his contemporaries. Here is a clue about the man. Only 16 of his centuries were double-centuries. Fifty-one of them ended between 100 and 110. Often, he was happy to forego a hundred because 50 or 60 was enough. His job was to score enough runs to set up victories, not to humble opposing bowlers, hog the limelight or boost his statistics. Like all the great batsman of first-class cricket's first 50 years, he was at his most valuable on bad wickets, when his team most needed him. 'That was the time you had to earn your living,' he once said. Significantly, he averaged six runs more per 'out' in Test cricket than he did in county cricket. Jack Hobbs saved his best for when it mattered most.

Two images of 'The Master'.
Above: The relaxed batting stance.
Left: On the defensive in Australia in 1924-25.

His statistics reveal an extraordinary consistency. Consider his Test batting record on a series by series basis:

Season	Opponent	Venue	Tests	Inns	NO	50s	100s	HS	Runs	Avg
1907-08	Aus	Aus	4	8	1	3	0	83	302	43.14
1909	Aus	Eng	3	6	1	1	0	62*	132	26.40
1909-10	SA	SA	5	9	1	4	1	187	539	67.38
1911-12	Aus	Aus	5	9	1	1	3	187	662	82.75
1912	Aus	Eng	3	4	0	1	1	107	224	56.00
1912	SA	Eng	3	5	1	2	0	68	163	40.75
1913-14	SA	SA	5	8	1	4	0	97	443	63.29
1920-21	Aus	Aus	6	10	0	1	2	123	505	50.50
1924	SA	Eng	4	5	0	1	1	211	355	71.00
1924-25	Aus	Aus	5	9	0	2	3	154	573	63.67
1926	Aus	Eng	5	7	1	2	2	119	486	81.00
1928	WI	Eng	2	2	0	1	1	159	212	106.00
1928-29	Aus	Aus	5	9	0	2	1	142	451	50.11
1929	SA	Eng	1	2	0	1	0	52	62	31.00
1930	Aus	Eng	5	9	0	2	0	78	301	33.44
Total			61	102	7	28	15	211	5410	56.95

It took him two years to settle into Test cricket, and his final two series, played after his 46th birthday, were unproductive by his high standards. In between, over nearly 20 years, he failed to average 50 in a series only once!

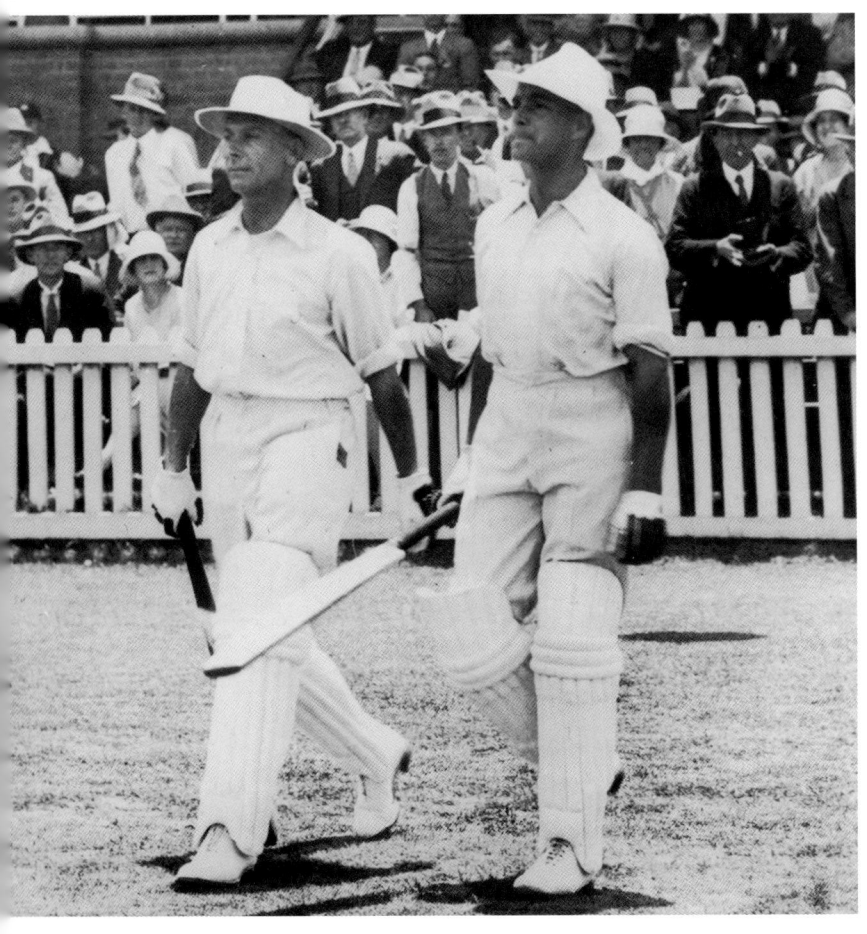

The great partnership: Hobbs with Herbert Sutcliffe.

Inevitably, as an opening batsman, Hobbs was outstanding against the quicks, most notably against the Australian pacemen — Tibby Cotter before the war and Jack Gregory and Ted McDonald afterwards. He was also magnificent against slow bowling, such as the South African wrist spinners of 1909-10, and the outstanding Australia 'leggies', Herbert Hordern, Arthur Mailey and Clarrie Grimmett. He was at the absolute height of his powers in 1914, when he scored 11 centuries and 2697 runs during the English county season. But then the world went to war, meaning that Hobbs lost four of what otherwise must have been his most productive years. He came back in 1919, aged 36, to immediately score another 2594 runs and eight centuries, but he was a different player. Now he went more onto the back foot, deflecting more, playing with less power, placing more emphasis on the short single. After the 1924-25 Ashes series, the former Australian captain Monty Noble wrote, 'Hobbs, as we know him today, is perhaps a more prolific run-getter than ever, but does not possess the compelling genius that he was a few years ago.' The man himself believed that he was 'twice the player' before the war that he was afterwards.

The First XI

However, he was more prolific post-war. Between 1919 and 1934 he scored 35,017 runs and 131 centuries. Before the war he had scored four Test centuries against Australia, afterwards he compiled another eight. Hobbs modestly claimed this was because the wickets after 1918 were flatter, the bowlers not as good, the lbw rules more in favour of the batsmen. The truth is that Hobbs understood the art of batting as well as anyone ever has, and was thus able to adapt his game to compensate for his advancing years. He equalled Grace's record of 126 first-class centuries in 1925, a season when, aged 42, he scored 3024 runs and a then record 16 centuries.

In 1926, Hobbs made a famous century on a wet wicket in the final Test, with Herbert Sutcliffe building the partnership that won the Test and regained the Ashes. 'It was a joy to watch the way Hobbs adapted his methods to the turf as it changed from docility in the early morning to its later viciousness,' wrote Neville Cardus. In 1928-29, the pair did it again, batting through the worst of a dreadful MCG sticky to set the stage for England to make 7-332 in the fourth innings and win the third Test, thus going an unbeatable 3-0 up in the series. George Hele, one of the umpires, wrote in 1974 that Hobbs' effort that day was 'the finest innings I've seen on a wet wicket'.

Hobbs' career Test batting average of 56.95 remains the second highest completed by a regular opening batsman who played more than 20 Test innings. Only Sutcliffe averaged more, but no one who saw the two bat has any doubt who was the better player — a fact which is no criticism of Sutcliffe at all. In England v Australia Tests, Hobbs still ranks second only to Bradman in terms of runs scored (3636 at 54.26 in 41 Tests) and most hundreds (12). In the eight decades since his farewell Test, there have been some opening batsmen who were more stylish or exciting, but none have equalled Jack Hobbs' consistency. He was known as 'The Master' because he was that little bit more efficient than anyone else.

The classic style that brought Jack Hobbs 197 first-class hundreds.

JACK HOBBS (ENGLAND)

Test Cricket

Tests	Inn	NO	Runs	HS	Ave	100	50	Ct	Balls	Runs	Wkts	Ave	Best	5/	10/
61	102	7	5410	211	56.95	15	28	17	376	165	1	165.0	1-19	–	–

First-Class Cricket

Mat	Inn	NO	Runs	HS	Ave	100	50	Ct	Balls	Runs	Wkts	Ave	Best	5/	10/
826	1315	106	61237	316*	50.65	197	270	340	5169	2666	107	24.92	7-56	3	–

No. 7 Malcolm Marshall

There are many contenders for the title of cricket's greatest fast bowler. For this study, it comes down to Malcolm Marshall versus Dennis Lillee. Trying to separate this pair is so difficult — in Lillee's favour is the manner in which he fought back from a back injury that would have ruined most cricketers' careers, and also the way he evolved as a bowler, from lethal tearaway to pace bowling master. However, Marshall was also a master of the art of pace bowling. His Test record — number of wickets (376), bowling average (20.94; the lowest of all those to take 200 Test wickets) and strike rate (a wicket every 46.77 deliveries) — is grand enough. But what is perhaps most impressive is the fact that in an era of stupendous West Indian fast men, Marshall is almost universally recognised as being the best of them. Take Allan Border's view: 'Day in, day out, in all conditions, Malcolm Marshall is my pick. He was something special.'

In 1986, Sir Donald Bradman wrote that he thought Marshall was one of the three fastest bowlers he had seen (Harold Larwood and Frank Tyson were the others). At 180cm (5ft 11in), Marshall was hardly tall for a fast bowler, but rather than his lack of height being a drawback, he skidded the ball through at the batsmen in a manner that made him extremely awkward, and very different to his partners in fast-bowling crime. His bounce was ultra-accurate and as a consequence lethal, and he developed an outswinger to go with his scare tactics. In his early days, Marshall raced in a long way, but later he cut his run-up, though never the bustling nature of his sprint to the crease, which ended with the ball being whipped with plenty of wrist down towards the batsman. 'So quick is his action,' Michael Manley wrote in A History of West Indies Cricket, 'that you might miss the perfection of his delivery stride, left (front) leg kicking and body laid out almost horizontal to maximise the whip effect of the delivery itself.'

The complete fast bowler.

Marshall learned to vary his pace by observing the champions, and was taught how to bowl an inswinger by the great Lillee. He could move the ball off the pitch too, especially the leg cutter. Few fast men have used the full width of the bowling crease better. And he was as effective from around the wicket as he was over, whether to give his bouncer more potency or to give a new angle to his inswinger. His accuracy is reflected in the fact that of the 77 men to take at least 100 wickets in one-day internationals, only Joel Garner, Richard Hadlee, Michael Holding and Curtly Ambrose have done so while conceding less than Marshall's 3.54 runs per over.

Though Marshall played Test cricket until 1991, it was in the mid '80s that he was at his absolute peak. Viv Richards described his bowling in the 1983-84 series in India as 'ferocious, his pace and accuracy were just mesmerising'. In one spell on a green pitch in Kanpur, he knocked the bat out of Sunil Gavaskar's hands before dismissing

The First XI

him, stunning the local fans and players. At the conclusion of his opening spell that day his figures read 4-9 from eight overs. With the bat, Marshall scored 240 runs in that series, including 92 in the first Test (the closest he came to scoring a Test century), and became the first West Indian to score 200 runs and take 25 wickets in one Test series. His batting was never accomplished enough for him to be considered a genuine allrounder, but his 10 half-centuries at the highest level confirmed that he definitely could bat.

At Leeds in 1984, Marshall produced the most extraordinary effort of his career. Earlier in the series, he'd ended the stillborn Test career of Andy Lloyd, who was struck on the helmet, suffered blurred vision, and didn't play again all season. While fielding on day one of this third Test, he broke his left thumb and it was assumed that he was out of the match, possibly the series. Consequently, on the fall of the ninth wicket of the West Indies first innings, the Englishmen headed for the dressing rooms, only to back-pedal when Marshall strode out onto Headingley, to bat one-handed so Larry Gomes could reach his century. Then, with his lower arm encased in plaster, Marshall took 7-53, operating at almost top speed, the ball swinging devilishly. The batsmen were reduced to complaining that the white plaster was putting them off, so Marshall covered it with pink elastoplast, which made it sort of skin-coloured. As it turned out, he missed just one Test and was back at The Oval to claim five wickets in an innings for the seventh time in 10 Tests, a run he extended to 11 in 14 when he dominated the 1984-85 Test series in Australia.

England's Allan Lamb (left) and Pakistan's Imran Khan (below) are both lbw to Marshall.

The 100 Greatest Cricketers

For all his skill in England, his bowling in Adelaide in late 1984 might have been his finest ever. The pitch was lifeless, and for once his fellow bowlers were struggling, but Marshall rose to the occasion, taking 5-69 and 5-38. It was not just the fact he took 10 wickets, it was the way he got them. Border remembers: 'Malcolm Marshall bowled a spell between lunch and tea — non-stop, we're talking two hours of bowling — in 100-degree heat. He just rushed in, having decided that he had to really have a red-hot go, bowled real good pace and broke the back of our batting.

Marshall in England 1984, when he established himself as the leader of the Windies pace attack.

Other bowlers, even the other great bowlers that the West Indies had at their disposal, wouldn't have been able to sustain their performance like Malcolm Marshall did that day.' Or perhaps he was at his greatest in England in 1988, when he grabbed a West Indies series record 35 wickets at just 12.65. Five of them came in an hour at Manchester, where he took 7-22 as England floundered to 93 all out.

In 1996, three years before Marshall's death at age 41 from colon cancer, Australia's David Boon had named Marshall as the best fast man he faced. 'There are a huge number of pacemen who earned my enormous respect,' he wrote, 'but Malcolm Marshall was just that little bit better. He had one of the best brains of any bowler I faced (which he coupled with a wicked sense of humour), and could bowl that quick and swing it both ways. Inevitably, you found yourself in trouble.'

Five years later, the sports TV network ESPN interviewed a large number of cricket identities for the series *ESPN's Legends of Cricket*. It was amazing how many people described Marshall as the 'complete' fast bowler. One was New Zealand's Martin Crowe. 'He was one of my favourite bowlers, not to face but to admire,' Crowe explained. 'He had a wonderful attitude and, obviously, a very strong ability to get the ball to kick and climb. He worked players out, he was very intelligent and knew exactly what he was trying to achieve. I thought he was the most complete fast bowler to come from the Caribbean.'

MALCOLM MARSHALL (WEST INDIES)

Test Cricket

Tests	Inn	NO	Runs	HS	Ave	100	50	Ct	Balls	Runs	Wkts	Ave	Best	5/	10/
81	107	11	1810	92	18.85	–	10	25	17584	7876	376	20.95	7-22	22	4

One-Day International Cricket

ODIs	Inn	NO	Runs	HS	Ave	100	50	Ct	Balls	Runs	Wkts	Ave	Best	4/
136	83	19	955	66	14.92	–	2	15	7175	4233	157	26.96	4-18	6

The First XI

Sachin Tendulkar No. 8

It is remarkable how quickly the cricket world moves these days. It seems so long since fans were debating which of Brian Lara, Steve Waugh or Sachin Tendulkar was the best batsman in the world. Yet it was only a decade ago. By a strong consensus, the winner was Tendulkar. However, the little Indian master has not been so dominant in the period from 2004 to 2009, when he has, in reality, been just one of the best batsmen in the world, rather than the undisputed No. 1. But we still have the memories of his true greatness, and the record books also offer ample evidence as to his total impact. As at June 30, 2009, he is in the top 20 for career batting average in both Tests and limited-over internationals, having scored 820 more runs than anyone else in Tests and 3533 more runs than anyone else in ODIs. He has scored the most hundreds in Tests and ODIs, and the most half-centuries in ODIs. In all, he has scored 29,457 runs in international cricket (12,773 in Tests; 16684 in ODIs), with 85 centuries and 144 half-centuries. These are truly monumental numbers, even more extraordinary when you consider the constant scrutiny and adulation that accompanies him.

Few teenagers had faced the kind of expectations that confronted Tendulkar when he was just 15. Already, he had achieved some mighty scores in schoolboy cricket. 'We have a young batsman in Bombay called Sachin Tendulkar, who is sent from upstairs to play the game,' boasted the Indian Test allrounder Ravi Shastri in 1988. 'He is only 15, a right-hand bat, five foot four inches tall, but I tell you, he's going to be a great player.' Even those who witnessed Don Bradman batting for Bowral when he was 15 could not have been *that* confident of the young Don's future greatness. However, nothing Tendulkar did in international cricket in the seasons from 1989 suggested that Shastri overrated him. Indeed, when talking to the Australian television journalist Ray Martin in 1996, Sir Donald said of him: 'I asked my wife to come look at him. I never saw myself play, but I feel that this fellow is playing much the same as I used to play, and she looked at him on the television and said yes, there is a similarity between the two. To me, his compactness, his technique, his stroke production, it all seemed to gel as far as I was concerned.'

The Little Maestro

Tendulkar made his first Test appearance at Karachi against a Pakistani attack marshalled by the great Imran Khan and also featuring Wasim Akram, Abdul Qadir and a young fast bowler also making his Test debut, Waqar Younis. In at 4-41 after Pakistan had been bowled out for 409 (Imran 109 not out), Tendulkar and Azharuddin added 32 before Waqar bowled his fellow first-gamer. Eight days later, Tendulkar became the youngest person to score a Test half-century (lbw Imran 59), and the youngest to share in a Test century partnership (143 for the fifth wicket with Sanjay Manjrekar), the start of a succession of 'youngest ever' Test records that included youngest to 1000, 2000, 3000, 4000, 5000, 6000, 7000, 8000, 9000, 10,000, 11,000 and 12,000 runs. The fastest bowling scarcely

The 100 Greatest Cricketers

Two famous landmarks. Above: Tendulkar reaches his double century on the way to 241 not out, his highest score against Australia, at the SCG in January 2004. Right: Nearly two years later in Delhi he becomes the new world record holder for most Test centuries.

worried him, bowlers the world over quickly learnt that he could hit the ball as hard as anyone, and he had that rare skill of scoring rapidly without looking as if he was trying to. Steve Waugh described Tendulkar's 155 not out at Chennai in 1998 as a 'lesson in how to pulverise an attack on a turning wicket and make it look like you were playing a knock against your brothers in the backyard'.

As well as being the Test batsman of the 1990s, a compelling case can be put that Tendulkar is the greatest ever one-day batsman. The magnificence really started in March 1994, in a one-day international at Auckland, when New Zealand could only set India 146 to win. The wicket, however, was seaming, Indian opener Navjot Sidhu had a stiff neck, and no one seemed keen to take his place at the top of the order. So Tendulkar volunteered — 'Let's give it a try, I'm pretty sure it's going to work,' is how he remembers his words to the tour selectors — and blasted 82 runs from 49 balls, including 15 fours and two sixes. He's been opening India's one-day innings ever since. It actually took Tendulkar 78 matches before he scored his first one-day century, against Australia in Colombo in September 1994. Four years later, aged 25, Tendulkar scored his 18th one-day international century, against Zimbabwe at Bulawayo, breaking Desmond Haynes' record. It was his 198th ODI. Another two years, and he became the leading runscorer in the one-day game. By June 2009, in terms of total ODI runs scored he had raced away from all other batsmen and he had taken 154 wickets as well, ninth highest among all Indian bowlers.

Tendulkar did not score a double century in Test cricket until his 71st Test, against New Zealand in Ahmedabad in late 1999, having already scored 20 single centuries. Incredibly, it was only in the previous year that he made his maiden first-class double ton. It was as if, after scoring so many runs in the '90s, he developed an even greater appetite. In the one-day tournament that followed that big innings against the Kiwis, he smashed an unconquered 186 from 150 balls at Hyderabad, just eight runs short of Saeed Anwar's world record score. Five years later, and having not scored a Test hundred for 12 months (in part because of injury), he finally completed his 35th ton, breaking Sunil Gavaskar's record for most centuries in Test

The First XI

cricket. Four of his previous 15 hundreds had been double centuries, and there had also been scores of 194 not out and 193. The trend has continued as he marches on: in 2008, he scored four centuries and in two of them he went past 150. His first Test century of 2009 was another big one, 160 against New Zealand at Wellington.

Hard markers worry that Tendulkar has not played sufficient match-winning innings, but his effort against England at Chennai in December 2008, when he scored an unbeaten 103 as India successfully chased 387 was brave and inspirational, not least because it came just weeks after an appalling terrorist attack in Mumbai. The nation was desperate for some good news and their hero provided it.

So much of this chapter has been about statistics, and they provide compelling evidence as to Tendulkar's greatness. But what gets him unequivocally into this First XI is the manner in which he dominated the game for four or five years around the turn of the century, when he had that gift Steve Waugh referred to — the ability to make batting in high-pressure Test matches look easy. Tendulkar's Test batting average climbed to over 50 in 1994 and hovered around the 50 mark for the next three years, before an orgy of runscoring in 1997-98 — when he made three hundreds against Sri Lanka and then smashed an Australian attack led by Shane Warne — seemed to set him on an upward spiral. In 36 Tests from August 1997 to December 2001, Tendulkar scored 3802 runs at 67.89 and was a class above his contemporaries. Considering those expectations that have never left him, and the inspiration but also stress the frenzied support he enjoys brings him, his displays during this period were phenomenal. As good as batsmen such as Brian Lara, Ricky Ponting and Rahul Dravid have been in the 21st century, they never came close to the dazzling heights reached by the Little Maestro.

The 16-year-old Test cricketer.

SACHIN TENDULKAR (INDIA)														
Test Cricket														
Tests	Inn	NO	Runs	HS	Ave	100	50	Ct	Balls	Runs	Wkts	Ave	Best	5/	10/
159	261	27	12773	248*	54.59	42	53	102	3934	2272	44	51.64	3-10	–	–
One-Day International Cricket														
ODIs	Inn	NO	Runs	HS	Ave	100	50	Ct	Balls	Runs	Wkts	Ave	Best	4/
425	415	39	16684	186*	44.37	43	91	129	8015	6806	154	44.19	5-32	6

The 100 Greatest Cricketers

No. 9 Sydney Barnes

Not long before Wilfred Rhodes died, Neville Cardus found himself in conversation with the former great Yorkshire and England cricketer. First, Cardus asked Rhodes what he thought of Ranjitsinhji.

The style that brought Barnes 189 wickets from just 27 Test matches.

'He were a good bat were Ranji. But I always fancied myself getting him leg before doin' that leg glance of his.'
'What did you think of Trumper?' Cardus asked.
'He were a good bat were Victor.'
'There was no advance on a good bat in Wilfred's vocabulary of praise,' Cardus recalled. 'Once, though, he let himself go. I asked him his opinion of Sydney Barnes as a bowler.
'The best of 'em today is half as good as "Barnie".'

Barnes was a tall, wiry, often moody bowler, who brought the ball down from his full height and could spin or cut it from leg or off. Jack Hobbs said he was 'undoubtedly the greatest bowler of my time'. Barnes' 189 wickets came at an average of just 16.43. No other bowler to take even 120 Test wickets has a bowling average less than 20.

He was one of those bowlers who, like Curtly Ambrose, because he used his full height in his delivery, had arms that looked longer than they were. His most dangerous delivery was the leg-cutter, bowled at genuine medium pace, even quicker at times; his greatest asset was his accuracy, which was relentless. Clem Hill couldn't remember ever getting a really bad ball from him. Because Barnes could move the ball away off the pitch at some speed, most critics put him in front of the greatest bowler of the 19th century, the 'Demon' Fred Spofforth.

In the second Test of 1911-12, in Melbourne, Barnes produced one of Test cricket's most famous bowling spells. After Hill, the Australian captain, had decided to bat, Barnes bowled five overs for one run and the wickets of Warren Bardsley, Hill, Charlie Kelleway and Warwick Armstrong. Trumper, in at 3-8, led a brief fightback, but relaxing against the considerable left-arm skills of Frank Foster, he was soon bowled. Barnes came back to get Roy Minnett, at which point his figures were 5-6 from 11 overs. The home team never recovered, and England won the final four Tests having lost the first, with Barnes dismissing Trumper four more times in the series. As HS Altham wrote in his celebrated *A History of Cricket*, Australian observers were now convinced that Barnes was 'the greatest bowler we had ever sent against them'.

This stayed the case while first-hand memories of Barnes remained. Johnnie Moyes recalled in his 1950 book *A Century of Cricketers* how as a teenager in Adelaide he doubted that any bowler could turn the ball on the rock-hard Adelaide Oval pitch while bowling at Barnes' pace. 'But I sat on the Hill and saw him do it.' 'Englishmen will tell you that Barnes stands supreme among bowlers of all ages,' Moyes concluded. 'If Barnes wasn't the greatest bowler ever born he was so close to it that it doesn't matter.'

The First XI

Seventy-five years after that 1911-12 Ashes series, Sir Donald Bradman decided to write a letter to a young allrounder by the name of Stephen Waugh. Throughout this correspondence, the message was positive: that the 21-year-old Waugh was a player of considerable promise who could go far in the game. To help him with his bowling, Sir Donald attached an instructional piece on bowling that had been written many years ago, the suggestion being that if you followed these pearls of wisdom you'd go all right. The author of that piece was Sydney Barnes.

Barnes' raw statistics are imposing. His international career stretched from December 1901 to February 1914, and by the time he was finished he had taken nearly 50 more Test wickets than any other bowler. He kept the wicket-taking record until 1936, when Clarrie Grimmett went past him, the Australian leg-spinner having bowled nearly 6000 more deliveries. In fact, Barnes bowled in only seven series, only once averaging less than five wickets per match in a series — when he took 24 wickets in five Tests in Australia in 1907-08. He took five wickets in a Test innings against Australia 12 times, a figure beaten today by just one man: New Zealand's Richard Hadlee. In his final three years in Test cricket, 1911-1914, Barnes took 122 wickets at 14.08.

When Barnes was first chosen for England, for the 1901-02 tour of Australia, he had played just six first-class games. Folklore has it that his stunning invitation to tour came after England captain Archie MacLaren faced him for a mere 30 minutes in the nets at Manchester. Barnes certainly justified his selection by taking 19 wickets in the first two Tests before his knee betrayed him. In the years that followed, Barnes could have played more Test cricket than he did, but he was a difficult man, prone to bouts of pique and clashes with authority. The drudgery of county cricket did not appeal to him. 'He preferred the easy and not less economically profitable life of a league professional,' wrote Cardus. From 38 seasons in the leagues, he took 3741 wickets, at the ridiculous average of 6.61.

He made his name in Test cricket. Like WG Grace before him, he would never sell himself short; like Shane Warne much later, he bowled best on the brightest stage, and for captains who fully appreciated him and let him run the show. 'In Barnes' heyday,' Cardus wrote in *Close of Play*, 'his best ball was known as the "Barnes ball". It pitched on the stumps between leg and middle, and then turned to threaten the off-stump or find the edge of the quickest bat.' Barnes was the first medium or fast-medium bowler to master the ball that moved from leg to off. Sure, the leg break existed in the first two decades of Test cricket, but bowled at pace as a leg-cutter it was rarely a stock ball because it was too risky. Barnes was so good he changed the game, and only the true legends of the game have managed that.

SYDNEY BARNES (ENGLAND)
Test Cricket

Tests	Inn	NO	Runs	HS	Ave	100	50	Ct	Balls	Runs	Wkts	Ave	Best	5/	10/
27	39	9	242	38*	8.07	–	–	12	7873	3106	189	16.43	9-103	24	7

First-Class Cricket

Mat	Inn	NO	Runs	HS	Ave	100	50	Ct	Balls	Runs	Wkts	Ave	Best	5/	10/
133	173	50	1573	93	12.79	–	2	72	31527	12289	719	17.09	9-103	68	18

No. 10 Adam Gilchrist

Few Australian batsmen outside Bradman have played as many game-turning innings in Test cricket as did Adam Gilchrist. He did so in Hobart, in Mumbai, Birmingham, Johannesburg and Cape Town. Think of the first week of 2003, at the Sydney Cricket Ground, when he played another gem — not a matchwinner in this instance — in which he decisively outscored Steve Waugh at a time when the then Australian captain was playing one of finest innings of his life. Waugh finished with 102 runs from 135 deliveries; Gilchrist 133 from 121. How about Christchurch in 2005, when he came to the wicket with Australia 6-201 after nightwatchman Jason Gillespie had been dismissed, and bludgeoned 121 from 126 balls, with 12 fours and six sixes? There have been so many times when Gilchrist has come out and quickly changed the game that he must be the best No. 7 in history, better even than Ian Botham. Yet in Kandy in 2004 he was promoted to No. 3 by new captain Ricky Ponting and hit 144 from 185 balls after the first 21 wickets of the Test had fallen for 342 runs. In doing this, he set the tone for the entire series.

After his first 47 Tests, Gilchrist had a Test batting average of 60.25, with nine centuries. Only four batsmen in Test history who have played even 20 innings have a career average above 60. In Gilchrist's next 33 Tests, to March 1, 2006, he averaged a mere 39.26, with six hundreds, and was tagged in some quarters as being out of form. Yet, apart from Gilchrist, at that time in Test history only three men who had kept wicket for any significant time had also averaged 40 or more with the bat over their career — Zimbabwe's Andy Flower (53.70), England's Les Ames (43.40) and South Africa's Denis Lindsay (40.00). Despite his 'slump', Gilchrist's career average was nearly twice as much per innings as that of Ian Healy or Rod Marsh, yet both Healy and Marsh were considered in their day to be better-than-average keeper/batsmen. For the final 16 Tests of Gilchrist's career, from March 2006 to January 2008, he averaged only 34.31 with the bat, yet he still made two superb hundreds, one a match-saving 144 (out of an innings total of 269) against Bangladesh at Fatullah; the other a crushing century from just 57 balls — one delivery more than Viv Richards' record for the fastest hundred in Tests — against England in Perth. He was also named man of the match in

The unique, exhilarating style of cricket's finest wicketkeeping all-rounder.

The First XI

the 2007 World Cup final against Sri Lanka, after hitting 149 from a mere 104 balls.

For most of the first 90 or so years of Test cricket, one of the game's time-honoured adages was that when it came to picking your wicketkeeper, skill with the gloves was the crucial measuring stick. Batting prowess was only an issue if you were choosing between two keepers of equal ability. As an example, in 1962 AG Moyes recalled the England XI selected for the first Ashes Test of 1946-47: 'By some strange process of reasoning, Evans was omitted from the English team for the first Test at Brisbane in 1946 so that Gibb could play. It was an over-emphasis on batting and a negation of the established principle that the second-best in wicketkeeping will not do. Of course, the plan failed ...'

In the 1970s, England's Alan Knott and Australia's Rod Marsh were able to demonstrate the true value of a wicketkeeper who could also bat. However, both Knott and Marsh were also great keepers, who most likely would have retained their Test places even if their runs had dried up (as Marsh's did to some degree in the 1980s). Still, they started a trend, and when the West Indies dominated the 1980s with an average gloveman — but excellent batsman — in Jeffrey Dujon, it became almost the accepted wisdom that a team couldn't afford a keeper who could not bat. England often preferred to have Alec Stewart behind the stumps, even if his Test batting average was nearly 12 runs worse when he donned the gloves. Yet it was Gilchrist who put the old thinking to bed for good; in series against Australia in 2004 and 2005, India and then England persevered with terrible keepers in the belief that the extra runs might somehow make up for the muffed chances.

Gilchrist, stand-in captain with Ricky Ponting injured, celebrates Australia's victory in India in 2004.

What these hapless jugglers really did was prove just how priceless Gilchrist was: an extra batsman as effective as any of the top six in the Australian order, and a capable gloveman who, managed an Australian-best 4.33 dismissals per Test. (By comparison, Marsh completed 3.70 dismissals per Test, Healy 3.32 dismissals per Test). He was the first Australian keeper to complete 400 Test dismissals. Further, he was a revelation as an opening bat for Australian one-day teams, scoring 9619 runs and 16 hundreds while averaging almost a run a ball with the bat.

In just his second Test, Gilchrist came to the wicket on the fourth day with Australia 5-126 chasing 369 against a Pakistani attack that included Wasim Akram, Waqar Younis, Shoaib Akhtar and Saqlain Mushtaq, and with Justin Langer added 238 for the sixth wicket. Gilchrist's contribution was 149 not out, from 163 balls.

Two and a half years later, and his captain, Steve Waugh, was calling him the 'Tiger Woods of cricket', suggesting that 'Viv Richards would be the closest to him for the freedom and expression of skills and the pure essence of what batting is about.'

The 100 Greatest Cricketers

Few captaincy ideas have been more inspired than Steve Waugh's decision in 1998 to move Gilchrist to the top of the Australian one-day team's batting order.

Some are critical of Gilchrist's glovework, but he has averaged more dismissals per Test than any other Australian keeper.

Gilchrist had scored what was then the fastest double century in Test history, from 212 balls, with 19 fours and eight sixes, against South Africa in Johannesburg. In the following Test in Cape Town, he smashed 138 from 108 balls, reaching his century in 91 deliveries. 'To "Gilly" (as it was for Sir Viv),' Waugh wrote, 'each ball is seen as an opportunity to score a boundary, rather than a chance to be dismissed.'

Waugh noted that Gilchrist had been on the winning side in 24 of his first 30 Tests, and wondered whether such a run could possibly continue. But for the rest of his career, Gilchrist's golden touch was still very much apparent: 96 Tests, for 73 wins, 12 draws and just 11 losses. Bradman, by comparison, was on the losing side 12 times in 52 Tests. The superb cricket website howstat.com.au notes that of all batsmen who have had their deliveries faced faithfully recorded (this information not having been recorded in earlier Tests), Gilchrist is the second fastest scorer, at 81.96 runs per 100 balls faced. Only Pakistan's Shahid Afridi (86.13) is ahead of him, but his Test batting average is 37.40.

Combining Gilchrist's batting average with his strike rate, and remembering that he was also a wicketkeeper who played nearly 100 Tests, makes him one of the most influential cricketers of all time. For all the great quality of modern-day Australian champions such as Waugh, Warne, McGrath and co, the strong suspicion is that without the unique contributions of Gilchrist — taking all his catches, scoring all his runs, always quickly — the Australian team's winning record could not have been as good.

ADAM GILCHRIST (AUSTRALIA)																
Test Cricket																
Tests	Inn	NO	Runs	HS	Ave	100	50	Ct	St	Balls	Runs	Wkts	Ave	Best	5/	10/
96	137	20	5570	204*	47.61	17	26	379	37	–	–	–	–	–	–	–
One-Day International Cricket																
ODIs	Inn	NO	Runs	HS	Ave	100	50	Ct	St	Balls	Runs	Wkts	Ave	Best	5/	10
287	279	11	9619	172	35.89	16	55	417	55	–	–	–	–	–	–	–

Graeme Pollock

No. 11

One of the reasons batting averages have continued to be recorded by the cricket statisticians is that, for all their faults, provided they are based on sufficient innings they still represent a good guide to a batsman's ability. And according to the batting averages, if you take Sir Donald Bradman out, Graeme Pollock was the greatest batsman of all time. Of all cricketers to bat 20 times in Tests, Bradman dominates with his average of 99.94. Next best, at 60.97, from 2256 runs in 41 innings, is Pollock.

To some degree, it is difficult to measure Pollock's greatness, because his international career was prematurely ended by the sporting bans placed on South Africa because of the apartheid policies of its government. His 19th Test ended on February 28, 1967, the day after his 23rd birthday. Three years later, he played the last four of his 23 Tests. He continued in first-class cricket until he was almost 43, still good enough to blast eye-catching hundreds, but unable to build the sort of imposing Test record that would have been expected of him. Imagine how exciting a clash between Pollock and Lillee and Thomson might have been.

Pollock was a schoolboy prodigy, maker of a first-class century before his 17th birthday. He made his Test debut in Australia in 1963-64, and after failing to get past 25 in the first two matches scored his maiden Test century in the third, becoming at 19 years 318 days the youngest South African to score a Test century. However, it was in the fourth Test in Adelaide that he made his reputation, joining Eddie Barlow at the wicket when South Africa was 2-70 in reply to 345, and with Barlow adding a South African record 341 for the third wicket. Barlow was out for 201, Pollock for 175, and South Africa went on to 595, then their highest ever innings total against Australia. 'The main subject for debate in the George Giffen Stand,' wrote the veteran cricket writer RS Whitington, 'was whether Garry Sobers, then representing South Australia, or Graeme Pollock was the more talented and attractive left-hander.'

Pollock in England in 1965.

45

Eighteen months later, at Trent Bridge, Pollock produced an innings that established his reputation in England. By the numbers, the effort is impressive enough: South Africa were 4-43 and then 5-80 on the first morning before Pollock scored a superb century and steered them to 269 all out. However, it was the way he dominated while those around him struggled that was most impressive. He scored 125 runs out of 160 in 140 minutes, on a pitch that Richie Benaud said was 'soft like Plasticine and reckoned by many experts to be too slow for strokeplay'.

The older Pollock, confined to South African first-class cricket because the apartheid boycott, but still the most imposing batsman in the country.

Back home in 1966-67, Australia lost the first Test heavily, the first time they'd lost a Test in South Africa, but in Cape Town they were delighted to not only make a huge first-innings total but then reduce the home team to 5-85. Handicapped by a bruised toe and a strained thigh muscle, but seemingly as unflustered as ever, Pollock this time made 209 out of 353, after the other five batsmen in the top six had scored 33 between them. During this innings, he also showed that the habit bowlers had relied on in previous years — of bowling at his pads to avoid his offside power — had turned him into an excellent onside player. 'He is now as close to a complete all-round batsman as one is likely to find,' wrote Benaud.

South Africa did not play another series until the Australians returned in early 1970 for four Tests. Pollock's first five scores in the series were 49, 50, 274, 52 and 87, before he failed twice in the last Test, as South Africa won the series 4-0. The 274 in Durban came after Barry Richards had scored his first Test century, and people who were there talk about the batting of the young opener and the great left-hander after lunch as perhaps the greatest 60 minutes in South African cricket history. 'That hour after lunch on the first day was unbelievable,' their teammate Lee Irvine told ESPN's *Legends of Cricket* in 2002. 'We talk about one-day cricket now and how people hit the ball. What happened that day was not hitting, it was strokeplay and it was the most brilliant cricket I've ever seen in my life. Two greats of the game trying to outdo each other in some way.' Pollock batted for 417 minutes, faced 401 balls, and hit a five and 43 fours.

Two Tests later, and Pollock's Test career was over. After South Africa's scheduled tour of England in 1970 was cancelled, Pollock was permitted to join a Rest of the World team that took part in a five-match series that served as a substitute for the originally programmed Tests. He managed one century, in the final international, a performance he matched in Australia in 1971-72 when again a South Africa tour was cancelled and replaced with a tour by a 'World XI' combination. For the next 15 years, Pollock's career was contained to Currie Cup cricket in South Africa, plus occasional series against rebel teams from Sri Lanka, England, the West Indies and Australia, and also private touring teams such as the 'International Wanderers' side that Richie Benaud brought to the republic in early 1976. How lethal he might have been in international one-day cricket was indicated by his fastest century in first-class cricket, made from 52 balls for the International Cavaliers against a Barbados XI in Scarborough (England) in 1969. In a one-day match in South Africa, he came in during the 12th over and at the end of 60 overs was 222 not out!

The First XI

Pollock with his elder brother Peter (right), who took 116 wickets in 28 Tests.

Throughout his career, Pollock made a habit of hitting good balls for four. He was immensely strong in the wrists and forearms, which allowed him to use a bat that weighed 3lbs, almost a pound heavier than the willow Bradman used. Some cynics thought he might have had a weakness against pace, but a century scored against the International Wanderers when Lillee was near his fastest set that myth straight. In the second innings of that same game, Lillee took 7-27, as if to prove he was fair dinkum. Pollock, despite not being far from his 40th birthday, also scored two hundreds against the West Indies rebels in the early 1980s, against two lively temperamental quicks in Franklyn Stephenson and Sylvester Clarke.

Pollock ended his career in 1987 with Currie Cup records for most runs (12,409) and most catches (157). In all, he'd made 20,940 first-class runs, at 54.67 with 64 centuries, despite never playing county cricket. As clearly as Don Bradman is cricket's greatest batsman, Graeme Pollock is the best runscorer to ever come out of South Africa.

GRAEME POLLOCK (SOUTH AFRICA)
Test Cricket

Tests	Inn	NO	Runs	HS	Ave	100	50	Ct	Balls	Runs	Wkts	Ave	Best	5/	10/
23	41	4	2256	274	60.97	7	11	17	414	204	4	51.00	2-50	–	–

First-Class Cricket

Mat	Inn	NO	Runs	HS	Ave	100	50	Ct	Balls	Runs	Wkts	Ave	Best	5/	10/
262	437	54	20940	274	54.67	64	99	248	3743	2062	43	47.95	3-46	–	–

The 100 Greatest Cricketers

Dennis Lillee

Viv Richards

The Second

Muttiah Muralitharan

Brian Lara

The Second XI

Richard Hadlee

Wally Hammond

Fred Spofforth

Len Hutton

Alan Knott

Victor Trumper

Ian Botham

No. 12 Dennis Lillee

In early 1971, Dennis Lillee burst on the Test scene, taking five wickets in his first innings, the only time an Australian managed a five-for in the 1970-71 Ashes series. As the team surged back to the top of the cricket tree, more than anyone else in the side, Lillee captured the team's hard, brash, give-'em-nothing image. Then, as the game in Australia, on the back of World Series Cricket, moved into the entertainment age, Lillee became its biggest star. On his retirement in 1984, he left a sport far different to the one he'd joined more than a decade before. And, despite the quiet complaints of some traditionalists, it seemed the game was better for the experience.

The most famous bowling action of the 1970s

Dennis Lillee might have taken five English wickets the first time he bowled in Test cricket, but it was not until the following season, 1971-72, that he established himself as a genuine force in international cricket. He did so in sudden, devastating style, against a 'World XI' team that had come to Australia after a scheduled series against South Africa was cancelled. In the second international, at the WACA in Perth, Lillee produced a spell of fast bowling as lethal as anything bowled by Harold Larwood, Ray Lindwall or Frank Tyson. In 57 deliveries he took 8-29 — the last six wickets in a spell of 31 balls for no runs — and demoralised a world-class batting order with steepling bounce and awesome speed. Soon after, Lillee took 31 wickets in the 1972 Ashes series, at that time the most ever by an Australian in England, and twice took three wickets in four balls. 'Like Tyson and Wesley Hall, he makes crowds gasp when they first see him bowl,' wrote John Arlott in *The Ashes 1972*. 'That is the measure of real speed in a bowler.'

A back complaint that restricted Lillee somewhat in the 1972-73 Australian season flared into a major injury in 1973, and ultimately cost the fast man the best part of two years of his cricketing life. Some had assumed that he was gone for good, but these cynics had severely underestimated their man. The fable of Lillee's long battle back to full fitness is one of the most inspiring in cricket's history. First, he endured a difficult and frustrating six weeks with his back in a plaster cast from his buttocks to his chest. Then, supported by Dr Frank Pyke and others at the physical education department at the University of Western Australia, he put himself through a strength-building and fitness program that evolved into something of a blueprint for the future preparations of young fast bowlers and the rehabilitation of injured pacemen. At the same time, he set about understanding the mechanics of his art, and modified his run-up and delivery into a classic approach that also limited the chances of his back failing again. These learning processes would continue for the rest of his career, and beyond.

The Second XI

The new Lillee saw no harm in trying to rile or intimidate the opposition, with words and actions, stating defiantly that he aimed bouncers at batsmen, hoping to scare them. 'When you are out in the middle,' he told journalist Keith Butler in 1976, ' you have to hate the opposition player. There's no doubt about that, but what I mean by hate is not to hate him personally — but to hate what he represents. You have to regard him as someone who is trying to steal something from you.' However, Lillee never bore grudges, and while occasionally his on-field demeanour looked boorish, it never harmed his bowling.

In Australia in 1975-76, Lillee and Jeff Thomson took on the West Indies' Andy Roberts and Michael Holding. There were plenty of bouncers, but the result was a no contest, Australia winning 5-1, with Lillee taking 27 wickets in five Tests, including his 100th Test wicket. During the following season, after Thomson wrecked his shoulder, Lillee was magnificent, taking 47 wickets in six Tests, including 11 in the Centenary Test against England at the MCG, an occasion which evolved into a major personal triumph. Australia was bowled out for only 138 on the opening day, but despite already bowling more than 1700 deliveries for Australia in the previous 11 weeks he gallantly took 6-26 from 13.3 overs, getting lift, swing and movement off the pitch, as England capitulated to 95, and then toiled through another 34.4 eight-ball overs, taking 5-139 to prevent England achieving an unlikely victory on the final afternoon. At game's end, he was chaired from the field as the conquering hero. Soon after, he announced his body desperately needed a rest and therefore he would not be available for the 1977 Ashes tour.

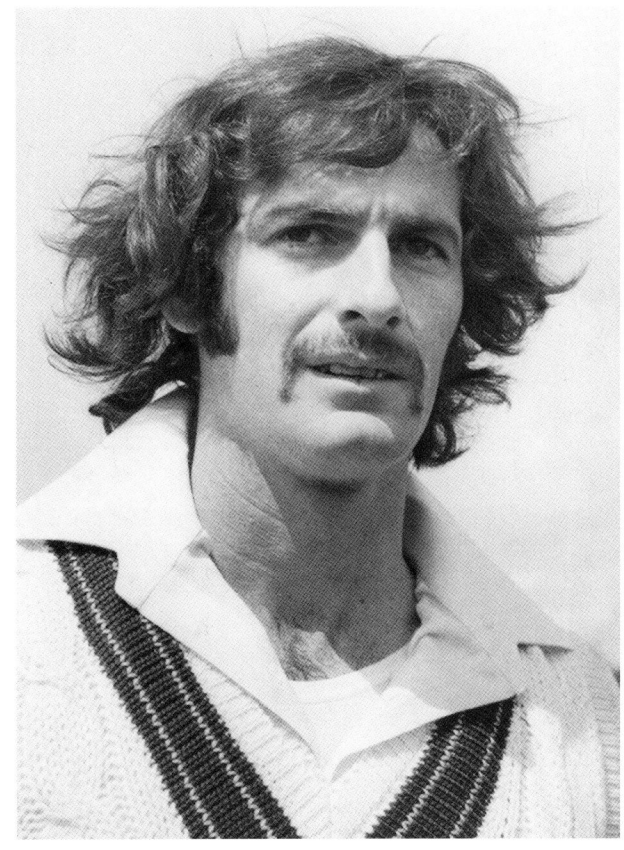

Lillee in 1972, the year he established himself as the spearhead of the next great era of Australian cricket.

The break paid dividends. In World Series Cricket, 1977-79, Lillee was supreme among a plethora of great pacemen — Roberts, Holding, Joel Garner, Mike Procter, John Snow, Imran Khan, et al. He took 79 wickets in the SuperTests, another 54 in the one-day internationals, all the time operating at an intensity that gradually won over the sceptics who'd reckoned WSC was not fair dinkum. Then, in the sixth Test of 1979-80, the season after traditional cricket and WSC made up, Lillee overwhelmed England through skill and strength of personality on a slow pitch that reduced other fast bowlers to bystanders. Cutting his run, he relied on changes of pace and a collection of leg- and off-cutters, and took 11-138 for the match. In the 18 months from the Centenary Test in England in 1980 to the end of the 1981-82 Australian season, Lillee took 122 wickets in 19 Tests at 18.95, in the process breaking Richie Benaud's then Australian wicket-taking record, beating Hugh Trumble to become the leading wicket-taker in Ashes history, becoming the only Australian since Fred Spofforth to take 10 wickets in an Ashes Test four times, and then taking a world record 310th Test wicket.

The 100 Greatest Cricketers

The infamous clash between Lillee and Pakistan's Javed Miandad at the WACA in 1981-82.

The most thrilling moment of this period came at the MCG on Boxing Day 1981: the dismissal of Viv Richards. It was the first day, and the crowd was already in a vibrant mood after a dynamic unconquered century by Kim Hughes. The West Indies had 35 minutes to bat, and Lillee was inspired, having Desmond Haynes caught at second slip, nightwatchman Colin Croft lbw and finally, dramatically, Richards bowled off the inside edge from the final ball of the day.

Lillee retired after the 1983-84 Australian season, having taken 355 Test wickets and 103 one-day international wickets. At the time, these were both world records. What made Lillee such a special sportsperson was that — because of serious injury and having already proved himself as a firebrand of the highest class — he was able to remake himself as the craftiest fast-medium bowler and most professional cricketer of his generation. He was the man all captains would have wanted on their team, whatever the conditions, whether it was the young Lillee pre-injury or the experienced campaigner post-injury, whoever was the batsman at the other end.

DENNIS LILLEE (AUSTRALIA)

Test Cricket

Tests	Inn	NO	Runs	HS	Ave	100	50	Ct	Balls	Runs	Wkts	Ave	Best	5/	10/
70	90	24	905	73*	13.71	–	1	23	18467	8493	355	23.92	7-83	23	7

One-Day International Cricket

ODIs	Inn	NO	Runs	HS	Ave	100	50	Ct	Balls	Runs	Wkts	Ave	Best	4/
63	34	8	240	42*	9.23	–	–	10	3593	2145	103	20.83	5-34	6

The Second XI

Viv Richards

No. 13

Though batting helmets came into international cricket in the late 1970s, when Viv Richards' Test career was just three-and-a-half years old, he never wore one. To him, it was an admission of fear, and while he was occasionally hit on the cap, he was never ruffled. He seemed invincible. For a decade, he was the best hooker in the game. In World Series Cricket, which featured a posse of fast bowlers pitching short on some suspicious surfaces, Richards was supreme, taking on the quicks while others tried to survive. Like all the game's truly great hitters, he was able to combine timing with savage force, and though he made a habit of moving straight onto the front foot, which often gave the illusion that he had committed himself too early, his eye rarely failed him. Just when a bowler thought Richards might be in trouble, he'd move sweetly back and play the correct shot with time to spare.

Given that he liked to plant that front foot, it is astonishing that no fast man, however quick, surprised him with a bouncer. Stop a video of him batting at the moment just after the ball was delivered and you might think him technically deficient, incapable of keeping his balance to play a decisive shot; forward on to the moment he hit the ball and everything seems right, even when he was hitting across the line. Adding to the package, Richards was a big-match player who revelled in a challenge. He saw his role as being to stride out on the fall of the first wicket and take the attack to his opponents, with his special mission being to destroy the other team's spearhead. In 1980, Richards tore at England's Bob Willis to the point that the bowler, in his own words, 'felt utterly helpless and depressed'. *Wisden* called what occurred in the third Test a 'vendetta-like attack', as Richards bashed 53 of his 65 runs from the man who had been England's No. 1 bowler. Willis was sacked after one more Test and didn't regain his confidence for 12 months. When the pair next faced each other in a Test match, four years had passed, but the offensive continued unabated. Willis' career was all but over.

Richards in England in 1976, his first great series.

The value of such assaults — on the bowler, the bowler's teammates and his own comrades — cannot be understated. It's very difficult to win the race if you're last after the first lap. Inevitably, the field placings were now more suited to a one-day game, so Richards could relax and pick his moments. His fellow batsmen, ever grateful, would face shattered

53

bowlers who had lost their ambition. The pressure was gone. The fans, though, were excited. When Viv Richards was scheduled to bat, the cricket was not to be missed.

Born in tiny Antigua in 1952, he first came to world cricket's attention when he ran out three of Australia's top-order batsmen in the 1975 World Cup final. As an all-round fielder, Richards was probably the best of his time, high praise given that this was an era in which fielding standards reached new heights. He was a sure catch in the slip cordon, with a goalkeeper's ability to dive sideways. At mid-wicket or in the covers his range was many metres wide. His Test career took off in 1976, when he scored an unprecedented 1710 runs for the calendar year, including seven centuries, at an average of 90. For much of the next decade, Viv was king, in cricket's great era of pace demonstrating time and again that he was one of the greatest players of pure pace bowling in cricket history. He didn't have to face his fantastic teammates, but still confronted Dennis Lillee and Jeff Thomson, John Snow, Garth le Roux, Richard Hadlee, Rodney Hogg, Geoff Lawson, Ian Botham, Imran Khan, Kapil Dev, Craig McDermott and Wasim Akram, all of them after revenge for the bouncers bowled upon them.

Richards hooks away during the 1984 Texaco Trophy one-day series in England

In 1981, Richards marked the first ever Test played in Antigua with a century, his sixth against England in 12 Tests, but it was a slow, deliberate innings, especially by his standards. Five years later, against the same country and again at St John's, he clobbered the fastest hundred (in terms of balls faced) in Test history. Twenty-eight runs came from his bat before tea from just 14 balls, he reached his fifty in 34 balls and his hundred in 56, hitting seven fours and seven sixes. Another astonishing innings was his 189 not out in a 55-over one-day international against England at Old Trafford in 1984. Made from 170 balls, it featured an undefeated last-wicket partnership of 106 in 14 overs with Michael Holding, who scored 12. One of Richards' five sixes went clean out of the ground.

The Second XI

Some parts of Richards' résumé are quite fantastic. His eight Test centuries against India has been matched only by Sobers. He reached a fifty against India at Kingston in 1983 in 32 balls. In New Zealand in 1987, he scored 119 and took 5-41 in a one-day international in Dunedin, the first instance of a player achieving a century/five-for double in a ODI. Between 1979 and 1986 Richards played in 12 Test series and only once failed to score at least one hundred in the rubber. In 1988, he became the first West Indian to score 100 first-class centuries. He is one of only two men in ODI history (India's MS Dhoni being the other) to play at least 40 innings, average over 40 (he averaged 47.00), and maintain a strike rate of more than 90 runs scored per 100 balls faced.

As a captain, there is a perception that his West Indies teams were not as dominant as the great outfits led by his immediate predecessor, Clive Lloyd. However, this is not fair. Discounting the occasions he filled in prior to Lloyd's retirement in 1985, Richards led the West Indies for six years (1985 to 1991), during which he never lost a series, and beat England and Australia home and away, and India and New Zealand at home. Certainly, the team was much less dominant in one-day internationals, but the team's loss to India in the 1983 World Cup final suggested this decline might actually have begun under Lloyd. Richards captained the West Indies in 50 Tests for 27 victories and 15 losses.

In building this top 100, Richards was one of the most difficult to rank. His final Test batting average of 50.23 is excellent, but still less than other great batsmen of his era such as Gavaskar, Greg Chappell, Javed Miandad and Allan Border who are always placed below him. In the end, why Viv Richards ranks highest of his generation is as much about his 'aura' as anything else. There might not have been a cricketer since WG Grace who had a more distinctive air on the cricket field *and* was able to follow it up with a succession of amazing deeds.

By 1988, Richards was the Windies captain and as imperious and successful as ever.

VIV RICHARDS (WEST INDIES)

Test Cricket

Tests	Inn	NO	Runs	HS	Ave	100	50	Ct	Balls	Runs	Wkts	Ave	Best	5/	10/
121	182	12	8540	291	50.24	24	45	122	5170	1964	32	61.38	2-17	–	–

One-Day International Cricket

ODIs	Inn	NO	Runs	HS	Ave	100	50	Ct	Balls	Runs	Wkts	Ave	Best	4/
187	167	24	6721	189*	47.00	11	45	101	5644	4228	118	35.83	6-41	3

No. 14 Richard Hadlee

Richard Hadlee's career total of 431 Test wickets was, at June 30, 2009, more than 200 wickets above that taken by any other Kiwi bowler bar Daniel Vettori (who has taken 293). His bowling average (22.30) is more than four runs better than any other Kiwi with even 100 Test wickets. He scored 3124 Test runs, ninth highest among all New Zealanders, even though he often seemed more intent on hitting than orthodox batting. He also took 158 ODI wickets and 1751 ODI runs, and achieved all this despite never having a high-class opening bowling partner to share the load, let alone soften up the opposition. He is as clearly New Zealand's greatest cricketer as Don Bradman is statistically the game's greatest batsman.

The consummate professional: Hadlee at Lord's in 1986.

Hadlee is the son of one of New Zealand's finest players, Walter Hadlee, and younger brother of Barry and Dayle, who both went on to represent their country in cricket (all three sons played together in the 1975 World Cup). Throughout his career, he brought to fast-medium bowling as complete and comprehensive an approach as is possible. If he did not take wickets, which was rare, it was never for lack of preparation and concentration. When he retired, he must have been satisfied that he had got everything out of his bowling talent that he possibly could.

Though he made his Test debut in February 1973, Hadlee was not a certain selection in his country's top XI until he destroyed India at Wellington three years later. This was only New Zealand's ninth Test victory, in their 119th match, and their first by an innings, and Hadlee's match figures of 11-58 were a New Zealand Test record (and remained so until Hadlee improved on them against Australia in 1985-86). When he next bowled in a Test, he was opening the attack, in Lahore in October 1976, and he responded by taking 5-121. In the third Test, in Karachi, he scored 87, his first Test half-century, and with Warren Lees added 186 for the seventh wicket. After three Tests in India, Hadlee returned home having, in the upbeat words of captain Glenn Turner, 'come of age'.

In early 1978, at Wellington, New Zealand defeated England in a Test match for the first time, at the 48th attempt. It was an astonishing victory, Hadlee taking 6-26 as England, chasing 137, were bowled out for just 64. However, in county cricket, playing for Nottinghamshire, Hadlee was disappointing for three seasons, often injured, until in 1981 he took advantage of a summer of peak fitness to become the only bowler to take 100 wickets in the season and to lead the county to the county championship for the first time since 1929. Significantly, he took his wickets using a shortened run-up, cut from 23 paces to 15.

The Second XI

Hadlee's view is that this abbreviated run-up made him more 'clinically efficient', and his cricket story through the '80s amply supports that view. Anything lost in pace was amply compensated by an extraordinary control and a broader range of deliveries. His stock delivery was the leg-cutter, but whenever he needed, he could nip one back the other way, usually after delivering the ball from a little wider on the bowling crease. He could also swing the ball both ways, always late. His slower ball usually swung into the batsmen. And he had a quicker bouncer, which always seemed to be bowled when the batsman least expected it.

From the moment he inspired a stunning and controversial victory over the West Indies in early 1980, the first time New Zealand had won a series at home, Hadlee was always rated as being among the game's elite. Any doubts were erased in Australia in 1980-81, when the media handed him the mantle of 'villain' during a tempestuous season that culminated in the infamous 'underarm' one-day international. Hadlee was booed by the Australian crowds, but (and because) he rivalled Dennis Lillee and Greg Chappell as the cricketer of the summer. In three Tests he took 19 wickets (Lillee managed 16) despite not getting even one lbw decision from the Australian umpires.

Hadlee took special pleasure from beating Australia. In 1985-86 he spearheaded arguably New Zealand's greatest performance in a cricket match, taking 9-52 and 6-71 and scoring 54 in the Kiwis' only innings at the Gabba. This might have been the finest, at the very least the most controlled, pace bowling performance in cricket history. Especially in the first innings, it seemed Hadlee could place the ball wherever he wanted. While it must be conceded that, Allan Border apart, he was facing an ordinary and dispirited Australian side, it should also be remembered that this was a good batting wicket, on which four centuries were scored and New Zealand, when they batted, reached 7 (declared) for 553.

Hadlee in Bangalore in November 1988, having just broken Ian Botham's Test wicket-taking world record.

For the next two years, Hadlee's wicket-taking was prodigious. He captured 33 wickets in that three-Test series in Australia, as New Zealand won a rubber against their neighbours for the first time, then took another 16 as they repeated the dose in three more Tests at home. The first wicket he took in the opening Test, at Wellington, was Border lbw, his 300th Test wicket. Fourteen Tests later, he went past Ian Botham's world record of 373 Test wickets, and against Australia in early 1990, in his final Test on home soil, he took five wickets in an innings for the 100th time in first-class cricket and the 35th time in Tests, as New Zealand won decisively by nine wickets. This result meant that in the decade of cricket, 1980-81 to 1989-90, the two countries had five victories each, from 17 Tests. Before 1980, Australia won five Tests to the Kiwis' one; between 1991 and 2008, the record was Australia 14 victories, New Zealand one.

The 100 Greatest Cricketers

Hadlee appeals for an LBW decision against England's Graham Gooch during his farewell Test series.

In June 1990, nine days before the second Test between England and New Zealand at Lord's, Hadlee was knighted, and he celebrated by slamming a belligerent 86 from just 84 balls. Then, a fortnight later, in the 86th and last Test match of his career, he took another eight wickets, including two wickets in his final over in Test cricket. One of these, Devon Malcolm, was his 431st victim, taken with his very last ball. Hadlee remained the leading Test wicket-taker until February 1994, when Kapil Dev took over.

Kapil and Sir Richard were two of the quartet of great allrounders who thrilled cricket fans through the 1980s, Ian Botham and Imran Khan being the others. Rating one better than the other is awkward, though it is fair to say that if all four were in the one team, Hadlee would definitely be the lowest in the batting order. In most circumstances, Kapil would have to accept bowling second change. Who would bowl the first over? It could easily be Imran from 1982, or perhaps Botham from 1978. If it was to be Sir Richard Hadlee, it could be the Hadlee of any year from 1980 to 1990, for he was proud, dangerous and productive right through that era. Very few pace bowlers in the game's history have been so good for so long.

RICHARD HADLEE (NEW ZEALAND)

Test Cricket

Tests	Inn	NO	Runs	HS	Ave	100	50	Ct	Balls	Runs	Wkts	Ave	Best	5/	10/
86	134	19	3124	151*	27.17	2	15	39	21918	9611	431	22.30	9-52	36	9

One-Day International Cricket

ODIs	Inn	NO	Runs	HS	Ave	100	50	Ct	Balls	Runs	Wkts	Ave	Best	4/
115	98	17	1751	79	21.62	–	4	27	6182	3407	158	21.56	5-25	6

The Second XI

Wally Hammond

No. 15

Wally Hammond scored 22 Test and 167 first-class centuries, four first-class triple centuries, 36 double centuries. He was the first batsman to score 6000 and then 7000 Test runs, one of only two men to score 900 runs in one Test series. However, because he played his cricket at the same time as Don Bradman, many of his grandest efforts were quickly more than matched by the unique runscoring of The Don, and the result is that Hammond does not always get the recognition his great achievements deserve, for he was as close to Bradman statistically as just about anyone. Only Bradman has scored more first-class double centuries (37 to 36) or first-class triple centuries (six to four) than Hammond. When the Englishman hammered 905 runs in the Ashes series of 1928-29, Bradman scored 974 runs in 1930. Hammond was the first to score double hundreds in successive Tests; in the following series Bradman scored a triple century followed by a double. After Hammond scored a magnificent unbeaten double century in the second Test of 1936-37, and England led the series 2-0, Bradman responded with 270, 212 and 169 in the last three matches and Australia retained the Ashes. Bradman only took two wickets in Test cricket, but one of them was Hammond.

The London *Times* correspondent Geoffrey Green once wrote that one of his fondest memories of cricket was 'Walter Hammond striding down the pavilion steps at Lord's like a stately white galleon in full sail'.

On the field, Wally Hammond was a supremely confident batsman, with an aura that often made bowlers seem more of a hindrance than a threat. He was a classic stylist, but his game was straight out of the textbook, and his cricket mindset was ruthless. The front pad was never far from the bat when he played forward, and when he went back he kept his head still and over the ball. Whether batting, bowling or taking lightning catches in the slip cordon, everything seemed in the right place. If contemporary accounts of his innings are a good guide, he might have been cricket's best ever cover driver.

Hammond arrived in Sydney for the second Test of 1928-29 having not made a century in his first nine Tests. As Steve Waugh was to do when he rescued his Test career 60 years later, Hammond decided to minimise risk, eschewing the hook and pull shots completely, and even avoiding the square cut until he was set. The results were fantastic: 251 in Sydney, 200 and 32 run out in Melbourne, 119 not out and 177 in Adelaide, and finally, with the first four Tests all won, 38 and 16 in Melbourne. Australia's attack was hardly potent in this series, but still in those middle three Tests Hammond was as close to impossible to dismiss as any batsman has ever been. Rarely in the years afterwards did Hammond let his guard down — perhaps because, the bodyline series apart, Bradman's Australia was always slightly in front — but there were moments, such as when he decided to end the 1932-33 Ashes series with a six. Philip Lee was promptly lofted into the crowd beyond the long-off boundary. That happened in Sydney, where Hammond was almost inevitably successful, scoring four hundreds in Test matches (251 in 1928-29, 112 and 101 in 1932-33, 231 not out in 1936-37) and averaged 256.67 in Tests before World War II.

No one ever questioned his courage. In the third Test of 1936-37 at the MCG he played an innings of 32 on a hazardous pitch on which 13 wickets fell for 98 runs during the day. But in doing so, he might have cost England the Ashes. By making the diabolical wicket appear playable, Hammond fooled his skipper Gubby Allen into procrastinating about his declaration. After he was dismissed to make it 4-68, caught in spectacular fashion by Len Darling at short leg, England lost 5-8 even though Bradman had instructed his bowlers not to get anyone out, and Australia lost only one wicket in the short time left before stumps, even though its batting order was reversed. The next day, after the pitch dried, Bradman came in at No. 7 and made 270, Jack Fingleton scored 136, and the momentum of the series was irreversibly altered. Had the Australians been put back in even half an hour earlier, immediately after Hammond was dismissed, the story might have been different. No wonder Neville Cardus called Allen's declaration a 'grim belated joke'.

Just 32 runs, but this was Hammond's greatest innings. Cardus, seeing a Melbourne sticky for the first time, was enthralled. One ball from O'Reilly 'rose straight from a good length to Hammond's cap', he wrote in his book, *Australian Summer*. 'I was lost in amazement and admiration of the way Hammond continued in the gyrating circumstances to maintain something of his own poise and reasonableness. He was like a cool, cultivated surveyor applying a spirit level in a volcanic region.' Cardus argued that Hammond had revealed himself as 'the world's greatest batsman, fair weather and foul', a wonderful tribute given that Bradman was the opposing captain. He was not dismissed, Cardus wrote grandly, rather 'dethroned'.

Hammond on his way to a double century against India at The Oval in 1936.

Ten years later, Hammond, now 43, played a similar innings on a gluepot in Brisbane. England's outstanding post-war opening bowler, Alec Bedser, said of that knock, against Keith Miller, Ray Lindwall and Ernie Toshack: 'When it was short, he stood aside and let it go. If pitched up, he let fly, playing straight past the bowler to eliminate risk. He hit cleanly and sensibly and in the circumstances, it was the best bad-wicket innings I've seen.' Hammond made 32 in two hours, his last great innings.

Hammond was cricket's greatest runscorer (7249 runs in 85 Tests) until Colin Cowdrey became the new record holder in November 1970. Cowdrey also matched Hammond as the leading English scorer of Test centuries when he scored his 22nd hundred, a feat matched by Geoff Boycott in 1981 but still to be beaten by an Englishman. Across all teams, only Bradman, Herbert Sutcliffe and Ken Barrington have a higher Test batting average of those batsmen to appear in

The Second XI

Hammond with his opposite number Don Bradman during the 1938 Ashes series.

50 Tests. Hammond's 336 not out in Auckland in 1933 remains the fastest triple century made in Test matches (288 minutes, including the third hundred in 48 minutes). The 10 sixes he hit in that innings was a Test record until Wasim Akram slammed 12 for Pakistan against Zimbabwe in 1996-97. And Hammond also took 83 Test-match wickets. 'Had he not been such a wonderful batsman,' Bradman argued, 'I think Wally Hammond may easily have proved equal to Tate and Bedser with the ball, for on some occasions, particularly when he failed with the bat, I have known him to bowl medium-paced stuff superbly.'

Wally Hammond was never as influential as WG Grace nor as technically perfect as Jack Hobbs. Where he matched these two legends, and stands above all the English batsmen who followed him, even Len Hutton, was the way he was *always* the key wicket during his career. 'From the moment he walked from the pavilion to begin his innings he looked the master,' wrote Hutton of Hammond in 1956. 'The moment he faced up to bowling that had held difficulties for the other batsmen, that bowling appeared to lose its venom.'

WALLY HAMMOND (ENGLAND)

Test Cricket

Tests	Inn	NO	Runs	HS	Ave	100	50	Ct	Balls	Runs	Wkts	Ave	Best	5/	10/
85	140	16	7249	336*	58.46	22	24	110	7969	3138	83	37.81	5-36	2	–

First-Class Cricket

Mat	Inn	NO	Runs	HS	Ave	100	50	Ct	Balls	Runs	Wkts	Ave	Best	5/	10/
634	1005	104	50551	336*	56.11	167	185	819	51449	22389	732	30.59	9-23	22	3

No. 16 Fred Spofforth

Frederick Spofforth was the greatest Test bowler of the 19th century. *Wisden*, in its obituary of the great bowler in 1927, called him 'one of the most remarkable players the game has ever known'. AG Moyes said he was 'the first great modern bowler ... control of length, flight, and spin are, and always have been, the basis of the art of bowling, and in Spofforth they were developed to the nth degree'.

The Demon Spofforth. The likeness to DK Lillee is remarkable.

Spofforth was also a natural athlete, able to run the 100 yards in 10.2 seconds, which in 1881 was a New South Wales' residents' record. An irony is that his celebrated nickname of 'The Demon' implies that he was a fast man, but in fact his extraordinary influence was as a slower bowler than that. Yes, as a boy, Spofforth did want to send 'em down as fast as he could; indeed, when he told the story of how he confronted WG Grace in the nets during WG's first tour of Australia, in 1873-74, he claimed that at the time he 'could bowl faster than any man in the world'. Later, though, having observed outstanding bowlers such as the crafty roundarm off-spinner James Southerton and the ultra-accurate slow-medium Alfred Shaw on James Lillywhite's team's tour of 1876-77, he evolved into an all-round bowler of the highest class. He could bowl quick if he wanted to, but he didn't often have to. It was not only in looks that he was a lot like Dennis Lillee.

Of bowlers to take 50 Test wickets for Australia, Spofforth has the best strike rate — a wicket every 44.52 balls. By comparison, Charlie 'The Terror' Turner, Australia's other great bowler of Test cricket's early summers, took a wicket every 51.44 deliveries. It should be noted that Jack Ferris, Turner's bowling partner in eight Tests between 1887 and 1890, captured 48 wickets for Australia, and then a further 13-91 in one Test for England against South Africa, giving him a career strike rate of 37.74 (for Australia it was 42.29), but few critics of the day thought Ferris a better bowler than Turner, or, by extension, as accomplished as Spofforth. Of course, the wickets of these long-gone days were more bowler friendly than those of later seasons, a fact reflected in the overall lower batting averages compared with the decades after World War I, but statistics still reflect the extraordinary capabilities of both Spofforth (94

The Second XI

wickets in 18 Tests, at 18.41) and Turner (101 wickets in 17 Tests, at 16.53). No other Australia bowler in cricket history has taken 75 Test wickets at an average of less than 20.

George Giffen, the Australian allrounder, thought it was impossible for anyone to be *more* venomous than the Demon on a sticky pitch. 'He was unique as a fast bowler and practically established a school of bowlers,' was WG Grace's verdict. When Spofforth was at his peak, from 1878 to 1885, Australia matched it with England, winning six Tests and losing five. The most famous victory came at The Oval in 1882, when he bowled out England for 77 when they needed 85 to win. Fired up by Grace's discredited run out of Sammy Jones, Spofforth told his team-mates that 'this can be done', and strode out to deliver 28 (four-ball) furious overs, 15 of them maidens, to get Australia home. His match bowling figures were 14-90 (7-64 and 7-44), his final 11 overs yielded four wickets for two runs. The next day, the *Sporting Times* published their mock obituary and the story of the Ashes was born, but it was the Demon, more so than the newspaper's editor, who was responsible for the birth of the legend.

The Australian team that toured England in 1878. The Demon is standing back left. Two other players featured in this top 100 are in this photograph: Billy Murdoch (front centre) and Jack Blackham (front right).

Spofforth had completed Test cricket's first hat-trick while taking 13-110 for the match at the MCG in January 1880. He'd take 10 wickets in a Test twice more after 1882: 11-117 in 1882-83 and 10-144 in 1884-85. Before any of this, on Australia's tour of England in 1878, he had inspired a remarkable victory over a Marylebone Cricket Club (MCC) XI at Lord's. WG Grace's finest biographer, Simon Rae, described this as the 'most momentous six hours in cricket history'. In the MCC XI's first innings, things proceeded fairly calmly until Spofforth came on first change, and promptly took 6-4 in

23 deliveries. Australia scraped together 41, enough for an eight-run first-innings lead, but then Spofforth had Grace dropped off the first ball and bowled by the second. Harry Boyle was actually the main destroyer in this second innings, taking 6-3, but the Demon managed 4-16, giving him 10-20 for the match, as the home side was all out for just 19. Australia managed the 12 runs needed for victory for the loss of a single wicket. At the start, there had only been a few hundred curious cricket devotees in attendance; by the climax, as word of the drama got out, there were around 5000 panicky Londoners at the ground. From this day, a match between England and Australia, would — in English and Australian eyes at least — overshadow all else on the cricket calendar.

> In Affectionate Remembrance
> OF
> **ENGLISH CRICKET,**
> WHICH DIED AT THE OVAL
> ON
> **29th AUGUST, 1882,**
> Deeply lamented by a large circle of sorrowing friends and acquaintances.
>
> **R.I.P.**
>
> N.B.—The body will be cremated and the ashes taken to Australia.

HS Altham, in *A History of Cricket*, described Spofforth as a 'tall, rather slim figure, but lissome, wiry and full of vitality; a very high action, an atmosphere of undisguised hostility, and a subtle and unresting brain behind it all.' That ability to 'think' a batsman out is the critical factor in measuring his quality; like Grace with batting, Spofforth changed the way the matter of bowling was approached, a point one of Australia's greatest captains, Monty Noble, fully recognised in his book, *The Game's The Thing*.

'What a debt we owe Spofforth, the "blue streak of cricket",' Noble wrote, 'who, before anyone else, mastered the art of deception in pace, at the same time spinning the ball and laying down the axiom for all who came after: "Disguise in action — surprise in effect." It was due to these qualities that his great success was chiefly due. What an influence his example has had on the game! Today no bowler's education is considered complete, nor does he create any degree of apprehension in the batsman's mind, until he has mastered this guile.'

In 1924, Neville Cardus described the Australian fast bowler Ted McDonald, then playing for Lancashire, as 'one of the great fast bowlers of all time', and then compared this 'modern' champion to the old master: 'He has Spofforth's pace, though not his many masks and contrivances ... McDonald also lacks Spofforth's unappeasable appetite.' It is hard to imagine that a bowler such as the Demon — who came to appreciate the art of bowling, who had such a desire to take wickets, who possessed a killer instinct that could win matches that seemed lost, who successfully grew from speed demon to medium-paced master, while still having a fast ball in his pocket that he could use when he needed it — would not have been a champion in any era.

FRED SPOFFORTH (AUSTRALIA)

Test Cricket

Tests	Inn	NO	Runs	HS	Ave	100	50	Ct	Balls	Runs	Wkts	Ave	Best	5/	10/
18	29	6	217	50	9.43	–	1	11	4185	1731	94	18.41	7-44	7	4

First-Class Cricket

Mat	Inn	NO	Runs	HS	Ave	100	50	Ct	Balls	Runs	Wkts	Ave	Best	5/	10/
155	236	41	1928	56	9.89	–	3	83	30536	12760	853	14.96	9-18	84	32

The Second XI

Len Hutton   No. 17

The opening bats in this Top 100's first XI were WG Grace and Jack Hobbs, two men whose influence on the development of modern batting was supreme. The first opener selected in this second XI is a cricketer who captured two crucial characteristics that all accomplished 'first men in' need: single-mindedness and pragmatism. Yorkshire and England's Len Hutton also epitomised cricket courage by the manner in which he fought back from the rigours of World War II to become the best batsman of his time.

In his debut Test match, against New Zealand in 1937, the 21-year-old Hutton scored just 0 and 1, but straight after, at Old Trafford, he made an even 100. The following year he began his Ashes career with another century, in a Test in which he was one of four English century-makers and Australia's Stan McCabe made his classic 232. Hutton failed at Lord's, missed the Leeds Test, but came back at The Oval to compile arguably cricket's most famous long innings, which cemented his reputation. The pitch for this match, it must be said, was tame, and the Australian attack, Bill O'Reilly and Chuck Fleetwood-Smith apart, was poor, but though England batted for 335.2 overs, and the ball refused to turn, O'Reilly was relentless, and at the end Hutton felt as if he'd earned every one of his 364 runs. He batted for 13 hours and 17 minutes until he hit an exhausted catch to cover.

Of course, World War II came at a bad time for everything, but from a cricket perspective it came at exactly the worst time for Len Hutton. His Test batting average when hostilities broke out was 67.25, from 21 innings. The loss of potentially the best six years of his cricket life was one thing; the physical disability he carried after being hurt during the war was another. 'After my arm was fractured, I had to move my left hand farther round the handle of the bat, so that the back of the hand faced cover-point,' Hutton explained in his autobiography. 'I never played so well again. In 1939 I could play every stroke in the book as and when I wished. After my disablement, I could not play certain shots the way I would have liked.'

Hutton hits out against South Africa at The Oval in 1947.

Eventually, after trying lighter bats and various methods, Hutton accepted that he would have to eliminate the hook and the pull shots from his game, which made life difficult when he first faced Ray Lindwall and Keith Miller in Australia in 1946-47. He was also hindered by the nagging back pain that had first annoyed him in 1938, but this did not prevent him playing one of the finest short innings in Test history, during the second Test. In 24 minutes, just before lunch, Hutton scored 37 in a manner that had veterans at the SCG recalling Victor Trumper. 'It was a glorious piece of batting, a choice miniature that I shall carry with me always,' wrote AG Moyes. 'The Hutton who scintillated that day was one of the masters.'

Hutton, the professional captain of England, and Alec Bedser lead England out at The Oval in 1953.

In 1947, Hutton scored a century in his first Test at Leeds. The fact that it took a decade for him to play a Test on his home turf in Yorkshire underlines the opportunities he missed because of the war. By 1950, with the retirement of Bradman, Hutton became the most dependable batsman in the world. His ability to watch the ball right onto the bat, his perfect balance, and skill in letting the ball come to him, finding the gaps, getting the ones, piercing the field, made him No. 1. His ability against the spinners was amply demonstrated against the West Indies' Sonny Ramadhin and Alf Valentine at The Oval in 1950, when he batted through England's first innings for 202 not out. In Australia straight after, against the pace of Lindwall, Miller and Bill Johnston, he was easily the batsman of the series, averaging more than double that of any other batsman on either side.

Hutton's 62 not out in Brisbane was perhaps his most notable innings of that 1950-51 tour, though he also became the second man (after Australia's Bill Woodfull) to bat through a Test innings twice when he made an unconquered 156, out of 272, in Adelaide. The effort at the Gabba was made batting at No. 8, out of an innings total of 122, circumstances brought about by a shocking wet pitch which made batting impossible for everyone else. Kept back as long as possible, but still in with the innings total just 30 chasing 193 to win, Hutton made some thrilling shots and added 45 for the final wicket with Doug Wright, of which Wright scored two. This was the eighth Test against Australia that England had lost in a run of 11 Tests. By series' end, they'd lost three more, but in the final match of the series, England got their first Ashes win since The Oval in 1938. Hutton, unbeaten on 60 out of 2-95, hit the winning runs.

The crowd at the conclusion of the fifth Test in 1953, after the Hutton-led England regained the Ashes.

The Second XI

When Australia returned to England in 1953, Hutton was his country's first professional captain. In the late 1930s, Wally Hammond had become an amateur so he could accept the captaincy, sustaining the tradition that cricketers untainted by professionalism were best equipped for the role, but Hutton quietly but firmly informed those in charge he would not do likewise. He was appointed anyway, simply because he was too clearly the best person available, and brought to the captaincy the pragmatism, caution and desire to win that had always typified his cricket. The impact Lindwall and Miller had made on him immediately after the war made him a strong believer in fast bowling, so when young pacemen such as Fred Trueman, Brian Statham and Frank Tyson emerged, Hutton built his bowling strategies around them. He also, controversially, slowed his team's over-rate, which conserved his bowlers' energies, frustrated his opponents and, because he won, bred a generation of imitators who robbed fans of many overs in the years that followed. He never lost a series as captain, from the home Tests against India in 1952 through to the 1954-55 Ashes tour; his career record as a Test captain reads 23 matches for 11 wins and only four losses. In the 41 Tests he played between the war and when he became skipper, England won 14 times, but lost 16.

In Australia in 1954-55, Hutton won some notoriety by sending his opponents in in the first Test, after going into the match with an all-pace attack, and losing by an innings and 154 runs. Some leaders might have lost their nerve, but this England captain refused to lose faith in his fast bowlers, and watched his pacemen, led by Tyson, win the next three Tests. He was knighted in 1956, purely for his services to the game, the second Englishman, after Sir Jack Hobbs, to be so honoured. He ended his career with 40,140 first-class runs at 55.52, and his Test aggregate included 19 centuries, but — revealing in its own way — he hit just two sixes. In Len Hutton's considered, pragmatic view of cricket and what an opening batsman was supposed to do, they just weren't worth the risk.

Don Bradman congratulates Hutton at The Oval in 1938, after the Yorkshireman went past The Don's 334, the previous highest individual score in Ashes Tests.

LEN HUTTON (ENGLAND)

Test Cricket

Tests	Inn	NO	Runs	HS	Ave	100	50	Ct	Balls	Runs	Wkts	Ave	Best	5/	10/
79	138	15	6971	364	56.67	19	33	57	260	232	3	77.33	1-2	–	–

First-Class Cricket

Mat	Inn	NO	Runs	HS	Ave	100	50	Ct	Balls	Runs	Wkts	Ave	Best	5/	10/
513	814	91	40140	364	55.52	129	177	400	9774	5106	173	29.51	6-76	4	1

The 100 Greatest Cricketers

No. 18 Ian Botham

The Ian Botham who made his Test debut as a brash, precociously talented 21-year-old able to immediately take five wickets in an innings was a very different cricketer to the man who scored 2 and 6 and took 0-9 in his final Test 15 years later. His first Test victim was Greg Chappell, the Australian captain, the finest Australian batsman of his generation. In his last Test, he was dismissed twice by Pakistan's Waqar Younis, then at the peak of his considerable form. Botham always mixed well with the best of company, but whereas he seemed made for Test cricket in his youth, at career's end he was there solely because of his reputation.

The young Botham, an exuberant success from his first day in Test cricket.

Botham's first Test century came on a bowler's wicket in New Zealand in early 1978, part of a brilliant all-round performance that also featured eight wickets, three catches and a quickfire 30 in England second innings that gave he and his fellow bowlers enough time to bowl the Kiwis out on the final afternoon. He also ran Geoff Boycott out in that second innings, reputedly because the veteran opener wasn't scoring quickly enough. Back in England, he belted hundreds against Pakistan at Edgbaston and Lord's, where he also took 8-34 in one innings, a Test record at the ground. Later in that season, he took 24 wickets in three Tests against New Zealand, including 11 at Lord's, before going to Australia where he became the first Englishman to score more than 275 runs and take more than 20 wickets in one Ashes series. At age 23, in his 21st Test, he became the seventh Englishman to achieve the 1000 runs/100 wickets double, 12 matches faster than any other Englishman had taken to reach this landmark, and two Tests quicker than anyone at all.

By the start of the 1980 English season, Botham was the face of English cricket, with a higher profile even than Kevin Keegan, the country's football captain. He had scored six Test hundreds and taken five wickets in a Test innings 14 times, 10 wickets in a Test three times. Best of all, in the one-off Test staged in India in February 1980 to celebrate the Golden Jubilee of the Board of Control for Cricket in India, he had produced an all-round performance unprecedented in the history of Test cricket. First, he bludgeoned 114 after England had collapsed to 5-58; then he took 13-106 for the match. Botham won the Test by 10 wickets.

The decision to make him England captain in 1980 was a bold one, but in his first 10 Tests in charge (nine of them against the West Indies), his team had no victories, and he compiled just 242 runs and took 29 wickets. The following year, England played without spirit, losing the first Test against Australia and drawing the second. Botham made a pair in the latter game, at Lord's, and returned to the pavilion to embarrassing silence, the mood reflecting the fact that his time as captain was over.

The Second XI

Yet within weeks, excited cricket patriots were joyfully chanting his name, as he came to dominate an Ashes series in a way no one has ever done. At Headingley and then Old Trafford, Botham smashed extraordinary centuries against an Australian attack starring Dennis Lillee and Terry Alderman — the first hundred to retrieve a position so dire that bookmakers had offered odds of 500-1 about an English victory, the second to emphatically confirm a series victory that just a few weeks earlier had seemed unlikely. In between, at Edgbaston, he took 5-1 in a spell of 28 balls, sparking a dramatic Australian capitulation just when it seemed they had the Test won.

In India in 1981-82, Botham became just the third allrounder to complete the 2000 Test runs/200 Test wickets double. Again against India, this time at The Oval in 1982, he smashed 208, his highest Test score, during which he managed to break some tiles on the pavilion roof. However, after the 1982 home season, Botham's struggles with a nagging back injury that had first emerged in 1980 began to hurt his cricket. So, too, did his rare ability to attract controversy, only some of it related to sport. His hotel room became, in his own words, his 'bat-cave', as cricket became less of an adventure, occasionally a chore. When he came out to Australia in 1982-83, he was overweight and his impact diminished, though one sensed he was still, with David Gower, the wicket the Australians wanted most. He did take 31 wickets in the 1985 Ashes series, and slaughtered an inexperienced Aussie bowling line-up at the Gabba while slamming 138 in the first Test of 1986-87, but more and more his greatness came in cameos rather than displays of sustained excellence. Strangely, throughout his career, he never scored a ODI century or took five wickets in a ODI innings.

Of the scandals he was involved in, all were media-driven and a few of them might have been true. On August 4, 1986, Botham celebrated his return from a suspension handed down after he confessed to occasionally using cannabis by bashing Worcestershire for 104 not out from 66 balls. Soon after, he made a record 175 not out, including 13 sixes, against Northants in a John Player League match. Back in the Test side, he took a wicket almost immediately equal to Lillee's Test wicket-taking record.

Botham's battles with the other great all-rounders of his time — Hadlee, Imran and in this case Kapil Dev — were a feature of the 1980s.

Botham traps New Zealand's Jeff Crowe LBW at The Oval in 1986 to become Test cricket's leading wicket-taker, breaking Dennis Lillee's record.

69

That was an out-swinger, then an inswinger that had the Kiwi batsman Jeff Crowe lbw. Just briefly, it was glory days again.

In the first half of Botham's career he was an allrounder of extraordinary influence, capable of almost impossible feats. In the second, he was — by his own standards — one of the most overrated players of all time. The statistics prove the point. Using the end of the 1982 English season as a dividing line, Botham's Test record looks as follows:

Years	Tests	Runs	HS	Avge	100	50	Wkts	Best	Avge	Cght
1977–1982	54	2996	208	37.92	11	12	249	8-34	23.32	60
1982/83–1992	48	2204	138	29.00	3	10	134	8-103	37.84	60

Herein lies one of the conundrums of trying to nominate the top 100 cricketers of all time. The Ian Botham of 1977-1982 was the best allrounder since Sobers; if not a member in the all-time first XI, then a certainty for the second. The Botham of 1983 to 1992 was different; many cricketers over the years have averaged more with the ball than with the bat. Some cricketers decline as their careers go on simply because they eventually face better opponents, or perhaps they get worked out and aren't talented enough or smart enough to adjust their games. Botham, in contrast, was beaten down in part because of a back ailment and mostly by his own celebrity. Those first 54 Tests are the true measure of his greatness.

Botham 'duck hooks' a wild delivery from Australia's Geoff Lawson during his stirring comeback century at Leeds in 1981.

IAN BOTHAM (ENGLAND)
Test Cricket

Tests	Inn	NO	Runs	HS	Ave	100	50	Ct	Balls	Runs	Wkts	Ave	Best	5/	10/
102	161	6	5200	208	33.55	14	22	120	21815	10878	383	28.40	8-34	27	4

One-Day International Cricket

ODIs	Inn	NO	Runs	HS	Ave	100	50	Ct	Balls	Runs	Wkts	Ave	Best	4/
116	106	15	2113	79	23.22	–	9	36	6271	4139	145	28.54	4-31	3

The Second XI

Victor Trumper
No. 19

Frankly, if you rely on statistics, it is very hard to find a place for Victor Trumper anywhere near the peak of this top 100. His Test batting average of 39.05 is very good for the era in which he batted, but hardly exceptional. After all, just among his countrymen in Tests up to World War I, Warren Bardsley averaged 45.15, Charlie Kellaway 39.62, Clem Hill 39.21, Vernon Ransford 37.84, Warwick Armstrong 35.67, Reggie Duff 35.59. Against England, Trumper averaged only 32.80. Billy Murdoch, who retired nine years before Trumper's Test debut and batted on inferior pitches, averaged exactly 32.00 in 18 Tests against England.

In Sheffield Shield cricket, Trumper averaged 48.36. However, Monty Noble averaged 68.00, Hill 52.28, Armstrong 50.47, Duff 49.98. And yet, in the opinion of those who saw him, Trumper was the greatest batsman of his time, perhaps of any time.

Armstrong remembered Trumper this way: 'He could hit as quick as lightning all around the wicket, appearing to favour no particular hit, yet one could never place a man against him to stop his onslaught. Wherever the ball was pitched, it was hit away for runs.' Johnnie Moyes wrote of him: 'I was privileged to play against him in Sheffield Shield matches, to field on the fence or in the slips and be amazed at his artistry. It made one wonder whether he was playing the same game or whether it was something he had made up for himself — some variation of cricket.'

In a Sydney grade match, Frank Iredale, a batsman good enough to average 36.68 in 14 Tests, complained to the bowler, Herbert Hordern, 'You don't bowl that rubbish to me,' after Trumper had played another of his spectacular shots. 'For your information Frank,' Hordern replied, 'the ball that Victor belts for four is exactly the same one with which you can barely make contact.'

The legendary Victor, jumping out to drive.

In 1936, Noble said that he had 'no hesitation giving the palm to Victor Trumper as the world's great batsman'. By this time, Don Bradman had played 28 Tests and scored seven centuries, six double centuries and two triple centuries, and was averaging almost 100 in Test cricket. After Jack Hobbs had scored 573 runs in the 1924-25

Ashes series, including his seventh, eighth and ninth Test centuries against Australia, Noble wrote, 'I would like to be able to bracket him with Victor Trumper, not as a record breaker but as a batsman, but it would not be honest to do so.'

'You can never speak to an Australian about Victor Trumper without seeing his eyes glisten with pride and affection,' wrote Neville Cardus in 1929. 'Trumper will always remain for your true Australian the greatest batsman that ever lived. But it was in England that Trumper achieved his most wonderful play ...'

Posed photographs from the first decade of the 20th century don't do justice to Trumper's celebrated grace as a batsman.

Trumper toured England four times, as a colt in 1899, in 1902 when he was superb, and again in 1905 and 1909, when he was moderately successful. He scored just two Test centuries there — 135 at Lord's in 1899 and his famous 104 at Old Trafford three years later, when he became the first man to score a century before lunch on the first day of a Test. Over those four tours, his Test batting average in England was 27.84, yet Cardus asked: 'Was it not genius that made Trumper a master batsman in conditions not common to Australian cricket?' And later in that same story he wrote, 'He was master of all the strokes, and he could use almost any one of them at his pleasure, no matter the manner of ball bowled at him.' Elsewhere, Cardus reckoned, 'Trumper was a great player whether he made 18 or 180.' It wasn't only Cardus either. CB Fry, a highly regarded captain of England, said Trumper played a defensive stroke 'only as a very last resort'. Archie MacLaren claimed 'Victor had half a dozen strokes for the same kind of ball'.

There is no record of Trumper playing a genuine defensive innings. His method was to attack or counter attack, as he did at Sydney in 1903-04 after England had built a huge first-innings lead of 288. Once again, he scored a century in a session, this time 112 between tea and stumps, on his way to 185 not out. In one 40-minute spell, he scored 60 runs, the *Sydney Morning Herald* stating that he 'was out on one of his hitting expeditions'. Later in the same report his batting was described as 'the very height of perfection and grace'.

As an opening bat, his preferred position in the order, Trumper averaged 33.00 in Tests. At No. 5, he averaged 69.38 in Tests and at six he averaged 48.20. Perhaps he was wasted at the top of the order. Against the South African spinners in 1910-11, Trumper helped himself to 661 runs at 94.43, including his highest Test score of 214 not out, at that time an Australian record. This time, the *Herald*'s correspondent called

The Second XI

him 'incomparable' and continued, 'Trumper took length balls on the off peg and hooked them to the leg boundary. He forgot that the best wicketkeeper in the world was crouching behind him, and drove fast and slows indiscriminately.'

'Believe me when I tell you that it was odds on Trumper hitting the first ball bowled to him for four,' Herbert Collins, Australian captain from 1921 to 1926, once said. 'That was always his objective.' England's Sydney Barnes suggested much the same thing: 'Victor, well, he always gave you a chance, almost daring you to bag his wicket.' This is a laudable batting policy, if you want to be popular with the fans in the outer, but it doesn't lend itself to heavy runscoring, especially for an opening bat. At the same time, Trumper's daredevil approach became the essence of his magic — despite going for his shots from the jump, he was still able to be the most acclaimed batsman of his day.

To measure Trumper's true quality, you need to ignore the records and consider two things. First, as Clem Hill put it, 'He never realised his own greatness.' It is easy to imagine Englishmen such as Fry and MacLaren actually dreading the thought of Trumper adopting a more disciplined approach, like everyone else. Of course, this carefree attitude makes him flawed, but does it diminish his talent?

Secondly, as Noble argued, Trumper changed cricket. This puts him on the same level as Grace and Hobbs, Bradman and Warne. In a famous essay in his book *The Game's the Thing*, Noble argued that before Trumper emerged, cricket in Australia was being slowly suffocated by a passion for orthodoxy and safety first. Trumper changed all that with an approach to cricket that could have been foolhardy, but because of his genius instead put him on a pedestal far above his teammates.

Probably the most loved player in Australian cricket history.

'How Victor's wonderful demonstrations shocked old ideas and brought light out of semi-darkness is well-known, particularly in Australia,' Noble explained. 'With his coming the old order passed for ever.'

VICTOR TRUMPER (AUSTRALIA)

Test Cricket

Tests	Inn	NO	Runs	HS	Ave	100	50	Ct	Balls	Runs	Wkts	Ave	Best	5/	10/
48	89	8	3163	214*	39.05	8	13	31	546	317	8	39.63	3-60	–	–

First-Class Cricket

Mat	Inn	NO	Runs	HS	Ave	100	50	Ct	Balls	Runs	Wkts	Ave	Best	5/	10/
255	401	21	16939	300*	44.58	42	87	172	3822	2031	64	31.73	5-19	2	–

No. 20 Alan Knott

Through the 1970s, England was fortunate to have two accomplished wicket-keepers: Alan Knott of Kent and Bob Taylor of Derbyshire. Taylor was probably the second best gloveman in the game during this time, but while he had many opportunities to witness Test cricket from the dressing-room, until Knott signed with World Series Cricket in 1977, he had only one chance to experience a Test while out in the middle. That came in New Zealand after Ray Illingworth's team regained the Ashes in 1970-71, when Knott stood down to give Taylor his international debut. That gesture done, Knott came back for the second Test and, straightaway, as if to prove how invaluable he was, all but became the first keeper to score a century in each innings of a Test, making 101 and 96.

After WSC, Knott played little Test cricket, ostensibly because he decided not to make himself available for overseas tours, and Taylor was able to enjoy himself in 57 Tests. But at home in 1980, and again in 1981, the selectors decided they needed the Kent man, after first trying Yorkshire's David Bairstow, and then recalling the 40-year-old Taylor for the first four Ashes Tests of 1981. Mike Brearley, England's captain for most of Taylor's Test career and one of his keenest supporters (but who was behind the decision to drop him in 1981), described Knott in the 1986 *Wisden* as 'a more or less automatic selection for any team on the strength of his keeping alone'. Then he added, 'When his batting was put in the scales, all doubt fell away, for he was a genius — a minor genius — with the bat'.

As Knott built his reputation through the 1970s, he was often likened to another great England keeper, Godfrey Evans, and not just because like Evans he kept for Kent. In trying to compare the two, supporters of Evans pointed out that Knott was reluctant to 'stand up' to the stumps for the medium pacers, but for the modern man this was not a matter of courage as logic, for he made few stumpings off the quicker bowlers while not being able to catch thick edges, especially down the legside. The fact that when standing back Knott moved sideways to snare catches as well and athletically as any keeper in history only added to the rationale.

Before Knott made his Test debut as a 21-year-old in 1967 against Pakistan, England had used eight keepers in the 1960s without ever appearing truly satisfied with any of them. Though the debutant took seven catches in his first appearance and four more catches and a stumping in his second, Jim Parks, reputedly a superior batsman, was preferred for the first three Tests of England's subsequent tour of the Caribbean. It proved an ironic strategy, given Knott's batting exploits over the next decade and more. After three draws, Knott returned to the team for the crucial Port-of-Spain Test and promptly scored a fighting 69 not

Knott, as pugnacious as ever, plays one of his favourite shots off the quicker bowlers.

The Second XI

out after the visitors slumped to 5-260 in reply to 7 for 526 (declared). England went on to win the Test after Garry Sobers got his second declaration all wrong. Before lunch on the final day of series, England slumped to 5-41 as they sought to save the match. Knott came out to bat for the rest of the game, mostly with his captain, Colin Cowdrey, and at the death with No. 11 Jeff Jones. The keeper finished 73 not out. There would be no further conjecture about who should fill the English wicketkeeping job until the advent of World Series Cricket.

In Pakistan in 1969, Knott was denied a first Test century because the Karachi crowd rioted when he was 96 not out. In Australia in 1970-71, he was outstanding with the gloves (21 catches and three stumpings), scored a critical 73 as a nightwatchman in the opening Test, and intrigued the locals with his idiosyncratic ways, not least his constant stretches between deliveries. Throughout his career, he was fanatical about his health and fitness. Had he not been superb, the boisterous crowds would have ridiculed him. Instead, the contrast with Australia's Rodney Marsh, who often struggled in his first series, was stark.

The Australian selectors kept faith with Marsh, and he responded by evolving into one of his country's greatest wicketkeepers. However, he never matched Alan Knott.

Knott had a presence behind the stumps, an impish eagerness that had him diving sideways and forwards to grab half chances. His work in support of his long-time Kent and England colleague, Derek Underwood, who bowled left-arm finger spin at almost medium pace, was always high-class. Knott was also innovative, adapting his keeping gear to suit his own style, and as a batsman he became more and more unorthodox, without ever losing that rare ability to score runs when they were most needed. His batting stance was such that it almost looked as if he was playing French cricket, and he specialised in either cutting or squirting the ball past backward point, or slicing it over the slips to third man, while against the spinners he would sweep at nearly everything, trusting his eye, and almost never miss.

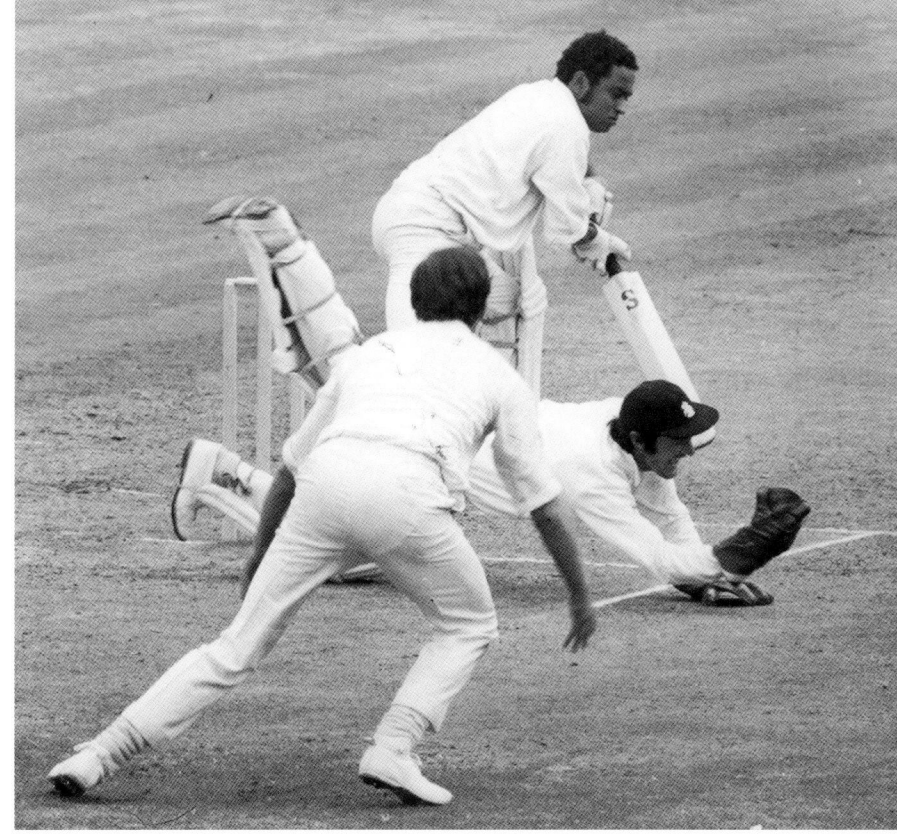

No keeper has had better reflexes, and was better equipped to scoop up catches others thought impossible.

If his eccentricity was a trademark, so too was his courage. More than once he drove Dennis Lillee to frustration, such as at The Oval in 1972 when he made 92, and in Adelaide in early 1975, when he scored his first Test century against Australia. He also hit a stirring hundred against Andy Roberts and Michael Holding at Leeds in 1976, in the same match in which he equalled Godfrey Evans' world record by completing his 219th Test-match dismissal. He'd played 77 Tests to Evans' 91. That record was broken a Test later, in a match in which he scored 50

The 100 Greatest Cricketers

and 57 while Holding was taking 14 wickets and bowling as rapidly and beautifully as any fast man has ever bowled in England. Twelve months later, against Australia at Trent Bridge, he helped Geoff Boycott through a trying period in the Yorkshireman's comeback to Test cricket, and then went on to 135, still the highest score by an English keeper against the Aussies, as he reached 4000 runs in Test cricket, the first keeper to do so. 'When Boycott was shocked almost runless early on, Knott provided the inspiration,' Greg Chappell recalled somewhat grimly. 'His flair and sense of urgency set up England's win.'

Knott catches Australia's Ray Bright off Bob Willis at Old Trafford in 1981.

Yet such was his keeping ability that now, approaching 30 years after his final Test (against Australia at The Oval, when his final-day 70 not out saved the game), his batting is remembered as being secondary to his glovework. Sunil Gavaskar is just one of many who have described him as 'the finest wicketkeeper I have seen'. The fact is that of all the glovemen who would have made their Test teams even if they'd hardly scored a run, Alan Knott was the best of them. His batting was just an incredible bonus.

ALAN KNOTT (ENGLAND)

Test Cricket

Tests	Inn	NO	Runs	HS	Ave	100	50	Ct	St
95	149	15	4389	135	32.75	5	30	250	19

First-Class Cricket

Mat	Inn	NO	Runs	HS	Ave	100	50	Ct	St	Balls	Runs	Wkts	Ave	Best	5/	10/
511	745	134	18105	156	29.63	17	97	1211	133	104	87	2	43.50	1-5	–	–

The Second XI

Brian Lara

No. 21

Brian Lara is, at the very least, one of the most intriguing cricketers of all time. The first man to score 400 in a Test. The first to score 500 in a first-class match. Twice, the holder of the highest score in Test cricket. After his retirement in early 2007, he was the leading runscorer in Tests. He was twice sacked as West Indies captain, despite averaging nearly eight runs more per innings when he batted as a Test-match captain. He has been on the losing side in Test matches more often than any other cricketer, and at times been almost demonised by sections of the Caribbean cricket community outside his native Trinidad.

'Probably the most destructive player in my 15 years in cricket,' is how Shane Warne described Lara in his life story. 'The thing that singles him out among others is his placement of the ball, you just think he's throwing the bat at them and give you a chance, but he actually always hits the gap. I remember the Sydney Test when he got 277. If we didn't run him out, I think he would still be batting now.'

That innings remains one of the greatest ever played at the SCG. It was his first Test hundred, and rarely, if ever, has a batsman announced his skill on the highest stage with such a flourish. Lara used a high backlift, and often in defence the ball seemed to squirt out towards cover point rather than be met with the full face of the bat, with a gap left between bat and pad. But when he was 'on song', which was often, trusting his extraordinary eye and following sweetly through, never has a batsman seemed more gifted than his contemporaries.

Lara's second Test century came against England at Georgetown in early 1994. Three Tests later, he broke Garry Sobers' world record Test score, going to 375, and a few weeks after that, hit the highest ever first-class score, 501 not out for Warwickshire against Durham in the county championship. However, the following year the West Indies were beaten at home by Australia — the first time the Windies had lost any series since early 1980, first time since 1973 they'd been conquered at home — and though in the next 12 months India and Sri Lanka were defeated, the veneer of indestructibility was gone. Lara would not have it easy as he sought to build his reputation.

When Australia next came to the Caribbean, in 1999, Lara's very career was in jeopardy. He had been West Indies skipper for two years, and though he started with victories over England, his men had been embarrassed in South Africa. Then, in the opening Test against Steve Waugh's team, the Windies were pitiful, bowled out for just 51, their lowest ever innings total, while being thrashed by an ugly 312 runs. One more defeat, and Lara knew his reign as captain was over. Australia

Lara in Sydney in 1993, during one of the greatest double hundreds ever seen at the famous ground.

was bowled out on the first day for 256, but the home side crashed to 4-37 at stumps, Lara 7 not out. But from there he saved his reputation, batting throughout the second day and going on to 213. An emphatic 10-wicket victory squared the series; a prelude to one of Test cricket's finest ever matches and maybe its greatest ever innings.

Chasing 308 on the final day in Bridgetown, against a bowling line-up featuring Glenn McGrath, Jason Gillespie, Shane Warne and Stuart MacGill, the West Indies fell to 5-105, then 8-248. But Lara remained, having completed his 12th Test century, and with Curtly Ambrose took the score to 302 before Gillespie had Ambrose caught at third slip. This was a fifth-day wicket, against an accomplished attack that expected to win but was hardly over-confident, and no other batsman made more than 38 in either team's second innings. Yet Lara was now 146 not out, an innings crafted rather than belted from 250 deliveries. Courtney Walsh survived the rest of Gillespie's over, which included a no-ball, and then Waugh brought back the great McGrath. Two runs came from an edge past first slip, then two dot balls, then Lara declined an easy run with the field back, then a wide as McGrath sought to keep the captain on strike. Now it was one to tie, two to win, two balls left, and Lara hooked a single from the first opportunity. Walsh survived the final ball, and then, after a short delay, Lara smashed the first ball from Gillespie's next over through the covers for four and the Test.

Australian captain Steve Waugh watches as Lara hits another four at Bridgetown in 1999 during the West Indies skipper's remarkable match-winning 153 not out.

Lara in Adelaide six-and-a-half years later, having just become Test cricket's highest run-getter.

The Second XI

By the time Lara passed Allan Border's Test runscoring record at Adelaide in late 2005, he had made another 19 Test centuries, all of them memorable. However, his resume was spoilt by the West Indies poor record over the previous decade. In all, Lara played 130 Tests for the Windies (and one for the ICC World XI), for 32 wins, 36 draws and 62 losses. He had lost the captaincy at the end of 1999, then been reappointed in 2002, before standing down again in 2004. During that second stint, the Windies won the ICC Champions Trophy, a one-day tournament featuring all the Test playing nations, and Lara averaged 66.37 with the bat in Tests, with eight centuries. His last five Test innings, in Pakistan, were 61, 122, 216, 0 and 49, but after the Windies' disappointing performances at home during the 2007 World Cup he announced his retirement from international cricket. In all likelihood, he would have been sacked again as captain anyway. His team's play was too often lacklustre and inevitably the blame was his.

The flamboyant Lara backlift that became instantly recognisable all over the cricket world.

We are left with a cricketer whose reputation is built mostly on individual performances rather than team achievements. In a ODI against Bangladesh at Dhaka in October 1999 he opened the batting and scored a century from 45 balls, the second fastest on record. At the end of 14 overs of the West Indies innings that day, he was 106 not out. In Sri Lanka in 2001-02, Lara scored 688 runs in a three-Test series, including a double century and single century in the third Test. Yet the West Indies lost all three Tests, two of them by 10 wickets. In Johannesburg in 2003-04, Lara took 28 (4, 6, 6, 4, 4, 4) from one over from the left-arm spinner Robin Peterson, the most runs hit from one over in Tests. Only Don Bradman has scored more than Lara's nine Test double centuries.

In October 2003, Australia's Matthew Hayden scored 380 against Zimbabwe in Perth. Six months later, Lara became the first man to twice hold the record for Test cricket's highest score, when he hit 400 not out against the same team, England, at the same venue, St John's, where he'd scored 375 in 1994. He also became the first captain to claim this record since Billy Murdoch in 1884. That world record, made from 582 balls, was one of only six of Lara's 232 Test innings to end with him undefeated. Of all the Test batsmen with a career average of 50 or more, no one with even 100 innings has fewer not outs. This study ranks him third among West Indian run-makers, behind Sobers and Viv Richards. But imagine if he batted four as Richards did, coming in after Gordon Greenidge, Desmond Haynes and Richie Richardson, instead of with the score at 2 for less than 50. In those circumstances, Brian Lara would have played on many more winning teams and might have established himself as the greatest West Indian batsman of them all.

BRIAN LARA (WEST INDIES)

Test Cricket

Tests	Inn	NO	Runs	HS	Ave	100	50	Ct	Balls	Runs	Wkts	Ave	Best	5/	10/
131	232	6	11953	400*	52.89	34	48	164	60	28	—	—	0-0	—	—

One-Day International Cricket

ODIs	Inn	NO	Runs	HS	Ave	100	50	Ct	Balls	Runs	Wkts	Ave	Best	4/
299	289	32	10405	169	40.49	19	68	120	49	61	4	15.25	2-5	—

No. 22 Muttiah Muralitharan

It is impossible to discuss the quality of Muttiah Muralitharan without focusing on his unusual bowling action. His most vehement detractors reckon he's a cheat. His supporters call him a genius. He is, most likely, the toughest off-spinner batsmen have ever had to confront. Given all that he's been through, and fact he has been such a prolific wicket-taker for so long, he also has to be one of the toughest cricketers to have ever played the game.

Muttiah Muralitharan at Kandy in December 2007, having just dismissed England's Paul Collingwood to become Test cricket's greatest wicket-taker.

As the laws of cricket read in 1996: 'For a delivery to be fair, the ball must be bowled not thrown — see Note (a) below. If either umpire is not entirely satisfied with the absolute fairness of a delivery in this respect he shall call and signal 'no-ball' instantly upon delivery'. Note (a) read: 'A ball shall be deemed to have been thrown if, in the opinion of either umpire, the process of straightening the bowling arm, whether it be partial or complete, takes place during that part of the delivery swing which directly precedes the ball leaving the hand. This definition shall not debar a bowler from the use of the wrist in the delivery swing.'

At first glance, the manner in which Murali bowled looked illegal. He often appeared to spear his off-break, the ball coming out with a jerk as his arm was propelled towards the batsman. Slow-motion replays added to the confusion: maybe he was okay...

When he was called by umpire Darrell Hair in the second Test against Australia at the MCG in December 1995, Murali had been a Test bowler for more than three years. Having taken 81 wickets in 23 Tests (at the not very impressive average of 33.89), he was already Sri Lanka's leading Test wickettaker, but it seemed his career would now go the way of other bowlers called for chucking in Test matches, such as South Africa's Geoff Griffin and Australia's Ian Meckiff, who never played again. Or would he change his bowling action, and lose his effectiveness? Murali did not appear in the final Test of that series, but did play in the one-day internationals (being called in one match) and was a part of the Sri Lankan team that won the World Cup in March 1996. Biomechanics then examined Murali's action in off-field experiments and concluded that a congenital defect in his arm meant he was incapable of straightening it, but that when he bowled there was an illusion that the arm did straighten, caused at least in part by way he flicked his wrist (which his fans said was more elastic than most). With that report in his pocket, cricket officials were happy for him to resume his Test career.

The first time he bowled at the Australians, in 1992, Murali totally befuddled Allan Border. The Australian captain seemed to think he was playing a leg-spin bowler. Many cricket fans were as confused by his action as the Aussie captain. The fault lay in the law that was ridiculously vague, but for the next eight years the administrators played only at the edges, and Murali had to battle stoically through a storm. The voyage became prodigious, and he became the game's leading Test wicket-taker, in the process reducing his career average to 22. As well, he developed a new delivery, the 'doosra', an off-spinner's wrong 'un, that turned from leg to off but which to the batsmen looked like another 'offie'. However, it looked more suspicious than his stock delivery.

The Second XI

Under regulations introduced in 2001, the ICC established three 'tolerance limits' on the degree of bending of the arm: five degrees for spinners, 7.5 degrees for medium-pacers and 10 degrees for quick bowlers. Finally, in November 2004, an ICC panel recommended that the limit be increased to 15 degrees for all bowlers. The logic was that when arms were bent less than 15 degrees, the naked eye didn't always see things straight; while Murali's doosra was crooked under the old limits, crucially so too to varying degrees were the actions of many other bowlers. His backers now hoped he would be recognised as the champion they always believed he was. If the sympathy was with the umpires in 1995, by 2005 it was definitely with the great bowler.

The former Australian captain Steve Waugh is a strong supporter. 'Batting against him was the ultimate challenge,' Waugh wrote in his autobiography, 'with the ball reaching you a split second later than you envisaged, as if he bowled two balls and you needed to focus on the second one. He controls the ball as if it is attached to a string, enticing then withdrawing, probing before striking, each delivery a mini-battle for the batsman to overcome.'

At June 30, 2009, Murali had taken 62 more Test wickets than any other bowler, and 274 more wickets in Tests and ODIs combined. Since those no-ball calls in that Melbourne Test, he had taken 689 wickets at 20.81. For all the fine efforts of the left-arm fast-medium Chaminda Vaas, in the main the great off-spinner has carried the Sri Lankan attack since 1996. It is no real surprise that he has taken five wickets in a Test innings and 10 wickets in a Test more often than any other bowler. His best performance, statistically at least, came against England at The Oval in 1998, when he bowled 113.5 overs to take 16-220 (7-155 and 9-65), the fifth best analysis in all Tests. He is the only man to have bowled more than 7000 overs in Tests and at June 30, 2009, was fast approaching 10,000 overs in Tests and ODIs combined. The stress such an unusual arm action puts on his body makes this longevity a marvel.

While Warne made leg-breaks trendy again in 1993, except on the dustiest of pitches, off-breaks remained unfashionable. Murali changed all this. By being different, he broke the off-spinner's mould, becoming the first of his type to be a weapon on all surfaces, not just on dusty or broken ones. Other unusual off-spinners, such as Pakistan's Saqlain Mushtaq and India's Harbhajan Singh, soon followed and Murali thus became the first Sri Lankan to have a profound influence on cricket's evolution. In an era when many observers were concerned that batsmen were starting to dominate, this was surely no bad thing.

MUTTIAH MURALITHARAN (SRI LANKA)
Test Cricket

Tests	Inn	NO	Runs	HS	Ave	100	50	Ct	Balls	Runs	Wkts	Ave	Best	5/	10/
127	157	53	1178	67	11.33	–	1	69	42020	17081	770	22.18	9-51	66	22

One-Day International Cricket

ODIs	Inn	NO	Runs	HS	Ave	100	50	Ct	Balls	Runs	Wkts	Ave	Best	4/
329	154	59	610	33*	6.42	–	–	127	17713	11485	505	22.74	7-30	24

The 100 Greatest Cricketers

Sunil Gavaskar

Greg Chappell

The Third

Herbert Sutcliffe

Glenn McGrath

The Third XI

Bill O'Reilly

Frank Worrell

Wasim Akram

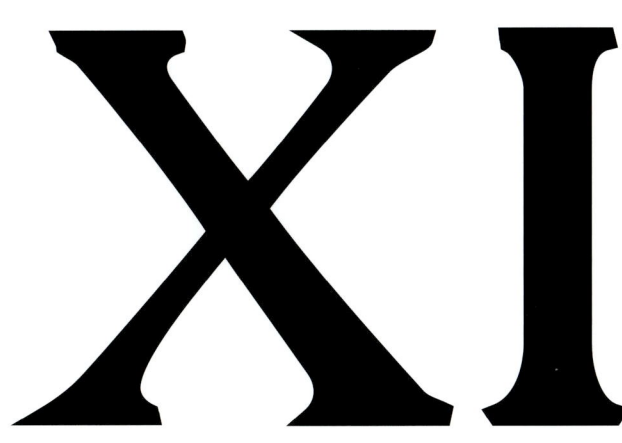

Kapil Dev

Jack Blackham

George Lohmann

George Headley

The 100 Greatest Cricketers

No. 23 Sunil Gavaskar

Between 1976 and 1991, the West Indies were undoubtedly the No. 1 team in Test cricket, a dominance built to a large degree on a succession of imposing fast bowlers. To make runs consistently against the Windies during this period was a sign of true greatness in a batsman. Of the few who did, only one was an opening batsman. He came from India, a nation whose batsmen had almost to a man exhibited a frailty against pace bowling, that until Kapil Dev emerged in the late '70s had never produced even a fast-medium bowler of much repute. This opening bat was just 163cm (5ft 4in) short, but he made his debut in spectacular style in 1971, scoring four centuries and 774 runs (average 154.80) in four Tests in the Caribbean, the most runs ever by a batsman in his maiden series. He was Sunil Gavaskar.

Gavaskar was a Test opener who could bat for nearly 12 hours for 172 (against England in Bangalore in 1981), but also score a hundred from 94 balls (against the West Indies in Delhi in 1983). When he retired from big-time cricket in 1987, he held a plethora of records, including most Tests (125), most innings (214), most runs (10,122), most hundreds (34), most scores of 50 or more (79), most hundred partnerships (58). But most praiseworthy of all, the fact you keep coming back to when considering his place in cricket history, his runs were made in an era dominated by superb, often intimidating opening bowlers. Consider the quicks he confronted apart from the West Indians: Dennis Lillee, Jeff Thomson, Rodney Hogg, Len Pascoe, Craig McDermott, Imran Khan, Wasim Akram, Richard Hadlee, John Snow, Ian Botham and Bob Willis. Most of all, consider the West Indians: Andy Roberts, Michael Holding, Joel Garner, Courtney Walsh, Malcolm Marshall, Sylvester Clarke, Wayne Daniel ...

Gavaskar drives off the back foot during his second tour of England, in 1974.

The Windies' opening bowlers he faced in 1971 were medium paced compared to the speed he'd confront later on. In 1976, Gavaskar scored centuries at Port-of-Spain in the second and third Tests, his third and fourth hundreds at the ground, against Roberts and Holding in the first match, just Holding in the second. In that third Test, India were set 403 to win, and scored 4-406 (Gavaskar 102, Gundappa Viswanath 112, Mohinder Amarnath 85), at the time the highest fourth-innings total ever made in Tests to win a match. In Australia in 1977-78, Gavaskar scored second-innings centuries in the first three Tests, against an attack led by Thomson. Then, in the following October, India were in Pakistan for the first Tests between the two nations for 17 years, and for the first time Gavaskar faced the bowling of Imran in a Test. 'The most compact batsman I've ever bowled to,' was the Pakistani spearhead's assessment, 'a masterful batsman with a great temperament.' Imran had just returned from a season of WSC, which made his rating telling. During the third Test, Gavaskar became his country's leading run-getter in Test cricket.

The Third XI

Two weeks after that Pakistan series concluded, India was involved in another home Test series, against the West Indies, and Gavaskar's statistical march continued. In the first Test, amid wild celebrations, he scored 205 in his home town, Bombay, becoming the first Indian to reach 200 in a home Test against the Windies. In the third Test, he became the first man to score hundreds in both innings of a Test three times, and the first Indian to score 4000 Test runs. For the second time in his Test career, he scored four centuries in one Test series. In January 1980, he made his 23rd Test century, putting him third on the then all-time list, behind Don Bradman and Garry Sobers. No other Indian had made more than 12. A little less than four years later, inevitably against the West Indies, he hit his 29th and 30th Test centuries, the ones that took him level, then past, Bradman's previous record, and

Left: Gavaskar, Allan Border and the prize that Indian and Australian Test teams now fight for — the Border-Gavaskar Trophy — at the Adelaide Oval in 1999.

they were two of his finest. No. 29 came in Delhi in the second Test, and was compiled from just 94 balls. The Windies had won the first Test by an innings, during which Gavaskar had had his bat dramatically knocked out of his grasp by Marshall. He saw it as his duty to reinvent himself and inspire a counterattack, which he surely did, starting with two electric hook shots off Marshall, for four and six. His first 50 came from just 37 deliveries, and during the innings he scored his 8000th Test run. But even when he was batting in such an explosive manner, he was still technically superb. *The Observer's* excellent cricket writer, Scyld Berry, who was covering the Test, noted that Gavaskar favoured 'neither offside nor leg, front foot nor back'.

The 30th hundred came in Madras in the final Test of that series. It was his last Test against the world champions. This time batting at No. 4 (but in before a run was scored), Gavaskar went all the way to 236 not out, his 13th hundred and third double century against the West Indies. Between March 1976 and

The relaxed batting stance that became a symbol of Indian cricket from 1971 to 1987.

The 100 Greatest Cricketers

December 1983, he made nine centuries against the Windies; the next best by any batsman against the best team on the planet in this period was four, by his teammate Dilip Vengsarkar. The only opener with even two was England's Graham Gooch.

Having long gone past Geoff Boycott's previous Test runscoring record of 8114, he reached 10,000 runs in his 124th Test, against Pakistan at Ahmedabad in March 1987. He was already the first batsman to play 200 Test innings, the fourth man to play 100 Tests (and the first to play 115), the first Indian fieldsman to take 100 catches, the first man to play 100 consecutive Tests. That 100th straight Test was the Tied Test in Madras against Australia in 1986. Set 348 to win on the last day, Gavaskar's 90 gave India a chance, setting the scene for a dramatic final hour which ended with India's 10th wicket falling off the second-last possible delivery.

Gavaskar glances Ian Botham during the 'Golden Jubilee' Test at Bombay in 1980.

Gavaskar's final first-class match was at Lord's in August 1987, when he scored 188 (his only century at the ground) and 0 for a Rest of the World XI against the MCC. From there it was back home to India, for the fourth World Cup, where he slammed 103 not out from 88 balls against New Zealand, his only one-day international century, before India were beaten by England in a semi-final at Bombay. In 1980, the West Indies' Gordon Greenidge explained in his autobiography *The Man in the Middle* how opening the batting was an onerous task that requires 'nerve, skill and an iron will' and that the little Indian had all these qualities. 'Gavaskar may not have the panache of my old (Hampshire) colleague Barry Richards,' Greenidge continued, 'but in the end a batsman is judged on what he actually achieves'. By the time he retired, Gavaskar had changed the way the cricket world perceived Indian batsmanship. In doing so, he paved the way for countrymen such as Sachin Tendulkar, Rahul Dravid and Virender Sehwag, the stars of the 1990s and into the 21st century.

SUNIL GAVASKAR (INDIA)

Test Cricket

Tests	Inn	NO	Runs	HS	Ave	100	50	Ct	Balls	Runs	Wkts	Ave	Best	5/	10/
125	214	16	10122	236*	51.12	34	45	108	380	206	1	206.0	1-34	–	–

One-Day International Cricket

ODIs	Inn	NO	Runs	HS	Ave	100	50	Ct	Balls	Runs	Wkts	Ave	Best	4/
108	102	14	3092	103*	35.14	1	27	22	20	25	1	25.00	1-0	–

The Third XI

Greg Chappell   No. 24

As Australia was thrashing Pakistan at the Sydney Cricket Ground in the final Test of the 1983-84 Australian summer, Greg Chappell farewelled the game's biggest stage by scoring 182 and taking three catches. He became the first batsman to score a century in his first and last Test innings, and the sixth batsman and first Australian to score 7000 Test runs. The second catch was his 121st in Tests, breaking Colin Cowdrey's previous record for most catches by a non-wicketkeeper. Completing the occasion, this would also be the final Test for the great bowler/keeper combination, Dennis Lillee and Rod Marsh, who had both commenced their international careers in the same season as Chappell (1970-71). It was definitely the end of an era; Australian cricket would take many years to recover from the loss.

Chappell was the younger brother of Ian Chappell, who played 75 Tests for Australia between 1964 and 1980, averaging 42.42 with the bat and led Australia with distinction between 1971 and 1975. When Ian had stood down as captain, Greg was the natural choice to replace him. In 1972, at The Oval, they'd provided the first instance of brothers both scoring a century in the same Test innings. Eighteen months later, in Wellington, they'd provided the only instance of brothers scoring centuries in each innings of the same Test. Chappell's aggregate in that Test of 380 (247 not out and 133) was a world record until Graham Gooch scored 456 (333 and 123) against India at Lord's in 1990. The Chappells' grandfather, Victor Richardson, had led Australia to South Africa in 1935-36, and played 19 Tests between 1924 and 1936. Their younger brother, Trevor, played three Tests for Australia in 1981, but is best remembered for doing what Greg, as Australian captain, told him to do: bowl the dreaded 'underarm' in a ODI against New Zealand at the MCG earlier in that year.

Chappell in England in 1972, his first overseas tour with the Australian team.

Being the younger brother of a future Australian skipper guaranteed an interesting upbringing, and their backyard Test matches were, as Greg puts it, 'pretty willing affairs'. A downside was that even though Greg scored almost 4000 runs, including 10 centuries, for South Australia between 1966 and 1973, he needed to transfer to Queensland to get captaincy experience at the first-class level. Queensland had long been the easybeats of the Sheffield Shield, but Chappell turned that around immediately, to the point that his side would have won the Shield in his first season in charge had they won their last game outright, in Sydney (they lost by 167 runs).

Although Chappell's first Test innings was 108 against England at the WACA in December 1970, for the remainder of that season and the first half of 1971-72 he was unable to cement his place in the side. However, an innings of 197 not out against a World XI in Sydney at the start of 1972, followed by an impressive Ashes

The 100 Greatest Cricketers

Chappell in dominant form against England at the MCG in 1980.

tour that featured memorable Test centuries at Lord's and The Oval established Chappell as the key wicket in the Australian side, a stature he never lost until he retired.

Chappell's first series as captain, against the West Indies in Australia in 1975-76, was seen as an unofficial world championship, coming straight after Australia had dominated two Ashes series and the Windies had won the inaugural World Cup (defeating Australia in the final). Chappell was superb against an attack that featured Andy Roberts, Michael Holding and the off-spinner Lance Gibbs, hitting three centuries (two of them in his maiden Test as captain) and 702 runs in the series, at an average of 117. This might have been Chappell's greatest season, though he was also magnificent during the two years of WSC, when he handed the captaincy back to his brother and scored 1416 runs in the SuperTests, 523 more than any other Australian. His aggregate in the one-day internationals of 1166 was also substantially higher than any of his comrades.

Chappell led the Australian team in every official Test he played from November 1975 until his final home season, when he handed the responsibility to Kim Hughes. In 1982-83, he matched his brother by leading his team to regain the Ashes on home soil. As a batsman, Chappell's Test average was slightly higher after WSC than it was before (4097 runs at 53.20 in 51 Tests between 1970 and 1977 against 3013 at 54.78 in 36 Tests, 1979-84), and he scored three of his four Test double centuries after his return. Like legendary batsmen of earlier eras, such as Grace, Hobbs and Bradman, he was more shrewd and effective towards the end of his career, even if he looked more imperious in younger days.

Chappell, the brilliant slips catcher, snares the West Indies Richard Austin off Dennis Lillee during a WSC Supertest in 1979.

The Third XI

Richard Hadlee described Chappell as 'the best batsman I encountered, in the all-round sense'. Comparing him to Geoff Boycott, whom he rated as the best batsman purely on the basis of technique, Hadlee commented that Chappell could 'tear attacks apart, which Boycott couldn't do — I never felt Boycott was in charge when I bowled to him even though he was very difficult to remove, but Chappell was a constant threat'. He then cited Chappell's superb 176 from just 218 deliveries on a seamer's wicket at Christchurch in the third Test of 1982, which included exactly 100 runs in the first session of the second day, as proof of his 'murderous artistry'. At his best, Chappell was graceful, clever and appeared well-organised, with the great player's ability to work the ball into gaps. He never bludgeoned the ball, even in one-day cricket, but his timing — especially when hitting through the covers of the front and back foot, and when driving the ball between mid-wicket and mid-on — was exquisite.

The memory of Chappell's skill and style remain vivid for fans who became hooked on Australian cricket during the 1970s. Chappell's medium-pace bowling was serviceable, good enough to get him 47 Test wickets and even one spell of 5-61 against Pakistan in Sydney in 1972-73. His magnificent catching, especially in the slip cordon, was foolproof; he ranks with Bob Simpson and Mark Waugh as the best catcher of flying edges Australia has ever had. But it was his batting that made Chappell special.

When ranking the greatest Australian batsmen after Don Bradman and Victor Trumper, a case can be made for any of Chappell, Allan Border, Ricky Ponting, Charlie Macartney, Steve Waugh and Neil Harvey to be put third. In 2003, for the book *Top 10s of Australian Test Cricket*, this author rated Border third best, followed by Macartney and Chappell. However, after giving more consideration to Chappell's Test batting record compared to his contemporaries, that batting order has been changed a little. Of batsmen Chappell faced at least once at Test level, and who played at least 30 Test-match innings during their careers, only eight — Javed Miandad (52.57), Sunil Gavaskar (51.12), Viv Richards (50.24), Geoff Boycott (47.73), Rohan Kanhai (47.53), Clive Lloyd (46.68), Dennis Amiss (46.31) and Martin Crowe (45.37) — averaged more than 45 in Test cricket. Only three teammates — Allan Border (50.56), Doug Walters (48.26) and Bill Lawry (47.15) — averaged more than 45. Chappell averaged 53.86. For most batsmen, the '70s and early '80s were tough times for scoring runs. But not for Greg Chappell.

The great triumvirate — Chappell, Lillee and Rod Marsh — after what proved to be their final Test, against Pakistan in Sydney in January 1984.

GREG CHAPPELL (AUSTRALIA)

Test Cricket

Tests	Inn	NO	Runs	HS	Ave	100	50	Ct	Balls	Runs	Wkts	Ave	Best	5/	10/
87	151	19	7110	247*	53.86	24	31	122	5327	1913	47	40.70	5-61	1	—

One-Day International Cricket

ODIs	Inn	NO	Runs	HS	Ave	100	50	Ct	Balls	Runs	Wkts	Ave	Best	4/
74	72	14	2331	138*	40.19	3	14	23	3108	2096	72	29.11	5-15	2

The 100 Greatest Cricketers

No. 25 Bill O'Reilly

Bill O'Reilly was to Australia's bowling in the 1930s what Don Bradman was to its batting. During a decade of sustained runmaking, O'Reilly took 102 English wickets, at 25.76. Of the remainder of the Aussie attack, Clarrie Grimmett took 59 wickets, Tim Wall 35, 'Chuck' Fleetwood-Smith 33, Ernie McCormick and Stan McCabe 21. None of these bowlers averaged less than 30. No one else managed more than 15 wickets.

The Tiger in his delivery stride, as threatening as any 'slow' bowler in Test-match history.

O'Reilly was a product of the Australian bush, born at White Cliffs in western New South Wales, the son of a schoolmaster. In 1917, Mr O'Reilly senior was transferred to Wingello, in the Southern Highlands, where Bill made his name in a number of sports, including cricket. But where young Don Bradman from the not-too-far-away town of Bowral was soon recognised as having freakish ability, Bill was a frustrated paceman who reluctantly switched to bowling quick leg-breaks. A wise old coach suggested that might give him a better chance of going somewhere in the game.

By 1925, O'Reilly was studying at teachers' college in Sydney, and close to Christmas, his train home was stopped at Bowral Station, when he heard his name being called by the stationmaster. When the young leg-spinner identified himself, he was promptly told he was required at the Bowral cricket ground, where the game between the locals and Wingello was about to begin. Of course, the Wingello skipper had lost the toss, and through O'Reilly troubled him early on, the 17-year-old Bradman went on to be 234 not out at stumps. Next Saturday, he was bowled first ball by O'Reilly. As the Tiger put it, 'The birds began to sing. The sun shone becomingly. One ball changed my whole sporting outlook.'

In 1926-27 O'Reilly was chosen in North Sydney seconds, but Johnnie Moyes, a NSW selector, saw him in action, and Tiger was immediately invited to state practice. A year later, he made his first-class debut against a New Zealand XI and played one Shield match (the game before Bradman made his first-class debut), but then the NSW Education Department dispatched him to the bush, and he was not seen in first-class cricket again until 1931-32. After four matches for NSW that season, he was in the Australian team for the final two Tests against South Africa (taking seven wickets), and from there didn't miss a Test until after World War II.

His first great performance in Tests came in the second match of the bodyline series, when, opening the bowling with Tim Wall, he took five wickets in each innings. Among O'Reilly's victims on the final day were Herbert Sutcliffe, comprehensively bowled, and Wally Hammond, caught at deep cover after losing his composure following a spell of wickedly tight bowling. Had the television camera been there for that Sutcliffe ball, which the great batsman said 'turned a bloody

The Third XI

yard', it might be as famous as Warne's 'Gatting ball'. In 1974, umpire George Hele, who was at the bowler's end, called it 'the best ball I've seen bowled in any class of cricket'. Hele continued, 'It pitched on his middle and leg stump and hit the off stump about six inches below the bail.'

Of O'Reilly's bowling in this Test, which ended in Australia's only win of the summer, Hele commented: 'Bill showed that, when the wicket gave a spin bowler some assistance, he was the one who could take fullest advantage of it. He delivered every kind of ball he owned, from the above-medium-pace leg-break to the high-popping wrong 'un. He used his faster straight ball occasionally. He had every batsman who faced him groping forward or scurrying back.'

O'Reilly at Old Trafford in 1934, when he took seven wickets in England's first innings.

O'Reilly's run-up — feet thumping, arms almost flailing as he bounded to the bowling crease — was inspired and belligerent, informing spectators, teammates and batsmen that he was fair dinkum. At delivery, he was slightly front-on, and maybe there was a suggestion of a stoop, but the ball fizzed through relentlessly. Like all the great bowlers, he knew what length the batsmen liked least. The English left-hand bat of the 1930s, Maurice Leyland, once told the story of an over from O'Reilly that featured six different deliveries. First, an off break, then a leg break, googly, almost a bumper, and one that went on with the arm. 'What about the last one?' Leyland was asked. 'Oh that,' he remembered with a wry smile. 'It was the straight 'un that bowled me.'

O'Reilly didn't spin the ball viciously sideways in the manner of Warne, but he was much quicker through the air and no wrist-spinner has ever got more bounce. His wrong 'un had a real buzz, which explains why he had so much success with men fielding close in on the on-side. In the first Ashes Test of 1934, O'Reilly rescued his captain Bill Woodfull, who earlier in the day had made a ridiculously conservative declaration. Woodfull dallied until England needed all of 380 runs in 285 minutes on a wearing pitch, and when Les Ames and Leyland batted well into the final session a draw seemed likely. But then the last five wickets crashed for seven runs, so Australia won by 238 runs with 10 minutes to spare. O'Reilly, who took five of the final six wickets, finished with 7-54. He also took seven wickets in an innings in the third Test, at Old Trafford, including three wickets in four balls before lunch on the first day. — the last of which was Hammond, bowled by a fast leg break that hit the top of off stump.

O'Reilly (far left) with his teammates, among them 'Chuck' Fleetwood-Smith, Lindsay Hassett, Don Bradman and Stan McCabe in the Aussie dressing-room early on the 1938 Ashes tour.

O'Reilly finished with 28 wickets in 1934, took 27 in the Tests in South Africa in 1935-36, another 25 in the Ashes series of 1936-37 and 22 more when he returned to England in 1938. Even at The Oval, when Len Hutton got 364 and England made 7-903 (declared), O'Reilly was never truly conquered. He finished that laborious innings which spread over more than eight sessions with figures of 3-178 from 85 six-ball overs. Straight after World War II, he appeared in one more Test, in New Zealand, where he bowled 19 six-ball overs and took 8-31 (5-14 and 3-19). But his knee wouldn't allow him to play any more big-time cricket, not with his old fire anyway, so he retired to the pressbox, where he wrote in a knockabout and perceptive style for the next 40 years. A feature of his articles was his constant promotion of the art of spin bowling, often when others were arguing that it had had its time. Tiger would have enjoyed watching Warne.

Strangely, O'Reilly bowled plenty of no-balls during his career, but such was his control it was said that he never bowled a wide. In 1992, Sir Donald Bradman wrote of O'Reilly: 'Although only slow medium, his bowling was accurately described by [Lindsay] Hassett as "savage aggression". Attack was his creed and there was never any respite from his relentless accuracy. Without doubt, he was the best bowler I ever faced or saw.'

Perhaps the clearest proof of Bill O'Reilly's greatness has been that, despite all his success, no one has ever able to successfully mimic him. He was one of a kind.

BILL O'REILLY (AUSTRALIA)
Test Cricket

Tests	Inn	NO	Runs	HS	Ave	100	50	Ct	Balls	Runs	Wkts	Ave	Best	5/	10/
27	39	7	410	56*	12.81	–	1	7	10024	3254	144	22.60	7-54	11	3

First-Class Cricket

Mat	Inn	NO	Runs	HS	Ave	100	50	Ct	Balls	Runs	Wkts	Ave	Best	5/	10/
135	167	41	1655	56*	13.13	–	1	65	37064	12850	774	16.60	9-38	63	17

The Third XI

Frank Worrell

No. 26

For its 2000 edition, Wisden set out to name the best cricketers of the 20th century. Its method was to ask 100 experts from around the world to each nominate his or her five greatest players, the cricketers with the most votes being recognised, and among the criteria for selection were 'leadership qualities, personality, character and impact on the public'. Thus Sir Frank Worrell was ranked equal sixth, even though — based purely on his ability to score runs and take some wickets — he was not entitled to be measured quite so highly. What this vote reflected was the undeniable fact that as the man most responsible for the rise of the West Indies teams in the 1960s and '70s, a case can be made that he was cricket's greatest ever leader. There was a touch of the Nelson Mandela about the way he transformed the West Indies team after he became captain in 1960, by looking forward and grasping an opportunity, rather than getting square. As a cricket statesman, his influence arguably went further than any other player in history.

Worrell was something of a schoolboy prodigy. He first made the Barbados senior team as a slow left-hand bowler, but one effort as nightwatchman was enough to convince his seniors that he was good enough to succeed higher up the batting order. At age 19, he hit a first-class triple century, 308 not out, for Barbados in an inter-colonial encounter with Trinidad in Bridgetown. Two seasons later, the Trinidadians were victims again, as Worrell hit 245 not out in Port-of-Spain. Such run-getting was remarkable for one so young, and he batted with enormous style, but he also possessed a brave and worldly attitude that bordered — in the view of the white upper classes at least — on insolence. Worrell recognised his place from an early age, but he didn't like it and wouldn't accept it. 'A proud and strong-minded man, [he] had grown up increasingly restless under the unyielding racial hierarchy that was Barbados society,' wrote Michael Manley in *A History of West Indies Cricket*. Thus, in 1947, Worrell moved to Jamaica, which he believed was an island less dominated by racial divides.

Worrell hits out in England in 1950.

Worrell made his Test debut in the second Test of the 1947-48 home series against England, making 97 and 28 not out, and then followed up immediately in Georgetown by scoring an unbeaten 131. On the strength of those two appearances, the English writer EW Swanton, who covered the series, commented, 'His (Worrell's) gifts exceed those of any modern player, Bradman and Compton excepted.' In the fourth and final Test Worrell made 38 (giving him a Test average at this stage of 147), but was overshadowed by an innings of 141 by Everton Weekes that was so explosive and impressive that England captain, Gubby Allen, rated Weekes fractionally superior to Worrell. Weekes' form on a tour of India (a trip Worrell declined, following a pay dispute with the West Indies Cricket Board), where he scored four hundreds, a 90 and a 56 in six Test innings, appeared to lock in this rating.

Worrell with another of the West Indies' famous 'Ws', Everton Weekes. Worrell, Weekes and Clyde Walcott were the stars of the Windies batting order for much of the '50s.

On the England tour of 1950, Weekes made one triple century and three double hundreds in first-class matches, and averaged 56 in the Tests, but Worrell produced an innings in the third Test, at Trent Bridge, of such quality that it suggested he was actually his team's finest batsman. What Worrell did was come to the wicket early on day two with the score 2-95 and left early on day three at 4-521, having scored 261 runs out of 426 while Weekes, one of the game's most powerful hitters, scored 129 but was obliged to play the supporting role. The West Indies won that Test by 10 wickets, and the fourth, too, by a prodigious innings and 56 runs, with Worrell making 138. This was the first time the West Indies had won a Test series in England.

Worrell's Test batting average, after seven Tests (all against England), was 104.13. By the time his Test career was over, 13 years later, that figure had dropped to 49.48, while Weekes' career average stood at 58.62. The third of the famous 'Ws', Clyde Walcott, averaged 56.69, despite keeping wicket in 15 of his 44 Tests. Worrell took 69 wickets in his career but, maybe, purely on cricket ability, he should be ranked third of this famous threesome. Then again, the toughest examination the West Indies batting line-up of the early '50s faced was against Ray Lindwall and Keith Miller in Australia in 1951-52, and the three Ws were restricted to just one century: Worrell's 108 in the fourth Test. Over their careers, Worrell was the only one of the three to average more than 50 in Tests against England: 54.97 from 25 games. Yet he had the lowest average of the trio against Australia: 32.79 from 14 Tests. Worrell is ranked highest of the trio in this study because of his leadership.

The Third XI

With hindsight, it seems bewildering that it took a decade for Worrell to finally be appointed West Indian captain, but the demise of colonial influence in Caribbean cricket took all of that time. When he was finally appointed, for the 1960-61 tour of Australia, he cared little for opportunities lost, instead concentrating on the way his men would play in the future. Through the 1950s, the team had often lacked cohesion. The new captain wanted to invoke the spirit that had invigorated the game of his youth, but not just for entertainment's sake. In his view, this was the most likely way to gain results. In Richie Benaud, he found an Australian skipper equally as pragmatic and ambitious. Consequently, the series, featuring three thrilling finishes including cricket's first tied Test, evolved into the most exciting in history. 'The spare parts came together to form a machine which could function efficiently under the guidance of a master mechanic,' Johnnie Moyes wrote after the tour.

Worrell acknowledges the applause during his masterpiece at Trent Bridge in 1950.

Having encouraged a brand of cricket that helped revitalise the game in Australia, Worrell then took his men to England in 1963 and they did the same thing there. Few sides have been more popular while defeating the home side. The Lord Mayor of London, in a post-tour reception, stated that 'a gale of change has blown through the hallowed halls of cricket'.

From the start of the Australian series to the end of that England tour, the West Indies won nine Tests out of 15, a telling statistic that reflects the fact that Worrell was more than just a diplomat. Just as important, even after Worrell tragically died of leukemia, aged just 42, in 1967, his messages were absorbed. 'The point is, if you weren't winning people from different islands could say you weren't picking him or you weren't doing this,' Clive Lloyd told ESPN's *Legends of Cricket* in 2002. 'But if you were winning you got rid of that. I learnt a lot from him in this respect, that winning was the key to being one entity, even though we were from different islands. Winning was the glue that kept us together.'

FRANK WORRELL (WEST INDIES)

Test Cricket

Tests	Inn	NO	Runs	HS	Ave	100	50	Ct	Balls	Runs	Wkts	Ave	Best	5/	10/
51	87	9	3860	261	49.49	9	22	43	7141	2672	69	38.72	7-70	2	–

First-Class Cricket

Mat	Inn	NO	Runs	HS	Ave	100	50	Ct	Balls	Runs	Wkts	Ave	Best	5/	10/
208	326	49	15025	308*	54.24	39	80	139	26740	10115	349	28.98	7-70	13	–

No. 27 Wasim Akram

Of all the left-arm fast bowlers, Wasim Akram was the greatest. Cricket has never had a great bowler with as quick and deceptive an arm-action as Wasim. The only man to take 400 wickets in Tests and also 500 in one-day internationals, Wasim came on the international cricket scene as a gifted teenager in 1984 and remained there — brilliant, lethal and controversial — for 20 years. Using a short explosive run-up, he would dash to the wicket and then fire the ball at the startled batsman, a whippy whirr of an action. If speed was his shock tactic, swing was his art; no bowler has been better at making the old ball swing, or more adept at swinging the new or old ball at pace.

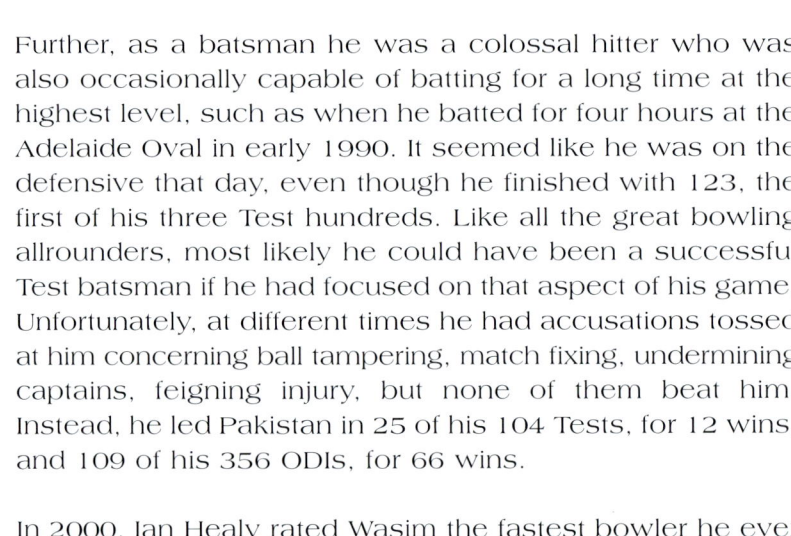

This page and opposite: Two views of arguably the great left-arm fast bowler in cricket's history.

Further, as a batsman he was a colossal hitter who was also occasionally capable of batting for a long time at the highest level, such as when he batted for four hours at the Adelaide Oval in early 1990. It seemed like he was on the defensive that day, even though he finished with 123, the first of his three Test hundreds. Like all the great bowling allrounders, most likely he could have been a successful Test batsman if he had focused on that aspect of his game. Unfortunately, at different times he had accusations tossed at him concerning ball tampering, match fixing, undermining captains, feigning injury, but none of them beat him. Instead, he led Pakistan in 25 of his 104 Tests, for 12 wins, and 109 of his 356 ODIs, for 66 wins.

In 2000, Ian Healy rated Wasim the fastest bowler he ever faced, based purely on one spell he survived during that 1989-90 season. It is perhaps strange then that the 18-year-old Pakistani's Test debut, in the second Test against New Zealand in 1984-85 at Auckland, passed almost without notice. A fortnight later, in Dunedin, he announced himself to the cricket world by becoming the youngest bowler to take 10 wickets (5-65 and 5-72) in a Test. From there it was to Australia for the World Championship of Cricket, a one-day tournament featuring all the then Test-playing teams. Wasim had not bowled in any of the one-day internationals in New Zealand, and had no success in Pakistan's opening match in Melbourne, but against Australia at the MCG he was stunningly magnificent, taking the first five wickets of the home team's innings (including Kepler Wessels, Dean Jones, Allan Border and Kim Hughes) and finishing with 5-21 from eight overs.

Scoring runs and taking wickets against the powerful West Indies at home in 1986 and against England away in 1987 boosted Wasim's ever-growing reputation, while his significant role in Pakistan's dramatic first-ever series win in India in 1987 was rewarded with a popstar-like reception back home. In 1989, he took his first hat trick in international cricket in a Champions Trophy ODI against the West Indies at Sharjah. Within 12 months, he'd done it again, in the final of the Austral-Asia Cup against Australia, a game in which he also hit 49 from 35

The Third XI

balls. His batting prowess was evident again in the Nehru Cup final, against the West Indies in Calcutta in 1989, when he slammed Viv Richards high over the mid-wicket fence to give Pakistan a thrilling victory with one ball to spare.

In five Tests at home in 1990-91 (he missed one through injury), Wasim took 31 wickets, including one remarkable spell in Lahore against the West Indies when he became the third bowler in Test history to take four wickets in five balls. Then in 1992, he played a key role in Pakistan's triumph in cricket's fifth World Cup. He was the leading wicket-taker in the competition, with 18 at 18.78, and in the final, after Pakistan had reached 6-249 (Wasim 33 from 19 deliveries), he dismissed Ian Botham for 0, then came back for a second spell to get Allan Lamb and Chris Lewis with successive deliveries, to earn the man-of-the-match award.

In a one-off Test in New Zealand in Hamilton in the first week of 1993, Wasim (5-45) and Waqar Younis (5-22) bowled Pakistan to a stunning 33-run victory after New Zealand had been set only 127 to win on a flat batting wicket. There is no doubt that Wasim and Waqar were one of the greatest of all fast-bowling tandems, a fact that had been fully apparent since the series in England in 1992, when the pair led Pakistan to an emphatic victory. Sadly, however, it was at this time that the Pakistani team began to be tarnished by controversies and scandals, involving ball tampering allegations that led to court cases in England, match-fixing allegations, numerous captaincy changes and sinister suggestions that players had not always given their best. All this meant that the high class of their best players was not always acknowledged.

Above left: Wasim, a man capable of hitting 12 sixes in one Test innings, hits out against Australia during a one-day international in 1999-2000.

Sri Lanka's defeat of Wasim's team in the 1996 World Cup quarter-finals was deplored across Pakistan, and his decision to miss the match because of injury was ridiculed in some quarters. He dropped out of one-day tournaments in Singapore and Sharjah after that disaster, but came back to lead Pakistan to a 2-0 series win in England, during which he became the 11th bowler and second Pakistani (after Imran Khan) to take 300 Test wickets. Then, back home, he smashed one of Test cricket's most memorable innings, against Zimbabwe in Sheikhupra, breaking a number of records. He scored 257 not out, his highest score in first-class cricket and the highest ever made by a No. 8 in Test cricket. His 12 sixes was the most ever hit by an individual in one Test innings, while his eighth-wicket partnership of 313 with Saqlain Mushtaq was a Test record. As if to emphasise his all-round greatness, he followed up by taking 6-48 and 4-58, his fourth 10-wicket haul in Tests, in the second Test of the series.

Wasim during the 1992 World Cup at the MCG, arguably his greatest day (and night) in cricket.

Wasim's Test career extended to 2002, his last ODI came at the 2003 World Cup. During this time he played under a succession of captains, led the side again (taking his team to the 1999 World Cup final), and established a series of records, such as first Pakistani and fourth bowler to take 400 Test wickets, third bowler to take two hat-tricks in Tests (in successive matches against Sri Lanka in 1999), the first to take Test hat-tricks in two different countries, first Asian bowler and first captain to take a Test hat-trick. He also bowled the most overs in ODIs, as at June 30, 2009 78.5 more than Muttiah Muralitharan and more than 400 more than anyone else.

Of all the men to play 100 Tests, Wasim was clearly the fastest bowler. This fact, and all his runs and one-day international performances are a wonderful tribute to his durability. None of his injuries stopped him for too long. The controversies he became a part of, especially the match-fixing allegations, were often relentless, as were the complicated politics that lurk just below the surface of Pakistani cricket. However, though they may have diminished his reputation until they were resolved, they do not detract from his greatness as a cricketer, nor his toughness — mental and physical — as a sportsman.

WASIM AKRAM (PAKISTAN)

Test Cricket

Tests	Inn	NO	Runs	HS	Ave	100	50	Ct	Balls	Runs	Wkts	Ave	Best	5/	10/
104	147	19	2898	257*	22.64	3	7	44	22627	9779	414	23.62	7-119	25	5

One-Day International Cricket

ODIs	Inn	NO	Runs	HS	Ave	100	50	Ct	Balls	Runs	Wkts	Ave	Best	4/
356	280	55	3717	86	16.52	–	6	88	18186	11812	502	23.53	5-15	23

Kapil Dev

No. 28

Until the late 1970s, India seemed a haven for spin bowlers, the general belief being that the hot and often dusty conditions were sufficient to stifle a young pace bowler's growth and ambition. But then, suddenly, an opening bowler with genuine fire arrived on the scene. When, in November 1994, Kapil Dev became the leading wicket-taker in Test history, perhaps his greatest achievement was the 217 Test wickets he'd captured on home soil.

Kapil made his Test debut in October 1978, during the first India-Pakistan series for 17 years, and first made an impact with some rapid bowling and a 33-ball half-century in the third Test. Straight after, at home against the West Indies, he established his reputation. The fourth Test, on an unusually bouncy wicket in Madras, developed into what *Wisden* called a 'bumper war'. Previously, India wouldn't have dreamed of such a confrontation; this time they won the match by three wickets, thanks to Kapil's hostility, seven wickets and 26 not out at the death. In the fifth Test, he hit his first Test century, a blazing 126 not out from 124 balls. Not only had India won the series, they had a new hero.

Kapil was never express in the way of Andy Roberts, Jeff Thomson or Michael Holding, but in the first half of his career he was more than fast enough and had that rare ability to hit the bat surprisingly hard. His greatest assets were late outswing, which came from a side-on action straight out of the cricket textbook, and the ability to effectively vary pace and length. Tall (188cm) and athletic, he was a better batsman than his final Test-match average (31.05) suggests. Most certainly, he was one of the most durable of the great Test cricketers: the body might often have been aching but from 1978 to 1994 he never once missed an international match because of injury.

India has just shocked the West Indies in the 1983 World Cup at Lord's.

To some degree, Kapil's fast bowling reputation was tarnished by the latter stages of his career, when he was more medium-paced than strike force. Years of carrying the load had clearly worn him down. He never had a Thomson, a Keith Miller, a Waqar Younis or a Jason Gillespie at the other end. Instead, he shared the new-ball with 20 different partners during his Test career, none of whom threatened to take the first over from him. His 300th Test wicket arrived in Sri Lanka in January 1987, but it was five more years before he reached 400 and two more before he staggered past Richard Hadlee's world mark.

Kapil has England's Geoff Boycott caught behind by Syed Kirmani at Eden Gardens in 1981-82.

The 100 Greatest Cricketers

Kapil was an unsuccessful captain of India — just four wins from 34 Tests, though in ODIs he had 40 wins and 32 losses. Clearly, his greatest day in charge came when India won the 1983 World Cup. In the final, his leadership as India defended a total of 183 was superb, his 11 overs for just 21 runs were important, and his beautifully judged running catch of Viv Richards at mid-wicket, 20 metres from the boundary, was perhaps the single most critical moment of the match. Three months earlier, in his first Test series as captain, in the West Indies in 1982-83, he had become the youngest man to that point to take 200 Test wickets and complete the 200 wickets/2000 runs Test double. He did this in Port-of-Spain, in his 50th Test, and marked the occasion by scoring a century from 95 balls. Four years later, 10 weeks after becoming the first man to captain India to a series victory in England, Kapil was the Indian skipper in cricket's second Tied Test, against Australia in Madras, and his role in the drama was significant. He scored a blazing hundred in India's reply to Australia's 7-574 (declared), racing from 50 to 100 with only 16 scoring shots. Then, on the final day, his team played in a manner befitting their captain's philosophy, pursuing the 348-run target with gusto.

Perhaps the best example at Test level of Kapil Dev's pure hitting skill occurred in the sixth and final Test against England, in Kanpur, in 1981-82. By then the match was certain to be drawn and the series decided in India's favour, so Kapil put on a show, racing to his century in 84 balls. Or did it come in Kanpur in 1986-87, when he scored 163 against Sri Lanka? The hundred mark was reached that day in 74 balls. Kapil also recorded three of the swiftest Test fifties ever made — one in 30 balls, two in 33 balls.

The style of one of the cleanest and most effective hitters the game has seen.

The last of Kapil's eight Test hundreds, 129 against South Africa at Port Elizabeth in 1992, was made out of a total of 188, after India had fallen to 6-31. Two years earlier, he had produced perhaps his most famous cameo. With India nine wickets down and needing 24 to avoid the follow-on at Lord's, Kapil hit the off-spinner, Eddie Hemmings, for four sixes, all of them over the boundary near the Nursery-end sightscreen. Easy.

The Third XI

However, Kapil Dev's greatest innings came not in a Test match, but at a place called Tunbridge Wells. An occasional venue for Kent in southern England, it was host in 1983 to a World Cup match between India and a Zimbabwean side that had surprised Australia earlier in the competition. India came into the game having won two of their first four qualifying matches so they could not afford to falter if they wanted to reach the semi-finals. As it turned out, they needed Kapil Dev at his absolute best to get them this vital win. Without him, the massive celebrations at Lord's seven days later would never have occurred.

This remains the most memorable fast-bowling action in the history of Indian cricket.

The first ball of the day kicked at Sunil Gavaskar off a length and the last ball of that over had him lbw. One for none. By the 10th over, Kapil Dev was in the middle, at 4-9. By the 13th over it was 5-17. From this unlikely launching pad, Kapil unleashed one of one-day cricket's most stirring fightbacks. First he added 60 with Roger Binny, who scored 22. Ravi Shastri fell almost immediately to make it 7-78, but, undeterred, in the 36th over Kapil reached his 50 and India their 100. At lunch it was 7-106, and afterwards Kapil and Madan Lal took the score to 140 in the 44th over before David Houghton took his fourth catch of the innings. After that, Syed Kirmani defended. Kapil's century came in the 49th over, and when the 60th over ended Kapil was 175 not out (six sixes and 16 fours), Kirmani 24 not out, the innings total 8-266

In this study, Kapil is rated above Keith Miller as an allrounder, the reason being that he produced more stupendous performances in international cricket than did the great Australian. He also never had a bowler like Ray Lindwall to support him. Miller did have a better Test batting and bowling average, and no doubt Miller would have been as great a success in one-day internationals as was Kapil, but for all Miller's enormous ability and popularity across the cricket world, he was never as important to Australian cricket as was Kapil Dev to India.

KAPIL DEV (INDIA)
Test Cricket

Tests	Inn	NO	Runs	HS	Ave	100	50	Ct	Balls	Runs	Wkts	Ave	Best	5/	10/
131	184	15	5248	163	31.05	8	27	64	27740	12867	434	29.65	9-83	23	2

One-Day International Cricket

ODIs	Inn	NO	Runs	HS	Ave	100	50	Ct	Balls	Runs	Wkts	Ave	Best	4/
225	198	39	3783	175*	23.79	1	14	71	11202	6945	253	27.45	5-43	4

The 100 Greatest Cricketers

No. 29 George Headley

George Headley was short, finely built, and on the cricket field he usually had his sleeves buttoned at the wrists and his cricket cap with its peak at a jaunty angle. First impressions, which might have suggested he was even a little frail, were wrong, because from the moment he arrived at the batting crease he was tough and strong. If one story of Headley sums up the man, it was of his only tour of Australia, in 1930-31, when he arrived with a weakness on the on-drive that the home team resolved to exploit, largely through the relentless accuracy of their No. 1 bowler, Clarrie Grimmett. However, Headley had the good fortune to observe Don Bradman and Archie Jackson savage Grimmett during a Sheffield Shield match in Adelaide, adding 334 in only 223 minutes. Then it was to the nets, where he practised for hour after hour. He scored centuries in the third and fifth Tests, and years later Grimmett commented, 'George Headley was a magnificent player, the best onside batsman against whom I ever bowled.'

Is this the 'Black Bradman'? Or was The Don the 'White Headley'?

As a teenager, Headley had been unlucky not to be selected for the West Indies' tour of England in 1928, thus missing the Windies' first-ever Tests. He was still not 21 when the Hon. Frederick Calthorpe brought a reasonable England team over for the first official Test series in the Caribbean in 1929-30, but he belted 703 runs during the series. Headley's 176 in the first Test remains the sixth highest innings by a batsman in his first Test, and the highest by a debutant in his team's second innings. His twin centuries in the third Test spearheaded the West Indies to their first ever Test-match victory, while the 223 he crafted in the final game of the series, on his home turf in Kingston, Jamaica, is still the highest score made by an individual batsman in the fourth innings of a Test.

His feats were celebrated *throughout* the Caribbean, and he was especially revered on his home island, where he gave a semblance of hope and pride to his community. 'That it is not generally realised is the almost inseparable obstacles the average cricketer in the West Indies has to overcome,' Headley explained years later. 'I was comfortable compared to many I knew, whose lot was unemployment, half-fed, and in dire circumstances. The powers-that-be make no attempt to help such fellows.' In the same way Viv Richards and Andy Roberts

The Third XI

gave validity to the cricket claims of Antigua, indeed the entire Leeward Islands, in the 1970s, so Headley boosted the status of the game in Jamaica between the wars and beyond.

On his first English tour, in 1933, Headley finished third on the season's first-class averages, scoring 2320 runs at 66.28, including seven centuries. No one else in the touring team averaged even 40, only three averaged 30 or more. At home in 1934-35, the West Indies won a Test rubber for the first time, beating a mid-strength English side 2-1 in four Tests. The series began in Barbados on a diabolical pitch and involved just 309 runs, two declarations, and an eventual four-wicket win for England, but much of the talk afterwards was about brave and extraordinarily skilful displays on the sticky wicket from Wally Hammond for the visitors (43 and 29 not out) and Headley (44 run out). Hammond was regarded as being at least the best batsman since Jack Hobbs on such surfaces, but Neville Cardus, for one, would rate the Jamaican ahead of him. Cardus especially remembered one Headley century on a dangerous pitch at Lord's, which was 'of such sure judgement and aim that if ever he edged a viciously spinning ball he did so with the edge's middle'. In the final Test of '34-35, in Jamaica, Headley came in at 1-5 on the first morning, and batted for over eight hours to finish on 270 not out. The West Indies passed 500 for the first time in a Test and went on to win by an innings and 161 runs.

Headley played no more Test cricket until 1939, when he undertook his second trip to England with a West Indies team. By this time, he was a hardened professional cricketer, having first signed with Haslingden in the Lancashire League for the 1934

Headley at Old Trafford in 1939, during a season in which his batting equalled, often even outshone, that of Wally Hammond, Len Hutton and Denis Compton.

season — in the process doubling his annual income — and had evolved into one of the shrewdest thinkers in the game. However, West Indies cricket was not yet ready for a black captain. Rather, Headley and his accomplished comrade, Learie Constantine, had to fight hard for a suitable financial deal for themselves and Manny Martindale, the other black professional in the squad. After this matter was resolved, Headley went on to top the English first-class averages for the season with 1745 runs at 72.60. No other West Indian scored 1000 runs on the tour, or averaged even half what Headley did. In the opening Test of the series, at Lord's, he became the second man, after England's Herbert Sutcliffe, to twice score a hundred in each innings of a Test.

That series ended on August 22, within days the world was at war, and for 30-year-old George Headley the best days of his cricket career were over. Named officially as captain of Jamaica in 1947, he made an immediate mark by successfully asking the local administrators for his black teammates to be given a transport and kit allowance. Headley played three post-war Tests, spread over six years, scoring 55 runs in five innings. In the first of these, against England in January 1948, he was the captain, the first black man to lead a West Indies Test side, but he had to miss the rest of the series because of a back ailment, and his appointment as leader hardly proved to be a watershed. The next time a black man led the West Indies was at Brisbane in December 1960.

Of all the batsmen who have played 20 innings in Test cricket, only Bradman (99.94) and Graeme Pollock (60.97) have higher averages than Headley. If you ignore his three post-war Tests, his Test career batting average is 64.70. Of the first 14 centuries made by West Indian batsmen in Test cricket, he made 10 of them. In the 35 Test innings in which he batted before the war, Headley top-scored 15 times. He hit eight hundreds against England in 14 Tests between 1930 and 1939. Only four men in Test history, Bradman (19 in 37 Tests), Garry Sobers (10 in 36), Steve Waugh (10 in 47) and Greg Chappell (nine in 35) and have scored more centuries against England.

Since World War II, the cricket world has seen a string of exceptional West Indies batsmen — Weekes, Worrell and Walcott, Sobers and Kanhai, Lloyd, Richards, Richardson and Lara — so it is possible to forget just how important Headley was to the story of West Indian cricket. During his career, Headley had been known as 'Atlas', because of the way he carried the West Indies side, and also as the 'Black Bradman'. Constantine, however, disagreed with this. He was sure that Bradman was the 'White Headley'!

GEORGE HEADLEY (WEST INDIES)
Test Cricket

Tests	Inn	NO	Runs	HS	Ave	100	50	Ct	Balls	Runs	Wkts	Ave	Best	5/	10/
22	40	4	2190	270*	60.83	10	5	14	398	230	0	—	0-0	—	—

First-Class Cricket

Mat	Inn	NO	Runs	HS	Ave	100	50	Ct	Balls	Runs	Wkts	Ave	Best	5/	10/
103	164	22	9921	344*	69.87	33	44	76	3845	1842	51	36.12	5-33	1	—

George Lohmann

No. 30

Of all bowlers to take 50 Test wickets, George Lohmann has the lowest bowling average: 10.76. Lohmann played 18 Tests between 1886 and 1896, for 112 wickets, taking five wickets in an innings nine times, 10 wickets in a match five times. He played in eight series (considering even one-off Tests as a series) and never averaged more than 18.06, averaging less than nine three times. In 15 Tests against Australia, Lohmann took 77 wickets at 13.01. Thirty-five of those wickets were taken at the Sydney Cricket Ground, in four Tests, at an average of 9.46. In England, his Test bowling average was 14.56; in Australia it was 11.66.

Of course, wickets came at a lower cost in the 19th century, but no other bowler took them as cheaply as this. Lohmann's three Tests against South Africa in 1895-96, when he was not in the best of health, brought 35 wickets at the ridiculous rate of 5.80 runs per wicket. For the tour, he took 157 wickets at 6.78. In the opening Test, at Port Elizabeth, after taking 7-38 in the home team's first innings total of 93, Lohmann took 8-7 in the second from 49 balls. South Africa were all out for 30. A fortnight later, he was kept back to first change after England made 482, and took 9-28 from 72 balls. Never in Test history has a team been so over-matched against one bowler.

According to HS Altham, Lohmann was 'the first English bowler really to master the revolutionary lessons of Spofforth, and to make length the handmaid of variety in pace and spin and flight'. Lohmann's stock delivery was on the slow side of medium pace, and though mostly he broke the ball back from the off, he could land a leg-break as well. Again quoting Altham, he was also 'a gallant dashing batsman and possibly the finest slip-fielder that the world has known'.

For a bowler whose final record was so fantastic, Lohmann's first two Tests were unproductive, even though England won fairly comfortably at Manchester and then by an innings at Lord's. Lohmann took just one wicket in his first Test, and none at all in his second, but then snared 7-36 and 5-68 on his home pitch at The Oval. Almost immediately, he set sail for Australia, to become the first man to take eight wickets in one Test innings (8-35), bowling unchanged through Australia's first innings of the second Test. As a professional cricketer, he was happy to accept another invitation to Australia 12 months later, for the second summer in a row taking more than 50 first-class wickets, nine of them (for 52) in the only Test of the tour. In the home Tests in 1888, Lohmann took only 11 wickets, jockeying with two other brilliant bowlers, Johnny Briggs and Bobby Peel, for overs against a disappointing Australian batting side. His greatest influence came in the second Test at The Oval, when on the first morning he dismissed both Australian openers with spectacular slip catches, and then clubbed 62 not out, batting 10, in England's only innings. One can imagine the way the spectators would have reacted to this display; WG Grace described Lohmann as 'the idol of the Surrey crowd', who 'almost lionised' him.

George Lohmann's Test career bowling average of 10.76 remains the lowest of all bowlers with 50 or more wickets.

Grace thought Lohmann was born for cricket, saying, 'The better the batsman, the better Lohmann bowled.' He was one of those brilliant bowlers who, because of his variety, had a fast, straight ball that could do considerable damage. By the time it was bowled, the batsman could hardly believe it wasn't going to do anything. Lohmann also had an unbreakable faith in his own ability. In Australia in 1891-92, Grace went up to him and said, 'George, it's time for a change, isn't it?' To which Lohmann responded, 'Don't you think I'd better go on at the other end?' He always fully expected to get a wicket; if not now, then soon.

'Most people, I believe, considered his action to be perfect,' Charles Fry wrote of Lohmann in 1900. 'To the eye it was rhythmical and polished.' Fry was in awe of his change of pace, and the manner in which, from that high delivery, he could deceive the batsman by getting the ball to dip and dive late, to land on the perfect length when at first it seemed it was going to be a half-volley, maybe even a full toss. Or maybe it looked like it was going to be short of a length, only to be the yorker. There was never any discernible change in action or effort, and the only time Lohmann pitched too full or too short was if it was all part of the plan. And like all the great medium-pacers, he hit the bat hard, his deliveries seeming to accelerate off the pitch. 'He was what I call a very hostile bowler,' Fry concluded. 'He made one feel he was one's deadly enemy, and he used to put many batsmen off their strokes by his masterful and confident manner with the ball. He was by far the most difficult medium pace bowler I ever played on a good wicket.'

So why then is so little heard of Lohmann today? For seven straight seasons from 1885, he had taken more first-class wickets than any other English bowler, but in 1892 his health broke down, and on Christmas Eve he sailed for South Africa, hoping that by avoiding the cold of winter he might win a battle with tuberculosis. Sadly, while he still had his grand days (especially, of course, in the Tests of 1895-96), playing first-class and Test cricket in England and South Africa, he was never able to sustain the great spells of his youth. Meanwhile, new bowling heroes — such as Wilfred Rhodes, Bill Lockwood and Tom Richardson — emerged and, critically in terms of how we remember the cricketers of those days, great writers such as Neville Cardus spent the next 70 years grandly recalling them. Cardus was 13 years old during the famous 1902 Ashes series.

Lohmann died in 1901, aged just 36. Fred Spofforth — because his fast ball was quicker and because he was the *first* great Test bowler — is entitled to ranked as the No. 1 bowler before Sydney Barnes. But the Demon aside, it is very difficult to mount a case that any other bowler from this era was better than George Lohmann.

GEORGE LOHMANN (ENGLAND)

Test Cricket

Tests	Inn	NO	Runs	HS	Ave	100	50	Ct	Balls	Runs	Wkts	Ave	Best	5/	10/
18	26	2	213	62*	8.88	–	1	28	3821	1205	112	10.76	9-28	9	5

First-Class Cricket

Mat	Inn	NO	Runs	HS	Ave	100	50	Ct	Balls	Runs	Wkts	Ave	Best	5/	10/
293	427	39	7247	115	18.68	3	29	337	71724	25295	1841	13.74	9-28	176	57

The Third XI

Jack Blackham

No. 31

Jack McCarthy Blackham, known in his day as the 'Prince of Wicketkeepers', was quite obviously Australia's first-choice keeper from 1877 to 1894. During that time he revolutionised the art of wicketkeeping. He was tough, superb and consistent, to the point that he is recognised in England as well as Australia as the man who made the use of a longstop obsolete. As the story goes, during a district game in Melbourne, the man fielding directly behind him on the boundary came up and said, 'I'm getting nothing to do, Jack. What say I field at fine leg?' Thus, the batsmen had an extra fieldsman to counter. When English spectators first saw Blackham keeping to Fred Spofforth without a longstop, they were simply astonished. 'He was actually spoken of in one quarter as a positive danger to the well-being of cricket,' remembered HS Altham, 'encouraging as he did by his example the abolition of the long stop!'

The Prince of Wicketkeepers.

In 1899, WG Grace wrote of Blackham: 'Clean, quick as lightning, and quiet, he stood as close to the wickets as the laws of cricket permit and took the fastest bowling with consummate ease. To stand up to Spofforth's fastest bowling was in itself an achievement, but to keep wicket against the Demon without permitting a bye to pass was a phenomenal performance. The batsman who stirred out of his ground when Blackham was at the wicket knew he had to hit the ball or his innings was over. There was no element of chance in Blackham's stumping; it was a case of inevitability. His hands might get damaged, or the ball might bump on a rough wicket, but Blackham was upon it. (Lancashire's Richard) Pilling was his only rival behind the wicket, and Pilling was only in the cricket field for a few years, while Blackham stuck to his guns for twenty ...'

One of Blackham's more incredible achievements was his role in Spofforth's first Test wicket, taken in cricket's second Test, at Melbourne in 1877. The *Argus* reported that Spofforth 'hurled the ball forwards with a velocity and recklessness as to the consequences enough to make all timid people tremble for the safety of the batsman'. Even so, Blackham stumped Alfred Shaw during the Demon's fourth over. In *On Top Down Under*, the great cricketer writer Ray Robinson thought Blackham taking Spofforth was 'as near as cricket ever got to the thrills of a knife-throwing act', even if it was true that from time to time Blackham did go back to take Spofforth's fastest. Against the Gentlemen of England in 1884, for example, the Demon was upset after an appeal for a slips catch was rejected, and for the next few minutes Blackham retreated while the bowler angrily sought revenge.

The 100 Greatest Cricketers

Blackham was only short, around 176 cm (5ft 9in), weighed 66kg (10st 6lb) and really was as tough as nails. Johnnie Moyes stated in *A Century of Cricketers* (published in 1950), 'Whether there is much difference between the techniques of 1877 and 1947 cannot be determined with any certainty, but my reading leads me to believe that the chief difference is in pads and gloves, not in science and the application of that science.' Blackham lost most of his front teeth before his career was over, his fingers were gnarled and misshapen, and Robinson claimed he also had a cavity in chest where a fast one had speared into his ribcage.

The Australian team that toured England in 1888. Blackham is in the back row, third from right. The acclaimed opening bowler, Charlie Turner, is seated second from left.

The 20-year-old Blackham was one of two future Victorian and Australian captains to make his first-class debut in a match against New South Wales in December 1874, a childhood friend from Fitzroy, Tom Horan, being the other. Spofforth made his first appearance for NSW in the same game. Blackham marked his debut with four dismissals, three catches and a stumping, and was a certain selection for his state for the next 20 years. His choice as Australia's keeper for the inaugural Test match was met with some controversy, chiefly after Spofforth refused to play because Billy Murdoch, a loyal friend and the NSW keeper, had not been selected. It was rumoured that the Demon didn't think Blackham could handle his fastest deliveries, but if this was true, the Victorian set him straight soon enough. In 1902, Spofforth was asked about the standard of wicketkeeping in England, where he was now living. 'I do not think at present that there is a wicketkeeper in the same street as Blackham,' he replied emphatically.

The Third XI

Blackham played in all of Australia's first 12 Tests (the only man to do so) without ever scoring a fifty. However, in his 13th appearance, played in a match in which a fresh pitch for each innings, he clubbed 57 and 58 not out as Australia won by four wickets. 'He was never a particularly reliable run-getter,' recalled George Giffen in 1899, 'yet few great batsmen have pulled a side out of a tight place more frequently than he has with his unorthodox batting. And how he could demoralise the bowling! Let him get a start and it was difficult to place the field for his strokes.' Blackham captained Australia in eight Tests, and in the last of them, the first Test of 1894-95, he achieved his highest Test score, 74 in 86 minutes, while adding 154 with Syd Gregory for the ninth wicket. This remains an Ashes Test record partnership for the ninth wicket.

In 1890, Blackham had been one of the first chosen for what would be his seventh tour of England. The biggest selection quandary was over who should be the second keeper, with most observers believing either NSW's Sid Deane or Victoria's Jack Harry would get the nod. However, Blackham pushed hard for the Tasmanian Kenny Burn, who had been a strong candidate for the 1888 side, having played for an Australian XI as a batsman in two matches in 1887-88. Blackham had noticed in the papers that 'Burn' had made some stumpings in Tasmania, and assumed that keeper to be Kenny, when in truth it was Kenny's brother, a fact that didn't become apparent until the touring team had set sail for England. 'Extraordinarily heavy work will fall on Blackham's shoulders, or should I say his hands,' wrote Horan in the *Australasian* after the mistake was revealed. 'But, like the keen cricketer he is, he looks forward cheerfully to his task.'

He had more than one nickname. Giffen claimed he was known as 'The Caged Lion', a title earned during a tour of England when he was prone in close finishes to pace around the rooms, fists clenched, chin on chest, bemoaning real and invented injustices. As captain against WG Grace in 1891-92, Blackham blamed stress for the stone in weight he lost as the Australians won the series 2-1. By the end of his career, he was known as 'Old Jack', which really was a wonderful tribute in that the revered racehorse Carbine also carried this sobriquet. Carbine was originally from New Zealand, but had become a hero in Australia after his courageous win in the 1890 Melbourne Cup. It was genuinely fitting that these two legends of Australian sport were known by the same name.

JACK BLACKHAM (AUSTRALIA)

Test Cricket

Tests	Inn	NO	Runs	HS	Ave	100	50	Ct	St
35	62	11	800	74	15.69	–	4	37	24

First-Class Cricket

Mat	Inn	NO	Runs	HS	Ave	100	50	Ct	St	Balls	Runs	Wkts	Ave	Best	5/	10/
275	442	61	6395	109	16.78	1	26	274	181	312	138	2	69.00	1-8	–	–

No. 32 Glenn McGrath

It is hard to pinpoint what made Glenn McGrath such a great bowler. There was not one single aspect of his bowling that he did better than anyone else. There have been quicker bowlers, men who have swung it more, seamed it more. His change of pace was clever, rather than astounding. Few bowlers of his pace have been more accurate. His temperament was usually on the level, but not always. The thing is, there have been precious few bowlers who have been as excellent at all these things as was McGrath. He was quick enough, swung it enough, seamed it enough, changed his pace enough, was accurate enough and certainly smart enough to be ruthless. The result was one of the finest exponents of pace bowling from the modern era.

McGrath's line was ultra-consistent, on or just outside off stump, forever pitching in what has become known as the 'corridor of uncertainty'. If one's idea of bowling is to get batsmen playing back when they should be playing forward and forward when they should be back, then McGrath was a master. Many was the time — whether the dismissed man had been caught behind, in the slips, at short leg or trapped lbw — when the cause of the wicket was the batsman misreading the length. The result was that McGrath took more Test wickets through leg-before decisions than by bowled, and more than a quarter of his total outs were caught behind, where Ian Healy and Adam Gilchrist loved working with him.

Perhaps in days of old when batsmen were more patient, McGrath may not have been quite as successful. However, in these more frenzied days, as run-rates increased and batsmen weren't happy to see out the tough times, he became the game's No. 1 paceman. It is interesting that the two countries against whom McGrath averaged the most runs per wicket were South Africa and New Zealand, the two teams in the modern era most likely to grind out a long innings. Significant, too, is the fact that on the six major Australian Test venues, even including the spin-friendly Sydney Cricket Ground, McGrath's highest Test bowling average was for the WACA in Perth, for everyone else the best fast-bowling ground in the world, but where he conceded just over 24 runs per wicket. Such a return, of course, is hardly dismal; the fact is, all grounds came alike to him. Most batsmen did, too, except the stars, who seemed to inspire an even greater effort. McGrath made a habit of targeting the opposition's best player, most notably England's Mike Atherton (whom he dismissed 19 times) and the West Indies' Brian Lara (15 times), and he was never scared to back himself publicly in regard to these duels.

The young McGrath, against New Zealand at Perth in 1993-94, his Test debut.

The Third XI

McGrath came into the NSW team in 1992-93, the Test side 12 months later. His third Test was the SCG, and was marked, as he ran up to deliver his first ball, with a cry from the outer of 'C'mon Narromine!' — recognition of his hometown in the bush. He lived in a caravan in his early days in Sydney, had been nicknamed 'Pigeon' because of the fragile look of his legs, and having taken only eight Test wickets in his first summer of international cricket, was hardly an overnight success. In each of his first five Test series, he was dropped at least once, but in the West Indies in 1995 he made his name by enthusiastically volunteering to bounce the local batsmen throughout the Tests. He did so knowing he was one of the game's worst No. 11s and that he'd cop plenty of bumpers in reply, but his actions inspired his comrades, who stood up to Curtly Ambrose and Courtney Walsh in a manner no team had done against the West Indies for 20 years. McGrath also took 17 wickets in the four Tests, and stayed at the wicket with Steve Waugh at Kingston so his mate could reach a Test double century. The only Tests McGrath missed from that tour of the Caribbean to his retirement in 2007, after he was named player of the tournament at the 2007 World Cup, were because of injury or for personal reasons, never because of the selectors.

With Shane Warne, he formed the greatest paceman-spinner partnership in cricket history, while between 1997 and 2004 he and Jason Gillespie opened the Australian bowling with telling effect. Having become the first Australian fast bowler to appear in 100 Tests, inevitably he took plenty of wickets, but it is in other areas that his statistics are so impressive. His strike rate of wicket every 51.95 balls and average of 21.64 per wicket would have been outstanding if he'd played in 1890, in 20 Tests, if he'd taken 50 wickets instead of 563. Of the 10 Australians with the best career bowling averages, only McGrath has played more than 44 Tests.

Strangely, he has never taken more than 10 wickets in a Test, but he does hold two of the four best innings analysis achieved by an Australian in Tests: 8-24 v Pakistan in Perth in 2004-05 and 8-38 v England at Lord's in 1997. A Test after he took 10-27 for the match against the West Indies in Brisbane in 2000-01, he took a hat-trick in Perth, dismissing Sherwin Campbell, Brian Lara and Jimmy Adams. The middle wicket was his 300th in Tests. Add to all this the fact he has taken more ODI wickets than any other Australian, been part of three World Cup winning teams, taken a World Cup best (and second best in any ODI) 7-15 against Namibia in 2003.

McGrath at Lord's in 1997, when he took 8-38 in England's first innings.

Healy compared McGrath to Ambrose in the way he can relentlessly deliver from a great height, ball after bouncing ball on the right line and length. But maybe Justin Langer got closest to the true reason for McGrath's success when he wrote, 'No one knows their own game better than our No. 1 bowler. Every ball seems to

The 100 Greatest Cricketers

McGrath bowls Courtney Walsh at Bridgetown in 1995.

McGrath with Adam Gilchrist (left) and Ricky Ponting at Old Trafford during the 2005 Ashes series.

be part of a plan. Like all of the great medium-pace and fast-medium bowlers, McGrath hits the bat hard, and the pronounced flick of his wrist as he delivers the ball often generates awkward bounce off a good length.' Further, the way McGrath worked on his batting, turning himself into much more than just a quick out, proves his commitment. After 20 Tests, his batting average was 2.24, by 50 Tests it had risen to 6.19, and at the end of his career it was 7.37. He scored a Test fifty and was part of two century partnerships for the 10th wicket in Test matches, with Jason Gillespie when he made that 61 and with Mike Hussey against South Africa at the MCG in 2005-06.

The Australian team has been remarkably successful during McGrath's career and clearly he has been a key reason for this. When he missed series against India away in 1998 and at home in 2003-04, the Australian attack suddenly seemed less imposing. In England in 2005, the two Tests McGrath missed because of injury were the two Australia lost. Following his retirement, the critics liked to suggest that at least a couple of his successors bowled like him, but the team was suddenly losing as many Tests as it won. Truth is, like Warne, he could be irreplaceable.

GLENN McGRATH (AUSTRALIA)
Test Cricket

Tests	Inn	NO	Runs	HS	Ave	100	50	Ct	Balls	Runs	Wkts	Ave	Best	5/	10/
124	138	51	641	61	7.37	–	1	38	29248	12186	563	21.64	8-24	29	3

One-Day International Cricket

ODIs	Inn	NO	Runs	HS	Ave	100	50	Ct	Balls	Runs	Wkts	Ave	Best	4/
250	68	38	115	11	3-83	–	–	37	12970	8391	381	22.02	7-15	16

The Third XI

Herbert Sutcliffe
No. 33

The lowest batting average Herbert Sutcliffe ever had in Test cricket was his final figure of 60.73, fourth best all time of all those to play at least 30 innings. He began his international career in 1924 against South Africa with an innings of 64, then made his first Test hundred in the second Test, and finished the series with an average of 75.75. Immediately, it was to Australia, where he averaged 81.56 after scoring centuries in his second, third and fourth innings of the series. The average didn't dip below 70 until his 20th Test, at Durban in 1928, and it was still 65.87 at the end of the bodyline series in 1932-33. By this time, Sutcliffe was 38 years old, but he played on for another two and a half years, scoring 471 runs at 36.23 in his final 11 Tests.

Sutcliffe never averaged less than 50 in a series against Australia, then clearly the toughest opponent in world cricket. His performances in his six Test series against the Aussies were as follows:

The style of a batsman whose Test batting average never dropped below 60 during a 54-match career.

Series	Tests	Inn	NO	HS	Runs	100	50	Avge
1924-25	5	9	-	176	734	4	2	81.56
1926	5	7	1	161	472	1	3	78.67
1928-29	4	7	-	135	355	1	2	50.71
1930	4	7	2	161	436	1	3	87.20
1932-33	5	9	1	194	440	1	3	55.00
1934	5	7	1	69*	304	-	3	50.67
Total	28	46	5	194	2741	8	16	66.85

These were all five-match series. Significantly, the Tests he missed in 1928-29 and 1930 were two of the three England lost in that time.

'Courage and concentration were his basic attributes,' recalled *Wisden* it its obituary for Sutcliffe in 1979. 'No prospect daunted him, no difficulty dismayed him, no crisis upset him.' There is a photograph that appeared in *Bodyline Umpire*, RS Whitington's biography of Australian umpire George Hele, of Sutcliffe batting during the first bodyline Test, in which he scored 194. When his score was on 43, he was lucky when a defensive shot against Bill O'Reilly spun back from the crease line and hit the stumps without dislodging a bail. The photo shows the fieldsmen and keeper Bert Oldfield with their heads thrown back, arms outstretched, clearly despairing of the near miss. Sutcliffe, his hair slicked back, arms by his side, unperturbed, has looked back at the ball lying near the stumps, little if any emotion in his body. One imagines him soon twirling his bat, resuming his stance, getting on with the next ball while everyone tries to regain their breath. Perhaps he'd lean on his bat for a moment, while equilibrium was elsewhere restored. Whoever invented the word 'unruffled' did so with Sutcliffe in mind.

Sutcliffe and Jack Hobbs stride out to face the Australians during the 1926 Ashes series.

He made his first-class debut for Yorkshire immediately after World War I, aged 24, and marked his debut season with five centuries, but it wasn't until 1922, when he first scored 2000 runs in a first-class season that he was truly counted among the top batsmen in the country. By the time he made his Test debut, he was in his 30th year, confident of himself and his technique, and hardly overawed by the thought of going in first with the great Jack Hobbs. In 38 Test innings, the pair would average 87.81 for the first wicket, clearly the highest average of opening partnerships to add 1000 runs together. Fifteen of those 38 stands went for more than 100 runs, only four for less than 10, including two in the fifth Ashes Test of 1924-25, when Hobbs was stunningly out for a duck in the first innings and Sutcliffe just as surprisingly for the same score in the second. The former Australian captain

The Third XI

Monty Noble wondered whether the Yorkshireman was 'stale' from all the runs he'd already scored in the series! Afterwards, in his book of the tour, *Gilligan's Men*, Noble wrote of Sutcliffe: 'The more we saw of him the more we admired his wonderful tenacity, the soundness of his methods, his greatness in defence, and his all-round ability in the field ... By the time the Test matches started he had gained so much confidence and was displaying so much ability that I venture to say no greater colt has ever come out of England. His stamina and self-control are wonderful ... Although never really aggressive, he always knew how to punish loose stuff, and many of his beautifully placed off-drives had great power behind them.'

Sutcliffe's two most famous innings were played on sticky wickets in Ashes Tests, one in 1926, the other in 1928-29, both, almost inevitably, in tandem with Hobbs. At the start of the third day of the fifth Test at The Oval, England were 0-49 after Australia had gleaned as first-innings lead of 22. It had rained for most of the night, and after an hour the sun came out to make the pitch a dreadful sticky. Yet Hobbs made 100, Sutcliffe 161. 'A mistake by either of them,' wrote Neville Cardus for the *Manchester Guardian*, 'and Australia could hardly have captured less than four wickets before lunch.' Of Sutcliffe, Cardus wrote simply: 'His assurance was endless.'

The wicket at the MCG in 1928-29 was even worse. Hobbs remembered the partnership in Jack Fingleton's book, *Masters of Cricket*: 'That old campaigner Hughie Trumble, then secretary of the Melbourne Cricket Club, told us in all seriousness that 70 would be a good score in our second innings. Well, as you know, we chased 332 and eventually won by three wickets.' In both partnerships, Hobbs was the first out. At Melbourne, Sutcliffe went on 135, not being dismissed until victory was all but assured. Yet for all he achieved in Test and first-class cricket (50,670 runs at 52.02, including 151 centuries), Sutcliffe tends to be somewhat underrated. EW Swanton, after listing many of his records, explained: 'When contemporaries and critics discuss Herbert Sutcliffe in the context of the other great names of history, they do so generally on a note of qualification. The fact is he was the perfect second string ...'

Patrick Murphy, in his study of Sutcliffe for the book *The Centurions*, suggested that 'Sutcliffe knew deep down that he was not a truly great player, that he achieved statistical greatness by a massive effort of character, tenacity and iron will'. Sutcliffe earned and valued every run, and got everything from his game that he possibly could. With such a philosophy and such ambition, he was entitled to become one of the most productive opening batsmen the game has seen.

HERBERT SUTCLIFFE (ENGLAND)

Test Cricket

Tests	Inn	NO	Runs	HS	Ave	100	50	Ct	Balls	Runs	Wkts	Ave	Best	5/	10/
54	84	9	4555	194	60.73	16	23	23	–	–	–	–	–	–	–

First-Class Cricket

Mat	Inn	NO	Runs	HS	Ave	100	50	Ct	Balls	Runs	Wkts	Ave	Best	5/	10/
754	1098	124	50670	313	52.02	151	229	474	993	563	14	40.21	3-15	–	–

The 100 Greatest Cricketers

Keith Miller

Everton Weekes

The Fourth

Archie MacLaren

Jim Laker

The Fourth XI

Clyde Walcott

Allan Border

Alan Davidson

Godfrey Evans

Curtly Ambrose

Wilfred Rhodes

Steve Waugh

No. 34 Keith Miller

For many cricket fans straight after the war, Miller was the hero, even more so than The Don.

Almost all of the cricketers profiled in this book were or are renowned for their commitment, their desire, their focus on their sport. These legends dedicated themselves to the pursuit of excellence and succeeded admirably. Keith Miller was certainly highly successful, but when it came to cricket, he could never be described as 'single-minded'. He was an instinctive, unpredictable genius, and an entertainer who loved adventure, who delighted in the unexpected, hated being bored and was keen to explore different ways to win, always believing that it was far from the end of the world if you happened to lose. He became, in his way, almost as big a hero as Don Bradman. His cricket needed to be vibrant, his physique was imposing, and his hair was dark, relatively long for the times, and the way he swept it back off his forehead became a trademark. For young women, he had definite sex appeal; for boys and young men his exploits were something out of a *Boy's Own Annual*.

He was born in 1919, made his first-class cricket debut in 1938, but twin sporting careers in Australian football and cricket were stifled by World War II. In 1945, he made a name for himself in the 'Victory Tests' staged in England after true hostilities had ceased, to the point that he was just about a certain selection for the Australian team that faced England in 1946-47. Many observers were already convinced of his greatness. The former NSW captain Alan Kippax rated him a better allrounder than Jack Gregory, the outstanding allrounder of the 1920s, explaining, 'Very few batsmen I have watched have his rare ability to blend beauty with power.'

Miller's shots and hundreds were worth the journey to the ground purely for the manner in which he made them. He liked to get on the front foot, to drive hard and on the up, but he could also hook and pull, and cut hard through point or delicately fine. AG Moyes, in 1954, described him this way: 'He always looks the complete batsman when he takes up his stance, and often plays that way, for his cover drive came out of the pages of the best textbook, his hits for six leave no doubt as to where the ball will go, while his forcing shots between mid-on and mid-wicket is a sight to make old men young.'

The Fourth XI

As a bowler, Miller's strongest trait was his unpredictability. 'I'm sure he often had no preconceived idea what he intended to bowl even as he turned to start his run,' claimed Denis Compton. 'As a batsman you never knew what was coming. It could be as fast a ball as anyone was entitled to expect on this planet, a slow leg break, a bouncer or a fast back-break off an immaculate length, which would land outside the off stump and, if missed with the bat, would smack the legs.' The Rev. David Sheppard, a Test opening bat of much ability, was once bowled by a Miller wrong 'un at Lord's. Len Hutton, who reckoned he never saw a bowler who cared less about where his bowling mark was, also commented that, 'I never felt physically safe against him.'

In his first full series, Miller averaged 76.80 with the bat and 20.88 with the ball. However, the rest of his career was not quite so statistically satisfying. Even so, Miller still did enough throughout his career to confirm that he was the greatest batting-and-bowling allrounder Australia has ever produced. As his Test career grew older, he evolved from a brilliant batsman who often bowled well to become an outstanding strike bowler whose batting, while still brilliant on occasions, was rarely reliable. He did play a number of famous innings in the years that followed his first Ashes series, but by the time he retired his Test batting average did not reflect his enormous talent. In contrast, his bowling returns improved to the point that, on his last Ashes tour in 1956, despite having celebrated his 36th birthday he bowled more balls and had a better strike rate and superior average than on his two previous tours there, in 1948 and 1953.

Miller sweeps during his 281 not out against Leicestershire during Australia's 1956 tour of England.

Miller was one of the most famous of Bradman's Invincibles, but when it came to scoring runs and taking wickets he was hardly the star of that tour, averaging 26 with the bat and taking 13 wickets in the Test series. His sacking for Australia's tour of South Africa in 1949-50 caused a furore, but the selectors at least had some ordinary form to support their decision. Miller eventually did go to South Africa as a replacement, after Bill Johnston was injured in a car accident, and played reasonably well in all five Tests. Seemingly revitalised, he topped the Australian batting averages in the 1950-51 Ashes series — the highlight being an unbeaten century in Sydney — and took 17 wickets as well. Against the West Indies a season later, he managed another century, again at the SCG, and also took five wickets in an innings twice. He was also heavily censured for bowling too many bouncers, especially at the Windies' best batsman, Everton Weekes, just as he had previously been criticised for bumping England's Len Hutton and Denis Compton. To Miller, this was all part of the entertainment.

In his next three Test series, at home against South Africa and then in Ashes encounters at home and away, Miller scored only one century — 109 at Lord's in 1953 (in eight other innings in that series he scored just 114 runs) — and never managed to take five wickets in an innings. Then came a run-scoring blitz against a poor bowling side in the West Indies that featured three centuries, including his highest Test score of 147 in the first Test, at Kingston, followed by an impressive beginning to the 1956 Ashes tour. A magnificent 281 against Leicestershire came a month before a stirring bowling performance at Lord's, when — leading a much-weakened Aussie attack — he completed the only 10-wickets-in-a-match performance of his Test career (5-72 and 5-80) and won Australia their only Test victory of the series.

Miller's Test record suggests he was a good batsman and an outstanding bowler. He averaged almost 37 with the bat, and took 170 wickets at less than 23, averages similar to those of Ian Botham during the Englishman's best years. Miller scored seven Test centuries, and took five wickets in an innings seven times. He also snared 38 catches. However, these are not the stats of one of the absolute greatest players of all time, which is what his vast number of admirers claim him to be. Was he, compared to other cricket legends, overrated? Ask any Australian cricket fan aged between 55 and 75 today and they'll tell you, almost to a man and woman, that 'Keith Miller was my hero when I was a kid'.

Miller with former England captain Len Hutton at the start of the 1956 tour.

They can't all be wrong. Can they?

KEITH MILLER (AUSTRALIA)
Test Cricket

Tests	Inn	NO	Runs	HS	Ave	100	50	Ct	Balls	Runs	Wkts	Ave	Best	5/	10/
55	87	7	2958	147	36.98	7	13	38	10461	3906	170	22.98	7-60	7	1

First-Class Cricket

Mat	Inn	NO	Runs	HS	Ave	100	50	Ct	Balls	Runs	Wkts	Ave	Best	5/	10/
226	326	36	14183	281*	48.91	41	63	136	28405	11087	497	22.31	7-12	16	1

The Fourth XI

Everton Weekes and Clyde Walcott

No. 35 & No. 36

Weekes and Clyde Walcott finished their Test careers with similarly exceptional batting averages: Weekes 58.62; Walcott 56.69. However, the two began their journeys to these finals figures by taking different paths. Weekes exploded out of the blocks, his average climbing as high as 88.00 after his eighth Test, the fourth Test against India in 1948-49, in which he was run out for 90 in his only innings, having scored 141, 128, 194, 162 and 101 in his previous five Testmatch innings. After this fantastic beginning, Weekes' career average 'slumped' to 53.59 during his next three series, but from 1952 until he retired in 1958 he had only one poor series, against England in 1957 when he struggled with sinus trouble. Otherwise, he averaged at least 50 in every series in which he played. Walcott averaged 40.36 as a wicketkeeper /batsman in his first 15 Tests, but after he surrendered the keeping gloves in Australia in 1951-52, he blossomed as a specialist batsman, averaging 64.66 in his final 29 Tests.

Weekes' blazing square cut, one of the most destructive shots ever played in cricket.

Walcott was solidly built, 185cm (6ft 2in) tall with the physique of a heavyweight champion more so than a Test wicketkeeper. He made his debut in the same Test as Weekes, the first against England at Bridgetown in January 1948, scoring 8 and 16 as an opening batsman. When he scored 152 and then 108 in India in 1948-49 he became the second keeper, after Les Ames, to score more than one century in Tests. He was batting at No. 6 and still the keeper when the West Indies won their first Test in England, at Lord's in 1950, and his contribution was critical, a barnstorming 168 not out in the second innings which gave the rookie spinners, Sonny Ramadhin and Alf Valentine, enough runs to bowl their side to a famous victory.

Weekes was shorter and more compact than Walcott. Neither had any formal coaching when they were young, but like George Headley they were keen observers of the game, with an innate gift to learn fast. Both were at the Bridgetown Test of 1935, though not sitting together, when Headley and Wally Hammond were superb on a sticky pitch, and went away hoping one day to be as good. Like Walcott, Weekes debuted in Test cricket against England in January 1948, but struggled in his first five innings before coming good in the final match when he hit 141. Following his run-fest at India's expense, Weekes smashed four double centuries and one triple century in first-class matches during the initial 10 weeks of the 1950 tour of England, and then scored 129 in the third Test at Trent Bridge.

It is amazing how many people use Don Bradman as their barometer when trying to measure Weekes' game. 'He was a magnificent hooker and cutter and a glorious driver, said by many Australians who saw him in action to be the closest in style to the pre-war Bradman,' wrote Richie Benaud in 1969. 'There was sometimes a machine-like quality about Everton Weekes' batting which reminded me of Sir Donald Bradman,' Trevor Bailey remembered. Wisden in 1951 began its tribute to Weekes as one of the five cricketers of the year by commenting, 'Perhaps no batsman since Bradman has made such an impression on his first English tour as a ruthless compiler of big scores.' Inevitably, there were comparisons with Headley, too. By amassing 2310 runs at an average of 79.66, Weekes was just 10 runs short of his predecessor's West Indies tour aggregate record achieved in 1933, even though he played five fewer innings. 'Weekes evoked comparison with Headley, whom he resembled in his compact build,' continued *Wisden*. 'Both showed the same instinct to dominate the bowling, and seldom indeed did Weekes allow any attack to tie him down to defence for long, although he was not so resourceful nor equipped with quite such a wide range of strokes as Headley. Yet the resemblance was strong ...'

Both Weekes and Walcott were among the hardest hitters of a cricket ball in the game's history. Walcott was more consistently powerful on the drive, on both the front and back foot (though

Walcott goes over the top (above) and sweeps to leg (right).

The Fourth XI

Weekes could get on the front foot and hit powerfully, too), perhaps not as ruthless on the pull and hook shots. In his autobiography, he recalled fondly how he loved batting with Weekes because opposing captains would invariably strengthen the field square of the wicket to protect their bowlers from Weekes' square cuts. That left more room for Walcott's off and cover drives. He also recalled the Nottinghamshire batsman of years gone by, George Gunn, commenting after Weekes scored 279 in 235 minutes at Trent Bridge on the 1950 tour, 'I have seen them all since Victor Trumper and including Bradman. I have never seen a more brilliant array of strokes nor heard the ball so sweetly struck.'

In Australia in 1951-52, Walcott and Weekes showed glimpses of their class, but that was all, as Ray Lindwall and Keith Miller targetted them. From 1953 to 1955, however, Walcott went on an incredible spell of runmaking, hitting 11 centuries in 16 Tests, while Weekes managed eight hundreds in 17 Tests between 1953 and 1956. Against Australia at home in 1955 Walcott scored 827 runs at 82.70 in the five Tests, including a record five centuries, twice scoring a hundred in each innings of the same game. The wickets might have been flat, but the Australian bowling attack — featuring Lindwall, Miller, Bill Johnston and Richie Benaud — was formidable. 'I have never seen a more powerful batsman than Walcott,' recalled Benaud, 'when he was "going" it was almost impossible to bowl a length to him.' Weekes scored 'only' 469 runs in the series, at 58.63, and when he and Walcott both scored hundreds at Port-of-Spain, it was, in Benaud's words, 'some of the most blazing batting I have ever seen'.

Walcott failed to score a Test hundred in England in 1957, but *Wisden* still named him one of their cricketers of the year, as if they were catching up for not nominating him earlier. The almanack remembered how in the mid '50s he had 'challenged Hutton for the title of the world's best batsman', and bemoaned the fact that a leg injury had hindered him on this latest tour. Originally, the 1957-58 home series against Pakistan was to be the last for both Weekes and Walcott, but two years later Walcott was asked by the selectors to come back and add some aggression to the West Indies batting line-up. This move was only partially successful, and straight afterwards he retired for good.

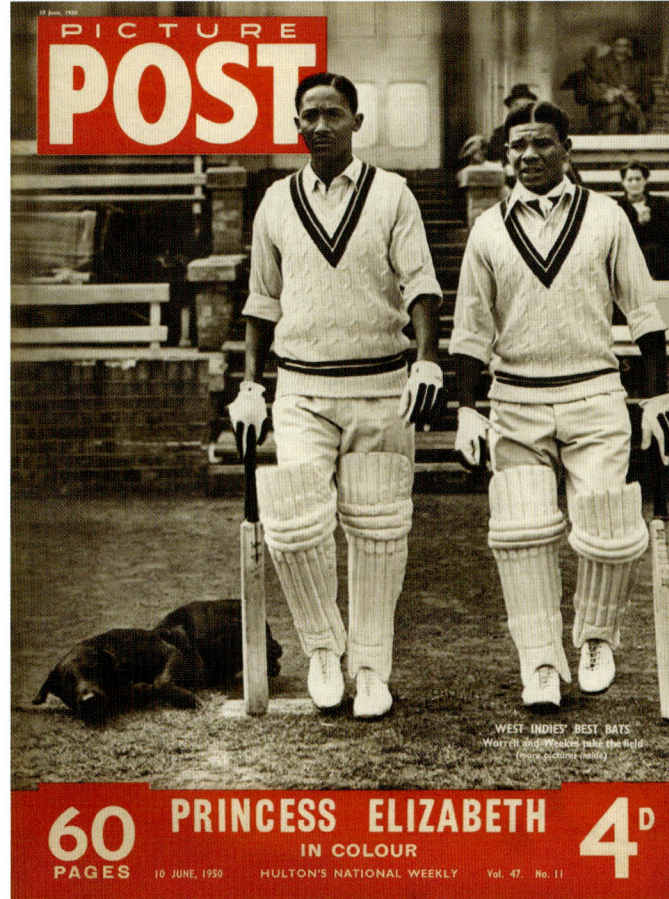

At times on the West Indies' 1950 tour of England, the three Ws could push even Royalty from the front covers of British magazines.

Weekes scored only 195 runs in the five Tests against England in 1957, but he still managed to produce one of the innings of the season. At Lord's in the second Test, he came to the wicket in the second innings with the game as good as lost and Fred Trueman and Brian Statham in rousing form, and made what Denis Compton later described as 'one of the finest knocks seen in contemporary cricket on the ancient ground'. Weekes broke a finger before he was finally out for 90, Garry Sobers made 66 (the pair adding 100 in 95 minutes), but no other West Indian scored more than 26. 'There was a ridge at the Nursery end and only the best technicians and the stout of heart survived for long,' Compton remembered. Then he added, in respect of Weekes' knock, which included 16 fours despite his handicap, 'In every respect, it was the innings of a genius.'

The 100 Greatest Cricketers

Weekes on his way to an unbeaten 304 for the West Indians against Cambridge University in May 1950.

With Frank Worrell, Walcott and Weekes were members of the famous Barbadian triumvirate: the 'Three Ws'. They were born within 18 months of each other, and all within a mile of the Kensington Oval in Barbados. It is very easy to say that all three were great players, much harder, though, to say who was the greatest. Statistically, Weekes and Walcott have marginally superior batting records in Tests than Worrell, though there were times between 1947 and 1952, especially in England in 1950, when Worrell seemed to be the finest run-maker. Worrell was the better bowler. Walcott, of course, could keep wicket, though he was hardly exceptional in this field. The thing that set Worrell apart was his leadership, but at the same time no one should underrate the personal qualities of either Walcott or Weekes, who as well as being wonderful cricketers were also clearly men of the highest calibre. Neither had the chance to captain the West Indies. Both fully deserved the knighthoods they received in the 1990s.

It seems natural that in this study Weekes and Walcott should go into the same XI. To do this, one of the pair will have to open the batting, something neither did often in Tests even though it is hard to imagine either being a long-term failure in the position. Weekes only did so once in Tests — from the start of his career, he was always the key man in the middle order. Most of his runs came as a No. 4. Walcott failed the three times he went in first, right at the start of his career, but in 23 innings as a Test No. 3 he averaged 51.86 and scored four centuries, including three against Lindwall and Miller in 1955. Certainly, either man would have been absolutely sensational going in first in limited-over cricket. In the modern era, middle-order regulars in Tests such as Sachin Tendulkar and Adam Gilchrist have revolutionised one-day international cricket by the way they open the batting. What might naturally hard-hitting, dynamic, aggressive batsmen such as Clyde Walcott and Everton Weekes have done, had they been given the opportunity?

EVERTON WEEKES (WEST INDIES)

Test Cricket

Tests	Inn	NO	Runs	HS	Ave	100	50	Ct	Balls	Runs	Wkts	Ave	Best	5/	10/
48	81	5	4455	207	58.62	15	19	49	122	77	1	77.00	1-8	–	–

First-Class Cricket

Mat	Inn	NO	Runs	HS	Ave	100	50	Ct	St	Balls	Runs	Wkts	Ave	Best	5/	10/
152	241	24	12010	304*	55.35	36	54	124	1	1125	731	17	43.00	4-38	–	–

CLYDE WALCOTT (WEST INDIES)

Test Cricket

Mat	Inn	NO	Runs	HS	Ave	100	50	Ct	St	Balls	Runs	Wkts	Ave	Best	5/	10/
44	74	7	3798	220	56.69	15	14	53	11	1194	408	11	37.09	3-50	–	–

First-Class Cricket

Mat	Inn	NO	Runs	HS	Ave	100	50	Ct	St	Balls	Runs	Wkts	Ave	Best	5/	10/
146	238	29	11820	314*	56.56	40	54	174	33	3449	1269	35	36.26	5-41	1	–

The Fourth XI

Allan Border

No. 37

Through the 1980s, or at least after the retirement of Greg Chappell, Allan Border often seemed to stand alone in the Australian batting order. Consider the records of Australian specialist batsmen who played at least 15 Tests between the first Test of the 1979-80 Australian summer (the first home Test after World Series Cricket) and the final Test of the 1988-89 season. Australia played 91 Tests in this span.

Batsman	Tests	Runs	100s	Ave
GS Chappell	36	3013	10	54.78
AR Border	91	6888	21	52.98
DM Jones	21	1546	4	45.47
GR Yallop	18	1268	4	43.72
KC Wessels	24	1761	4	42.95
DC Boon	36	2410	7	38.87
KJ Hughes	53	3299	7	37.48
GR Marsh	27	1670	3	35.53
GM Ritchie	30	1690	3	35.20
BM Laird	21	1341	-	35.28
DW Hookes	17	950	1	35.18
WB Phillips	27	1485	2	32.28
AMJ Hilditch	18	1073	2	31.55
GM Wood	44	2421	7	31.44
SR Waugh	26	1099	-	30.52
J Dyson	27	1258	2	27.95

Clearly, Chappell and Border stand out. Both men also captained Australia in this period — Chappell from the start of the span to the inaugural Australia-Sri Lanka Test in 1983 (missing a couple of overseas series during this period); Border from the third Test against the West Indies in 1984-85 to the end of the span. Chappell led Australia to 13 in 31 Tests; Border to just seven wins in 39 Tests, only one of them overseas, a reflection of how unsuccessful the Australian team was during the second half of the 1980s, and how hard it must have been for Border to be so often fighting a lone hand. Greg Chappell usually had high-quality batsmen alongside him in the Australian batting order; Allan Border, from 1984 on, was often on his own. To average more than 50 in Tests under these circumstances was remarkable.

Border made his debut in the third Test of the 1978-79 Ashes series, was dropped for the final Test, came back for Australia's next match, against Pakistan at the MCG, where he scored his first Test century, and was never left out again. He retired in 1994 holding the following Test records: most matches (156), most innings (265), most runs (11,174), most fifties (63), more scores of at least 50 (90), most catches by a non-wicketkeeper (156), most matches as captain (93) and most successive Test appearances (153).

For a period from 1984 to 1989 Border was clearly Australia's finest batsman in both forms of the game.

On his second overseas Test tour, to Pakistan in 1980, Border became the first, and to this day only, player to score 150 in both innings of a Test match. His style of batting was becoming known throughout the world. He stood upright as the bowler approached and then crouched slightly as the ball was delivered. A master in nudging the ball into the gaps and working the bowlers for ones and twos, he drove often and effectively through the covers and played horizontal bat shots such as the pull and the cut quite fiercely. He was masterful against the spinners, always eager to use his feet to drive through the offside or past mid-on. At the end of 1981, after 33 Tests, Border's Test batting average was 51.86. Three years later, on the eve of the 1985 Ashes tour having now played 61 Tests, his average had barely dropped, to 51.59. Consistency was his calling card.

Of all his great innings, Border believed his double in Trinidad in 1984, against Malcolm Marshall, Joel Garner and co, was his finest batting effort. Brian Lara, a native of Port-of-Spain, specifically mentioned this performance as an inspiration when he went past Border's Test runscoring record in 2005. In the first innings Border made 98 not out (the innings he considers his greatest ever); in the second, not out again, he went two runs better. Border went past 4000 runs during that series in the Caribbean, in which he scored 521 runs at 74.42. No other Australian batsman scored even half that many, or averaged more than 26. At career's end, he was to lament that he was in the absolute best form of his career in a period, 1984 to 1987, when the Australian team was very ordinary.

Border needed time to blossom as a captain. He really wasn't seen at his best in Test matches until 1989, though his tide had begun to turn when the Australians won the 1987 World Cup in India. They went into that tournament as rank outsiders but captured the ultimate prize thanks to a plan developed by Border and new coach Bob Simpson that deliberately separated Australia's style of cricket from other nations. In doing so, they changed the way all teams approached one-day cricket. Their formula revolved around opening batsman Geoff Marsh anchoring the innings, as more aggressive batsmen around him tried to keep the run-rate moving. The hope was that wickets could be kept for a dash in the final 10 overs, while throughout the batsmen adopted a bolder approach to running between wickets. Bowlers had a strong idea at which point of the innings each one would be required, which helped them focus on when they would be needed. Most important of all, endless hours of hard work made the Australians the fittest and the best fielding team in the world. Border, lurking at mid-wicket and deadly when throwing at the stumps, became a symbol of this excellence in the field.

Border in England early on the 1981 Ashes tour.

The Fourth XI

In 1987-88, Australia won a Test series for the first time under Border's captaincy, though it was a close-run thing: No. 11 Mike Whitney having to keep out Richard Hadlee in the third and final Test at the MCG to give his captain a draw and a 1-0 series win. In the second Test, Border had scored 205, his highest Test score, during which he passed 7000 Test runs and then Greg Chappell's Australian record 7110. This was his 22nd century in his 91st Test.

For a captain who'd been on the wrong end of decisive losses in the Ashes series in 1981, 1985 and 1986-87, the 1989 adventure — which saw Australia win 4-0 after the team had been tagged the 'worst ever' by the English tabloids (and by Jeff Thomson) before the first Test — was a joy. Suddenly, he was captain of a winning team, in part because batsmen such as David Boon, Dean Jones and Steve Waugh, who had struggled to various degrees early in their Test careers, all became accomplished Test cricketers at around the same time. Australia won 25 of Border's last 54 Tests, and lost only nine. And in the years since Border's retirement, the Australian teams led by Mark Taylor, Steve Waugh and Ricky Ponting have been remarkably successful, not least because of the new culture and grit that Allan Border brought to the men who wear the baggy green cap.

Border and his vice-captain Geoff Marsh enjoy the ticker-tape parade in Sydney that welcomed home the 1989 Australians after their stunning 4-0 triumph.

ALLAN BORDER (AUSTRALIA)
Test Cricket
Tests	Inn	NO	Runs	HS	Ave	100	50	Ct	Balls	Runs	Wkts	Ave	Best	5/	10/
156	265	44	11174	205	50.56	27	63	156	4009	1525	39	39.10	7-46	2	1

One-Day International Cricket
ODIs	Inn	NO	Runs	HS	Ave	100	50	Ct	Balls	Runs	Wkts	Ave	Best	4/
273	252	39	6524	127*	30.63	3	39	127	2661	2071	73	28.37	3-20	–

No. 38 Alan Davidson

Alan Davidson made his Test debut in 1953, but until Australia's tour of South Africa in 1957-58, by which time Keith Miller had retired and Ray Lindwall was dropped, he was hardly the spearhead of the bowling attack. In 12 Tests, he had taken the grand sum of 16 wickets at 34.06. Australia had been humiliated during the Ashes tour in 1956, a tour that for Davidson was unproductive, ruined by injury and also by captain Ian Johnson's decision to experiment with him as left-arm finger spinner. Yet for the first Test, at Johannesburg, in late December 1957, new captain Ian Craig gave his NSW teammate the opening over and in the second innings Davidson responded by taking 6-34 as the South Africans, firm favourites to win the series, were bowled out for 201. The second Test started with Colin McDonald and Jim Burke adding 190 for the first wicket, Davidson, Richie Benaud and Lindsay Kline then bowled Australia to an innings-and-141-run victory. A new era in Australian cricket had begun.

From the first Test in South Africa until he retired at the end of the 1962-63 Ashes series, Davidson took 170 wickets in 32 Tests, at 19.26, without ever having a regular opening partner in the way Lindwall had Miller, Fred Trueman had Brian Statham, Dennis Lillee had Jeff Thomson. Davidson's most regular accomplices were Ian Meckiff early on, and Graham McKenzie late. In Test history, only six bowlers have taken 100 wickets in their career and averaged less than 20: George Lohmann (112 wickets at 10.76), Sydney Barnes (189 at 16.43), Charlie Turner (101 at 16.53), Bobby Peel (101 at 16.98), Johnny Briggs (118 at 17.75) and Colin Blythe (100 at 18.67). None of these men bowled an over in Test cricket after World War I. Only Barnes took more than 120 wickets.

Bob Simpson said emphatically in 1979, 'If I had one ball hanging between me and death, I'd give it to Alan Davidson.' Richie Benaud wrote of Davidson in 1998, 'He will remain in Australia's history as one of the greatest cricketers ever to set foot on a ground for NSW and Australia.' England allrounder Trevor Bailey thought Davidson's bowling in 1953 was 'accurate rather than devastating', but that he became 'the greatest new ball bowler of his time'. Part of this transformation must have come simply from the opportunity the left-hander was given with the departure of Lindwall and Miller; part, too, from the lessons learned watching close-up such masters in action. In Bailey's view, the key was that 'Davidson mastered the art of moving the ball into the right-handed batsman from on and outside the off stump'. He continued, 'His run-up was comparatively short, about 13 paces, and his very powerful body action was near perfection.

The young Davo, before he established himself as Australia's greatest ever left-arm bowler.

The Fourth XI

Although not exceptionally quick in a Lindwall or a Tyson sense, he was capable of producing a distinctly unpleasant bouncer — made all the more effective because he employed it sparingly — and he hit the bat hard enough to jar the hand if you were lucky enough to remain at the crease for long.'

That run-up's length was 'Fifteen Paces', which became the title of Davidson's autobiography. On Australia's tour of the sub-continent in 1959-60, which involved three Tests in Pakistan and five in India, it was often in operation, to the extent that he bowled 393.4 six-ball overs, taking 41 wickets at 17.78. At Kanpur, in the second Test against India, Australia went into the game with two wrist spinners, Benaud and Kline, but the new turf pitch was much better suited to finger spinners. Indian off-spinner Jasu Patel took 14-124 for the Test, including 9-69 in the first innings. Davidson responded by cutting that run, bowling slow-medium cutters and spinners, and taking 5-31 and 7-93, his best match return in Tests.

Davidson, the attacking left-hand batsman, swings at Johnny Wardle during the 1954-55 Ashes series. Godfrey Evans is the wicketkeeper.

'Great allrounder that Garry (Sobers) is,' Neil Harvey wrote in *My World of Cricket* in 1963, 'I regard Alan Davidson as his equal. There is so little between the pair in ability, with Sobers superior in the batting department and Davidson undoubtedly a more talented bowler.'

Sobers, of course, still had much of his cricket career ahead of him when Harvey made that assessment, but to even be spoken in the same breath as the great Barbadian is a tribute in itself. In 1960-61, Sobers and Davidson had been two of the stars of the remarkable Australia-West Indies series in Australia. The first Test, at the Gabba, ended in a famous tie, with the two great left-handers having pivotal roles, Sobers by scoring a wonderful century on the opening day and Davidson by producing one of the most complete all-round performances in a cricket match. He became the first man to score 100 runs and take 10 wickets in a Test, by scoring 44 and 80 and taking 5-135 and 6-87. The great drama came on the final afternoon, when Australia crashed to 6-92 chasing 232, but Davidson and Benaud still went for the win.

From 15 paces, Davidson could make the ball swing both ways, usually at good pace.

With a maximum 13 balls remaining, Australia needed seven runs to win, and Benaud tried to pinch another single after a pushing a ball into the legside. But Joe Solomon was on it in a flash and 'Davo' was run out by metres. Had Solomon muffed that opportunity, with Davidson so much in control, most likely Australia would have won with a few balls and wickets to spare. Instead, arguably the most famous over in Test history followed, which was great for cricket but meant Davidson, through no fault of his own, missed out on completing one of the greatest match-winning innings by a lower-order batsman in Test history.

Eight months later, came the compensation. With the series level at one-all, Australia began the final day of the fourth Ashes Test, at Old Trafford, at 6-331, with Davidson and Ken Mackay both 18 not out. With England having had a first-innings lead of 177, Australia were effectively 6-154, the game — and the fate of the Ashes — seemed evenly poised. However, when play resumed, David Allen immediately took 3-0 in 15 balls, and Davidson had only 20-year-old McKenzie with him to set England a reasonable target. Allen was turning the ball appreciably, and McKenzie was all at sea, so Davidson took the initiative and hit the off-spinner for 20 in over (6, 0, 4, 0, 4, 6). England captain Peter May panicked and made a change immediately, McKenzie settled in, and the pair added 98 for the last wicket with Davidson unconquered at the end on 77. Then, after Ted Dexter, played brilliantly for 76, Benaud spun through the rest of the innings, before 'Davo' took the final wicket and the Ashes were retained.

A false impression created by these two Tests is that Davidson was an accomplished lower-order batsman at the highest level. This might have been true in the Sheffield Shield, and there is no doubt that he could hit the ball a long way, but besides these two great innings, he scored only three other half-centuries in Tests, in 59 innings. It is as a bowler that Davidson earns his rating as a Test cricketer of the highest class. In recent times, many observers, including Sir Donald Bradman, have rated Pakistan's Wasim Akram as the greatest left-hand paceman of all time. This might be right, but a strong case can be put that Alan Davidson is at least right up with him.

ALAN DAVIDSON (AUSTRALIA)

Test Cricket

Tests	Inn	NO	Runs	HS	Ave	100	50	Ct	Balls	Runs	Wkts	Ave	Best	5/	10/
44	61	7	1328	80	24.59	–	5	42	11587	3819	186	20.53	7-93	14	2

First-Class Cricket

Mat	Inn	NO	Runs	HS	Ave	100	50	Ct	Balls	Runs	Wkts	Ave	Best	5/	10/
193	246	39	6804	129	32.87	9	36	168	37704	14048	672	20.90	7-31	33	2

The Fourth XI

Godfrey Evans

No. 39

England's selectors during the 1950s had a habit of making changes. Accomplished cricketers such as Fred Trueman, Tom Graveney and Jim Laker seemed to miss as many Tests as they played. The one constant, it so often appeared, was the man behind the stumps: Godfrey Evans.

Evans was, in the words of Fred Trueman, a wicketkeeper who 'made good bowlers look very good and helped very good bowlers live out their dreams'. Evans was the first man to appear in 90 Test matches, finishing with 91 from a career that ran from 1946 to 1959. He was also the last of the great keepers who preferred to stand up to the stumps to the medium pacers. His partnership with Alec Bedser was legendary — after the first few overs, Bedser preferred his keeper up close, and Evans wanted to be there. Both men felt the advantages outweighed the disadvantages, chief among the positives being that the batsman feels more restricted if the keeper is right behind him. Further, Evans believed that the entire fielding side got a lift from seeing their keeper standing up. 'They know where he is,' he commented in a letter to *The Cricketer* in 1966. 'They can relate their position to him at all times, and their work is nothing like as sloppy as it is when the wicketkeeper is running backwards and forwards all the time.'

The primary argument of those who preferred to stand back to the medium pacers was that they were much more likely to catch the edges, especially the thick edges which were hard to react to when standing up to the stumps. Evans countered by arguing that the fellows standing back also miss opportunities, through nicks that don't carry and stumpings lost.

Evans on his toes, a genuine attacking presence behind the stumps.

So in one sense, Evans was the last of the 'old style' glovemen. However, in many other ways, he was the first of his kind. Photographs of him crouched behind the stumps, waiting for the bowler's delivery, show him with his weight forward on his toes, unlike pre World War II keepers who had their heels on the turf. He also made himself noticed, which went against the accepted wisdom that the best keepers were the ones who kept themselves quiet. There was nothing unobtrusive about Godfrey Evans as he bounced about the field, a manner that became his trademark. 'What was the secret of his success?' asked Trevor Bailey. 'Apart from sheer ability and a superb eye, it was very largely a matter of vitality. Many people can be brilliant for a short period of time, but it takes a very exceptional person to be just as full of life and just as spectacular an hour before the close of play on a really hot day at Adelaide after five sessions in the field.' Another of Evans' virtues was that he could shrug off a mistake, never let it affect him. Not all keepers have had this skill.

Bradman cuts in 1948, with Evans decisive as ever as he hopes for a nick. A classic study of a great batsman and a great keeper.

Brian Statham believed that Evans was as important to England's victory in Australia in 1954-55 as Frank Tyson. Bailey thought Evans' best series came in Australia in 1950-51. Johnnie Moyes, in his book of the tour, was lavish in his praise: 'Evans was magnificent from start to finish. This thickset man with the hairy arms was a continual inspiration to his team, and the delight of the onlookers. Evans took the ball with equal certainty on either side of the wicket, rarely made a mistake, and took innumerable catches which showed the quality of genius. Like the star boxer, he was amazingly quick on his feet; and just as footwork is essential to batsmanship, so was Evans always in the right position for whatever happened. His anticipation was superb, and his stumpings so quick that they bordered on the miraculous. Normally batsmen get the headlines in cricket. Sometimes a star bowler will be featured. During this tour, Evans challenged them all for a popularity based on excellence. He outshone (Australia's Don) Tallon, and must surely rank with the greatest of English wicketkeepers ...'

Evans played his first Test against India in 1946, and made his name in Australia during the tour that followed soon after, when he made his Ashes debut in the second Test and didn't concede a bye until the second innings of the third — more than 1000 runs were scored before a ball got away from him. A naturally aggressive batsman, he achieved a certain notoriety in Adelaide by batting for 95

The Fourth XI

minutes without scoring a run, in doing so ensuring the fourth Test finished in a draw rather than an English defeat. When he finished his career 12 years later, he had scored two Test centuries, but hardly done his batting talents justice.

Evans lost his place because of form for two Tests in South Africa in 1948-49, but regained his spot for the home series against New Zealand three months later and was a constant for the next decade. During this time he took catches that, in Len Hutton's words, 'no one else could have held'. Take, as an example, Evans' catch of Richie Benaud at Trent Bridge during the opening Ashes Test of 1953. Because the second new ball had just been taken and the ball was swinging, the keeper was standing back to Bedser. In *Test Match Diary 1953*, John Arlott described the

Evans spectacularly tries to run out Frank Worrell during the 1950 series in England.

dismissal this way: 'Benaud's leg glance was an authentic and — in view of the field set — apparently safe stroke. Evans was standing a bare four yards back and, even as the stroke was made, it seemed, he took off and went through the air like a leaping salmon. Just before he landed he got his left hand under the ball and, as he hit the ground we saw his arm lift from the elbow, and it was a catch.' Two weeks later, at Lord's during the second Test of the same series, Evans stumped Arthur Morris off Bedser's bowling even though the ball took a clear deflection from Morris' pad on the way through.

His final tally of 219 Test-match dismissals remained a record until Alan Knott went past him in 1976. Clearly, he was a keeper of the highest class. That his Test career ran for 13 seasons further underlines his quality, and also reflects his toughness. Add this to the vibrant personality he brought to his sport, and you have one of the most important cricketers, and characters, to ever play for England.

GODFREY EVANS (ENGLAND)
Test Cricket

Tests	Inn	NO	Runs	HS	Ave	100	50	Ct	St
91	133	14	2439	104	20.50	2	8	173	46

First-Class Cricket

Mat	Inn	NO	Runs	HS	Ave	100	50	Ct	St	Balls	Runs	Wkts	Ave	Best	5/	10/
465	753	52	14882	144	21.23	7	62	816	250	286	245	2	122.5	2-50	—	—

The 100 Greatest Cricketers

No. 40 Steve Waugh

Steve Waugh was born in the south-western suburbs of Sydney on 2 June 1965, four minutes ahead of brother Mark. Six months short of his 21st birthday, he was brought into the Australian team when it was at perhaps its lowest ever ebb, having lost four series straight — to the West Indies twice, England and New Zealand — since the retirement of Dennis Lillee, Rod Marsh and Greg Chappell. On top of the loss of those great players, a rebel Australian team to South Africa had further sapped the available talent pool. Waugh was abundantly talented, but hardly street smart, and he found the expectations placed on him as the great new hope suffocating.

Waugh goes through the offside again during the 1989 Ashes series, which he started with scores of 177 not out, 152 not out and 21 not out.

In a sense he was lucky. Few cricketers have had such a long apprenticeship at the top level, as between 1986 and 1988 he became one of those cricketers who always seemed to do just enough to retain his place. Being a good, often excellent all-rounder in one-day cricket (especially at the 1987 World Cup) helped him keep his Test place, but even so had he failed on the 1989 Ashes series, he may well have been cast aside. Instead, for much of the tour he was unstoppable, especially in the first two Tests, when he made 177 not out, 152 not out and 21 not out, as Allan Border's suddenly indomitable side went two-up in the series. His Test average for the rubber finished, Bradman-like, at 126.50. Back home in Australia, the team were greeted as all-conquering heroes.

Disappointingly, Waugh's exploits in England that golden summer were a false dawn. For the next four seasons, he rarely dominated in the Test arena. He even missed a season and a half of Test cricket through 1991 and 1992, when his place was taken by his twin. A thorough re-assessment of his technique, especially against short-pitched fast bowling, an acceptance that patience is a virtue and that it didn't matter how you coped so long as you did, and hours of hard yakka in the nets helped fix the problems. That he was cured was clearly demonstrated in Rawalpindi in 1994, when Wasim Akram and Waqar Younis peppered him with bouncers but he remained brave, defiant and made 98. It was the same against the West Indies in the Caribbean in 1995. The cricket tutorial Waugh went through during his first decade in international cricket was brutal and comprehensive, but when he graduated he was a man armed with an enormous knowledge about the game and extraordinary confidence in himself, his strategies and his technique.

The Fourth XI

Waugh's Test career is one of two halves. Until as late as the fourth Test of the 1993 Ashes series he was a moderate Test cricketer, a batting allrounder capable of the occasional outstanding performance. His Test average as he walked out to bat in the second innings of the third Test, at Trent Bridge, was 36.76. Had he failed, he may well have been dropped again; instead he scored 47 not out and helped save the game. From the start of that innings to the end of his career, he averaged 58.16, and built a reputation as one of the greatest batsmen of his generation.

Beyond statistics, the true measure of the cricketer was the way he observed, absorbed and applied lessons learnt on the international cricket stage, and the circumstances in which he made his most important contributions. Take, for example, that experience in the Caribbean in 1995, when Australia beat the West Indies in a Test series for the first time in 20 years. Waugh's stupendous 200 in the series-deciding fourth Test in Jamaica was the crucial innings of the rubber. Just as significant was the manner in which he stood up to the leader of the much vaunted West Indies pace attack, Curtly Ambrose, on a dangerous wicket in the third Test, in Trinidad.

In the 1997 Ashes series in England, the home side led 1-0 after two Tests before Waugh scored a century in each innings of third Test, at Old Trafford, making his runs on a pitch on which only one other batsman passed 55, and on which no-one else could reach three figures. Especially important was his batting on the first day, when he made an undefeated 102 out of 7-224, which justified captain Mark Taylor's decision to bat first and gave Shane Warne sufficient runs to bowl Australia into a commanding position on the second day.

At the 1999 World Cup, Australia were on the brink of an early departure, but crept into the second round and as a result gave Waugh, the one-day captain since December 1997, an opportunity to add considerably to his legend. In the final match of the second round — for the Australians a knockout match — he came in at 3-48 to score an unbeaten 120 from 110 balls, as his team achieved a successful chase of South Africa's 7-271 with two balls to spare. Considering the state and status of the match, Waugh's remarkable effort might have been the greatest one-day century ever made. Four days later, in a semi-final at Edgbaston, he scored 56 and then marshalled his men superbly as the South Africans' final batsman, Allan Donald, was run out off the game's last ball, to miss the final by one run. The Australians then went to Lord's to rout Pakistan and win the tournament.

Waugh tries a hook shot against the West Indies at the Gabba in 1988-89.

Following this success, Waugh and his Test and one-day teams set off on an unprecedented run of success. After a hiccup in Sri Lanka, the Test team won 16 Tests in a row —against Zimbabwe (1), India (3), Pakistan (3), New Zealand (3), West Indies (5) and India (1). The previous best such run was 11. Meanwhile, the one-day team won 13 matches straight in January-February 2000. Of all men to captain their team in more than 30 Tests, Waugh has the best win rate: 41 victories from 57 matches. Critically, a number of players, most notably Justin Langer, Matthew Hayden, Ricky Ponting and Damien Martyn, revived their careers under his leadership. Having scored 17 Test hundreds before he became skipper, he hit another 15 before he retired in January 2004.

A hero's farewell at the Sydney Cricket Ground, after the last of his 168 Test appearances.

Strangely, there was a sense at the end of his career that while the fans adored him, he was under appreciated by some parts of the cricket community, most notably the Australian selectors, who seemed strangely keen for him to retire during the 2002-03 Ashes series. Only a stirring century in the fifth Test, at the SCG, which featured a last-ball-of-the-day boundary that took him to his hundred, saved his career. Waugh had been in mediocre form, but if ever a cricketer deserved reassurance rather than retirement, especially with the Australian side going so well, it was the captain.

There have been a number of more talented run-makers in Test history than Steve Waugh. But perhaps only Grace, Hobbs and Bradman in the history of the sport had as good an understanding of and appreciation for the batting art while they played. In the modern game, no one understood more about what it takes to make runs and to win, when to be brave and when to be cautious, and how to get the best out of himself and his team.

STEVE WAUGH (AUSTRALIA)

Test Cricket

Tests	Inn	NO	Runs	HS	Ave	100	50	Ct	Balls	Runs	Wkts	Ave	Best	5/	10/
168	260	46	10927	200	51.06	32	50	112	7805	3445	92	37.45	5-28	3	—

One-Day International Cricket

ODIs	Inn	NO	Runs	HS	Ave	100	50	Ct	Balls	Runs	Wkts	Ave	Best	4/
325	288	58	7569	120*	32.91	3	45	111	8883	6761	195	34.67	4-33	3

The Fourth XI

Wilfred Rhodes

No. 41

No all-round cricketer has had quite the career that Wilfred Rhodes did. As a 20-year-old in 1898, his debut season, he took over from Bobby Peel as Yorkshire's frontline spinner and became one of *Wisden's* five cricketers of the year. The following year he made his Test debut at the same time as Victor Trumper in WG Grace's farewell Test match. Rhodes was then a genuine tailender, scoring 10 runs in three innings as either last or second-last man in. Dropped after two matches, he was recalled for the final Test and scored eight not out batting 11, but couldn't spin England to victory on the final day. Because his county directed him not to tour Australia with Archie MacLaren's team in 1901-02, he didn't play Test cricket again for three years.

The best part of a decade after he played his fourth Test, Rhodes opened the batting in the final four Ashes Tests of 1911-12 but bowled just 19 overs in six separate spells. He did, though, outscore his famous opening batting partner, Jack Hobbs, three times in eight innings. In the fourth Test at the MCG they added 323, Hobbs making 178 and Rhodes 179. Fast forward another 14 and a half years, to 1926, and Rhodes was recalled to the England team to bat seven (scoring 28 and 14) and bowl 45 overs (2-35 and 4-44) as England regained the Ashes. Rhodes was still to become the oldest man to play Test cricket (at 52 years, 165 days, in the West Indies in 1929-30) and the only player to have a Test career spanning more than 30 years (1899 to 1930). He took a record 4187 first-class wickets, at 16.71.

Wisden had this to say of Rhodes after his first season: 'His qualities as a slow bowler struck everyone as being exceptional. He bowls with a high, easy action, his pitch is wonderfully accurate, and whenever the ground gives him assistance he can get a lot of spin on the ball.' In the first Test of 1902, he made 38 not out as the No. 11 and then, with the pitch having turned sticky after overnight rain and with fellow Yorkshireman George Hirst as his foil, spun Australia out for 36, its lowest ever total, of which Trumper made 18. Rhodes finished with 7-17 from 11 overs. However, further rain saved the visitors, who then won at Sheffield and Manchester and might have won again at The Oval but for a hundred in 85 minutes by Gilbert Jessop and a last-wicket stand between Hirst and Rhodes of 15 which got England home by the narrowest of margins.

'Rhodes gets his men out before the ball pitches; spin with him is an accessory after the act of flight — flight which disguises the ball's length, draws the batsman forward when he ought to be back, sends him playing back when he ought to come forward, and generally keeps him in a state of mind so confused that in time he begins to feel it might be a mercy to get out.' Neville Cardus wrote that in 1928, when Rhodes was past his 50th birthday but still bowling successfully for Yorkshire (115 first-class wickets that season at 19.63), which gave him much joy, not least because it stopped the youngsters suggesting that the heroes of yesterday were really not that good.

England's first great left-arm slow bowler of the 20th century.

Had Rhodes stayed totally focused on his bowling, who knows what Test records he might have set? Some sceptics had reckoned he would struggle on the plumb wickets in Australia in 1903-04, but at the earliest opportunity he set them straight. In the first Test at Sydney, on a pitch that the Sydney Morning Herald's correspondent described as a 'shirtfront', Rhodes took 2-41 (from 17.2 overs) and 5-94 (from 40.2) while batsmen such as Trumper, Clem Hill, Monty Noble and Reg Duff were in outstanding form. The Herald's man was effusive in his praise of Rhodes, counting a grand total of three loose balls from him on the fourth day, when Australia went from 0-16 to 5-367 and Trumper scored a dazzling century between tea and stumps. At one point, Trumper was reputed to have pleaded with Rhodes, 'For God's sake, give me a minute's rest!' In the second Test, 10 or 12 catches were missed from Rhodes' bowling (the Herald lost count!), yet he still took 15-124 for the match. He was, simply, in the words of an unidentified member of the Australian XI, a 'champion'.

Rhodes' Test bowling average at the end of that series in Australia was 17.65 (66 wickets in 13 Tests). From this point, he seems to have focused at least as much on his batting as his bowling. He remained at county level a prolific wicket-taker while scoring more runs, but in Tests he seemed happy to be a support act with the ball while working towards achieving his ambition to 'go in first for England'. He took five wickets in a Test innings only once after his third series, but scored 11 fifties and two centuries in his career despite not going past 40 not out in any of his first 34 innings, from 1899 to 1908.

In the years immediately before 1914, Rhodes bowling fell away even at county level, but straight afterwards, the war having decimated Yorkshire's attack, he revived his considerable skills. In 1919, at age 41, he topped the first-class averages, taking 164 wickets at 14.42. Rhodes took at least 100 wickets in a season nine times between 1919 and 1929 (scoring more than 1000 runs in each of these seasons), but except for that Test at The Oval in 1926 he had little impact with the ball at the highest level.

He retired as the only man to have scored more than 2000 runs and taken more than 100 wickets in Test cricket, a feat unmatched until Keith Miller scored his 2000th Test run at Lord's in 1953. Rhodes also took 60 catches in his 58 Tests. Only 12 players in Test history have managed the trifecta of 2000 runs, 100 wickets and 50 catches: (in order the feat was achieved) Rhodes, Richie Benaud (in December 1963, 43 years after Rhodes), Garry Sobers, Tony Greig, Ian Botham, Kapil Dev, Carl Hooper, Jacques Kallis, Shane Warne, Shaun Pollock, Anil Kumble and Andrew Flintoff. Yet in a sense, it is hard to think of Wilfred Rhodes as a classic allrounder, for rarely at Test level was he both frontline bowler and top-order batsman at the same time. Most of his records are on account of his longevity; he was around long enough to be a great bowler then a capable batsman. The closest he came to cricket genius was when he was the best spinner in the world during his second and third series of Ashes cricket.

WILFRED RHODES (ENGLAND)

Test Cricket

Tests	Inn	NO	Runs	HS	Ave	100	50	Ct	Balls	Runs	Wkts	Ave	Best	5/	10/
58	98	21	2325	179	30.19	2	11	60	8231	3425	127	26.97	8-68	6	1

First-Class Cricket

Mat	Inn	NO	Runs	HS	Ave	100	50	Ct	Balls	Runs	Wkts	Ave	Best	5/	10/
1110	1534	237	39969	267*	30.82	58	197	765	185799	70322	4204	16.73	9-24	287	68

The Fourth XI

Curtly Ambrose   No. 42

One of the most difficult tasks for cricket historians is to rank the West Indian fast bowlers of the last 50 years. This study has included Andy Roberts, Michael Holding, Joel Garner, Malcolm Marshall and Curtly Ambrose in the top 100. The two omissions that were most troubling were Wes Hall, the spearhead in the '60s, whose record against India is magnificent, against Australia and England not quite as impressive as his reputation suggests, and Courtney Walsh, taker of 519 Test wickets at 24.44 in a career that ran for 20 years from 1984 and between 2000 to 2003 the holder of the world wicket-taking record. The sense, though, was that throughout his career, Walsh was never quite 'up there' with first Marshall, Holding and Garner, and then Ambrose. Between 1960 and 1990, these great bowlers benefited from some excellent support, from men such as Charlie Griffith, Keith Boyce, Bernard Julien, Wayne Daniel, Sylvester Clarke, Colin Croft, Patrick Patterson and Ian Bishop.

As was stated in the chapter on Malcolm Marshall, there is a general consensus that Marshall was the best of the West Indian quicks. Of Roberts, Holding and Garner, perhaps Roberts was the most lethal, Holding the fastest, Garner the most relentless. Curtly Ambrose was something else, something of a concoction of all three. When Ambrose emerged in 1988 it was as if the prototype of the West Indian fast bowler had been taken to yet another level.

He was born 61 years to the day after Lord Constantine, in 1963, the year Hall and Griffith blazed through England with Frank Worrell's magnificent West Indies side. He debuted in international cricket against Imran Khan's outstanding Pakistan team in April 1988, and while his influence on that series was relatively minor, he was impressive in the Tests straight after in England, chiefly as Marshall's foil, and nasty in Australia, when he took 26 wickets in five Tests and broke tailender Geoff Lawson's jaw with a riser in Perth. During the first three Tests of that series, and indeed for the next few years, Ambrose seemed to have a psychological hold over certain batsmen, and could make a grave impact on the opposing dressing room. The fall of one wicket was often the prelude to a batting collapse. Few batsmen started badly in a series against Ambrose and lived to tell the tale. In England in 1991, there were high hopes for the Zimbabwean import Graeme Hick, but instead of flourishing Hick was dropped before the end of the series and never went on to fulfil his considerable promise.

Ambrose walks off The Oval after his final spell in Test cricket.

One adjective often associated with Ambrose is 'steepling' — as in 'steepling bounce'. He sort of half bounced, half glided to the wicket, and there was a definite acceleration as he let go of the ball from his full 201cm (6ft 7in) height. His half-pitched bouncer wasn't as frightening as that of Roberts, but the one short of a length would often rip horribly up into the ribs or the helmet grille. Only Garner bowled a better yorker. Ambrose's pace came not just from his rhythmical run-up, but also from his wrist snapping forward at the instant of release, to impart extra thrust to the ball as it began its downward trajectory. His accuracy was renowned;

there were days when there seemed no way the besieged batsman could get to the other end. On pitches that helped a little he could get a slow seamer's movement at top speed, and he knew where the stumps were. In 1990, his 8-45 against England in Bridgetown included the last five wickets all lbw, each man forced back onto his stumps before the gun was finally fired.

Few bowlers have produced more match-winning spells. At Port-of Spain in 1994, Ambrose took 6-24 in 10 overs as England was shot out for just 46. A year before in Australia, the series came down to a decider at the WACA, but in truth it was no contest. David Boon, never one to exaggerate, said the wicket 'had more than a bit of juice in it'. In fact, with Ambrose among the opposition, it was frightening, and the rubber was decided on the first day when he took 7-1 in 32 balls. 'Undoubtedly the best bowling I've ever faced,' was Mark Waugh's verdict.

Even though the West Indies won both those series, the team's dominance was actually fading. Richie Richardson and Brian Lara were the only batsmen capable of consistently giving Ambrose and Walsh reasonable scores to defend. The only bowler to debut for the West Indies since 1990 and take more than 125 Test wickets was Mervyn Dillon, whose career Test bowling average is 33.57. In the '80s, it had always seemed that when one fast bowler departed there were more waiting in the wings; now the cupboard behind the two spearheads was bare, and the Windies attack lost its trademark — the sense that there was no escape.

Ambrose in England in 2000, his last Test series, as intimidating as ever.

Ambrose attacks England's Hugh Morris in 1991.

The Fourth XI

Two confrontations with Australians captured the change in mood. In January 1993, Dean Jones came out and asked Ambrose to remove a white wristband, which Jones claimed was distracting him even though the fast man had been wearing them for years. Ambrose reluctantly did so, and promptly launched into a match-turning spell of 5-32. The general consensus was that Jones had stirred up a hornet's nest. Two and a half years later, Steve Waugh stood toe to toe with Ambrose at Port-of-Spain, an act that became symbolic of the turnaround in fortunes in West Indies-Australia Tests. Almost forgotten about that Waugh clash is that the home team won the game by nine wickets, with Ambrose taken 9-65 for the match. 'To me, Curtly Ambrose was the supreme fast bowling machine,' is how Waugh described Ambrose in 2005, making special note of the way he could find an extra gear when necessary.

Steve Waugh is caught behind off Ambrose at St John's in 1999.

While the West Indies lost series to Australia, South Africa, Pakistan, New Zealand and England between 1995 and 2000, Ambrose's individual Test-match bowling stats actually improved. At the end of that home series against Australia in 1995, his career average was 21.05 from 54 Tests. When he retired following the series in England in 2000, it was 20.99 from 98 matches. He had become the second West Indian (after Walsh) and the fifth bowler (after Richard Hadlee, Kapil Dev, Walsh and Wasim Akram) to take 400 Test wickets when he dismissed Michael Atherton in the fourth Test of that series.

Perhaps the way the West Indies declined on his watch should have a bearing on how we measure Ambrose's greatness. Then again, the manner in which he sustained his excellence while those around him could not is a credit to him. He and Walsh were fully entitled to the guard of honour formed for them by their opponents at The Oval following the final Test of 2000. They were the last of the West Indian fast men.

CURTLY AMBROSE (WEST INDIES)
Test Cricket

Tests	Inn	NO	Runs	HS	Ave	100	50	Ct	Balls	Runs	Wkts	Ave	Best	5/	10/
98	145	29	1439	53	12.41	–	1	22	22103	8501	405	20.99	8-45	22	3

One-Day International Cricket

ODIs	Inn	NO	Runs	HS	Ave	100	50	Ct	Balls	Runs	Wkts	Ave	Best	4/
176	96	36	639	31*	10.65	–	–	45	9353	5429	225	24.13	5-17	10

No. 43 Jim Laker

It is extremely difficult to leave the only man to take more than 17 wickets in a Test match out of this top 100. Just on one performance — 19-90 (9-37 and 10-56) against Australia at Old Trafford in 1956 — Jim Laker must be in; it's just a question of how high is his ranking.

The classic off-spinner's action.

There was something impossible about what Laker did in that Test. Yes, the pitch, which was so broken it resembled a beach, was perfect for him. But at the other end, the left-arm finger-spinner Tony Lock, despite spinning the ball away from the bat, couldn't get a wicket even though he bowled more overs in the match (69) than did Laker (68). This was Laker's fifth Test at Old Trafford. In four previous matches, dating back to 1950, he'd taken exactly eight wickets. He hadn't even been selected for Tests there in 1954 and 1955. He would never play another Test at the ground. A schoolboy spinner dreaming about his greatest day would have given Lock at least a quarter of the wickets, but Laker, magically, went way beyond that.

Replying to England's 459, the first Australian innings started after lunch on the second day without drama, with Jim Burke and Colin McDonald taking the score into the forties. Then Laker switched to the Stretford End, and almost immediately he dismissed McDonald and Neil Harvey. Burke and Ian Craig added 14, and then Lock — bowling with a slip, a gully and two short legs — had Burke caught by Colin Cowdrey at slip with one that turned appreciably away from the bat. Craig was out to a ball Bill O'Reilly in the press-box called 'a scorcher and unplayable'. The last seven Australian wickets fell for 22 runs, all to Laker, and the follow-on was enforced, the visitors 375 behind. McDonald had to retire hurt with a knee injury, and then Harvey was caught at short mid-wicket off a rank full-toss for his second duck of the game. Laker had taken 10 wickets in less than two sessions.

The last three days were remarkable. On the third day, only 45 minutes play were possible, and one wicket fell, Burke, caught in the 'leg trap'. There was scarcely more play on day four, and McDonald and Craig took the score to 2-84 as the dampness continued to hold the pitch together. On day five the weather cleared

The Fourth XI

and there was little drama until after lunch, when the pitch began to disintegrate. Laker enjoyed a beer and a sandwich during the interval, and that did the trick, for soon afterwards Craig was lbw, and the Australian middle order fell apart worse than the pitch. In a spell of nine overs, Ken Mackay, Keith Miller and Ron Archer were all dismissed for ducks. McDonald's rearguard stand didn't end until after tea, when he was caught at leg gully for 89, and it was only then, with three wickets in hand, plenty of time to get them and the wicket shattered, that the idea of Laker taking all 10 wickets really took hold.

Laker's eighth wicket, Richie Benaud, meant he equalled Sydney Barnes' record for the most wickets in one Test. Five runs later, Ray Lindwall was caught by Lock at leg slip (his third catch of the match), and almost immediately Len Maddocks was plumb lbw. Laker's appeal was understated, and as he walked off the field, sweater over his shoulder, there was little emotion. Still, everyone sensed they'd witnessed something that would never happen again.

Laker at The Oval in 1951, when he took 10 wickets in the fifth Test against South Africa.

Lock finished the match with figures of 1-106. Laker finished the series with 46 wickets, at 9.61. He also took 10-88 in one innings for Surrey against the Australians during the tour. However, if you put the Ashes of 1956 to one side, and ask Australian followers of Ashes cricket in the 1940s and 1950s for their other memories of Jim Laker in Test cricket, they would probably nominate the manner in which Don Bradman and Arthur Morris took to him at Leeds in 1948 (when Australia scored 3-404 on a spinning pitch on the final day), or perhaps his tour of Australia in 1958-59, when he bowled well without luck and took 15 wickets for a losing side in the Tests while Benaud was capturing 31 for the victors. Was Laker a one-series wonder?

Hardly. A simple study of Test bowling averages demonstrates that. Of all the spinners to take 150 wickets in Test history, as at June 30, 2009, only three have career averages of less than 25 runs per wicket: Clarrie Grimmett (216 wickets at 24.22), Muttiah Muralitharan (770 at 22.18) and Jim Laker (193 at 21.25). Take the 1956 Ashes series out, and Laker's return is 147 wickets at 24.89. He averaged less than 20 against each of Australia, New Zealand, Pakistan and South Africa, just 23.63 against India. It was only on the flint-hard pitches in the West Indies, where he toured twice (in 1947-48 and 1953-54) that Laker's wickets were more expensive. However, even that first trip to the Caribbean was hardly catastrophic for him. He'd been chosen as a 25-year-old after just a couple of months in first-class cricket, and afterwards, having taken 18 wickets in the four Tests at 30.44, Wisden suggested that, 'undoubtedly, he was the find of the tour'.

The biggest knock on Laker's reputation is that in the period between his first Test and his last, England were involved in 99 Tests, but he played in only 46 of them. For reputedly such a tremendous bowler, until 1956 the selectors had remarkably

The 100 Greatest Cricketers

Laker (middle) with his Surrey and England colleagues Peter May (left) and Tony Lock.

little faith in him. Part of this was because his unhurried, take-it-as-it-comes body language sometimes suggested a certain frailty. Trevor Bailey remembered that Laker used to 'wilt' when the batsmen went after him in his early days, but added, 'There was no comparison between the callow off-spinner who played against the Australians in 1948 and the polished artist he later became.' Experience was the making of him. 'I sometimes used to wonder, in Jim's playing days, if he realised just how great a bowler he was,' Fred Trueman said in 1977. 'When he was really spinning the ball, you could actually hear his fingers click as he delivered. He really was a prodigious finger spinner.' A few months *before* the 1956 Ashes series, Len Hutton nominated Laker as 'the best off-spinner on all classes of wickets during my time'.

Laker once took 8-2 in a Test-match trial, but wasn't chosen for either of the 1950-51 or 1954-55 tours of Australia, the logic apparently being that an off-spinner of his type would struggle on the hard wickets down under. He did play the final three Ashes Tests in 1953, taking nine wickets but bowling just 58.5 overs, his most important contribution being his 48 in the fourth Test which allowed England to escape with a draw and keep the series alive. Laker played only two home Tests in the next two years: the first of 1954 (1-17 and 1-22 against Pakistan) and the last of 1955 (2-28 and 5-56 against South Africa). It is not surprising that when Jim Laker finally got his real chance in 1956, he was not going to let it go.

JIM LAKER (ENGLAND)

Test Cricket

Tests	Inn	NO	Runs	HS	Ave	100	50	Ct	Balls	Runs	Wkts	Ave	Best	5/	10/
46	63	15	676	63	14.08	–	2	12	12027	4101	193	21.25	10-53	9	3

First-Class Cricket

Mat	Inn	NO	Runs	HS	Ave	100	50	Ct	Balls	Runs	Wkts	Ave	Best	5/	10/
450	548	108	7304	113	16.60	2	18	270	101352	35791	1944	18.41	10-53	127	32

The Fourth XI

Archie MacLaren   No. 44

Neville Cardus called Archibald Campbell MacLaren the 'Noblest Roman', writing lyrically of his 'grandeur' and 'romantic attitude'. Few cricketers inspired Cardus to write more extravagant prose. 'Magnificence was enthroned at the wicket when MacLaren took his stand there and surveyed the field with a comprehensive eye,' he enthused. 'He was an England captain by divine right; every cricketer who came into his company — great players like Ranjitsinjhi, Fry, Hirst, Lockwood and Shrewsbury — knew at once that this man was their master and that he would brook no denial.'

In this era of amateur 'gentlemen' and professional 'players', the temptation is to immediately picture Archie MacLaren as something akin to cricket royalty, and also as something of a martinet promoted because of status rather than talent. The truth is, of course, that many amateur cricketers, especially those from before World War I, could actually play a bit, especially the batsmen. Of course, WG Grace was the best of them; after him came MacLaren, with Ranji, the Hon. FS Jackson, Gilbert Jessop and CB Fry next in a regal line.

First, quickly, the statistics. MacLaren debuted in Australia in 1894-95, but it was on his second tour, in 1897-98, that he struck top form. From the start of that series until 1905 he appeared in 23 Tests, scoring 1565 runs at a very impressive 42.29, with four centuries. After 1905, he was often preoccupied working as Ranji's private secretary, but was recalled at age 37 for the 1909 Ashes series, only to have an unhappy time, scoring 85 runs in seven innings. At first-class level, MacLaren scored 22,236 runs at 34.16, batting from 1890 to 1923, but it was always the big occasion that got the best out of him. 'He would have gained still higher renown on the playing field but for periods of poor health and the calls of business,' *Wisden* noted in its tribute to him after he died in 1944. 'Test matches were the only kind of cricket which he found completely fulfilling and challenging,' wrote Michael Down in his book *Archie: A Biography of AC MacLaren*. All of his 35 Tests were against Australia.

One of the most compelling figures of English cricket before World War I.

The 100 Greatest Cricketers

MacLaren was the first to score 400 in a first-class innings: 424 for Lancashire against Somerset at Taunton in 1895. He scored 1000 first-class runs in a season on nine occasions: eight times in England and once in Australia, in 1897-98, when he made five hundreds in 11 matches. In the Tests that summer he made big hundreds in Sydney and Adelaide, but it was at the SCG where he was truly king, his scores for the season there being 142 and 100, 109 and 50 not out, 61 and 140, 65 and finally, stunningly, a first-ball duck. That one ball from Ernie Jones changed the game, reflecting MacLaren's importance to his side, as England sacrificed a first-innings lead of 106 to lose by six wickets. Four years later, his scores at Sydney were 145 and 73, 116, 167, 92 and 5. 'His masterly batting earned him esteem as the greatest Englishman seen on that ground up to that time,' Johnnie Moyes wrote in 1950. 'Of those who have played there since he retired, only Hobbs and Hammond approached his standard.'

MacLaren, the England captain, goes out to bat with Jack Hobbs at Edgbaston in 1909.

'There have been few finer batsmen to watch,' HS Altham explained in *A History of Cricket*. 'Every stroke was played in the "grand manner" with a full back-lift, perfect fluency and a free follow-through.' MacLaren loved to hit the good length ball wide of mid-on, and when he played back could cut and hook powerfully. Altham continued: 'There was about all his play a certain spaciousness and majesty that stamped him as no mere master of technique, but as one of the very few who, from time to time, have lifted batting from the level of accomplishment into the rarer atmosphere of an art.'

MacLaren was a controversial captain. Overall, his captaincy record in Tests is hardly flattering: four wins and 11 losses in 22 Tests. He made a study of the intricacies of cricket tactics, but unfortunately others did not always share his views. He was criticised when Victor Trumper hit a hundred before lunch at Old Trafford in 1902, but replied in part, 'I exploited the inner and outer ring — a man

The Fourth XI

there, and another man covering him. I told my bowlers to pitch on the short side to the off: I set my heart and brain on every detail of our policy. Well, in the third over of the morning, Victor hit two balls straight into the practice ground, high over the screen behind the bowler. I couldn't very well have had a man fielding in the bloody practice ground, now could I?' At Lord's in 1909, he caused such a kerfuffle after the selectors left out Jessop, Wilfred Rhodes, Sydney Barnes and the fast bowler Walter Brearley that Monty Noble sent England in, correctly sensing the negativity that had pervaded the home dressing-room.

MacLaren was at times a brilliant leader but also an unlucky one. The Yorkshire committee wouldn't let him take Rhodes and George Hirst to Australia in 1901-02, and then Sydney Barnes was injured early in the third Test. He could have won in 1902, if only Fred Tate had held a skied catch at Old Trafford, and should have been captain in Australia in 1903-4 (when England did win under Pelham Warner) but he found himself in dispute with the Marylebone Cricket Club and stayed at home. In the lead-up to the 1909 season, the *Daily Mail* commented, 'Players and public alike are clamouring for the return of AC MacLaren, who is perhaps the greatest captain England has ever had, though FS Jackson is more adept at spinning the coin and winning the toss.' By series' end, however, with Australia 2-0 victors, the general consensus was that he'd played one rubber too many.

MacLaren's reputation would be restored, but not until 1921, when he engineered a remarkable win over Warwick Armstrong's Australians. The tourists were unbeaten, triumphant and near the end of their tour when they faced up to 'An England XI' at Eastbourne, that side to be captained by none other than the silver-haired MacLaren, then three months short of his 50th birthday. As sole selector, he chose accomplished veterans such as Brearley and the South African allrounder Aubrey Faulkner alongside a group of young amateurs, among them the future England captain Percy Chapman, and did what everyone else thought was impossible. This astonishing victory was achieved after his men had been bowled out for 43, after the Australians reached 1-80 in their first innings, after Brearley was hurt and could not bowl an over. The first-innings deficit was kept to 131, and then MacLaren strode out late in the day to open the batting. He was bowled first thing the next morning, but his boldness had changed the mood, and after gleaning a lead of 196 on the back of Faulkner's magnificent 153, the Australians panicked in their run chase while every move MacLaren made worked as if he was directing a stage play.

He really was the master strategist. Maybe there should never have been any doubt.

ARCHIE MACLAREN (ENGLAND)

Test Cricket

Tests	Inn	NO	Runs	HS	Ave	100	50	Ct	Balls	Runs	Wkts	Ave	Best	5/	10/
35	61	4	1931	140	33.88	5	8	29	–	–	–	–	–	–	–

First-Class Cricket

Mat	Inn	NO	Runs	HS	Ave	100	50	Ct	Balls	Runs	Wkts	Ave	Best	5/	10/
424	703	52	22236	424	34.16	47	96	454	321	267	1	267.0	1-44	–	–

The 100 Greatest Cricketers

Frank Woolley

Ricky Ponting

The Fifth

Syed Kirmani

Alec Bedser

The Fifth XI

Denis Compton

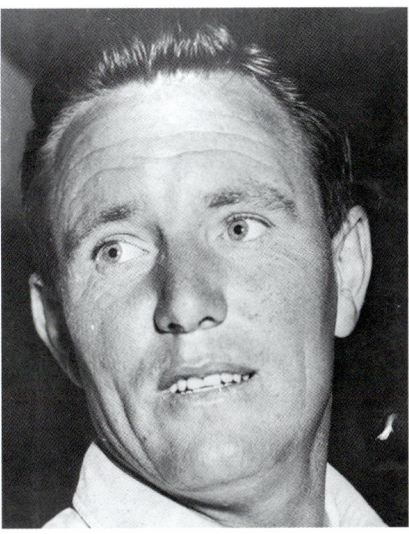
Ray Lindwall

Kumar Shri Ranjitsinhji

XI

Richie Benaud

Arthur Shrewsbury

Barry Richards

Fred Trueman

No. 45 Frank Woolley

In a sense, Frank Woolley is England's answer to Victor Trumper. Almost to a man, Woolley's contemporaries rated him the greatest left-handed batsman of his time, perhaps of all time. He was revered in his home county, known throughout the cricket world as 'The Pride of Kent'. Yet like Trumper, Woolley's Test statistics do not reflect such excellence. He played some wonderful hands, and was also — as first-class level — an excellent left-arm slow bowler, but a Test batting average of 36.08 from 64 Tests, just 33.28 from 32 Tests against Australia, and 83 wickets at 33.92 (43 Australian wickets at 36.16) are hardly the stuff of greatness.

The most revered of all English left-handed batsman.

Yet the hype about Woolley's batting was, and remains, avid. Consider the following quotes:

Neville Cardus (in 1928): 'He can be as powerful and brilliant a batsman as any other cricketer living, but it is not in this aggressive way that I prefer to think of Woolley. He is essentially a gracious batsman — and violence does not go in tune with grace.'

HS Altham (in 1938): 'Great batsmen come and go, but Woolley's batting has a personality that places him right apart. When he walks in for the last time something will go out of cricket which can never be recaptured.'

Arthur Mailey (in 1958): 'I don't know what Frank Woolley's batting average is and I don't care. I tremble to think what would happen to some of the present-day purveyors of slow leg-break half-volleys if Woolley was still in circulation.'

Mailey, the crafty leg-spinner, remembered an innings of 123 in Sydney in 1924-25, when the 185cm (6ft 1in) tall Woolley gave him a 'merciless hiding'. He thought Woolley's driving off his bowling during that innings was the finest he had ever seen, and that the Englishman hit the ball so hard that after delivering the ball he was best to dive back and take refuge behind the umpire. Mailey was proud of the fact that he could sometimes keep Jack Hobbs quiet. Woolley, however, was another matter. Ian Peebles, one of the better wrist-spinners in England between the wars, recognised that because Woolley's main form of defence was attack, he was not as impregnable as some others. But Peebles added, 'Once he was going there was no area in which the bowler could seek shelter.'

When the *Daily Mail* asked Len Hutton to pick a best-ever England XI to play a 'computer Test' against Australia in 1977, Woolley was in the middle order. The great sportswriter Ian Wooldridge summarised this selection this way: 'Woolley, towering, commanding and also left-handed to challenge O'Reilly, was a natural.'

The Fifth XI

Never was Woolley's class better demonstrated than at Lord's in the first Ashes series in England after World War I, when he scored 95 and 93 against Mailey, Jack Gregory and Ted McDonald. 'To have seen one of other or both of Woolley's two nineties at Lord's in 1921 is to be in possession of a kind of ringside ticket to a vision of immortality,' wrote Ronald Mason in his book Warwick Armstrong's Australians. 'There are not many innings in the long panorama of Test history that have collected such enduring glamour.' Woolley thought these to be his finest innings. At Lord's in 1930, he opened the batting and scored just 41, but it was a sensational short innings that left his two famous batting partners — Hobbs and Wally Hammond — looking almost pedestrian. Woolley scored 34 of the Test's first 37 runs, including seven fours, most of them drives either straight or through the covers. After 45 minutes, he had reached 41, when he square cut Alan Fairfax like a bullet but straight and low to Tim Wall at point and the masterpiece was over. 'The ease and grace of his poise denied his power,' Cardus wrote in the Manchester Guardian, yet the force of his strokes left the fieldsmen helpless — reduced them to white pillars of immobility.'

Woolley goes out to bat with South of England XI opening partner 'Gubby' Allen in a match against a North of England XI at Old Trafford in 1932.

The unfortunate punchlines to this innings were that England lost the Test — Don Bradman making a clinical, technically superb innings of 254 — and with Herbert Sutcliffe fit again, Woolley did not go back down the order, but was dropped completely. Those who rely solely on averages might have agreed with this decision; to the romantics it was reprehensible.

For all his panache, Woolley was still the sixth batsman and first left-hander to score 100 first-class hundreds. However, only five of them came in Test matches, just two of them against Australia. He amassed 58,969 first-class runs from 1906 to 1938, an aggregate bettered only by Jack Hobbs, but averaged only 40.75, 10 runs an innings less than Hobbs, many runs per innings less than many less

The 100 Greatest Cricketers

gifted individuals. Woolley also captured 2,068 first-class wickets at 19.86 and he held 1015 first-class catches, mainly at slip, 131 more than WG Grace, who remains second on the 'most catches' list.

As a Test bowler, Woolley's most successful season came in 1912, when he took 17 wickets in the 'Triangular Tournament' involving England, Australia and South Africa, from 57.5 overs at an average of just 8.94. Yet he bowled only 16 overs for a single wicket in the first four Tests, before taking 5-41, 1-24, 5-29 and 5-20. Twelve and a half years later, Woolley and another left-armer, Roy Kilner, almost spun England to victory at the Adelaide Oval, and in New Zealand in early 1930, he took 7-76 at Wellington, but otherwise he was rarely a frontline Test bowler. At first-class level, he used his height cleverly and took 100 wickets in a season eight times between 1910 and 1923, each time at an average of less than 20. He also kept wicket in the fifth Ashes Test of 1934, at The Oval, aged 47, after Ames hurt his back, but conceded 37 byes.

Woolley bats against Australia at Leeds in 1926.

In his life story, the great umpire Frank Chester told the story of how in 1937, Kent were set 218 to win a county game at Dover against Gloucestershire. Between innings, Bryan Valentine, the Kent captain, asked Chester if he reckoned they had any chance. 'If Frank Woolley knocks 50 in the first two overs, there's slight hope,' the ump replied jokingly. 'Very well, I'm going for them,' Valentine reacted.

Chester recalled that Woolley hit 44 in less than two overs. After he was dismissed, Les Ames came out and smashed 70 in 36 minutes, and Kent went on to win with 19 minutes to spare. Woolley, who was 50 years old, had scored an even century in the first innings. His bowling over the previous 30 years had been invaluable at county level, reasonable in Tests. His fielding was excellent, and his run-scoring ability was impressive enough. But it was manner in which he made his runs, and continued to make them for so long, that set him apart.

FRANK WOOLLEY (ENGLAND)

Test Cricket

Tests	Inn	NO	Runs	HS	Ave	100	50	Ct	Balls	Runs	Wkts	Ave	Best	5/	10/
64	98	7	3283	154	36.08	5	23	64	6495	2815	83	33.92	7-76	4	1

First-Class Cricket

Mat	Inn	NO	Runs	HS	Ave	100	50	Ct	Balls	Runs	Wkts	Ave	Best	5/	10/
978	1530	84	58959	305*	40.77	145	295	1018	94649	41058	2066	8-22	19.87	132	28

The Fifth XI

Ricky Ponting

No. 46

In the entry for June 30 in his *1997 Ashes Diary*, Steve Waugh wrote this about two of his young teammates: 'My tip for (Jason) Gillespie is 250-plus Test-match wickets. And while I'm making predictions, on the batting side of things I'll back Ricky Ponting to score 5000-plus Test runs. These two are players of rare calibre and temperament, who both possess a deep desire to not only play at the top level, but also to enjoy it. And, perhaps most important of all, they believe in themselves ...'

Despite often battling injuries, Gillespie finished his excellent career with 259 Test wickets. Ponting, who when Waugh made his prediction was not even in the Australian Test XI (he returned to the team three-and-a-half weeks later for the fourth Test and scored his maiden Test century), has now established himself as the best Australian batsman since ... Steve Waugh. Maybe, some critics have argued, since Bradman.

Experts who saw Ponting bat as a teenager, David Boon and Rod Marsh among them, knew he'd be a star. He made his Test debut in December 1995, against Sri Lanka in Perth, and was desperately unlucky not to begin with a hundred, being wrongly adjudged lbw for 96. Three months later he was playing in a World Cup final, by the following November he was batting three against Curtly Ambrose and Courtney Walsh. But two Tests after that he was rudely cast aside and was even a little fortunate to make the '97 Ashes tour. (The Australian selectors picked a 17-man squad that included nine batsmen and Adam Gilchrist as the second keeper. A better-balanced side would have carried one, perhaps two less batsmen, which might have left Ponting at home.) However, he was back into the side for the Leeds Test, batting six, and made a polished 127 after coming in with the score at 4-50.

Ponting has just hit the winning runs in his 100th Test match, at the SCG in 2005-06. He scored a century in each innings, a feat he would repeat when Australia toured South Africa later in 2006.

Ponting would lose his place again during the 1998-99 Ashes series, but by then everyone knew his absence from the team was only temporary. Sure enough, he returned for the third Test of the 1999 West Indies series and again scored a hundred at the earliest opportunity. There was a fear that Ponting might be a streaky player, prone to 'slumps'. A couple of off-field contretemps earned him further demerit points. Instead, he matured into one of the most consistent and prolific batsman of his generation, and the captain of his country. He went into the 2009 Ashes series having scored 63 international centuries: 37 in 131 Tests and 26 in 315 ODIs.

A critical game for him was the fourth Ashes Test of 2001, at Headingley. He had scored just 319 runs in his previous 18 Test innings, at an average of 19.94. He was back at No. 3 even though his Test career batting average was a mediocre

40.51, and in early on the first day when, third ball, he might have been caught in the slip cordon but the umpire gave him the benefit of the doubt. For an hour he was scratchy, but gradually he regained something like his best form, and finished with 144. In the second innings, he made another 72, then 62 at The Oval. In ODIs in 2001 he was magnificent, averaging 55.20 with two hundreds. The following Australian season he was consistent, made a big Test hundred against New Zealand at Hobart, but was still only averaging 43.78 as a Test cricketer when he was named as Australia's new one-day captain for a tour of South Africa, after Steve Waugh was sacked.

Right: Another catch for one of the finest all-round fieldsmen the game has seen.

The responsibility seemed to be the making of him, or perhaps it was the confidence that came with playing one of modern cricket's finest hands to win the second Test at Cape Town. Australia needed an imposing 331, and Ponting saw them home, reaching his hundred and hitting the winning runs with a six. In the 46 Tests Ponting played from that Cape Town Test to the New Year's Test in Sydney in 2005-06, his 100th Test, he averaged 72.72 and hit 19 centuries. Not since the days of Bradman has an Australian No. 3 scored so heavily and with such surety.

Ponting hits another six during his wonderful 140 not out in the 2003 World Cup final.

In one-day cricket, Ponting has had few setbacks. It is as if the game is made for him, rewarding as it does those who 'have a go' and appreciate the value of going for their shots. His often breathtaking all-round fielding skills are also on full display when wearing his country's colours. His biggest triumph in ODIs came at the 2003 World Cup, when he led his men superbly, and crowned the tournament with an extraordinary 140 not out in the final, as India was destroyed by 125 runs. When Waugh stood down as Test captain at the start of 2004, the Tasmanian was a natural choice to succeed him.

The Fifth XI

For such a naturally attacking batsman, it is somewhat ironic that arguably Ponting's best Test innings came while saving a Test. At Old Trafford, in the third Test of the 2005 Ashes series, he was in during the second over of the final day and batted until the final ball of the fifth last over, when he was out for 156, the ninth wicket to fall. Glenn McGrath and Brett Lee then batted out the remaining 24 balls to complete the save. Typical of the man, even though the target was out of reach, Ponting never went on the defensive. Australia eventually lost the series, making Ponting the first Australian captain since Allan Border in 1986-87 to lose an Ashes series, but at the SCG six months later, when he scored a century in both innings of his 100th Test match, he was still able to nominate that knock at Old Trafford as his favourite. 'To be able to bat in really tough conditions as long as I did and save a Test match was very satisfying,' he explained.

The characteristic that dominated this and most of his best innings was that he always stays true to the classic technique and pragmatic attitude that have served him well. As Viv Richards used to do, when in top form, he takes balls off middle stump and puts them consistently through mid-wicket for four. His running between the wickets is as dazzling as his fielding. He hooks the fastest bowlers with aplomb, and rarely resorts to slogging in the one-dayers because he doesn't need to do so to score rapidly. Ponting ended 2005 having scored 1500 runs in a calendar year for the second time in three years, and then came the glory of his 100th Test, followed by clean-sweep series victories in South Africa and Bangladesh. In 2006-07, he led Australia to a five-match clean sweep as the Ashes were regained in devastating style. From there, though, as some of his greatest team-mates retired, his team lacked some of its lustre, losing series to India, South Africa and England. But the captain remained one of the game's best batsmen, always at No. 3, his Test career average staying well above 56. Who would have thought that when Steve Waugh was making those bold predictions back in 1997 he was seriously underrating his man.

At Headingley in 2009, Ponting produced one of his greatest innings — a thrilling counterattack on a lively wicket that set up his team's only win of the series.

RICKY PONTING (AUSTRALIA)
Test Cricket

Tests	Inn	NO	Runs	HS	Ave	100	50	Ct	Balls	Runs	Wkts	Ave	Best	5/	10/
131	221	26	10960	257	56.20	37	46	148	539	242	5	48.40	1-0	–	–

One-Day International Cricket

ODIs	Inn	NO	Runs	HS	Ave	100	50	Ct	Balls	Runs	Wkts	Ave	Best	4/
315	306	35	11523	164	42.52	26	67	137	150	104	3	34.67	1-12	–

The 100 Greatest Cricketers

No. 47 Denis Compton

Denis Compton is generally considered to be one of the most dynamic, the most entertaining, of all English batsmen. He was one of those cricketers — in the manner of Trumper or Botham — whose greatest days were often wonderful and whose unproductive days (most of which happened in the second half of his career) were not just tolerated but considered part of the charm. His worth, to his teams and the game, always went beyond the scorebook.

Compton blazes away against the Australians in 1953.

All descriptions of Compton suggest he was a man who didn't care much for his statistics, yet they make for interesting reading. Certainly, for large parts of his career — most notably between 1946 and 1949 when he rivalled Len Hutton as England's finest batsman — he was statistically superb. He averaged more than 60 with the bat in 36 Tests before 1950, but less than 41 in 42 matches afterwards. Only four of his 17 Test centuries came in the 42 Tests he played from 1950 to 1957, and eight of his 10 Test ducks. Part of this decline can be blamed on the severe knee injury that struck him down in 1950, but terrific reflexes more so than classic technique were among his most important assets, so a decline with age was probably inevitable. Yet it was not as if he lost all his skill, or any of the phenomenal popularity he earned in the seasons immediately after the war. He was always Test class.

In 1947, Compton scored an unprecedented 3816 runs during the English first-class season, including 18 centuries. In the five-Test series against South Africa that summer, he amassed 753 runs at 94.13. A year later, against Don Bradman's 'Invincibles', Compton scored 562 runs in the Tests, gallantly standing up to everything Ray Lindwall and Keith Miller could bounce at him. 'A glorious natural cricketer' is how Bradman described Compton after that series. 'He does things that are unexpected and which nobody else can copy.'

Wisden's obituary in 1998 led with the fact that Compton was 'not just a great cricketer but a character who transcended the game and became what would now be called a national icon'. In part, this was due to the way his style and personality helped make cricket so popular in the testing times straight after the war, but more than anything it was simply about the way he played cricket as if it was an adventure. He was enjoying himself and the fans enjoyed the game with him. Compton was also, like Keith Miller in Australia, in part celebrity as well as cricketer, a face who became almost as well known for his Brylcreem advertisements as he was for his runs. He was cricket's answer to *Roy of the Rovers*, a good-looking sportsman who not only scored centuries against Australia, but also played FA Cup Finals for Arsenal.

The Fifth XI

Compton made his county debut in 1936, a week past his 18th birthday, a left-arm wrist-spinner batting 11, but in less than a month he'd scored his maiden first-class century and in little more than a year was batting four for England against New Zealand. The following year he marked his Ashes debut with 102 at Trent Bridge, becoming at 20 years 19 days England's youngest ever centurion, but also managed to be clean bowled for one at The Oval, when England famously scored 7-903 (declared). Neville Cardus commented on Compton's 'leisurely elegance', but also criticised his technique, most notably 'his way of reaching forward in front of the left leg'. The young batsman was not the type to change his style, yet during 1939 only Hutton and Wally Hammond outscored him. After the war, Bradman thought that Compton had a weakness against the short ball, and asked his fast men to bounce him as often as they dared. Compton responded by scoring a century in each innings in the Adelaide Test of 1946-47, and then at Old Trafford in 1948 he edged a bumper from Lindwall into his face, had to retire hurt, but came back to make 145 not out.

The teenage Compton with his Middlesex teammate, the former Test batsman 'Patsy' Hendren

'There was a touch of genius in him,' wrote Johnnie Moyes in 1950, 'the genius that enables the natural player to scoff at textbooks.' In the foreword to *Compton on Cricketers Past and Present* (1980), Alec Bedser recalled how someone had described Compton as the 'eternal schoolboy', before writing: 'Unfettered by techniques and the restrictions binding an ordinary player he hooked and cut with deadly precision and his cover driving was a treat to the eye (unless you happened to be bowling). Then there was the sweep. Ah ... the Compton sweep! I wonder just how many times in all parts of the world a bowler's heart leapt in exultation as Denis played his sweep at the very last second, and often to a ball arrowing straight at his stumps. And I wonder just how many times joyous anticipation turned to disbelief as the ball was turned to the boundary.'

In 1977, Fred Trueman called Compton 'one of the great instinctive cricketers', and also 'the cheekiest batsman I ever saw'. Trueman rated his 133 at Port-of-Spain in 1954 as an 'an incredible exhibition of batting', a standout performance in a Test in which Everton Weekes, Frank Worrell, Clyde Walcott and Peter May also scored centuries, and Tom Graveney made 92. Later that year, Compton hit his highest Test score, 278, against Pakistan at Trent Bridge. Either side of these big innings, he scored the winning runs at The Oval in 1953 when England regained the Ashes and was at the bowler's end when Godfrey Evans played the series-deciding shot at Adelaide in 1954-55. Of the latter innings, a crucial 34 not out, Moyes wrote in *The Fight for the Ashes 1954-55*, 'Compton batted stubbornly and without the d'Artagnan touch, a Cavalier turned Puritan for the good of the cause.' Again like Miller, Compton's image might have been carefree, but winning mattered.

Jubilant scenes greet Compton and Bill Edrich as they return to the pavilion after England regained the Ashes at The Oval in 1953.

In November 1955, Compton had his right kneecap removed, and it is now stored in the archives at Lord's. This operation allowed him to play two more seasons of first-class cricket, to play in one more Ashes Test — the final Test of 1956, when he scored 94 and 35 not out — and to end his international career with a tour of South Africa. His Test aggregate of 5807 was, at the time of his retirement, cricket's fourth best behind Hammond, Bradman and Hutton. His Test average of 50.06 is excellent by any standards, but his reputation is much greater than that.

DENIS COMPTON (ENGLAND)

Test Cricket

Tests	Inn	NO	Runs	HS	Ave	100	50	Ct	Balls	Runs	Wkts	Ave	Best	5/	10/
78	131	15	5807	278	50.06	17	28	49	2716	1410	25	56.40	5-70	1	—

First-Class Cricket

Mat	Inn	NO	Runs	HS	Ave	100	50	Ct	Balls	Runs	Wkts	Ave	Best	5/	10/
515	839	88	38942	300	51.85	123	183	416	36640	20074	622	32.27	7-36	19	3

The Fifth XI

Ray Lindwall

No. 48

Alan Davidson calls Ray Lindwall 'the best fast bowler I ever saw'. Simple as that. In 1980, Denis Compton described him as 'unequivocally the greatest fast bowler of them all'. In 1982, Harold Larwood rated Dennis Lillee the equal of Lindwall, 'but not ahead of him'. Len Hutton remembered his great Australian rival 'had the capacity to strike at will'. When Lindwall bowled the first ball in a Test match, smoothly accelerating towards the crease before slinging the ball at the batsman, the atmosphere was invariably electric. Alec Bedser, the great medium-pacer, once said of Lindwall: 'In 1953, I think Lindwall was at the peak of his ability. Of course, in 1948 he was quicker. I've never seen anyone as fast having such control. Ray could bowl the short one if he wanted to, but he didn't overdo it. To me, he's the best fast bowler I've seen, because of his variety and control.'

The fast bowlers ranked ahead of Lindwall in this study are all from the 'modern' era, almost post World Series Cricket, if you like: Imran, Marshall, Lillee, Hadlee, Wasim Akram and McGrath. The art of fast bowling might still be evolving. As far as the first 100 years of Test cricket is concerned, however, Lindwall was No. 1. Even the great Lillee had not done enough in his first six years as Test-match bowler to take that ranking away from him.

What separated Ray Lindwall from other fast bowlers was that he could pinpoint his late outswinger at high speed. Fred Trueman reckoned that Wes Hall and Lindwall were the only fast bowlers of his time (besides himself) who could do so. Of course, Lindwall could do much more than that — the fast yorker, the searing bouncer, the change of pace — but the outswinger was his calling card.

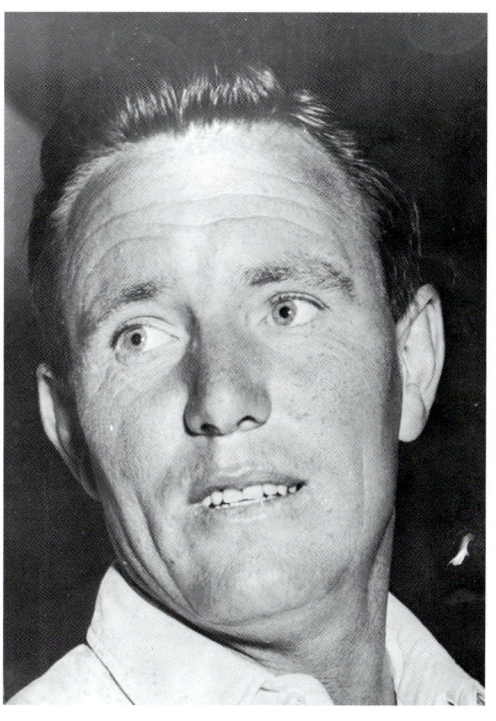

The face and classic action of Australia's greatest post-war fast bowler before Dennis Lillee.

The 100 Greatest Cricketers

The era between the wars had been dominated by batsmen, with Jack Gregory, Ted McDonald, Harold Larwood and Ken Farnes the only frontline fast bowlers worthy of the adjective. From 1946, things changed, and Don Bradman could hardly believe his luck. In Lindwall and Keith Miller, he had the best two fast men in the game, and with the second new ball now due after just 55 overs, the Australian captain took advantage. The best English batsmen, notably Hutton and Compton, were targeted with short-pitched bowling that would have been frowned upon in the years immediately after bodyline, and because Lindwall was able to marry this intimidation with high-class pace bowling he created a new mould. In Hutton's view, Lindwall bowled the best bouncers he faced: 'They did not go two or three yards over he batsmen's head; you had to play them or be hit.' When England finally found themselves fast men of a similar kind — Frank Tyson, Brian Statham and Fred Trueman — Hutton was captain and they implemented a similar strategy. Later, the West Indies would take the concept of intimidatory bowling to a new level. In this sense, Lindwall paved the way for all the famous quicks of the last six decades, from Tyson to Pakistan's Shoaib Akhtar and Australia's Brett Lee.

England's Frank Tyson leaves the SCG after being struck by a Lindwall bouncer in 1954-55.

Yet it would be so wrong to tag Lindwall as simply a bumper merchant. Of his 228 Test wickets, 98 were bowled, another 31 lbw.

Lindwall was a genuine sporting allrounder. He might have played rugby league for Australia but for the war, and did play 31 first-grade games for the mighty St George club before Bill O'Reilly apparently convinced him to focus on his cricket. Lindwall was also a good enough batsman to slam two Test centuries, and bat 15 times at No. 7. Lindwall actually scored a Test hundred before Miller, in his third Test (100 in the third Ashes Test of 1946-47) to Miller's fifth (141 not out in the fourth match of the same series).

Lindwall's first experience of Test cricket had been as a spectator, when with his older brother Jack (another outstanding footballer) he ventured to the Sydney Cricket Ground for the second day of the first bodyline Test. This was a famous day, as Stan McCabe scored 60 of the last 70 runs of the Australian innings while Larwood and Bill Voce bowled bodyline, and for an impressionable 11-year-old lad who opened the bowling for his junior team, the contrast between the Englishmen and Australia's mainly slow attack must have been stark. Years later, Lindwall admitted he was captivated by Larwood: 'He was the most famous fast bowler in the world and I naturally wanted to copy him.'

Perhaps Lindwall's greatest day in cricket came at The Oval in 1948, when he took 6-20 as England crashed to 52 all out. Yet at this stage of his career, according to Compton, he was still to master the inswinger. By 1953, however, the lesson had been so well learned he stunned the crowd at Headingley by bowling the local hero, Hutton, second ball of the fourth Test with

The Fifth XI

a wicked inswinging yorker. 'One wonders once more at Lindwall's amazing capacity to bowl this ball whenever he feels like it,' wrote the former Test batsman and journalist, Jack Fingleton. Lindwall took 5-54 in that innings, one of 12 occasions he took five wickets in a Test innings. The first time had come, fittingly, at the SCG when he took 7-63 against the Englishmen in 1946-47; the last occurred nearly 10 years later at Madras, when he ran through India's second innings to claim 7-43. Lindwall led Australia in the following Test of that series, at Bombay, filling in for Ian Johnson, but the following season he was a shock omission from the team that toured South Africa, even though he had taken 212 Test wickets — just four short of Clarrie Grimmett's Australian record — at 22.16. This decision cost him any chance to be the full-time captain, but he still fought back to play two Ashes Tests in 1958-59 and then tour India and Pakistan with Richie Benaud's Australian team.

Bradman's 'Invincibles' of 1948, featuring Lindwall (back row, fourth player from left), Keith Miller (back row, second player from right), Don Bradman (front row, fourth from left) and Neil Harvey (front row, far right).

'He had the subtleties of a slow bowler's mind,' said Compton of Lindwall. '(He) raised what is considered to be the labouring force of cricket to an art form with his tactical shrewdness, control and variations.' After the 1970-71 Ashes series ended, Australia's newest fast bowler, Dennis Lillee, walked up to Keith Miller seeking advice about the craft. Lillee asked for Ray Lindwall's address, saying, 'He might be able to teach me how to bowl.'

Given all that Lillee achieved in the seasons that followed, one assumes that the advice he got must have been okay. Most certainly, he could not have sought guidance from a better man.

RAY LINDWALL (AUSTRALIA)

Test Cricket

Tests	Inn	NO	Runs	HS	Ave	100	50	Ct	Balls	Runs	Wkts	Ave	Best	5/	10/
61	84	13	1502	118	21.15	2	5	26	13650	5251	228	23.03	7-38	12	—

First-Class Cricket

Mat	Inn	NO	Runs	HS	Ave	100	50	Ct	Balls	Runs	Wkts	Ave	Best	5/	10/
228	270	39	5042	134*	21.83	5	19	123	43215	16956	794	21.36	7-20	34	2

No. 49 Kumar Shri Ranjitsinhji

In 1900, after 23 years of Test cricket, 16 players had scored 800 runs during their careers. Only two of these men had a batting average of more than 37. One of these was Surrey's Tom Hayward, who after an excellent series against Australia in 1899 (413 runs at 68.83, with two centuries), had scored 976 Test-match runs at 44.36. The other was the Indian, Kumar Shri Ranjitsinhji, known as 'Ranji', who in 12 Tests had compiled 970 runs at 53.89.

Ranji brought a grace to world cricket it had not seen before.

It is not the intention here to study Ranji's life as His Highness The Jam Saheb of Nawanagar, the question marks over whether he was entitled to that title and the manner in which he managed his life before he became an Indian prince. Simon Wilde's superb book *Ranji: A Genius Rich and Strange* offers a well-researched and unbiased study of these aspects of the great batsman's life. Further, while the fact Ranji was the first non-white sportsman outside boxing to achieve international fame is highly significant, as was the fact that he became the first Indian to achieve a genuine international profile, the focus here is on runs and style more than on racial or political prejudice he had to overcome.

If Ranji didn't introduce the late cut and leg glance to cricket, he certainly turned them into an art form. He became a master of back-foot play, going right back on his stumps to not just defend but to elegantly place the ball into gaps when the general view was that forward defence, bad and pad together like Arthur Shrewsbury, was a more effective way to go. When he arrived at Cambridge from India in 1888, Ranji had hardly played serious cricket, but so hard did he work on his game that when he debuted for Sussex, against the MCC at Lord's seven years later, he scored 77 and 150 and was suddenly a contender for the England side. His Test debut came the following year, against Australia at Manchester, and with scores of 62 and 154 not out he became the first man to score 200 runs on his first appearance. On the third day, he went from 41 runs to 154 in the 130-minute pre-lunch session, from 50 to 100 in 45 minutes.

Ranji scored more than 1000 first-class runs in every English season from 1895 to 1904 (including more than 3000 runs twice and more than 2000 runs a further three times), and in Australia on his one cricket trip there, in 1897-98, when he scored 1157 runs at 60.89, including 457 runs at 50.78 in the Tests. In 1896, he broke WG Grace's 25-year-old record aggregate for a single season when he hit 2780 runs at 57.92. From 1905, Ranji

The Fifth XI

was obliged to spend more time in India but in the two seasons in which he played regularly (1908 and 1912) he again went passed 1000 first-class runs for the season. His name, and that of Charles Fry, became synonymous with huge run-getting at Sussex, but as Fry almost proudly admitted years later, 'There were no eyes for me. I played in Ranji's shadow.'

Ranji was one of *Wisden's* cricketers of the year for 1896. In its tribute, the almanack wrote, 'As a batsman Ranjitsinhji is himself alone, being quite individual and distinctive in his style of play. He can scarcely be pointed to as a safe model for young and aspiring batsmen, his peculiar and almost unique skill depending in large measure on extreme keenness of eye, combined with great power and flexibility of wrist. For any ordinary player to attempt to turn good length balls off the middle stump as he does, would be futile and disastrous. To Ranjitsinhji on a fast wicket, however, everything seems possible, and if the somewhat too-freely-used word genius can with any propriety be employed in connection with cricket, it surely applies to the young Indian's batting.'

Ranji had been left out of England's team for the opening Test of 1896, apparently because political pressure was put on the MCC committee not to choose him because he was from India. This was not so much a question of racial prejudice as a fear of an increasing Indian influence on matters of British Empire. When he did come into the Test side for the second Test at Old Trafford — because the Lancashire committee, perhaps influenced by public opinion, insisted — he was superb; despite his slight build he hit powerfully, his timing apparently coming through his wrists because there was no extravagant flourish about his play. Every time, whatever the Australians bowled at him, he was in the right position and then there was just a flick of those wrists and the ball was gone. He was masterful at putting the ball into the gaps. 'He seemed to take a fiendish delight in putting the ball from where we had moved a fieldsman,' remembered one of the Australians, Frank Iredale. 'His play was a revelation to us, with his marvellous cutting and his extraordinary hitting to leg,' George Giffen marvelled. 'I have never seen anything to equal it.'

To the world of cricket he will always be known simply as 'Ranji'.

To get into Australia in 1897, Ranji had to pay a special levy imposed on non-whites, but with that account settled he scored 189 in the first match of the tour, against South Australia in Adelaide, and then 175 in 223 minutes in the first Test (despite suffering a bout of quinsy that meant he came in at No. 7). Later, he had to overcome an injured hand, and after stating in a newspaper article that local fast bowler Ernest Jones was a chucker he was subjected to some spiteful barracking, some of it racially motivated, but still he finished the series with 457 runs at 50.78, the third highest aggregate for the series behind his close friend Archie MacLaren and Australia's Joe Darling. Ranji was again second in the English aggregates in the 1899 Ashes series (behind Hayward), and except for an ill-fated return to Test cricket in 1902, when he was out of form and totally distracted by a personal financial crisis, that was the end of Ranji's Test career.

It is no coincidence that the drawer of this caricature focused on Ranji's elegance on the legside.

He is commemorated today by the Ranji Trophy, the premier prize in Indian domestic cricket, which was introduced in 1934 (the year after his death) even though he played no first-class cricket in the country of his birth. Before Ranji, there was no indication that India could produce a world-class cricketer, so he became, in the words of the cricket writer and historian Mihir Bose, 'India's cricket ambassador'. He did this through his style, his glamour, but most of all through his unique skill. One of the best English amateur batsmen of his time, Gilbert Jessop, wrote of Ranji, 'He was indisputedly the greatest genius who ever stepped on to the cricket field, the most brilliant figure in what, I believe, was cricket's most brilliant period.'

KUMAR SHRI RANJITSINHJI (ENGLAND)

Test Cricket

Tests	Inn	NO	Runs	HS	Ave	100	50	Ct	Balls	Runs	Wkts	Ave	Best	5/	10/
15	26	4	989	175	44.95	2	6	13	97	39	1	39.00	1-23	–	–

First-Class Cricket

Mat	Inn	NO	Runs	HS	Ave	100	50	Ct	Balls	Runs	Wkts	Ave	Best	5/	10/
307	500	62	24692	285*	56.37	72	109	234	8062	4601	133	34.59	6-53	4	–

The Fifth XI

Richie Benaud

No. 50

It has been quite a trick by Richie Benaud to become such a mighty figure in the cricket media that we sometimes almost forget what a superb cricketer he was. Perhaps only a crafty leg-spinner and 'lucky' captain could have managed it. As far as this top 100 is concerned, we are not concerned with Benaud, the impeccable TV host, smooth and discerning commentator, and perceptive journalist, but with the classy allrounder who completed the double of 2000 runs/200 wickets in Tests in December 1963, seven-and-a-half years before it was achieved by anyone else. Today, 15 cricketers have done this double; only two — Benaud and Garry Sobers — appeared in a Test match before 1971.

Benaud's Test career took a long while to get going. His record from 1952 to 1956 suggests he was a mediocre leg-spinner and an inconsistent though hard-hitting batsman, a promising player who might have received more opportunities than he was entitled to. But he usually did just enough to keep his place — batting okay if his bowling was collared, getting a couple of wickets if the runs dried up, always fielding superbly. When he left England in 1956 after what for Australia had been a miserable tour, his Test record read: 23 Tests; 755 runs at 20.97; 49 wickets at 34.44. The selectors were anxious for a return on their investment.

To a degree, Benaud had been a victim of circumstances. For his first two seasons in the Test side, he was usually third or fourth change bowler at best, coming on after veterans from Bradman's famous 1948 side such as Ray Lindwall, Keith Miller, Bill Johnston and Doug Ring. Ian Johnson — another 'Invincible' and an off-spinner — was recalled to lead Australia after Lindsay Hassett retired after the 1953 tour of England, and he usually bowled himself before any other slow bowler. A watershed came in India on the way home from the '56 Ashes tour, when Benaud found himself bowling first change during the opening morning of the first Test at Madras. He took 7-72, and then 6-52 and 5-53 in the third Test at Calcutta, giving him 23 wickets at 16.87 for the three-match series.

Between 1956 and 1963, Benaud's leg-breaks were a dominant part of each Australian summer.

With Johnson retiring, most critics expected the next Australian captain to be one of Neil Harvey, Ron Archer or Benaud, with Harvey the popular choice. Instead the selectors went for Ian Craig, part of youth policy brought on by the retirement of Miller, Johnson and keeper Gil Langley and the decline of Lindwall. Benaud was suddenly a senior player and he responded in South Africa in 1957-58 with one of the finest all-round performances in a Test series. In the fourth Test, a critical game with Australia leading 1-0 in the series, he hit 100 batting four and took 4-70 (second change) and 5-84 (first change) to inspire the side to a 10-wicket win. For the series, he had 30 wickets at 21.93 with four five-wicket hauls and scored 329 runs at 54.83 with two centuries. 'It was on this tour that Richie really emerged as the world's best leg-spinner,' recalled Harvey in 1963.

Benaud goes round the wicket to win the fourth Test at Old Trafford in 1961.

'Richie earned this success with his sweat,' keeper Wally Grout wrote in his autobiography. 'He was the most enthusiastic and diligent member of the team, the first to practice and the last to leave. He was also the best spin bowler I have seen.'

This was also Alan Davidson's 'breakout' series, as he took 25 wickets at 17.00. The Benaud-Davidson combination evolved into the best fast man/slow man bowling partnership Australia ever had until Glenn McGrath and Shane Warne. Benaud's control was as good as any leg-spinner before Warne, and though he didn't spin either his leg break or his wrong 'un all that far, it did turn far enough. His high delivery could sometimes generate unusual bounce and got the ball to dip and drift, while his experiments with the 'flipper', a ball squirted out by the thumb and the index finger, paid handsome dividends during the second half of his career. Again like Warne, he disguised this ball better than his googly.

After Ian Craig was struck down by hepatitis, Benaud became Australian captain and first up he stunned England in 1958-59 by leading his men to a emphatic 4-0 triumph. While his batting return declined (he made only five fifties and no hundreds as captain, in 28 Tests), one of his greatest strengths as a skipper was that he was aware he was one of his team's leading bowlers and gave himself plenty of overs, unlike some captains who get preoccupied trying to give everyone else a fair go. Benaud took 31 wickets against the Englishmen, and then in eight trying Tests in Pakistan and India managed 47 more as Australia won both series. His contribution as captain to the clash with Frank Worrell's West Indians at home in 1960-61 is well remembered, as the two teams produced a run of inspiring and entertaining cricket. Benaud took 23 wickets, but most important for cricket history was his decision to go for the win when Australia needed 123 with four wickets in hand at tea on the last day of the first Test. He and Davidson had the batting skill to almost get Australia home, and then came the last-over drama that ended in Test cricket's first tie.

The key wicket at Manchester: Dexter, caught Grout, for 76. From 1-150, England fell to 201 all out, with Benaud taking 6-70.

The Fifth XI

Benaud's second famous performance in nine months came at Manchester in 1961, when he went around the wicket to aim at the rough outside the right-handers' pads, and took 5-12 in 25 balls to win a Test many thought lost. It was after this win that some people said facetiously that he was a lucky captain. The truth was that he had the courage to back his players, and himself, which sometimes turned around games, even series. 'He regularly thumbed his nose at convention, and often took the initiative when, by all the rules, he should have been on the defensive,' recalled Davidson. Jim Laker wrote in 1979 that Benaud was the best captain of Australia he'd seen, 'and that included Sir Donald Bradman'. Benaud had the diplomat's skill of being generous while never being too charitable. He always played Test cricket as hard as he knew; all the risks he took were calculated. As a trained journalist, he quickly realised that the cricket world was changing, especially when it came to his and his team's relationship with the media. He knew what the public wanted *and* what was good for the game.

Benaud during the fifth Ashes Test of 2005, when his unique career as a master player, captain and commentator was acknowledged by the full house at The Oval.

Benaud had struggled with fibrositis in his shoulder during the 1961 tour, and though he continued on until the end of the 1963-64 season, he was not quite the dynamic bowler he had been from the end of the 1956 Ashes series to the start of the '61 trip. In that 'golden' period, he took 170 wickets in 31 Tests, at 22.83, the figures of a genuinely great bowler. When you add his batting, the leadership, plus all that he has given the game in the years since his retirement, you have one of the true giants of the game.

RICHIE BENAUD (AUSTRALIA)

Test Cricket

Tests	Inn	NO	Runs	HS	Ave	100	50	Ct	Balls	Runs	Wkts	Ave	Best	5/	10/
63	97	7	2201	122	24.46	3	9	65	19108	6704	248	27.03	7-72	16	1

First-Class Cricket

Mat	Inn	NO	Runs	HS	Ave	100	50	Ct	Balls	Runs	Wkts	Ave	Best	5/	10/
259	365	44	11719	187	36.51	23	61	254	60481	23370	945	24.73	7-18	56	9

The 100 Greatest Cricketers

No. 51 Fred Trueman

Fred Trueman was the first man to take 300 Test wickets. Considering the fact that he played in 67 Tests between his first appearance, against India in 1952, and his last, versus New Zealand in 1965, but in that time England played 118 Tests, he should have taken many more. Few if any great players have been treated so disdainfully. In his first five years as a Test cricketer, it seemed the selectors needed little reason to omit him, sometimes none at all. In his last five years, his reputation was such that he was judged by different standards to other bowlers. In 1961, he was sacked two Tests after taking 11 Australian wickets in a match. He missed five major tours during his career — Australia in 1954-55, South Africa in 1956-57 and 1964-65, India and Pakistan in 1961-62, India in 1963-64 — but always came back for more.

One of cricket's most technically admirable bowling actions.

'Trueman and Statham', as in Brian Statham, is remembered today as one of England's best ever pace-bowling partnerships. Statham was a superb fast-medium bowler, more seam than swing, renowned for his accuracy. He, too, often struggled to win the selectors' favour. Statham made his debut before Trueman and played his final Test after Trueman's farewell, and appeared in 70 Tests; there were no less than 53 Tests between 1952 and 1965 when England went into the game without one, sometimes both of them. The pace bowlers who took the new ball for England during this time ranged from the famous to the forgotten: Alec Bedser, Trevor Bailey, Frank Tyson, Peter Loader, Alan Moss, 'Dusty' Rhodes, Les Jackson, Jack Flavell, Derek Shackleton, Len Coldwell, David Larter, John Price, Fred Rumsey, Ian Thomson, John Snow. Between 1954 and 1965, Trueman blamed his spells on the sidelines on the fact that he spoke his mind. He had certainly been brash and overly aggressive, sometimes rude, on his first overseas tour, to the Caribbean in 1953-54, and some people in high places took a long while to forget about it.

In 1952, Trueman had taken 29 wickets in his first four Tests, including 8-31 in one innings at Old Trafford. At Leeds, in his maiden Test, he and Bedser took the first four wickets before India scored a run and *Wisden* thought he might become a 'second Harold Larwood'. But in the ensuing four years, he played in just seven Tests, before taking 22 wickets in the 1957 home series against the West Indies. At Trent Bridge, in a match in which Peter Richardson (126), Tom Graveney (258), Peter May (104), Frank Worrell (191) and Collie Smith (168) all scored big

The Fifth XI

hundreds, Trueman took 5-63 and 4-80. A full seven years after his debut, the Trueman-Statham partnership finally came into its own when Trueman faced India again and captured 24 wickets in a five-Test series. Statham took 17 wickets, despite missing the third and fourth matches through injury, India were embarrassed 5-0 and Trueman and Statham were regulars in the England team until the end of the tour to Australian and New Zealand in 1962-63.

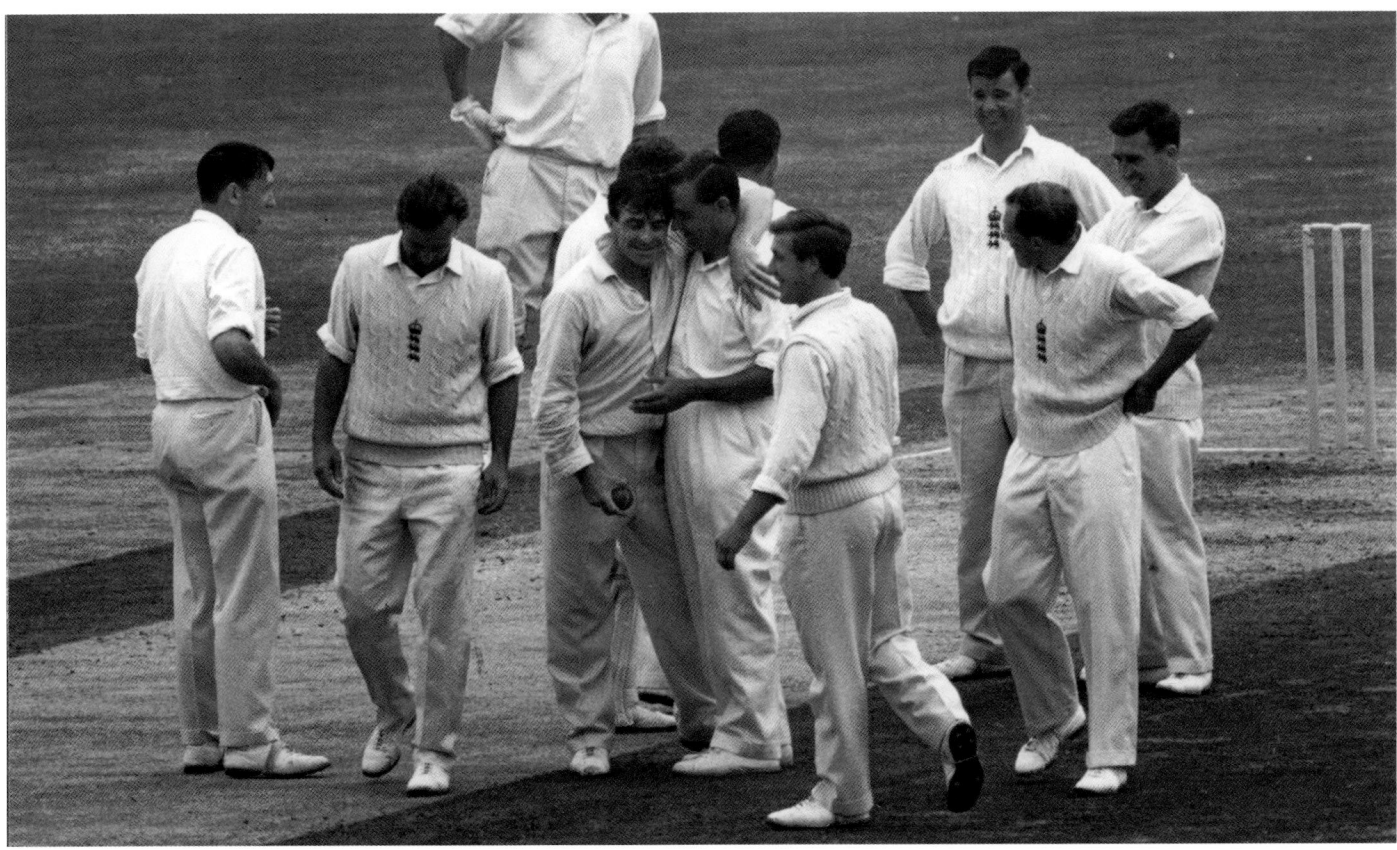

The pair were at their finest in the Caribbean in 1959-60. While Statham was outstanding in the three Tests he played (missing the first and fifth through injury), Trueman was simply magnificent. His 21 wickets for the rubber look quite good on paper, but statistics don't tell the true story of how he often rose above the agitated crowds and stormy atmosphere to spearhead an English counterattack. He was especially grand in the second Test at Port-of-Spain, when he took 5-35 as the home side collapsed to 112 all out in reply to England 382. On day three, the crowd rioted; four days later, the West Indies lost by 256 runs, the result that ultimately decided the series.

As good a bowler as Statham was, the general consensus seems to be that Trueman was superior. 'I put Trueman in front of Statham because he was more often capable of producing the type of delivery to defeat the best batsmen, no matter how well set,' reckoned Denis Compton. Bob Simpson agreed with this assessment. 'Both fine and classical bowlers, both always capable of getting quality batsmen out,' he wrote in *The Reasons Why* in 1996. 'Fred, though, was the more likely to do it because his methods were a little more unpredictable.'

Trueman with Colin Cowdrey, the man who took the catch that gave him his 300th Test wicket, v Australia at The Oval, 1964.

John Arlott's biography of Trueman, *Fred: Portrait of a Fast Bowler*, is one of the best cricket books ever written, not least because the author had a very rich character to portray. The chapter entitled 'In His Pomp' captures a tremendous competitor and a master of his craft. 'At times he was lit by the fire of greatness,' wrote Arlott of his subject. 'The most stirring memories of him recall days when, in face of completely discouraging opposition, conditions, and state of the game, over-bowled and ill-supported, he tried harder than any captain could fairly ask, and sometimes succeeded beyond the bounds of reasonable possibility.'

The 300th wicket: Neil Hawke, caught Cowdrey at first slip.

Trueman could bowl fast, especially early in his career when he roared in from a long run, but for the most part he was just below express. Only just, though, and at this pace he could move the ball both ways off the pitch as effectively as any medium pacer (which he never was, unless he needed to be). He had command of inswing and prodigious outswing, something the bowlers of the 21st century cannot do, could get the ball to lift quickly and learned how to disguise an adroitly delivered slower ball. One of his greatest performances was at Leeds in 1961, when against Australia he took 5-58 and 6-30 on a slow deck. In the first innings, he bowled fast and took his wickets by skill and reputation; in the second, he reverted to cutters delivered at various speeds to snare 5-0 in a spell of 24 balls. Two years later, during his last great series (34 wickets at 17.47), he took 5-75 and 7-44 at Edgbaston against Frank Worrell's champion West Indies side, after shortening his run-up but not so much his pace on the final day to win a match that seemed to be heading for a draw.

Frank Tyson saw Trueman as something of a Muhammad Ali of fast bowling. 'Whilst he did not always state he was the greatest,' he wrote in 1968, 'one always felt that his mastery was founded on this confidence.' Crucially, behind this bravado — and a liking for showmanship that won him many fans in the outer — was great skill, a shrewd cricket instinct, and that stamina that allowed him to bowl forever. From the start of the 1959 English season to the end of the 1963 English season, he bowled 37,183 deliveries in first-class matches (the equivalent of almost 6200 six-ball overs). Few men are better equipped to sneer when the stars of today complain about having to play too much cricket. Little wonder that when asked if anyone would ever break his Test wicket-taking record, he replied flatly, 'If anyone does, they'll be bloody tired.'

FRED TRUEMAN (ENGLAND)

Test Cricket

Tests	Inn	NO	Runs	HS	Ave	100	50	Ct	Balls	Runs	Wkts	Ave	Best	5/	10/
67	85	14	981	39*	13.82	–	–	64	15178	6625	307	21.58	8-31	17	3

First-Class Cricket

Mat	Inn	NO	Runs	HS	Ave	100	50	Ct	Balls	Runs	Wkts	Ave	Best	5/	10/
603	713	120	9231	104	15.57	3	26	439	99701	42154	2304	18.30	8-28	126	25

The Fifth XI

Barry Richards

No. 52

Of the 100 cricketers featured in this book, South Africa's Barry Richards has the least Test experience. He makes the list largely on reputation, and because, though he played so little Test cricket (because his country was banned from international sport from 1971 to 1992), he was still able to produce some extraordinary performances on the rare occasions he did play at the highest level. His Test career amounted to four matches, all against Australia at home in early 1970. Yet, many who saw him suggest he was among the best of all time. 'Greg Chappell, Viv and Barry Richards would have been great, truly great, batsmen in any era,' argued Jack Fingleton in 1981. 'Once in two or three generations there comes a virtuoso batsman who beguiles even his opponents. Such is Barry Richards,' wrote John Arlott, the doyen of English commentators. 'He was a great player,' said Garry Sobers, who then added, '"Great" is a misused word. I see it applied to so many players who have not qualified for such an accolade.'

Just four Tests, but still a certainty for any top 100.

In 1970, Sobers and Graeme Pollock were the best batsmen in the world. Some, including Sobers, expected the 24-year-old Richards to soon be a contender for that title. When he walked out to bat in a Test for the first time, against an Australian team that had beaten the West Indies and India in the previous 12 months, South Africa had not played a Test since early 1967. Given the protests that were growing ever stronger about the South African government's apartheid policies, there was no guarantee that they would play too many more. To some, this series between Ali Bacher's South Africans and Bill Lawry's Australians was a battle for the cricket world title. For Barry Richards, it was his last chance at Test level, if only he'd known it at the time.

South Africa won the first Test by 170 runs, with Richards scoring 29 and 32. Less than two weeks later, he made his mark. In the long history of Test cricket only four men — Trumper, Macartney, Bradman and Majid Khan — have scored a century before lunch on the first day of a Test. At Durban, in his *second ever* Test, the score at lunch was 2-126 and Richards, despite defending throughout the session's penultimate over, was 94 not out. At the time, he cared little for the hundred before lunch, being concerned only about his maiden Test century. This he reached off the fourth ball after play resumed. Had he known his Test career was nearly over, he admitted years later, he might have been more aggressive in those few minutes before the break in play.

The batting in the hour after lunch is celebrated today in South Africa as the greatest ever seen in that country. The strokeplay was awesome and dazzling, Richards and Graeme Pollock almost trying to outdo each other for brilliance, and 103 runs were added before Richards' epic innings ended when Eric Freeman bowled him for 140. Pollock went on to dismember the bowling for 274. After that, Richards hit 65 and 35 in the third Test and 81 and 126 in the fourth, giving him 508 runs for the series, at 72.57. South Africa swept the series.

Richards never again had the challenge of true Test cricket to inspire him. His highlight years came from late 1977 to early 1979, during World Series Cricket, when he played two of his finest hands. In a SuperTest at Perth, Richards opened with Gordon Greenidge. Often when they played together at Hampshire, Richards would let Greenidge take the lead. However, here Richards took 30 less deliveries to reach his hundred, and when Greenidge reached 114 the West Indian had to retire hurt, to be replaced at the crease by Viv Richards.

The comparison between the two Richards had been heavily talked about during this first WSC season. Australian fans had seen Viv in 1975-76, remembered him from the 1975 World Cup final, knew that he'd blasted two double centuries against England in 1976, and seen him smash two hundreds in earlier SuperTests. Barry's reputation in Australia revolved around those Tests in 1970 and one outrageously successful season with South Australia in the Sheffield Shield. Most Australians, if asked who was the better, would have plumped for the West Indian. On this day, at least, they were wrong. In 90 minutes, Viv scored 41 runs, while Barry hit 93 before he miscued Ray Bright to Greg Chappell at long off to be out for 207. In all, 136 of Barry's score had come in boundaries. The scoreboard read 1-369, after 60 overs.

A little more than 12 months later, Richards crafted a superb 110 not out in the 1978-79 SuperTest final at the SCG. This match was as tough a cricket test as has ever been played in Australia, and Richards' batting proved the difference. For most of the game the bowlers were in charge, and the World side were set 224 to win. Richards and Mike Procter, both literally playing the game of their lives, had come together at 4-84 and added 91 before Procter was bowled by Bright. Still a tricky 49 to get, but Richards launched an assault on Gary Gilmour and Dennis Lillee that quickly and brutally won what until then had been a tense affair.

Richards batting for Hampshire in English county cricket.

In all, Richards scored 28,358 first-class runs, at 54.75, with 80 centuries. He scored four centuries in one Currie Cup season four times for Natal. At Hampshire, against Nottinghamshire in 1974, he batted through the innings unbeaten for 225 out of 344, one of three times he batted through a first-class innings. He scored a hundred before lunch nine times, five times on the first day. Twice he scored a century in both innings of a county match. But maybe the most amazing innings of his career was his highest score in first-class cricket, 356 for South Australia against Western Australia in Perth in 1970-71.

The Fifth XI

He scored his first fifty in 70 minutes, but for much of the day he scored quicker and quicker. His century came in 125 minutes, 200 in 209 minutes, 300 in 317 minutes. In all, Richards faced 322 deliveries and hit 44 fours and one six during the day's play. He was the third man to score 300 in one day in an Australian first-class match. Only five men in the history of first-class cricket anywhere had scored more runs in one day than his eventual stumps score of 325 (the most ever is 345 by Charlie Macartney for Australia against Nottinghamshire in 1921).

The WA bowling attack for the match in Perth featured five past, present or future internationals, including Dennis Lillee and Graham McKenzie, who both opened the bowling for Australia that season, and the WA captain Tony Lock, formerly of Surrey, Leicestershire and England. Richards finished that season with 1538 first-class runs, including scores of 224, 356, 146, 155, 178 and 105, at an average of 109.86. His performances that Australian summer, though they weren't at Test level, were more than enough to suggest he was a champion.

Richards wears his World Series Cricket colours during a single-wicket tournament at The Oval in 1979.

BARRY RICHARDS (SOUTH AFRICA)

Test Cricket

Tests	Inn	NO	Runs	HS	Ave	100	50	Ct	Balls	Runs	Wkts	Ave	Best	5/	10/
4	7	–	508	140	72.57	2	2	3	72	26	1	26.00	1-12	–	–

First-Class Cricket

Mat	Inn	NO	Runs	HS	Ave	100	50	Ct	Balls	Runs	Wkts	Ave	Best	5/	10/
339	576	58	28358	356	54.75	80	152	367	6120	2886	77	37.48	7-63	1	–

No. 53 Arthur Shrewsbury

Next to WG Grace, Arthur Shrewsbury was England's finest batsmen of the 19th century, a fact summed up by one simple, famous remark. It came from WG himself, after he was asked with whom, of all the men he's shared a partnership, he'd most like to bat. 'Give me Arthur,' he quickly replied.

Few if any batsman in 19th-century cricket were harder to dismiss bowled than was Arthur Shrewsbury.

Shrewsbury had made his first appearance at Lord's in 1873, aged 17, for the 'Colts of England' against the MCC. Within two years he was a regular in county cricket, but it wasn't until he toured Australia under Alfred Shaw's leadership in 1881-82 — a tour he helped organise — that his true quality came to the fore. Never an overly robust individual, the warm weather seemed to invigorate him, starting with the second first-class game of the tour, against Victoria in Melbourne. This was the first time in Australia, and just the third ever, that a team won after being forced to follow on. The home side, batting first, totaled 251, Shaw's team struggled to 146, and in the second innings were 4-73 when Shrewsbury arrived in the middle. Despite the awkward pitch, he proceeded to make 80 not out, in a little more than three hours from an innings score of 198, while none of his partners made more than nine. Victoria crashed to 6-7 and finally 75 all out resulting in a stunning win for the England XI by 18 runs.

Later in the tour, Shrewsbury played another masterly innings on a wet MCG wicket, this time scoring 72 not out before the home side were shot out for just 92. In the third Test match, he top-scored in both innings (82 out of 188 and 47 out of 134), the first man to do so in a Test, but otherwise for him it was a largely frustrating series. England failed to gain a victory and his missed catch of Percy McDonnell in the third Test, when the Australian went on to score 147 of an innings total of 260, was just about the most crucial moment of the entire summer.

Shrewsbury didn't play Test cricket again until 1884, but by 1886, the first English season in which he topped the first-class averages, he was, besides Grace, recognised as the best batsman in the country. He was, on averages at least, the season's No. 1 on five occasions between 1886 and 1892 (missing the 1888 season when, with Alfred Shaw, he organised a tour to Australia by a British rugby football team), including three times straight from 1890. In 1887 he averaged 78.71 for the first-class season, with eight hundreds. Yet, perhaps more so than any other batsman of his time, it was not the weight of runs but more the manner in which he so reliably accumulated them on wet and dangerous tracks that set him apart.

'A great player on all wickets, it was on difficult pitches that he was seen at his very best,' wrote HS Altham in 1926. 'His mastery of the back stroke, which he played with a good deal of wrist action rather than in the now popular dead-bat method; his capacity for watching the ball right onto the bat; his inexhaustible patience — these combined to make him probably the greatest batsman on sticky wickets that has ever lived. For, indeed, some of the best contemporary judges are agreed that some of his innings under these conditions could have been played by no other batsman, not even the Champion himself.'

The Fifth XI

It is said that Shrewsbury, as brave and pragmatic as they come, revolutionised the use of the pad-play when on the defensive. 'His judgment of the length of bowling was almost unequalled,' was *Wisden's* view. 'It was said of him that he seemed to see the ball closer up to the bat than any other player.' Shrewsbury also knew where his stumps were, so with the laws of the day demanding that ball pitch wicket to wicket for an lbw to be achieved, he could be awfully difficult to dislodge.

In the second Test of 1886, at Lord's, against an Australian attack featuring Fred Spofforth, Shrewsbury made a then England Test record score of 164. It was his second Test hundred, following on from the 105 not out he'd scored in Melbourne (when he became the first England captain to make a Test-match century) 16 months earlier. At Lord's, he was masterful on a pitch that was at various times dangerous, slow and wet during his seven-hour innings. It all came alike to him, but not the Australians, who were promptly bowled out for 121 and 126 when it was their turn to bat. Seven years later, again on an awkward pitch at Lord's and this time against the 'Terror' Turner, Shrewsbury scored 106 and 81, in the process becoming the first Englishman to score three Test hundreds, and the first batsman to score 1000 runs in England-Australia Tests. Shrewsbury had becoming Test cricket's leading runscorer in 1886, surpassing Australia's Billy Murdoch, and he kept the record until Joe Darling scored his 1278th Test run, at his hometown Adelaide Oval in January 1902.

Sadly, by the following year, Arthur Shrewsbury was dead. In the 1902 season, at age 46, he scored five centuries and averaged exactly 50, better even than Victor Trumper, whose efforts that year in England were regarded as phenomenal. However, during the winter both Shrewsbury's health and his mindset deteriorated, and in May 1903 he shot himself, first in the chest, then in the head. The best guess was that he had convinced himself he had an incurable disease, though experts could find no evidence of that. The 1904 *Wisden* wondered whether the impending end of his career might have been a factor in his grave depression.

The renowned cricket historian Peter Wynne-Thomas, in his book *Give me Arthur: A Biography of Arthur Shrewsbury*, argues that Shrewsbury 'created modern professional batsmanship and, over 20 years, developed it to perfection'. If you accept this argument — and there is much evidence to support it — then it is difficult not to rank Shrewsbury among the finest batsman of them all. As talented, pragmatic and professional as he was, it is hard to imagine that he would not have been able to adapt to the demands of any cricket era.

ARTHUR SHREWSBURY (ENGLAND)

Test Cricket

Tests	Inn	NO	Runs	HS	Ave	100	50	Ct	Balls	Runs	Wkts	Ave	Best	5/	10/
23	40	4	1277	164	35.47	3	4	29	12	2	–	–	0-2	–	–

First-Class Cricket

Mat	Inn	NO	Runs	HS	Ave	100	50	Ct	Balls	Runs	Wkts	Ave	Best	5/	10/
498	813	90	26505	267	36.66	59	115	377	16	2	–	–	0-0	–	–

The 100 Greatest Cricketers

No. 54 Alec Bedser

In his book *Cricket Crossfire*, Keith Miller told a story against Don Bradman that related to Bradman's dismissal in the fourth Ashes Test of 1946-47, at the Adelaide Oval. England had made 460, and Bradman was the second wicket to fall, for a duck, bowled by a delivery that swung in late to pitch on leg stump and hit the top of middle and off. 'When he came back to the dressing room, Bradman was at great pains to tell everybody that he considered this was one of the best balls ever bowled to him,' Miller wrote. 'Personally, I thought that was a lot of blarney. He would have done better to keep the opinion to himself. He did no service to those who still had to face Alec.'

This page and opposite: Two views of Bedser's classic swing-bowler's action, a style of bowling that is as rare today as was high-class leg spin in the 1980s.

'Alec' was Alec Bedser. Bradman never altered his opinion about the delivery, calling it in his autobiography published in 1950, 'the finest ever to take my wicket'. As for Miller's view, it seems somewhat churlish and sadly typical of his anti-Bradman mindset. The Don was one of the sharpest cricket brains in the business, and he would hardly have set out to deliberately destroy dressing-room morale. More likely, he was bowled by a beauty, and in a series where Australia had been dominating saw the bonus in England having a bowler who could conjure up such a freakish delivery. For the next five years, until the emergence of fast bowlers such as Fred Trueman, Brian Statham and Frank Tyson and the maturity of Jim Laker, Bedser carried the England attack.

Of course, this was often hard work, a fact reflected in his figures. Going into the 1951 home series against South Africa, Bedser had taken 132 wickets at 29.97, with a strike rate of a wicket every 81 deliveries. People liked to compare him to Maurice Tate, the outstanding English medium pacer of the 1920s, noting especially the way both bowlers appeared to get the ball to accelerate off the pitch, but not even Bradman was game to suggest that the new man might have been superior. Bradman did point out that Bedser had a higher action than Tate, which gave him more lift off the pitch, though he beleievd that Tate had the better outswinger.

In the next four seasons, 1951 to 1954, involving home series against South Africa, India, Australia and Pakistan, Bedser captured 99 wickets at 16.53, with a strike rate of 47.20. In the Ashes series of 1953, Bedser took 39 wickets, including 14-99 in the opening Test at Trent Bridge, producing a leg-cutter to hit Lindsay Hassett's off stump in Australia's first innings that might have even better than the ball that

The Fifth XI

bowled Bradman. Hassett was past his hundred at the time, having batted for more than six and a half hours. Keeper Godfrey Evans didn't appeal so much as offer a shout of astonishment as a bail went flying, while Hassett later quipped that the ball had moved three ways.

Len Hutton made the point that Bedser was the best medium pacer in the world from 1948 to 1953 on all wickets. When the wicket was flat and hard, he could swing the ball and was a workhorse, as fit and enduring as any bowler who ever lived; if there was a little in the wicket for him he was precise and dangerous, mostly because of that famous leg-cutter. Denis Compton couldn't recall him bowling a really bad ball. Because of World War II, Bedser didn't make his Test debut until a month before his 28th birthday, yet he was often such a one-man band that in 1953 he went past Sydney Barnes' England record (189) and then Clarrie Grimmett's world record (216) for the most Test wickets. In the only series of his career when he consistently had a fast bowler working with him — against India in 1952, when Trueman made his debut — he took 20 wickets in four Tests at 13.95.

For left-handers, he could be a nightmare, as they had to always be wary of the ball that cut in to them, while also trying to cope with what was the inswinger to the right-hander, the outswinger to them. Compton told of a spell in Melbourne on the 1950-51 tour when Neil Harvey couldn't get bat on ball, as hard as he tried, while Arthur Morris became known as 'Bedser's bunny', falling to the Englishman an amazing 18 times in 21 Tests. Bedser also had Bradman caught behind square on the legside in five consecutive Test innings, once in 1946-47 and four times in 1948, as the great batsman tried to cover the leg-cutter but kept falling victim to the inswinger that bounced more than he expected.

In paying tribute to Bedser in his book Just My Story, Hutton told his version of that Adelaide Test of 1946-47. He recalled that the game was played in searing heat. 'Nevertheless, Alec bowled long and unsparingly. He put so much effort into his bowling that, after one particularly exacting over, he staggered from the wicket to an incorrect position in the field, rather like a boxer going to the wrong corner at the end of a punishing round. He was too exhausted to notice his mistake, yet he carried on and was able, miraculously, to produce the wonder ball that captured Don Bradman's wicket.'

Bedser's accuracy brought him nearly 100 Test wickets through bowled or lbw decisions.

Hutton's memory is awry here, because the key wicket fell with the Australian score on just 18. However, Bedser did go on to bowl 30 eight-ball overs during the innings, so he was entitled to be weary. When he retired in 1955, no Test bowler, fast, medium-pace or slow, had sent down more deliveries. Few cricketers have better combined enormous skill with such a brave and enduring spirit, but after Hutton went into the first Ashes Test of 1954-55 with four quicker bowlers — Bedser, Tyson, Statham and Trevor Bailey — and was thrashed by an innings, he dropped Bedser for the rest of the series. Instead, he relied on pure speed, England retained the Ashes by three Tests to one, and the veteran medium pacer's international career was all but over.

This raises the question as to whether a bowler of Bedser's ilk would be successful in the modern era. Had Len Hutton recognised earlier than most that the game was changing? Perhaps, but given the absence of quality swing bowlers in 21st century cricket, if Bedser re-emerged today, most likely he'd be highly successful because he'd be one of a kind. No one in the modern game can swing the ball like he could. His accuracy and understanding of his craft would make him highly effective in limited-overs cricket, while a batsman who struggles to cope with the concept of 'reverse swing' might find Alec Bedser's special brand of bowling particularly difficult to deal with.

ALEC BEDSER (ENGLAND)
Test Cricket

Tests	Inn	NO	Runs	HS	Ave	100	50	Ct	Balls	Runs	Wkts	Ave	Best	5/	10/
51	71	15	714	79	12.75	–	1	26	15918	5876	236	24.90	7-44	15	3

First-Class Cricket

Mat	Inn	NO	Runs	HS	Ave	100	50	Ct	Balls	Runs	Wkts	Ave	Best	5/	10/
485	576	181	5735	126	14.52	1	13	289	106118	39279	1924	20.42	8-18	96	16

The Fifth XI

Syed Kirmani

No. 55

'Obviously, the quality of a wicketkeeper is judged when he is standing up to the wickets,' Syed Kirmani once said. 'Anybody can stop the fastest of balls. Standing behind, the keeper has enough time to move and stop the ball. But for a spinner, only a fraction of a second is available to collect the ball and complete the stumping.'

Kirmani is regarded by most experts on the subcontinent to be India's best ever wicketkeeper. He made his reputation in the 1970s keeping to the four great spinners — Bedi, Chandrasekhar, Prasanna and Venkat — and then into the '80s maintained his excellence both as an accomplished gloveman (to both spinners and the pace of Kapil Dev) and a worthy late-order batsman. In a time when men such as Alan Knott, Rod Marsh and Jeffrey Dujon were confirming that a Test-class keeper had to make runs as well as dismissals, Kirmani's final Test batting average of 27.05 compares adequately with his contemporaries (Knott 32.75, Dujon 31.94, Marsh 26.52, New Zealand's Ian Smith 25.56, West Indies' Deryck Murray 22.91). Perhaps this is not too surprising, given that he topped the averages as a specialist batsman for the 1967 Indian Schoolboys team that toured England. In this top 100, Kirmani's batting also puts him ahead of the outstanding Pakistani wicketkeeper Wasim Bari, who might have been his equal with the gloves, but averaged more than 11 runs less per Test innings with the bat.

In 1984, Sunil Gavaskar claimed that Kirmani was universally recognised, 'even by the Australians', as the best wicketkeeper in the world. Former Pakistan captain Asif Iqbal agreed with him. Alan Knott was no longer in Test cricket at this time, and where Kirmani had it over Rod Marsh, Gavaskar asserted, was in keeping to the spinners. The stats offer some support for this — Marsh had 12 stumpings in 96 Tests to Kirmani's 38 in 88 — though Kirmani inevitably had more opportunities, given that in Marsh's career Australia never had a top-class spin bowler while India had some masters. 'I learned something from watching Kirmani,' England keeper Paul Downton told the writer David Lemmon in 1984. 'He is such a good mover, so supple, and, above all, completely unflappable.' Of all Test keepers, only Bert Oldfield (52 in 54 Tests between 1920 and 1937) and Godfrey Evans (46 in 91 Tests, 1946-59) have more stumpings.

In most people's eyes, India's best-ever wicketkeeper.

Kirmani had made his Test debut in 1976, in New Zealand, and as early as his second appearance became just the fourth keeper (after Australia's Wally Grout, South Africa's Denis Lindsay and England's John Murray) to complete six dismissals in one Test innings. Having failed to make an out on his Test debut, these were thus the first six dismissals of his Test life. Though he struggled in the

The 100 Greatest Cricketers

Kirmani behind the stumps, and England's Geoff Boycott, in 1981-82.

Caribbean after impressing against the Kiwis, a series of exemplary performances at home in 1976-77 soon had Indian fans realising they'd uncovered a more than worthy replacement for the popular Farokh Engineer. In three Tests against New Zealand, Kirmani scored 88, 64 and 44 as the series was won 2-0, but the visitors seemed even more impressed with his glovework than his runs. 'To see Kirmani keeping to Chandrasekhar throughout a long, very hot day, and see him as sharp at the end as he was at the beginning was a revelation,' opposition keeper Warren Lees told Lemmon. 'We found it hard enough to bat against him. Goodness knows what he was like to keep wicket to.'

Late in his career, his haircut became almost as notable as his immaculate glovework.

The following year, Kirmani was so impressive in Australia that Kerry Packer's World Series Cricket sounded him out about joining the rebel group, a development that might have led to his shock sacking from the England tour in 1979. There was no other logical explanation. Quickly, he was brought back for the home series against Australia, during which he was three times used as a nightwatchman, for scores of 57, 30 and 101 not out, his first (of two) Test centuries. The second would come against England in 1984. He might have scored a third on his 34th birthday (December 29, 1983), against Marshall, Roberts and Holding, had Kapil Dev not declared on him in Madras. He had added 143 for the ninth wicket with Gavaskar (236 not out) and was unconquered on 63 when the innings ended, leaving the West Indies to bat out a pointless hour and a half at the end of a rain-interrupted match.

The Fifth XI

Kirmani was an important figure in India's victory at the 1983 World Cup, completing 14 dismissals during the tournament, including five in one innings against Zimbabwe at Leicester (then a World Cup record). He also played an important knock in the return match against the Zimbabweans, only 24 not out, but with Kapil Dev (175 not out) the total climbed from 8-140 to 8-266 at the end of India's 60 overs. This remains a world record for the ninth wicket in one-day internationals. After Kapil held the Cup trophy aloft at Lord's a week later, Kirmani was named the keeper of the tournament.

Kirmani at Madras in January 1985, with a close-up view of Mike Gatting as the Englishman scores 207.

Kirmani was a very religious man, and following a trip to Mecca decided to shave his head. Soon his new look became something of a trademark. He also made something of a habit of not conceding byes in long innings. He did so in three straight Tests in 1981, while England scored 1563 runs, in the third of these also taking his 100th Test-match catch, the first Indian to do so. A year later, he was blemish-free again while Pakistan scored 652 at Faisalabad (then the second highest innings total without a bye), in the same first innings in which he took five catches, having already scored 66 with the bat.

His final series was in Australia in 1985-86, when his smooth glovework offered a stark contrast to the mediocre efforts of the home team's Wayne Phillips, who was struggling with the dual roles of keeping and opening the batting. Kirmani finished just two dismissals shy of the 2000 runs/200 dismissals double that to June 30, 2009, had been completed by just 10 keepers in Test history, none of them from Asia. One slight irony of Kirmani's record is that 51 of his 160 catches, nearly a third, came from the bowling of the fast man, Kapil Dev. For a gloveman who made his name keeping to the spinners, this statistic — easily the most successful keeper/bowler combination for India in Test cricket — reflects the fact that he was a wicketkeeper of the highest class in any situation.

SYED KIRMANI (INDIA)

Test Cricket

Mat	Inn	NO	Runs	HS	Ave	100	50	Ct	St	Balls	Runs	Wkts	Ave	Best	5/	10/
88	124	22	2759	102	27.05	2	12	160	38	19	13	1	13.00	1-9	–	–

First-Class Cricket

Mat	Inn	NO	Runs	HS	Ave	100	50	Ct	St	Balls	Runs	Wkts	Ave	Best	5/	10/
275	383	64	9620	161	30.16	13	38	367	112	175	126	1	126.0	1-9	–	–

The 100 Greatest Cricketers

Javed Miandad

Harold Larwood

The Sixth

Virender Sehwag

Les Ames

The Sixth XI

Mike Procter

Rahul Dravid

Charlie Macartney

XI

Joel Garner

Bhagwat Chandrasekhar

Bishan Bedi

Geoff Boycott

No. 56 Javed Miandad

Javed Miandad was cricket's version of the street fighter. He had all the shots and could use them, but the memory of him is as an accumulator of runs, as arguably the best player of spin bowling of his generation, and of being something of an agent provocateur. The England off-spinner John Emburey thought Javed was 'high-class', and made special note of his 'brilliant' footwork. 'He can play right back on his stumps and manipulate the ball into the most frustrating areas,' Emburey said. Javed was also a bloke who, at the MCG in early 1979, ran out Rodney Hogg while the Australian fast bowler was innocently out of his ground, patting down the pitch. Nine days later, Javed made a hundred against Hogg on the bouncy WACA wicket. Most famously, he clashed with Dennis Lillee in Perth in 1981-82. After a single was completed, there was a minor collision between the two, then Lillee aimed a tiny, silly kick at Javed's calf which made it obvious who was winning this battle. Javed reacted by raising his bat above his head as if he was about to bludgeon the great fast bowler. Umpire Tony Crafter had to come between them; everyone knew the Pakistani champion wasn't going to back away from anyone.

In his autobiography, Richard Hadlee used a variety of adjectives and phrases to describe Javed: 'exceptional', 'deserves the utmost admiration', 'outstanding player against all types of attacks', 'awkward, 'so annoying', 'adventurous', 'can make Test runs anywhere, whatever the cynics might say'.

In fact, Javed was a more prolific run-scorer in Pakistan that he was in other countries, averaging 61.38 in 60 Tests at home, 45.80 in 64 Tests away. However, just about all Pakistani batsmen of his era scored more runs at home. In the period from Javed's first Test in October 1976 to his last in December 1993, Pakistan as a team averaged more than 39 with the bat at home, just a fraction more than 30 away. Javed himself scored 14 centuries at home, and nine away, but 17 fifties at home and 26 away. Further, that 45.80 away-from-home average is still very good, especially for a man who made his cricket living in the 1980s. The statistic the 'cynics' jumped on was that he was never dismissed lbw in Pakistan; in fact he was out this way eight times at home, 25 times away. But a batsman of his skill and pragmatism was entitled to know how to survive and prosper in conditions he knew best. Perhaps the biggest knock on his record is that he only averaged 38.07 in 16 Tests in Australia, and only 33.75 in seven Tests in the Caribbean.

However, even these stats are a little misleading. Javed toured the West Indies three times, once right at the start of his career (when he was dropped after scoring 2 and 1 in the first Test) and once near the end. In between, in 1987-88, in

Javed drives at Malcolm Marshall in Lahore, during the first Test of the 1980-81 series.

The Sixth XI

arguably the highest standard Test series of the 1980s, he was the leading run-scorer from either side, making two centuries in three matches against Malcolm Marshall, Curtly Ambrose, Courtney Walsh and Patrick Patterson. His second-innings century at Port-of-Spain, which lasted more than seven hours, almost brought a famous victory after Pakistan had been set 372 to win on a pitch on which 15 wickets had fallen on the opening day.

Javed acknowledged that he was a 'controversial character', but also a 'fierce competitor and a proud Pakistani'. To opponents, his every action stated emphatically that he'd fight you for every run, that from this day forth Pakistan cricket was not to be taken lightly. If Imran provided the grandeur, and Wasim Akram and then Waqar Younis gave them firepower, Javed was the man in the engine room, stoking the fires. 'He had the qualities of confidence and arrogance all great players possess and they rubbed off on his colleagues,' wrote Ian Botham of Javed in 1994. 'A master improviser, able to conjure runs out of nothing. Pakistan were fortunate to have some great stroke players during the period I played against them, but he was the best of all.'

Javed at the 1992 World Cup final, as he and Imran Khan launch the revival that eventually gave Pakistan a match-winning total.

Emburey called Javed 'a big-innings man'. He had started his Test career with a big hundred: 163 against New Zealand at Lahore, and then followed up with 206 in his third Test, at Karachi. It was not until his fourth Test that his batting average slipped below 100, and it never dropped lower than 51.75. After he scored 145 against India at Lahore in his 100th Test, becoming the second man after Colin Cowdrey to crown the milestone with a century and the first to make a hundred in his first and

The 100 Greatest Cricketers

100th Test, his average was 57.42. Ten of Javed's 23 Test centuries went past 150, six past 200, three to 260 or beyond. Only Don Bradman, Brian Lara and Wally Hammond have scored more Test double centuries. At The Oval in 1987, after he was dismissed for 260, Javed expressed his disappointment at throwing away a chance to break the world record for the highest score in Tests. Still, the resultant draw was enough for Pakistan to win a series in England for the first time.

Javed and Wasim Akram celebrate their World Cup success at the MCG.

When asked by Patrick Murphy in his book, *Declarations*, to nominate his best innings, Javed named his effort against India in the final of the 1986 Austral-Asia Cup at Sharjah, a thrilling ODI won by Pakistan by one wicket from the last ball of the 50th over. Of course, Pakistan v India matches are always important and Javed was in at 2-39 chasing 246. The required run rate climbed towards nine an over, and with an over from Chetan Sharma to go 12 were needed with two wickets left and Javed past his century and on strike. Seven runs came from the first three balls, then the keeper, Zulqarnain, was bowled. A sharp single meant four to win ...

'I hit a big six over mid-wicket,' Javed told Murphy. 'It was a pressure innings. I finished 116 not out, but only 20 of them came in boundaries. I had to run many sharp singles in great heat. I feel I won that game single-handedly, and I was very proud.'

In 1996, Javed, at age 38, became the first cricketer to appear in six World Cups. Four years earlier, he had played a crucial hand in the 1992 final at the MCG, making 58 and restoring Pakistan's innings with Imran following the loss of two early wickets. The total eventually reached 249, which was too many for England. In a way, the one-day game was made for him, because few batsmen have been better able to deflect the ball, steer it into gaps, run like lightning between the wickets and judge run chases so astutely. Steve Waugh once made the telling observation that Javed 'was the player the Pakistanis all loved to bat with'. He was also an outstanding fieldsman. Whether it be Tests or one-dayers, with Javed Miandad about something was always likely to happen.

JAVED MIANDAD (PAKISTAN)

Test Cricket

Tests	Inn	NO	Runs	HS	Ave	100	50	Ct	St	Balls	Runs	Wkts	Ave	Best	5/	10/
124	189	21	8832	280*	52.57	23	43	93	1	1470	682	17	40.12	3-74	–	–

One-Day International Cricket

ODIs	Inn	NO	Runs	HS	Ave	100	50	Ct	St	Balls	Runs	Wkts	Ave	Best	4/
233	218	41	7381	119*	41.70	8	50	71	2	436	297	7	42.43	2-22	–

The Sixth XI

Harold Larwood

No. 57

At first glance, Harold Larwood's Test record is not overly impressive. He took nine wickets in two Tests against Australia in 1926, six more in two Tests against the West Indies in 1928. He played in all five Tests against Australia in 1928-29, taking 18 wickets at more than 40, and then captured eight wickets in three Tests against South Africa at home in 1929. The four wickets he took in three Ashes Tests in 1930 came at a cost of 73 runs per wicket, and in the only Test he played between the end of that series and the bodyline Tests of 1932-33, the third Test against New Zealand at Old Trafford in 1931, he did not bat or bowl.

When Larwood stepped aboard the *Orontes* for the voyage to Australia in 1932, he had been a Test cricketer for six years but had played in just 16 Tests, taking 45 wickets at 34.84. At first-class level, however, he had been consistently outstanding for Nottinghamshire, taking more than 100 wickets in every season from 1926 to 1932, except for 1930 when he finished with 99. Some Australians might not have been trembling at the thought of Larwood opening the England attack, but wiser pundits would have recalled how *Wisden*, after naming 22-year-old Larwood as one of its cricketers of the year in 1927, told of how he generates 'great pace off the ground, probably because he has a perfect run up to the wicket, and at times makes the ball come back so much that he is almost unplayable.' They might also have remembered how devastating he had been early in the 1928-29 series, especially when he took 6-32 in Australia's first innings of the series and made batsmen such as Bill Woodfull and Bill Ponsford look slow-footed. The England captain Percy Chapman had overbowled his spearhead in what became a batsmen's series, so it was little wonder Larwood had little left for the final two Tests, in which he took two wickets. Larwood also admitted he'd been undermined by the constant jibes of the Australian barrackers. He was four years older now, and determined to prove them wrong.

As history well knows, England's new leader, Douglas Jardine, had a special plan in which Larwood was the principal player. The Englishmen called it 'leg theory', the Australian press, players and fans quickly tagged it 'bodyline' — a strategy in which the right-hand fast man, Larwood, and the left-hand fast-medium, Bill Voce, would aim on and often outside the batsmen's leg stump, usually pitching short looking for catches to one of the three, four or five fieldsmen up close on the leg side, or the two men back on the boundary behind square leg. It worked brilliantly. Bradman, whose Test average going into this series was 112.29, averaged only 56.57 for the series. The Ashes were regained by four Tests to one. One of the Australian batsman, Alan Kippax, confessed that Larwood was simply 'too fast' for him. Ponsford was reduced to turning his back on the short balls, and cruelly wearing them on the back and buttocks. Bodyline needed

The man who made bodyline such an effective and dangerous strategy.

The 100 Greatest Cricketers

a bowler of extreme pace, guts, endurance and magnificent control if such a policy of intimidation was to work. No wonder that one of Larwood's few prized souvenirs from his cricket life was an ashtray given to him by Jardine at tour's end. It was inscribed, 'To Harold for the Ashes. 1932-33. From a grateful skipper.'

Sadly, Larwood became a pariah from the time the English authorities decided that bodyline actually wasn't in the spirit of cricket. They asked him to apologise, but he refused — fundamentally because he'd just been doing as he was told and he hadn't broken any rules. He had played his last Test, at age 28, having taken 33 wickets in his last series (including Bradman four times in eight innings), at 19.52. In county cricket, he missed all but one game of 1933 because of a broken foot, but continued to take plenty of wickets until 1938, when his body finally gave up on him. As late as 1936, he topped the English first-class bowling averages, for the fifth time in 11 years. Straight after the bodyline tour, he hadn't helped his reputation in Australia by putting his name to a series of newspaper exclusives that stated, among other things, that Bradman was 'too frightened' and Woodfull 'too slow'. But he was hardly the only one to express such sentiments. George Duckworth, the reserve keeper on the tour, was quoted in an interview as saying, 'The whole thing boils down to the simple fact that some of the Australian wizards were frightened to death of Larwood.'

Grainy, black-and-white, slow-motion film from the Adelaide Test of 1932-33 captures perfectly one of the most rhythmical and famous run-ups in cricket. That was

Above and opposite: two views of an action that inspired a generation of fast bowlers, not least Australia's Ray Lindwall.

Larwood bounces Australian captain Bill Woodfull in 1932-33.

The Sixth XI

the Test in which Larwood hit Woodfull over the heart and Bert Oldfield on the forehead, and mounted police had to ride onto the field to maintain the peace. Only 173cm (5ft 8in), but powerfully-built with broad shoulders and long arms, Larwood titled his head slightly left as he brought his right arm over, his back foot parallel to the crease and dragging through the delivery stride. 'The whole of his action was so well-co-ordinated that everything he had in him reached its peak at the precise moment of the delivery of the ball,' remembered Bob Wyatt, vice-captain in 1932-33. Like Michael Holding years later, umpires could hardly hear Larwood as he approached the bowling crease. His speed was exceptional, yards faster than any other front-line bowler of his time, and partly because of his slightly slinging action and also because he was hardly tall, his bouncer tended to skid, spearing into the ribcage rather than ballooning over the batsman's head. His stock delivery cut back from the off, sometimes prodigiously. He claimed he never aimed to hit anyone, but no one in the Australian dressing room in 1932-33 believed him and nor did the county batsmen who had heard stories of men such as Pasty Hendren, 'Jock' Cameron and Reg Sinfield being carried from the field unconscious after failing to avoid Larwood bumpers.

The huge irony of Larwood's life is that in 1950 he emigrated to Australia (sailing again on the *Orontes*). Two decades earlier, he'd been roundly hooted but now he was warmly greeted. The former Australian batsmen Jack Fingleton, who'd made a pair in the third bodyline Test, helped organise his arrival. Ex-prime minister Ben Chifley helped meet Larwood's hotel bill until he was settled. For a man who'd been working in the Nottinghamshire mines before he signed to play county cricket, his career had moved in some remarkable ways. Sadly, today he is remembered first as the villain to Bradman's hero. Just about the only other bad guy in The Don's cricket story is Eric Hollies, who bowled him for nought in his last Test and therefore prevented him from achieving a century average in Test cricket. Had it not been for Harold Larwood and bodyline, Bradman's average would have been well past the hundred before Hollies sent down that fateful ball.

HAROLD LARWOOD (ENGLAND)

Test Cricket

Tests	Inn	NO	Runs	HS	Ave	100	50	Ct	Balls	Runs	Wkts	Ave	Best	5/	10/
21	28	3	485	98	19.40	–	2	15	4969	2212	78	28.36	6-32	4	1

First-Class Cricket

Mat	Inn	NO	Runs	HS	Ave	100	50	Ct	Balls	Runs	Wkts	Ave	Best	5/	10/
361	438	72	7290	102*	19.92	3	25	234	58027	24994	1427	17.52	9-41	98	20

No. 58 Mike Procter

Mike Procter played just seven Test matches, all against Australia, the last four in 1970 when he was 23 years old. In those games he took 41 wickets at 15.02. Otherwise, because of the sporting boycott of South Africa that ran from 1971 to 1992, Procter was, like Barry Richards, obliged to forge his considerable reputation in the Currie Cup, in English county cricket and, during Australian summers, in World Series Cricket. In the former England captain Keith Fletcher's view, expressed in 1983, Procter was 'the best overseas cricketer to come into the English game'.

The batting stance of the third man to score a century in six consecutive first-class innings.

Procter was an extremely exciting player capable of scoring six first-class centuries in six consecutive first innings, and of scoring a first-class century before lunch and then taking a hat-trick later in the same day. An innings of 203 in 165 minutes against Essex at Gloucester in 1978 was described by Wisden as 'the best innings seen at the ground since Hammond's heyday'. Procter's bowling was explosive, a rapid-fire run-up ended with his shoulders almost square to the stumps, a whirl of the arms and ball was catapulted towards an apprehensive batsman. In his first-class career he took 1417 wickets at 19.53, five wickets in an innings 70 times, 10 wickets in a match 15 times, four hat-tricks (including two where all three batsmen were lbw), scored 21,936 runs, 48 centuries. Given a healthy Test career, and Procter might have gone close to matching the all-round exploits of Richard Hadlee, Ian Botham, Imran Khan and Kapil Dev. He might even have been better.

'Most of the time he bowls inswingers, but he can vary this with a ball that keeps going on straight,' Australia's Doug Walters wrote in his book *Looking For Runs* in 1971, 12 months after Australia had been demoralised 4-0 in four Tests in South Africa. 'He doesn't need to have an outswinger or, as far as I can see, is he ever likely to have one with that action.' Walters went further, explaining that though Procter usually seemed to be trying to bowl a leg cutter, more often than not it seamed into the right-handers rather than away. But when the leg cutter really gripped, it was almost unplayable as it seamed away. 'A combination of inswing, straight ball and movement either way off

The Sixth XI

the pitch is enough to make Procter, in my opinion, one of the best bowlers of the next five years in international cricket …'

But then Walters added, ominously, 'Always providing, of course, that South Africa continue in that sphere.'

Procter never batted higher than No. 7 in Test cricket, for a highest score of 48. Though he'd been a batsman/wicketkeeper as a boy, capable of scoring a double century at age 12, his batting didn't really take off until the 1970-71 South African domestic season, when in eight innings he made 956 runs for Rhodesia at 119.50, including six hundreds in six straight innings (equalling the world record held by Don Bradman and Charles Fry). One of those hundreds went all the way to 254, against Western Province, his highest first-class score. He also took 27 wickets at 16.11. Immediately after, for Gloucestershire, he scored another seven centuries while hitting 1786 runs and taking 65 wickets for the county season. Against Yorkshire at Sheffield, he took 1-11 from nine overs, which suggested quick run-scoring might have been difficult, before Geoff Boycott declared, setting a target of 201. Gloucestershire crashed to 3-11, before Procter strode out to score 111, and the match was won in 40.3 overs. Had he played, say, 10 Test matches during this period, as is the way in the 21st century, Procter would surely have been a sensation.

After the Australia-South Africa Test series in early 1970, Procter was established as the best fast bowler in the game. Sadly for him, he never played another Test.

Twice, he scored a century and took a hat-trick in the same first-class match. Against Worcestershire in 1977, he scored 108 and took 7-35 and 6-38. And then there was the big hitting. For Western Province against the Australians 1969-70, he scored 155 in 130 minutes, the last 55 of them in 12 minutes. The story goes that after Ashley Mallett was hit for another six, one of nine hit by Procter this day, Walters sidled up to the bowler and quipped, 'That's the end of the reds, now we can get on to the colours.' In the space of a week in 1979, Procter hit 93 in 46 minutes against Somerset at Taunton (the first 50 in 25 minutes) and then 92 in 35 minutes against Warwickshire at Bristol (the first 50 this time in 21 minutes). He and the future Test batsman Chris Broad added 80 for the fourth wicket, Broad's contribution being two. Three days later, Procter's century against Northants took 57 minutes. Yet back in 1965-66, batting for Natal against Transvaal, Procter had taken nearly seven hours to amass 129, his maiden first-class century.

First-class records are not everything, but in the case of Procter they are most of what we have. Consider the following:

Allrounder	Matches	Runs	Avge	100s	Wkts	Avge	5/	Score
IT Botham	402	19,399	33.99	38	1172	27.22	59	1.25
RJ Hadlee	342	12,052	31.71	14	1490	18.11	102	1.75
Imran Khan	382	17,771	36.79	30	1287	22.32	70	1.65
Kapil Dev	275	11,356	32.91	18	835	27.09	39	1.21
MJ Procter	401	21,936	36.02	48	1417	19.53	70	1.84

The 'score' column at far right is calculated simply by dividing the allrounder's batting average by his bowling average, the higher the score the better. While hardly perfect, it's not a bad measure — the basis of winning cricket matches is to score more runs than your opponents, so if you score your runs at a higher average than you take your wickets, you should be going okay. Of course, Procter's four rivals from the 1970s and '80s played a lot of their cricket at Test level, so many of their returns were harder earned, but surely this table indicates that the South African is entitled to be spoken of in the same sentence.

'He was probably the most naturally talented of them all, an extraordinary cricketer,' said Ali Bacher, the South African captain in 1970, comparing Procter to the other members of his famous side. 'He was another Garry Sobers, not in the same class, but probably second to him.' In 1970, *Wisden* thought Procter was the second most valuable 'import' in the county championship, behind only Sobers. 'He represents what the ancient game needs everywhere — a real personality, a gifted performer, and, what is equally important, one who is seen to enjoy every minute on the field,' wrote Alex Bannister in the Almanack. Selecting Procter in the sixth XI might be underrating him.

First-class statistics strongly suggest Procter was in the same class as any of Imran, Botham, Hadlee and Kapil Dev, the great allrounders of the 1980s.

MIKE PROCTER (SOUTH AFRICA)

Test Cricket

Tests	Inn	NO	Runs	HS	Ave	100	50	Ct	Balls	Runs	Wkts	Ave	Best	5/	10/
7	10	1	226	48	25.11	–	–	4	1514	616	41	15.02	6-73	1	–

First-Class Cricket

Mat	Inn	NO	Runs	HS	Ave	100	50	Ct	Balls	Runs	Wkts	Ave	Best	5/	10/
401	667	58	21936	254	36.02	48	109	325	65404	27679	1417	19.53	9-71	70	15

The Sixth XI

Rahul Dravid
No. 59

There has always been a lack of fanfare to Rahul Dravid's batting that means he'll never have the immediate appeal of a Sachin Tendulkar or an Adam Gilchrist. Think of Dravid and the words that come to mind are professional ... dependable ... reliable. Or should that be ultra-reliable. Unusually for an Indian batsman, he averages substantially more batting away rather than at home (56.90 to 47.24 as at June 30, 2009; in contrast Tendulkar averages 54.98 at home, 54.28 away), which suggests a strong adaptability about his method. His figures were also significantly better for the second third of his career than in the first, which suggest a talent for learning. Since 2007, his output has declined, but he remains the most reliable No. 3 batsman to ever play for India. He has also taken more catches in Tests than any other non-wicketkeeper, having overtaken Mark Waugh's old record in April 2009.

The style of arguably the most technically correct batsman of the early 21st-century.

Run-getting in the last 15 years has entered a new era, with the finest batsmen averaging more per innings than their predecessors. Where once a fifty average was considered exceptional, now that high benchmark is more like 55, perhaps 57. In part, this is due to an overall decline in bowling standards, especially in the West Indies (though, of course, there have still been a number of champions about, such as Shane Warne, Muttiah Muralitharan and Glenn McGrath). Boundary ropes have made the grounds slightly smaller. As in golf, technology has made for better bats.

Dravid's career batting average, which from December 2003 to December 2007 was always more than 55, reaching a peak of 58.76 in mid 2006, compares admirably with any of the modern masters. Having started in Tests with innings of 95 and 84 against England in 1996, Dravid's average declined to the mid 30s by the beginning of 1997, but a maiden century against South Africa in his ninth Test set things right. For a while, he was a batsman unable to turn starts into big hundreds, making 12 half-centuries in 20 Test innings before his second hundred, against Zimbabwe at Harare in October 1998. However, he made three more Test tons in nine innings before becoming the leading runscorer at the 1999 World Cup (hitting two of the six ODI centuries he'd make during this calendar year) and appeared to be on the verge of becoming a major star. Along the way he was smart enough to seek out the experience of men such as Ian Chappell and Steve Waugh, to discover what it takes to go from good to great.

Strangely, though, rather than flourishing, Dravid's 1999-2000 Test season was a difficult one. He went 16 innings without a fifty, apparently struggling to meet the higher expectations his success had brought him. Earlier criticisms that he was merely a stonewaller now appeared to haunt, and though he made runs against Zimbabwe at the end of 2000, three straight failures at home against Waugh's great Australian team had many questioning his calibre. For the second innings of the second Test, at Kolkata, Dravid was relegated from No. 3 to No. 6, one step away, it seemed, from losing his place altogether.

What happened next is the stuff of legend. With VVS Laxman, his replacement at No. 3, Dravid became involved in what was arguably the greatest substantial partnership in cricket history. After India had been obliged to follow on, they were still 42 runs down when Laxman and Dravid came together; when the stand finally ended more than a day later, the two had added 376 and set the stage for India's greatest ever Test victory. Laxman had made 59 in the first innings, and his confidence seemed to help Dravid, whose assurance grew the longer the fightback continued. By the time he was out for 180, it was as if he had finally learned to truly believe in himself.

In one-day cricket, he became the perfect foil to Tendulkar's blazing starts, especially adept at getting the most from the final 20 overs. Sometimes, he was also the part-time wicketkeeper. But his greatest days were in Tests, as he became his country's most valuable player, saving matches in South Africa, the West Indies and England,

Dravid's wicketkeeping in one-day cricket is another string to his bow.

The Sixth XI

and then contributing mightily to victories against England, Australia and Pakistan. In England in 2002 he hit centuries in three straight Test innings, and then followed up immediately with another Test hundred at home against the West Indies. Between 2002 and 2004, he hit four double-centuries in 15 Tests. During the last of these — a massive 270 at Rawalpindi — Pakistan's Yasir Hameed dropped an easy catch at a point when Dravid was on 71. When asked how he could have missed such a sitter, the fieldsman replied, only half-jokingly, that he was preoccupied 'watching a master at work'.

Dravid and VVS Laxman walk off at the end of day four in the second Test against Australia at Calcutta, having batted throughout the day to set the scene for a dramatic Indian victory.

Few modern batsmen are as balanced at the crease as Dravid was at his finest, or more adept at playing right back on the stumps against pace and slow bowling. A bowler pitching even fractionally to the legside of middle was inevitably forced through the onside field. He has never been overly stylish, in the manner of a David Gower, a Mark Waugh or a Kumar Sangakkara, but is technically correct, head still over the ball, and always willing for the fight, one of those cricketers never totally on the defensive. In 2004, Shane Warne described him as India's 'rock'. When Steve Waugh compiled his career-ending autobiography, he asked Dravid to contribute a foreword. Dravid responded by stating, with much admiration, that Waugh 'gave grit a good name'. Waugh, for his part, wrote of Dravid, 'As an opponent I respected his professionalism, and as a friend I admired his balanced views and the way he treated people from all walks of life equally.'

In late 2005, when he was appointed India's captain, Dravid was asked by the cricinfo website what style of team he wanted to lead. 'Tough, competitive, a team that is looking to improve and have some fun along the way,' he responded. Such a philosophy had worked supremely well for his batting, why not for all of India as well?

RAHUL DRAVID (INDIA)

Test Cricket

Tests	Inn	NO	Runs	HS	Ave	100	50	Ct	Balls	Runs	Wkts	Ave	Best	5/	10/
134	233	27	10823	270	52.54	26	57	184	120	39	1	39.00	1-18	–	–

One-Day International Cricket

ODIs	Inn	NO	Runs	HS	Ave	100	50	Ct	St	Balls	Runs	Wkts	Ave	Best	4/
333	308	40	10585	153	39.50	12	81	193	14	186	170	4	42.50	2-43	–

No. 60 Charlie Macartney

In 1921, in a tour match against Nottinghamshire, Charlie Macartney scored 345 in less than a single day. He reached his 300 in 205 minutes, with one hit going clean out of the ground. In the dressing room during the tea break, having passed 200 in much better than a run a minute, he was seen rummaging through his kit. 'What are you doing?' he was asked. 'I'm looking for a heavier bat,' he replied. 'I'm going to have a dip.'

Macartney doffs his cap after playing what many regard as his greatest innings, 151 at Headingley in 1926.

Macartney was Australia's greatest batsman of the 1920s. Before World War I, he was a fair all-rounder, making 879 runs with one hundred at 26.04 and taking 34 wickets at 26. His century was taken from the South Africans in 1910-11; his best pre-war score against England was 99, made at Lord's in 1912 when he was dismissed trying to reach three figures with a six. At Leeds in 1909, his left-arm spinners and cutters had been so effective he took 11-85, opening the bowling, after he'd batted at No. 8. After the war, he was a batting master, scoring 1252 runs with six hundreds at 65.89. He still took the bowlers on, but no longer tried to cut fast bowlers off middle stump. His 11 post-war wickets, however, came at an average of 32.64. His most successful series as a run-maker was his last, in 1926 when he was 40 years old, as if his whole cricket life had led to this remarkable personal triumph. He hit three hundreds, including a century in 103 minutes on the first day at Leeds after the England captain Arthur Carr had sent Australia in, Warren Bardsley was caught first ball of the match and then Macartney was dropped — by Carr! — four deliveries later. At lunch he was 112 not out. No man had hit three hundreds in a Test series in England before.

Of Macartney's batting in England in 1921, his captain Warwick Armstrong wrote, 'The brilliant way in which he made his runs was also of the greatest service to the side. It was like champagne to watch him.' Earlier that year, an open-eyed 12-year-old boy from Bowral had been taken by his father to the Sydney Cricket Ground, to see two days' play during the fifth Ashes Test. 'In that memorable Test match I was privileged to see Macartney, in all his glory, make 170 runs,' Don Bradman recalled in 1949. 'I can picture his delicate leg glances and one flashing drive — not through the covers but over the top.'

'As a batsman, Charles Macartney was arrogantly hostile,' wrote his Test teammate from 1920 to 1926, the leg-spinner Arthur Mailey. 'Brimful of confidence, he would boast of his capacity to knock a bowler right off his length.' Macartney was self-taught, having forged his own style after watching big games at the SCG, relying on plenty

The Sixth XI

of practice. His whole career was like a work in progress, but nothing ever taught him that defence was better than attack. Legend has it that as his confidence grew from strong to supreme he liked to smash a ball back at a bowler's head early in an innings, just to let them know who was boss.

Mailey described him as 'short, thickset, with Napoleonic features, tremendously thick wrists'. Because many profiles of him focus on his stately manner and his unshakeable confidence (which led to his nickname, 'The Governor-General'), a picture emerges of a batsman who routinely destroyed attacks. But this is not quite right. Armstrong appreciated the fact that his No. 1 batsman could play sensibly when the situation demanded it, a trait Macartney had to learn and probably didn't fully master until after the war. Mailey never forgot his footwork, the way he danced down the pitch to turn perfectly pitched leg-breaks into half volleys. Sir Pelham Warner said of that dynamic hundred at Leeds in 1926 that Macartney 'pulverised' the bowling, but then added, 'His timing of the ball was perfection itself, and every sort of stroke came in rapid succession.' This suggests a kind of controlled fury, an audacious genius.

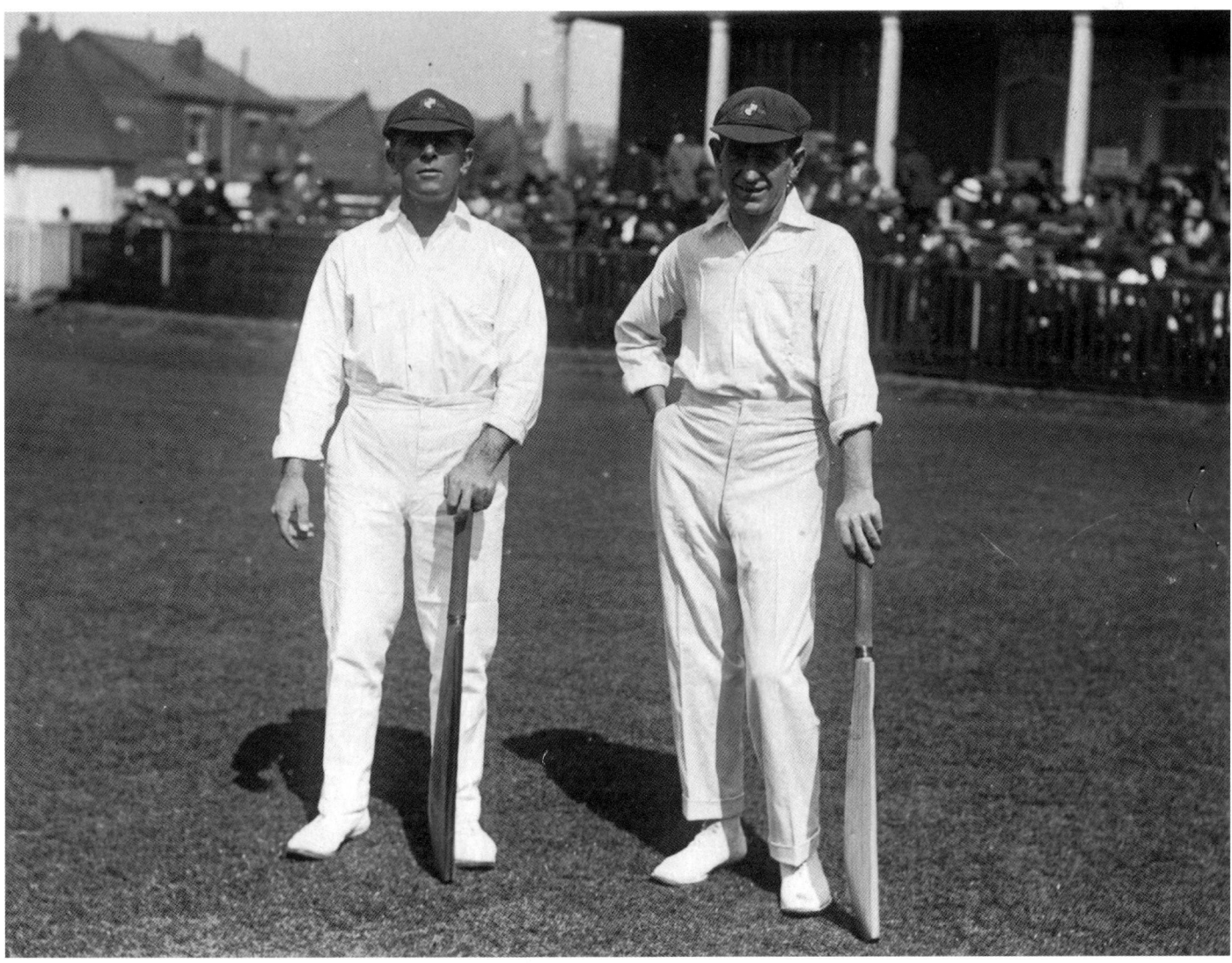

Macartney with Herbert Collins, the Australian captain between 1921 and 1926.

Armstrong reckoned that Macartney played 'all the orthodox strokes and a few of his own', making special reference to a 'drive behind point off the half volley'. He explained: 'To make this stroke he gets right down to the ball and guides it to its destination with his wrists. His square drive through the covers is very effective, so also are his square and late cuts, the former of which is a most powerful stroke. As his short arm hooking is also excellent, it may easily be imagined that few bowlers can remain entirely calm and unruffled while he is batting.'

Macartney at Leeds in 1921, on his way to his first Test hundred in England.

Although most of Macartney's Test runs were scored after 1919, his first-class figures in 1912-12 and 1913-14, when he averaged 107.67 and then 111.50, suggest his Test batting career might have blossomed earlier but for World War I. In first-class matches at the SCG in 1913-14 his scores were 195, 117, 54, 142, 201 and 110, four of the five hundreds featuring a century in a session. On a private tour to America in 1913, he topped the batting and bowling averages. After the war, when he was at his greatest, Macartney still had a difficult period through 1922-25, when the runs temporarily dried up as his health failed him. Three first-class innings in 1924-25 brought him just 11 runs, and there was little chance of him being selected for the first Ashes Test, but then it was revealed he'd suffered a breakdown and he was out for the season. That he fought back from this malady to dominate the 1926 Ashes series, playing with all his old verve, adds to his story.

The hard part of ranking Macartney is what to do with that career average of 41.78. He is not the only cricketer who was brilliant for half of his career, but only reasonable for the other half. Arthur Morris, for example, averaged 61.67 in Tests for Australia during the first half of his career, 36.82 in the second. Another Australian, Doug Walters, averaged 74.17 in his first 16 Tests, 41.49 in his final 58. In stark contrast, Macartney improved as his career went on, as he came to understand his game and what it takes to be a champion. A valid comparison might be with Steve Waugh, not least because both men, 70 years apart, grew to greatness in their own irresistible way.

CHARLIE MACARTNEY (AUSTRALIA)

Test Cricket

Tests	Inn	NO	Runs	HS	Ave	100	50	Ct	Balls	Runs	Wkts	Ave	Best	5/	10/
35	55	4	2131	170	41.78	7	9	17	3561	1240	45	27.56	7-58	2	1

First-Class Cricket

Mat	Inn	NO	Runs	HS	Ave	100	50	Ct	Balls	Runs	Wkts	Ave	Best	5/	10/
249	360	32	15019	345	45.79	49	53	102	24228	8782	419	20.96	7-58	17	1

Joel Garner

No. 61

First impressions of Joel Garner were wrong. He was so tall (208 cm, or 6ft 10in) and gangling and consequently so far removed from the fast-bowling prototype that it seemed impossible he would last long as a frontline paceman. There really hadn't been a fast bowler like him. The way he lumbered up to the wicket, he looked more like cricket's version of Lurch from the Addams Family than Big Bird from Sesame Street, from where he got his nickname. But then you noticed that in his delivery stride he was well co-ordinated and technically magnificent, and that because he had rhythm and power through the shoulder and upper torso his height was a monstrous advantage; he was coming at the batsman at pace from a higher storey than any other bowler had ever done. England's Mike Brearley complained that the sightscreens weren't tall enough for him. Garner's clever change of pace (not just a slower ball, but a very fast ball as well) and the fact that his devilish yorker always seemed to be fired in at precisely the right moment revealed an astute cricket mind. He had the precision of a sharpshooter, and could stay sharp for overs on end. In the field, he was strong and athletic.

As a complement to Andy Roberts and Michael Holding, coming on after the two great fast men had bowled longish opening spells, Garner was perfect, offering no escape for the shell-shocked batsmen. The former England captain Bob Willis was one who was grateful that he wasn't brought on earlier. 'Garner bowls enough unplayable deliveries when the ball is 80 overs old to make me wonder what he would do if he was given the new ball after six or seven overs,' Willis wrote in *The Cricket Revolution*. After Roberts left Test cricket in 1983, Garner would get the new ball and prove Willis right, to the point that with Malcolm Marshall now in full cry often Holding had to accept bowling first or second change.

'On his day, he could bowl as fast as anyone and was probably the most accurate paceman of recent years,' wrote Imran Khan of Garner in *All Round View*. 'He didn't do a lot with the ball, but with his great height he could extract a steep bounce, and he had a well-concealed change of pace. He often had to perform the role, of stock bowler for the West Indies, while Holding and Roberts were resting; and had he been the strike bowler more often he would probably have taken even more wickets. In any event, his record stands comparison with the best.'

Few have delivered the ball from such a great height as did the fearsome bowler known as 'Big Bird'.

The 100 Greatest Cricketers

That record reads 259 Test wickets at 20.98, and 146 ODI wickets at 18.85. Of Test bowlers who played since 1900 and have taken more than 100 Test wickets, only Sydney Barnes, Alan Davidson, England's Johnny Wardle (102 wickets at 20.39) and Malcolm Marshall have a lower average. No bowler with 100 ODI wickets has taken wickets at a smaller cost. 'I think any great batsman of the past would have been troubled by "Bird",' is Sir Garfield Sobers' view.

Garner, seen here bowling with great effect for Somerset in the Benson & Hedges Cup, had a fine career in county cricket from 1977 to 1986.

Though he was a Test bowler of the highest class, his most memorable performance came in a one-day match — the 1979 World Cup final. Viv Richards had already crafted a big hundred, and with allrounder Collis King (86) had pushed the West Indies total to 9-286, just five short of their match-winning score from 1975. England's reply was reasonable, though there was always a sense that they were falling further behind, a point made emphatically when Garner stepped up and ended the contest by taking five wickets, four of them bowled, for four runs in the space of 11 balls.

Garner is from Barbados, birthplace of Malcolm Marshall, Wes Hall and Charlie Griffith as well as Sobers and the three Ws. He was fortunate in that injuries to Holding and Wayne Daniel gave him a chance to make the West Indies Test side in early 1977, and 25 wickets against Pakistan in his debut series was enough to get him a deal with World Series Cricket. At the same time, some extraordinary wicket-taking feats in league cricket in England won him a contract with Somerset in 1979, and the county immediately won its first ever competitions, the Gillette Cup and the John Player League. In the county championship, he took 55 wickets at 13.84; in the Gillette Cup he took 17 wickets at 5.41, including 6-29 in the final.

Garner terrorises injured England batsman Paul Terry at Old Trafford in 1984.

The Sixth XI

Garner remained one of the leading bowlers in international cricket for most of the following seven years, capturing 27 wickets in his last full series, against England at home in early 1986, before finishing up by taking 12 New Zealand wickets in two Tests in February-March 1987. In 58 Tests, he was involved in 30 West Indian victories and only five losses. He took five wickets in a Test innings only seven times, and never 10 wickets in a Test, reflecting the fact that he rarely opened the bowling, but countering that he took 25 or more wickets in a series on five of the six occasions he was involved in a five-match series, and really had only one ordinary Test series in his life, away to India in 1983.

Garner may have lumbered somewhat to the wicket, but at the bowling crease he was technically superb.

The first thing Allan Lamb referred to when commenting on Garner was the Barbadian's hostility. 'I know he got steep bounce because of his height,' Lamb wrote, 'but the hostility thing is something that is mental as well as physical. Bowlers like Joel lope in and bowl well enough — then suddenly they find an extra gear from somewhere.' Lamb scored three centuries against the West Indies in 1984, but England was swept 5-0 with Garner taking 29 wickets, including nine at Edgbaston in the first Test when the match was won by an innings and 180 runs. The critical moment came at the start of the home team's second innings, which they started 415 runs behind. Holding and Eldine Baptiste had added 160 for the West Indies' ninth wicket, which suggested there was little in the pitch for the bowlers, but then Garner came out and dismissed Graeme Fowler, Derek Randall and David Gower to reduce England to 3-37. The tone for the rest of the summer had been well established. In summing up the series in the 1985 *Wisden*, Christopher Martin-Jenkins claimed that Marshall was the fastest of the West Indian bowlers, but that Garner, 'towering above the batsmen, was the most consistently dangerous'.

JOEL GARNER (WEST INDIES)
Test Cricket

Tests	Inn	NO	Runs	HS	Ave	100	50	Ct	Balls	Runs	Wkts	Ave	Best	5/	10/
58	68	14	672	60	12.44	–	1	42	13169	5433	259	20.98	6-56	7	–

One-Day International Cricket

ODIs	Inn	NO	Runs	HS	Ave	100	50	Ct	Balls	Runs	Wkts	Ave	Best	4/
98	40	14	238	37	9.15	–	–	30	5330	2752	146	18.85	5-31	5

No. 62 Geoff Boycott

In a one-day international at Sydney in December 1979, Geoff Boycott of Yorkshire and England scored 105. It wasn't so much that he scored a one-day hundred — though, of course, that is an achievement in itself — it was the way he played, against an Australian attack led by Dennis Lillee and Jeff Thomson, with Max Walker in support. 'Boycott scored his runs off 124 balls, often being prepared to chance his arm in an innings out of character with his usual approach,' reported *Wisden*. What impressed the regulars in the Sydney crowd was that Boycott never needed to slog; instead he proved, against the best of bowlers, that a mixture of great skill, cunning and aggression was enough to score at nearly a run a ball. He was masterful.

Boycott pushes warily against Australia in 1977, the season he came back to Test cricket and reaffirmed his status as one of the best defensive batsmen in the world.

It was unfortunate that, outside of his county, Boycott was hardly a popular cricketer. Even in Yorkshire, there are those who revere him and those who struggle to forgive him for the battles he had with the cricket committees there in the 1970s and 1980s. Through his career, a picture emerged of a batsman who was prone to play for himself, who often batted too slowly, as if the result of the match depended not so much on his runs as on him not getting out. Ian Botham once ran him out in a Test, because that gave England a better chance of victory. In 1970-71, he was the first to work out how to read the Australian 'mystery' spinner, Johnny Gleeson, but for a while kept the secret from his teammates. Sadly, this reputation clouds the fact that Boycott was also the wicket the opposition usually wanted most of all. An image that remains for most fans of Ashes cricket in the 1970s was the reaction of the Australians at Trent Bridge in 1977 after Rick McCosker dropped Boycott in the slips when the Englishman was making his comeback to Tests after a self-imposed three-year exile. It was as if McCosker had spilt the Ashes, that everyone from captain Greg Chappell down knew that there would be no second chance. And there wasn't. Boycott overcame his nerves and reservations to score 135. In the next Test, he made 191. England won the series 3-0.

The Sixth XI

Though Boycott might not have been loved, he was definitely respected. 'He was the best, technically,' Richard Hadlee explained to Patrick Murphy, for Murphy's 1989 book *Declarations*. 'I never felt he was in total control, but he would wear you down. I only got him out twice in my career.' Later in the same publication, Murphy asked Michael Holding who was the most difficult batsman Holding had bowled to, and the West Indian nominated Boycott and Ian Chappell. 'He was a great technician,' Holding said of the Yorkshireman. 'He had the shots for the bad balls but otherwise he grafted and accumulated. You had to bowl very well to get Boycott's wicket, his defence was immaculate.'

Botham described Boycott in 1994 as 'the best made batsman I have ever come across'. He continued, '[He] possessed total dedication to the business of scoring runs and unshakeable belief in his own ability. You knew that once he was "in" he would never give his wicket away.' Boycott achieved this by adopting a rigidly single-minded approach to his cricket, convincing himself that what was best for him was also best for his teams. He had needed time to develop his game at the highest level — though he scored a century in each of his first two Test series, against Australia in 1964 and then in South Africa in 1964-65, he was a good but not great batsman for the next five years. He even made three ducks in four Test innings at home in 1969, and asked not be considered for the first three matches of the England v Rest of the World series staged in 1970 to replace the cancelled South Africa Tests. While 'away', he hit 260 not out for Yorkshire against Essex (cheekily making the point in his autobiography that he scored these runs at a faster rate than had Herbert Sutcliffe and Percy Holmes when they added 555 for Yorkshire against Essex in 1932), and then came back to ensure his selection for the 1970-71 Ashes tour by making 157 against the World XI at The Oval.

Boycott scores a second-innings century in the 'Centenary Test' against Australia at Lord's in 1980.

In Australia, he was a revelation. In 1965-66, he had been a good, solid, defensive batsman. Now, no opener since Len Hutton had looked more assured at the crease. Against a mediocre bowling attack, it appeared at times that Boycott would never get out. In the fourth Test, he scored 77 and 142 not out, the true quality of the second dig not being apparent until after England captain Ray Illingworth declared, when Australia was promptly bowled out for just 116. 'Boycott demonstrated himself clearly the outstanding batsman on either side — technically and temperamentally,' wrote RS Whitington. 'More than ever he reminded me of the "Surrey Master", Sir Jack Hobbs.' The only rider Whitington put on this view was that Boycott scored too slowly, a fact that might have been one reason why it took until the final Test for England to regain the Ashes.

The 100 Greatest Cricketers

Boycott in the West Indies in 1968, when he scored four fifties and a century in eight Test innings during the series.

For the next three years, he was undoubtedly the most dependable opening bat in Test cricket, a reign that culminated with a stirring performance in the deciding match of the 1974 England-West Indies series at Port-of-Spain. On a wicket that offered plenty for the finger spinners, Boycott scored 99 and 112 in a Test the tourists won by 26 runs. However, there were rumours about that he was upset at being passed over for the captaincy after Illingworth was sacked, and after some inexplicable failures against the Indian medium-pacer Eknath Solkar, Boycott withdrew from the England camp and stayed away for the next three years.

On his return, Boycott became the first man to score his 100th first-class century in a Test match (191 v Australia, Leeds, 1977) and the second after Colin Cowdrey to appear in 100 Tests (v Australia, Lord's, 1981). When he finally got the chance to captain England he wasn't very good at it, but in his 107th Test, at Delhi in December 1981, he scored his 8000th Test run and soon after went past Garry Sobers to become Test cricket's leading run-getter, a landmark he'd hold until November 1983, when Sunil Gavaskar overtook him. Boycott's Test career ended within days of breaking Sobers' record, when he left the England party mid-tour after falling ill and soon after revealed that he was joining a rebel tour of South Africa. He continued at first-class level to 1986, finishing with 48,426 runs at 56.84, the highest aggregate of any batsman whose career started after World War II. Of all batsman to score 30,000 first-class runs, only Don Bradman (28,067 at 95.14) has a better average.

The paradox of Boycott is that in scoring so many runs, he seemed to alienate as many people as he impressed. Perhaps if he had adopted a more traditional approach to being a team player he might now be regarded as a more balanced cricketer, as well as being a great one.

GEOFF BOYCOTT (ENGLAND)

Test Cricket

Tests	Inn	NO	Runs	HS	Ave	100	50	Ct	Balls	Runs	Wkts	Ave	Best	5/	10/
108	193	23	8114	246*	47.73	22	42	33	944	382	7	54.57	3-47	–	–

First-Class Cricket

Mat	Inn	NO	Runs	HS	Ave	100	50	Ct	Balls	Runs	Wkts	Ave	Best	5/	10/
609	1014	162	48426	261*	56.84	151	238	264	3685	1459	45	32.42	4-14	–	–

The Sixth XI

Bishan Bedi and Bhagwat Chandrasekhar

No. 63 & No. 64

In India's first three decades of Test cricket, they hardly ever won. The first Test to involve them occurred in 1932, at Lord's, and resulted in a comfortable England victory. The initial Indian success came in February 1952, at Madras, over a below-strength England XI. The first series win came in the inaugural India-Pakistan Test series, in 1952-53, a second came three years later, against New Zealand. Australia was beaten in one Test in late 1959, England twice in 1961-62, but the West Indies not at all until 1971. The problem for India was twofold: the batting was too often frail against quality pace bowling; their own pace 'attack' was poor.

In the late 1960s, there was something of a change. India was competitive in 1966-67 in a series against a West Indies team captained by Garry Sobers that had just overwhelmed England in England. For a while, this seemed like a false dawn, as India were then swept in a series in England and Australia. But then came a decisive 3-1 home victory over New Zealand, followed by a competitive series against a powerful Australian side and then three straight series wins: over the West Indies in the Caribbean and, most famously, over England, away and then home.

There were quite a few reasons for this improvement, not least the emergence of batsmen of the ilk of Gundappa Viswanath and Sunil Gavaskar. But the single most important factor in the rise of Indian cricket was the development of a posse of high-class spin bowlers, who shaped the image of Indian cricket across the world so powerfully that today, 30 years after the last of them played his final Test, cricket fans link spin and India as naturally as we think of pads and lbws.

In fact, India had produced quality spinners earlier than the late '60s. In 1988, Garry Sobers described Subash Gupte, who took 149 Test wickets between 1951 and 1961, as 'the best leg spinner of my time in cricket'. Clyde Walcott also rated Gupte highly, calling him the 'best leg-break and googly bowler I played against'. However, it was the four men who vied for selection from 1966 to 1979, led usually by the left-arm finger spinner Bishan Bedi and the dynamic wrist-spinner Bhagwat Chandrasekhar, popularly known as 'Chandra', who forged India's cricket image.

The most famous and popular turban in 20th-century cricket.

Bedi and Chandra's brothers in spin were the off-spinners — Erapalli Prasanna, the master of flight, and the taller Srinivasaraghavan Venkataraghavan, better known as 'Venkat', later an international umpire. Bedi was the ringmaster, his turban as well-known across the cricket world as his loop and turn. Chandra was an enigma,

205

The 100 Greatest Cricketers

unique, a medium-paced leg-spinner against whom you were never truly 'in'. Bedi's bowling action was simple, rhythmic, classically side on, with subtle variations in flight and pace his signature. He was the master of deception. Chandra charged at the wicket, his bowling arm — withered by childhood polio — whirred over, the ball fizzed through.

Bedi was a first-class cricketer at 15, Test bowler at 20. His run up was no more than half a dozen paces on tip-toes, and then the ball was sent on its way from his full height. Everything seemed in order, in rhythm. In a way, he looked liked one of those tough old veterans you find at every level of cricket, not exceptionally athletic but able and happy to bowl all day. The difference with Bedi was that he was aggressive, too, if in his own way. Writing in *The Cricketer*, the former England captain Tony Lewis recalled how he once asked him if he bowled differently in attack than in defence. 'I have never bowled defensively,' was the craftsman's quick reply.

Against Australia in late 1969, he took nine wickets as India won easily in Delhi and then followed up by taking 7-98 two weeks later in Calcutta. 'Bedi, calm and phlegmatic, and possessing everything possible in accuracy, flight and change of pace, was the one who seemed to force the Australians in to most errors,' wrote Doug Walters in *Looking For Runs*. Two years later, while playing for a World XI in Sydney, Bedi bowled Ian and Greg Chappell with successive balls. He could spin the ball on the slowest pitches, and had that rare ability to make batsmen look silly, such as the day at the SCG in 1977-78 when, after being smashed by Kim Hughes into the Members Stand, he exacted immediate, total revenge. Hughes could not have known that the next delivery was a quicker, full pitched delivery, because Bedi's action did not change at all. Out of the hand it was a long hop, in reality it was a yorker, and Hughes had his middle stump knocked out of the ground as he gave himself room to cut.

The famous 'spin twins', Chandra (top) and Bedi.

In all, Bedi took 266 Test wickets between 1966 and 1979, a mark beaten by only seven spinners in Test history — Muttiah Muralitharan, Shane Warne, Anil Kumble, Harbhajan Singh, Lance Gibbs, Derek Underwood and Daniel Vettori. He also captained India in 22 Tests, not always successfully, sometimes causing storms with his forthright actions and comments.

Chandra was less consistent, but perhaps more of a matchwinner. It was no coincidence that some of India's greatest victories came when Chandra was on song. At The Oval in 1971 he took 6-38 as the home team collapsed for just 101 and

The Sixth XI

India won a Test and series in England for the first time in their history. At the MCG in 1977-78, he took 12-104 as an Australian team weakened by World Series Cricket was thrashed by 222 runs. The Indian spinners captured the Aussie public's imagination that summer, as WSC's speed merchants were compared, often unfavourably, with the subtleties of the spinners. Chandra was the most intriguing, a man who bowled right-handed but threw from the outfield with his left. Four slow steps, then six quick ones, and quickly the batsman was reacting to a sharp wrong 'un, more likely a bouncing top-spinner or maybe a fast leg break that deviated just enough to beat the outside edge. He finished with 242 Test wickets, despite missing three and a half years of Test cricket between 1968 and 1971 because of injury, with a strike rate of a wicket every 65.96, good for any spinner, quite exceptional for an Indian bowler of his time. (By way of comparison, Warne's career strike rate was 57.49, Muralitharan's (at June 30, 2009) is 54.57; Bill O'Reilly's was 69.61, Jim Laker's 62.32, Bedi's 80.32).

The great quartet — Chandra, Bedi, Prasanna and Venkat — in 2003.

Chandra made his Test debut in January 1964 as an 18-year-old, just three months out of club cricket, taking four English wickets at Bombay in his first innings. However, he was unable to spin his new team to victory on the final day. Later that year, at the same venue, he took eight wickets for the match, his first match-winning effort at the highest level, as India beat Australia for the first time in a Test. Only Peter Burge in the first innings and the left-handers Bill Lawry and Bob Cowper in the second played him with any confidence, though Burge had no chance with the fast leg break that took his off bail and dismissed him for a duck the second time round. At Bombay in December 1966, another left-hander, the West Indies captain Garry Sobers, led his all-conquering team to a six-wicket win, despite Chandra's 11 wickets, including 7-157 in the first innings. So bare was the fast bowling support that Chandra came on first change to bowl the third Indian over of the Test! Bedi debuted in the second Test of this series, a match marked by a riot over forged tickets that prevented play on day two, and came on second change after another spinner, Rusi Surti, opened the bowling.

207

At the same time, Wes Hall and Charlie Griffith were opening the bowling for the visitors, with Sobers as first change. Perhaps it was the total injustice of this imbalance that made Chandra aim a bouncer at Griffith at Madras in the final Test? Earlier in the tour, during a break in play, Hall had been skiting in the dressing room about how he could 'pick' Chandra when none of the specialist batsmen, Sobers apart, could do so. The truth was that Sobers had been signaling to Hall between deliveries as to what was coming next. When play resumed, Sobers left the fast man to his own devices, and he quickly became another Chandra victim.

The two great spinners' careers ended in England in 1979, ironically Kapil Dev's first tour outside the subcontinent. Imagine if the three could have bowled together when all were at their peak! The spin quartet had 853 Test wickets between them, a reflection of their enormous ability and also the manner in which they worked together. Further, inevitably, it illustrated the absolute dearth of faster bowling support they received during their time. No wonder the four felt a strong camaraderie. Often, when a wicket fell, the successful bowler went not to his captain, or perhaps the catcher, but rather to his fellow spinner. A well-planned coup had to be celebrated with someone who knew the art and scheming that had gone into it.

Bedi and Chandra had certainly had plenty of opportunity to do this in 1972-73, when England were beaten in India for the first time. The two bowled 664 six-ball overs between them in this series, Chandra taking 35 wickets and Bedi 25. The other nine Indian bowlers managed 15 wickets between them; Venkat took none in the first Test and one in the fifth, Prasanna 10 in the middle three. All four bowlers were in the middle of their long careers at this point, and perhaps this series captures their comparative talents. Venkat was a good Test bowler, but certainly behind his three co-conspirators. Prasanna was outstanding, not too far outside this Top 100. Bishan Bedi and Bhagwat Chandresekhar were one of the best spin-bowling partnerships there has ever been.

BISHAN BEDI (INDIA)

Test Cricket

Tests	Inn	NO	Runs	HS	Ave	100	50	Ct	Balls	Runs	Wkts	Ave	Best	5/	10/
67	101	28	656	50*	8.99	–	1	26	21364	7637	266	28.71	7-98	14	1

First-Class Cricket

Mat	Inn	NO	Runs	HS	Ave	100	50	Ct	Balls	Runs	Wkts	Ave	Best	5/	10/
370	426	111	3584	61	11.38	–	7	172	90354	33843	1560	21.69	7-5	106	20

BHAGWHAT CHANDRASEKHAR (INDIA)

Test Cricket

Tests	Inn	NO	Runs	HS	Ave	100	50	Ct	Balls	Runs	Wkts	Ave	Best	5/	10/
58	80	39	167	22	4.07	–	–	25	15963	7199	242	29.75	8-79	16	2

First-Class Cricket

Mat	Inn	NO	Runs	HS	Ave	100	50	Ct	Balls	Runs	Wkts	Ave	Best	5/	10/
246	244	114	600	25	4.62	–	–	107	54119	25547	1063	24.03	9-72	75	19

The Sixth XI

Les Ames

No. 65

As the England cricket team of 1932-33 travelled over the Nullarbor Plain from Perth to Adelaide, to kill the time they set out to pick the greatest ever England XI. As wicketkeeper, they didn't pick any of 'Dick' Lilley, 'Tiger' Smith, Herbert Strudwick or George Duckworth, the four most regular custodians since 1900. Neither did they go further back into history, so glovemen such as Richard Pilling and the Hon. Alfred Lyttelton (who once took four Australian wickets in a Test bowling underarm lobs) missed out, too. Instead, they chose a man from among themselves, a keeper who to that point had played in only nine Tests over four series, four of them as part of the below-strength England squad that toured the Caribbean in 1930.

At this time, Australians who had seen Duckworth perform splendidly during the 1928-29 Ashes series assumed he was still the first-choice keeper. Les Ames had also gone on that tour, aged 23, but never played a Test. He had, however, amassed some phenomenal figures for Kent in county cricket, completing more than 100 dismissals in a season (many of them off the leg-spinner 'Tich' Freeman's bowling) on three occasions since 1928. Furthermore, in England's most recent four Tests at home — three against New Zealand in 1931 and one against India in 1932 — he had been in good form with the gloves and had also batted beautifully, especially during an innings of 137 against the Kiwis at Lord's. During that knock, he and 'Gubby' Allen added 246 for the eighth wicket, still the England record for that wicket. Before that, Ames had scored two Test hundreds in the West Indies, which matched the grand total of centuries scored by keepers in Tests prior to 1930 — 134 by Harry Wood for England v South Africa in 1892 and 115 by South Africa's Percy Sherwell v England in 1907.

The scorer of eight of the first 11 Test centuries made by a wicketkeeper.

So he was something of a new concept for a wicketkeeper: an allrounder. By the time his career ended at the outbreak of World War II, Ames had scored eight of the first 11 Test hundreds made by a keeper. He was ahead of his time, a hitter who liked to get down the pitch to the slow (and not so slow) bowlers, a brilliant runner between the wickets, and an athlete with the reflexes to be able to hit Harold Larwood for six, something precious few men could do. In 1935, against South Africa at The Oval, he belted 123 runs between start of play and lunch on the final day. Yet he could also knuckle down when he needed to, such as at Lord's in 1934 when on the first day England had slumped to 5-182. Four and a half hours later, he was out for 120, England finished with 440 and though Bill Brown scored 105 the visitors were forced to follow on, and were then trapped on a sticky and lost by an innings. Don Bradman was out for 13 that day, swinging wildly at Hedley Verity and sending the ball so high any one of seven fieldsmen could have caught it. Ames stepped forward, held his nerve, and claimed one of the most important scalps of his life.

As a keeper, Ames was less showy than Duckworth, to whom he was often compared and who possessed the loudest appeal for a catch or lbw of his time. This, plus the fact that for the bodyline series he was often back away from the stumps to catch the flyers of Larwood and Bill Voce, led to a suspicion that he needed his runs to make the Test team. But as good a judge as Bert Oldfield, the Australian keeper from 1920 to 1937, thought otherwise. Comparing Ames to Duckworth, he commented, 'I have noticed that Ames was able to achieve the same result and still retain his poise whilst taking similar bowling.' When Len Hutton picked his best-ever England team in 1956, he chose Ames over Godfrey Evans.

Cynical Australian observers suggested that Ames had been preferred to Duckworth during the bodyline series purely because, with Larwood and Voce bowling bouncers, all England needed was a backstop. Little did they know that Ames had actually been concerned that because he had little experience standing back to the quicks, he might be a liability. Ironically, he ended up having a lousy series with the bat, but kept well, most notably in the Brisbane heat when he achieved two stumpings off Wally Hammond's sharp medium pace. The first one was critical, breaking Australia's opening partnership on the first day after it had reached 133. The home side trailed one Test to two at this point, early in the fourth Test of a five-match series, but for once they'd seen off the bodyline attack. Vic Richardson, on 83, tried a leg glance, missed, overbalanced slightly, and Ames had the bails off in an instant. 'I doubt if even George Duckworth could have done better,' wrote an admiring Jack Hobbs in the press box.

For the rest of the decade, whenever he was fit Ames was first choice for England. He missed the final two Ashes Tests of 1938 after fracturing a finger at Lord's, and Charlie Macartney, writing for the *Observer*, wondered whether Ames and Len Hutton's absence at Leeds cost England the series. With these two missing, and even with Bradman and O'Reilly in imperious form, Australia just snuck home by five wickets, their only, crucial victory of the season.

After the war, Ames was happy for Evans to do the glovework for Kent, while he set about becoming the first keeper to score 100 first-class centuries. He'd already become the first man to complete more than 400 first-class stumpings, yet today he is most remembered as a batsman who kept. This is unfair. Back in 1929, the year of his Test debut, when he was named one of Wisden's cricketers of the year after catching 69 batsmen, stumping 52 and scoring almost 2000 runs in the previous season, the Almanack's correspondent seem impressed most of all by his glovework. 'It has been said of him that he makes wicketkeeping look easy, which appears to be true,' he wrote. 'It is the greatest compliment which can be paid to a wicket-keeper.' There is nothing to indicate that Les Ames dropped that standard, even by a fraction, at any time in the next decade.

LES AMES (ENGLAND)
Test Cricket

Tests	Inn	NO	Runs	HS	Ave	100	50	Ct	St
47	72	12	2434	149	40.57	8	7	74	23

First-Class Cricket

Mat	Inn	NO	Runs	HS	Ave	100	50	Ct	St	Balls	Runs	Wkts	Ave	Best	5/	10/
593	951	95	37248	295	43.51	102	176	703	418	1383	801	24	33.38	3-23	–	–

The Sixth XI

Virender Sehwag — No. 66

Back in 2006, when the first edition of this book was published, Virender Sehwag was the hardest current-day player to measure, because there was a fear that he was such a dynamic batsman that he could lose form and make a high ranking look silly. Of course, it was also possible that he would continue to blossom, and earn an even better rating. As I wrote back then, 'For all the dynamics of today's highly-charged Australian batting order, starring Ricky Ponting, Matthew Hayden, Adam Gilchrist and partners, there is no doubt that the most thrilling Test batsman of the 21st century has been Virender Sehwag.' His Test batting average then was 52.24; by June 30, 2009, it had declined (caused by a slump that for cost him his Test place for eight months), but only slightly, and was still just above 50. The website howstat.com.au lists players who have scored 1000 Test-match runs and have a strike rate of at least 50 runs per 100 balls faced. The list is not complete, because the number of balls faced by individual batsmen was not always recorded, but of those who can be so measured, as at June 30, 2009, Sehwag (78.69 runs per 100 balls) sits third, behind only Pakistan's Shahid Afridi (86.13) and Gilchrist (81.96). Of this trio, Sehwag has the highest batting average (50.06), ahead of Gilchrist (47.61) and Shahid Afridi (37.40). No other batsmen in the table had a strike rate above 70.00.

More impressive than his batting average is the fact that Sehwag is an opening batsman. Never does he get the chance to come in at four or five wickets down for 350 to swing the bat. He began his Test career at No. 6, starting with 105 against South Africa at Bloemfontein after coming in at 4-68, and was promoted to the top of the order — reluctantly on his part and because, with the middle order made up of Rahul Dravid, Sachin Tendulkar, captain Sourav Ganguly and VVS Laxman, there was nowhere else for him — for his sixth Test, at Lord's in 2002. Straightaway, he scored 84 (from 96 deliveries), then 106 at Trent Bridge and 147 against the West Indies at Mumbai, in his first home Test as an opener, and was entrenched.

He is 21st-century cricket's rough diamond, with an exuberant batting style all his own, and though captains and coaches must think they're about to work him out, he just keeps going, fast and furious. His ability to wait for the ball, often beside its line rather than in behind it before it races away four backward of point, reflects his amazing eye. He is diminutive like Tendulkar, and is similarly strong off the back foot, especially through the offside, but while he has never appeared as naturally gifted as his hero, Sehwag has more than matched him for sheer audacity.

The young Sehwag in Sri Lanka in August 2001, having just completed his maiden one-day international century.

He has scored three hundreds against Australia: 195 at Melbourne in 2003-04 when the

The 100 Greatest Cricketers

local bowling line-up was without Glenn McGrath, Shane Warne and Jason Gillespie; 155 at Chennai in October 2004, one his finest innings; and 151 in Adelaide in 2007–08, made after he had been left out of the team for the first two Tests of the series. In that second knock, this time with the Aussie attack at full-strength, he was in with 13 overs remaining to be bowled on the first day, after Australia had been bowled out for 235. India had been thrashed in the opening Test of this series (Sehwag 39 and 0), and he had just endured a dismal run in one-day cricket, so perhaps it was no surprise that during that late afternoon he was circumspect against McGrath and Gillespie. But to the one ball he faced from the great leg-spinner, he did something quite exhilarating. The ball pitched outside the leg stump, right where Warne wanted it, but Sehwag went down the pitch, moved his front foot not to the pitch but outside it, and clipped the ball against the spin to deep mid-wicket for a single. Neither Warne nor keeper Gilchrist could quite believe it. He finished the day 20 not out, and the next day went on to one of his slower hundreds, from 221 balls with 21 fours. On a slow pitch, he was more reserved than usual against the quicker bowlers, but he had decided that merely defending against Warne would never work and though the ball was spinning he was always on the attack, usually sweeping or driving through mid-wicket.

Sehwag celebrates with Sachin Tendulkar after reaching 200 — on the way to becoming the first Indian to score 300 in a Test innings and eventually to 309 — against Pakistan at Multan in 2004.

He was asked afterwards by the Cricinfo website if he had ever thought of just padding the ball away if Warne pitched outside leg stump. 'In my batting,' Sehwag flatly replied, 'the pad has no role.'

His 309 against Pakistan at Multan in March 2004 was Sehwag's sixth Test hundred in 21 Tests, each made against a different team, only two of them scored at home. His seven Test centuries between December 2003 and January 2006 were all more than 150: 195, 309, 155, 164, 173, 201 and 254. When he made the 201 against Pakistan in Bangalore from 262 balls, Cricinfo's Amit Varma wrote of his 'aggressive watchfulness'. During that innings he scored his 3000th Test-match run, reaching the landmark nine innings faster than any had been achieved by any other Indian. Against Pakistan at Lahore in January 2006, when he scored 254, he and Rahul Dravid added 410 for the first wicket, at the time just three short of the Test record. After that series, his average in nine Tests against India's fiercest rival was 91.14, from nine Tests. 'Even on his bad days he can be destructive,' reckons Shahid Afridi.

The Sixth XI

To play as Sehwag does in Tests and survive you need confidence and ultra-sharp hand-eye co-ordination. To do this and average well over 50 in more than 40 Tests, he must have an astute cricket brain, which can tell him that while the shot he is about to play is flamboyant, it is also logical. 'He answers to no one, refuses to be intimidated and has abundant self-belief, which allows him to play with a clear head and a simple formula,' wrote Steve Waugh in 2005. That he has absolutely no fear of failure is a rare gift. At Multan, he thought nothing of reaching his century with a four and then six off Shoaib Akhtar; when he reached 295 he did it again, swinging Saqlain Mushtaq over wide long on to become the first Indian to score a Test triple century.

'Can he keep going at this frenetic pace?' we asked in 2006. Since then, he has spent that time out of the Indian Test side, but he has made three more Test hundreds, all of them more than 150 (his last 11 Test centuries have all been more than 150), the best of them a stunning 319, made at better than a run a ball, against South Africa. He thus joined Sir Donald Bradman and Brian Lara as the only men to have scored two Test triple centuries. And he has enjoyed something of a resurgence on one-day matches, averaging more than 40 in five successive series between June 2008 and March 2009. There is a temptation to move Sehwag out of this Sixth XI, perhaps replace him with Matthew Hayden or Bob Simpson, but both Hayden and Simpson had spells out of Australia's Test team. For the game's sake (and this Top 100), let's hope Virender Sehwag can blaze on in his unique style in all forms of the game for at least a few more years.

Sehwag, the youngest member of this top 100, and to many observers the most dynamic high-class batsman of the 21st century.

VIRENDER SEHWAG (INDIA)

Test Cricket

Tests	Inn	NO	Runs	HS	Ave	100	50	Ct	Balls	Runs	Wkts	Ave	Best	5/	10/
69	119	4	5757	319	50.06	15	18	55	2455	1265	29	43.62	5-104	1	–

One-Day International Cricket

ODIs	Inn	NO	Runs	HS	Ave	100	50	Ct	Balls	Runs	Wkts	Ave	Best	4/
205	200	8	6592	130	34.33	11	35	79	4015	3531	87	40.59	3-25	–

The 100 Greatest Cricketers

Neil Harvey

Charlie Turner

The Seventh

Matthew Hayden

Wasim Bari

The Seventh XI

Ken Barrington

Monty Noble

Andy Roberts

Michael Holding

Rohan Kanhai

Johnny Briggs

Bob Simpson

No. 67 Neil Harvey

Neil Harvey is one of only three Australian teenagers to score a Test century, the others being Archie Jackson (1928-29) and Doug Walters (1965-66). Harvey made his debut in January 1948, aged 19, scoring 153 in his second Test innings, during the final Test against India at the MCG. In England later that year, he struggled early, found some form before the first Test and forced his way into the top side for the fourth Test at Leeds. There, he became the fifth Australian (after Charles Bannerman, Harry Graham, Bill Ponsford and Jackson) to score a century in his first innings of England-Australia cricket, making 112 and then hitting the winning runs as Australia went 3-0 up in the series. After the tour, Don Bradman retired and next up Australia went to South Africa where Harvey averaged 132.00 in the five-Test series. From there, it wasn't until Norm O'Neill came into the Australian team for the 1958-59 Ashes series that the little left-hander was challenged for the title of Australia's No. 1 batsman.

For a decade after the retirement of Don Bradman, Harvey was Australia's No. 1 batsman.

Harvey was a kid from a working-class family in an inner-city suburb of Melbourne who found fame in the game he loved. He was the most athletic and second youngest of seven children, six boys and a girl. Four of those brothers played first-class cricket; one of them, Mervyn, played a solitary Test match in 1946-47, scoring 12 and 31 as an opening bat. Neil, the one left-hander in the tribe, learned the game from his father, his elder brothers and his mates, at school, in the park and on a cobblestone lane next to the Harvey home, where a 'Test match' was played every Sunday.

At 13, he scored 101 and 141 not out for Fitzroy in the third-grade grand final. At 15, he was in the firsts, part of a batting order that began Harvey, Harvey, Harvey, Harvey. In 1946-47, he was picked for Victoria, first for two games against Tasmania, then for a Sheffield Shield game in Sydney, where in his first innings he was stumped by Ron Saggers off the googly merchant Fred Johnston for a duck. In the second, he made 49 against the Test bowlers, Ray Lindwall and Ernie Toshack. Three weeks later, he scored 69 against the MCC after coming in at 3-32, and never forgot Godfrey Evans congratulating him on reaching fifty by saying, 'Well played son, we'll be seeing you in England next year.'

Having hit four hundreds in South Africa in 1949-50, Harvey scored four more when the South Africans toured Australia in 1952-53. Thus, he had 10 Test hundreds in 24 Tests, another in England in 1953 gave him 11 before his 25th birthday. Despite his slight frame, he could hit with genuine power, and he was one of those batsmen who never forgot that a half volley was meant to be hit for four, in an era when some batsmen did. In the first Ashes Test of 1954-55, he and Arthur Morris ruined Len Hutton's decision to bowl first by both scoring big

The Seventh XI

hundreds, and then came perhaps his greatest innings, not a century but 92 on a dodgy Sydney wicket against 'Typhoon' Tyson at his fastest. 'After this old men can talk to us of Spofforth or Tom Richardson or Barnes and Jack Gregory,' wrote Keith Miller and RS Whitington in their book *Cricket Typhoon*. 'They can talk to their hearts content about Trumper and Ranji. We shall stick our chests out and say, "But were you out at the Sydney Cricket Ground on December 22nd, 1954, to see Tyson and Harvey?" There can have been no greater bowling or batting than theirs.'

Harvey drives during a tour game against Sussex on the 1956 Ashes tour.

Harvey was at his best when facing the champions in the conditions that suited them. In a Test against South Africa in Adelaide, he'd scored a century in even time on a pitch that everyone said was too slow for quick run-scoring. In his autobiography *Fifteen Paces*, Alan Davidson captures the genius of Harvey by recalling three of his mate's finest Test innings. None of these gems was a hundred. There was that 92 against Tyson, a knock of 69 against Jim Laker at Leeds, and a 96 against Pakistan at Dacca in November 1959, made on a matting wicket, against the 'spiteful cutters' of Fazal Mahmood. In each case, the conditions were in the bowler's favour. Laker called Harvey the 'finest left-hander I bowled against'. Of the 19 wickets the off-spinner took at Leeds in 1956, the one he treasured most was Harvey in the first innings — bowled by a ball that drifted in to pitch on about middle and leg, before biting back to take the top of the off stump. Seeing their star batsman bowled in this manner set off a panic in the Australian dressing room that resulted in eight wickets falling, all to Laker, for 22 runs.

The 100 Greatest Cricketers

Many expected Harvey to be named Australian captain following this tour, but instead the selectors went for young Ian Craig. Immediately after this was announced, Craig's NSW played Harvey's Victoria in a Shield game in Sydney. At the toss, Craig surprised by sending the Victorians in, and Harvey returned to his teammates to discover that the opening bat, Colin McDonald, had broken his nose while practising in the nets. Exasperated, Harvey went out to the middle himself, hit three fours in Davidson's first over and finished with 209. A feature was a duel between Harvey and Richie Benaud after lunch, with the leg-spinner always on line but the batsman brilliantly using his feet to stifle any turn. Benaud finished with 0-73 from 20 overs, having seldom bowled better.

Harvey with captain Richie Benaud as the Australian team arrives in England for the 1961 Ashes series.

As a senior Australian cricketer, Harvey was not quite the thrilling shotmaker he'd been in his youth. In *Ins and Outs*, O'Neill recalled a conversation he had with Harvey after the 1958-59 series against England, in which the experienced batsman told of how his outlook on the game gradually changed. From the moment he felt that he had to score runs for the sake of the side, he became more conservative, still trying to dominate but not always prepared to play risky shots that had previously brought him plenty of runs. Harvey averaged 48.40 in that Ashes rubber, then 52.42 on the sub-continent in 1959-60, but after this his run-scoring fell away a little. His career average at the start of the 1960-61 series against the West Indies was 52.21, from 65 Tests; when he retired three seasons later, it had dropped to 48.42.

In 1966, the former England captain Ted Dexter wrote a column for the *Observer* in London. This was the year Garry Sobers had his greatest ever series, scoring 722 runs in five Tests, at 103.14. In early July, Dexter had this to say of the West Indies captain: 'English bowlers still think they can get him out by bowling outside his off stump and making him impatient. But though this used to be true, it isn't any longer: he has learned, in his own phrase, "to govern himself". But in my view, despite his protestations, I would still rather bowl to him there than I would to Neil Harvey.'

NEIL HARVEY (AUSTRALIA)
Test Cricket

Tests	Inn	NO	Runs	HS	Ave	100	50	Ct	Balls	Runs	Wkts	Ave	Best	5/	10/
79	137	10	6149	205	48.42	21	24	64	414	120	3	40.00	1-8	–	–

First-Class Cricket

Mat	Inn	NO	Runs	HS	Ave	100	50	Ct	Balls	Runs	Wkts	Ave	Best	5/	10/
306	461	35	21699	231*	50.94	67	94	228	2574	1106	30	36.87	4-8	–	–

Charlie Turner

No. 68

If Fred Spofforth was clearly Australia's greatest bowler of the 19th century, then Charlie Turner, 'the Terror', was just as decisively No. 2. Some of his bowling figures are simply breathtaking, perhaps none more so than his achievements on his first tour of England in 1888, when he took an incredible 283 first-class wickets in 36 matches. In one match against 'An Eleven of England' at Hastings he took 17-50, including 14 men out bowled, two lbw and one stumped. In other words, every dismissal involved the ball beating the bat. In the 1887-88 Australian season, Turner took an unprecedented 106 wickets at 13.59 (in 12 matches), a year after taking 70 wickets at 7.68 (seven matches). He was the first Australian and second bowler (after Johnny Briggs) to take 100 Test wickets, in 17 games.

Strangely, Turner took time to establish himself as a frontline bowler at the highest level, even after he took 17 wickets in a match (including all 10 in one innings) for a Bathurst and District XXII against Alfred Shaw's England team in December 1881. His first game for New South Wales came as early as 1882-83, but it was four years before he was opening the bowling for NSW and then Australia on a regular basis. There were times when he was selected as a middle-order batsman who didn't bowl. Then, for eight seasons, he was the best bowler in Australia, but after taking 3-18 and 4-33 in the fourth Ashes Test of 1894-95, his co-selectors — Jack Blackham and captain George Giffen — stunningly dropped him for the fifth and deciding Test. 'I'll never play cricket again,' he is reputed to have roared when told of his sacking. He did play a little more, but never another Test.

In his place for that crucial Test came another bloke from Bathurst, one who when he wasn't bowling medium-paced cutters was repairing sheep-shearing equipment, named Tom McKibbin, who had taken 34 wickets his past three first-class matches. Still, when England made 4-298 (McKibbin 1-47) on the final day of the series to win a Test most thought lost, many critics couldn't help thinking that Blackham and Giffen (who with Turner missing now quickly took the chance to open the bowling himself) had got it very wrong. One of the English players,

The first Australian bowler to take 100 Test-match wickets.

The 100 Greatest Cricketers

Archie MacLaren, admitted as much to the *Manchester Guardian* on the voyage home. He explained that not only was Turner still an exceptional bowler, but he had a psychological advantage over many of the tourists, and MacLaren himself, and that if Turner had played, 'we might just have left those Ashes instead of bringing them back'.

The Australians of 1888, with Turner the only man standing and wearing a top hat. Jack Blackham is also in the back row, at far left

If one single performance announced Turner as a great bowler it came at the SCG in February 1887. He had played his first Test three weeks earlier, taking 6-15 and 2-53 in a most satisfactory debut, but then — in a match between New South Wales and another England XI led by Shaw, Turner did the impossible, twice bowling Arthur Shrewsbury for a duck. He finished with the figures of 14-59 for the match, including 8-32 in the first innings, when seven of his victims were bowled and the eighth was caught and bowled.

WG Grace reckoned no man's bowling seemed to accelerate off the pitch quicker than did Turner's deliveries. The former Australian captain Tom Horan, who claimed he was the man who first used the 'Terror' sobriquet, recalled a day in Sydney when Turner was cutting the ball back from outside the off-stump so far and so fast that 'he was almost unplayable'. Stanley Jackson, who made his Test

220

The Seventh XI

debut for England during Turner's final (and least successful) Ashes tour in 1893, always rated Turner as the best medium-pacer he faced. *Wisden*, in its obituary written after Turner died at age 81 on New Year's Day 1944, recalled 'his rather long rhythmic run and beautiful right-arm action without any effort to make the most of his medium height — five feet nine inches'. The Almanack continued: 'He delivered the ball almost facing square down the pitch, and, added to his off-break with slightly varied pace about fast-medium, was ability to turn the ball from leg, send down a fast yorker, and, above all, to get quick lift from the turf.'

Between 1886-87 and 1890, Turner and Jack Ferris forged a prolific wicket-taking partnership, but they were rarely supported by the batsmen. Australia won only one of eight Tests in this period, even though Turner took 56 wickets at 11.93 and Ferris 48 at 14.25. In *A Century of Cricketers*, Johnnie Moyes quoted MacLaren as saying of Turner, 'With a sudden swing around, he would come tripping up to the wicket in the most cheery and, at the same time, graceful manner imaginable. His action was perfect, likewise his length, and he put heart and soul into every ball he bowled.'

'It is a delightful picture,' Moyes commented, 'of the bowler as artist.' Add MacLaren's word picture to the fact that one of Turner's most lethal attributes was his ability to make the ball kick off a wet pitch, and you have something of a 'smiling assassin', a terror indeed.

One day in the late 1920s, Turner was at the nets during a practice session for the North Sydney grade club. Bowling that day was an up-and-coming spinner by the name of Bill O'Reilly, and Turner heard no less than the Test bowler, Arthur Mailey, advising O'Reilly that he'd have to change his grip if he wanted to succeed in this game. When he also heard the young leggie from the bush politely say, 'Thank you Mr Mailey for your interest, but I've been gripping like this since I was a small boy, and I guess I'll have to sink or swim by it now,' Turner had to walk up and offer his support. The same thing had happened to him, he explained, when he came down from Bathurst in the early 1880s. He studied O'Reilly's unusual grip, and then, as he stated that being different wasn't necessarily a bad thing, showed off his own grip.

'He bent the top joint of his first finger until it was touching the palm of his hand,' O'Reilly recalled years later. 'I had never seen another bowler do this, still haven't.' Like so many of the great bowlers, the Terror was one of a kind.

CHARLIE TURNER (AUSTRALIA)

Test Cricket

Tests	Inn	NO	Runs	HS	Ave	100	50	Ct	Balls	Runs	Wkts	Ave	Best	5/	10/
17	32	4	323	29	11.54	–	–	8	5179	1670	101	16.53	7-43	11	2

First-Class Cricket

Mat	Inn	NO	Runs	HS	Ave	100	50	Ct	Balls	Runs	Wkts	Ave	Best	5/	10/
155	261	13	3856	103	15.55	2	11	85	41808	14152	993	14.25	9-15	102	35

No. 69 Ken Barrington

Of the cricketers who batted at least 30 times in Tests and played the majority of their Test cricket in the 1960s, how many have a Test batting average greater than 50? The answer is three: Graeme Pollock (60.97), Garry Sobers (57.78) and England's Ken Barrington.

Barrington hits Keith Stackpole for six over wide mid-on at the MCG during the fifth Ashes Test of 1965-66.

Barrington's final career average was 58.67. This single statistic is so impressive, given that fourth on this list — South Africa's Colin Bland (49.09) — is so far behind, that is can surely be taken as proof in itself that Barrington was a great Test batsman. The negative on Barrington is that there were times when his runs came too slowly, and that too few of his innings led to English victories. In fact, his style went against his natural instincts. He remodeled his game to best suit his team and also ensure that he kept his place in the side, the pity being that for much of his career the England bowling attack lacked firepower. As Barrington reached the absolute height of his powers, Fred Trueman and Brian Statham were approaching the end of their careers, John Snow just beginning, and none of the off-spinners or medium pacers being selected ever seemed likely to consistently go through opposition batting line-ups.

'A thickset 5ft 9ins (175cm), crinkly haired and strong-featured,' is how the cricket writer John Thicknesse described him. 'In anything but batting gear Barrington was jovial and gregarious, always ready to see the best in everyone and every situation.' A heart attack forced his premature retirement in early 1969 at age 38, but he returned to the game in a managerial capacity, where he was both respected and popular, not always an easy combination. His death while acting as assistant-manager on the England tour of the West Indies in 1981, was mourned across the cricket world.

Barrington made his Test debut back in 1955, the year he was awarded his county cap. However, in two Tests he scored just 52 runs, and didn't appear again for four more years. During those seasons in the 'wilderness' he revamped his game, eschewing aggression for pragmatism, maximising runs by eliminating risk. He opened his stance, stayed on the back foot (except against the spinners), and forgot all about trying to look glamorous. He never lacked courage. After England's thrashing in Australia by Richie Benaud's team in 1958-59, Barrington was brought back for the home series against India, and in his first five innings, spread over four Tests, scored 56, 80, 80, 87 and 46. Straight after, in the West Indies, he promptly scored his maiden Test century — 128 in Bridgetown — and he followed up with another hundred at Port-of-Spain, and for the next eight years he was a fixture in the England side. During these brave innings, Wes Hall and his new-ball partner Chester Watson targeted Barrington with a bumper barrage, as if that was the only way to dislodge him, but he never blinked, instead at one point doffing his cap after it was almost knocked off, and then pointing his bat at Hall as if it was a shotgun. It seemed a better response than rubbing the spot. The experience seemed to further toughen his run-making soul.

The Seventh XI

Barrington stands impassively at second slip as the Sydney crowd invades the field thinking the third Test of 1962-63 was over. In fact, Australia still needed two runs to win. Bob Simpson at the bowler's end is much keener for the spectators to leave the field.

'Ken was the undisputed prudent prince of percentage players who set aside shots he rated as unprofitable and awaited balls suitable for riskless strokes with his reduced repertoire,' remembered the great Australian journalist Ray Robinson in *The Wildest Tests* in 1972. 'For all his self-imposed restrictions, I thought him his country's surest cutter and sweeper and a good hooker — until Hall and Watson had him flopping on his back.'

Bill Lawry was a huge admirer. In his book *Rundigger* he wrote, 'When I watch Ken Barrington at the crease — and I have had the opportunity for many, many long hours! — my thoughts are that I only wish I could have been as good a cricketer.'

In 1964, Lawry's opening partner Bob Simpson batted for nearly 13 hours in a Test at Manchester to score 311. Barrington responded by turning his first Test hundred made at home into 256, his highest Test score. In all, 18 wickets fell in five days and both teams were slammed for forgetting about everyone but themselves. A year later, as criticism of the cautious ways of '60s batsmen grew louder, Barrington was dropped after making 137 in 437 minutes against a poor New Zealand attack at Edgbaston. At one point, he didn't manage a run for over an hour, but when he came back into the team he immediately accumulated 163 in less than six hours, a much more acceptable run-rate. In the following Australian summer, he hit centuries in the fourth and fifth Tests, the latter one at the MCG coming on the first day from just 122 balls and crowned by a six over long on. It was the second time in Ashes Tests that Barrington had cleared the boundary to reach three figures. In Adelaide in 1962-63, he did so as the game petered out to a draw, but on this second occasion, England needed a win to regain the Ashes, so Barrington set out to give them every advantage. What might have happened if he'd always played this way?

223

The 100 Greatest Cricketers

In Test cricket, Barrington averaged 77.24 in 40 innings as a No. 3, 59.18 in 44 innings as a No. 4, but only 41.96 from 31 innings as a No. 5. This was not so much a case of him scoring most of his runs when batting at the top of the order, but more a reflection of just how prolific he was in his greatest years, from 1962 to 1968. He was first promoted full-time to the No. 3 spot for England's tour of Pakistan and India in 1961-62, and responded by scoring a hundred in each of the first four Tests of the tour. The accomplished Indian slow men grew sick of the sight of him. When he retired, he had scored a century at every Test venue in England and in every Test-playing country of his time.

As he proved in 1965-66, Barrington was a batsman who could score a century in 325 minutes trying to save a Test, and then another hundred in 147 minutes just 10 days later, when England were desperate for a win.

England won 31 of Barrington's 82 Tests, and in those matches he averaged 64.42. His average in the 39 drawn Tests he was involved in was 67.05. But when England lost, which happened only 12 times, he averaged just 30.50. It wasn't quite as simple as if Barrington scored runs, England were safe, but often it seemed that way. 'The players of a generation pitted against him admired and respected a real competitor, a true Englishman who fought for his country as hard as they fought for theirs and then smiled his broken smile over a beer afterwards,' recalled Bob Simpson in 1996.

'It always seemed to me that he never received the recognition he deserved.'

KEN BARRINGTON (ENGLAND)

Test Cricket

Tests	Inn	NO	Runs	HS	Ave	100	50	Ct	Balls	Runs	Wkts	Ave	Best	5/	10/
82	131	15	6806	256	58.67	20	35	58	2715	1300	29	44.83	3-4	–	–

First-Class Cricket

Mat	Inn	NO	Runs	HS	Ave	100	50	Ct	Balls	Runs	Wkts	Ave	Best	5/	10/
533	831	136	31714	256	45.63	76	171	514	17301	8905	273	32.62	7-40	8	–

The Seventh XI

Monty Noble   No. 70

In 1947, officials at the Sydney Cricket Ground made the decision to name their newest, biggest grandstand, which had been opened in 1936 and since then had been known as the new member's stand. It became the 'MA Noble Stand', named after one of New South Wales and Australia's most respected cricketers. Montague Alfred Noble had been a trustee of the SCG in the years before his death in June 1940, but still it was a marvellous tribute to his achievements and contribution to the game to have such a landmark named after him. NSW had produced some outstanding and famous cricketers in the previous 100 years — among them the first Australian captain Dave Gregory, the Demon Spofforth, Charlie Bannerman, Billy Murdoch, Charlie Turner, Victor Trumper, Charlie Macartney, Don Bradman, Archie Jackson, Stan McCabe and Bill O'Reilly. Noble was honoured above them all.

The reason for the SCG Trust's decision was actually quite simple. Noble was a superb and influential cricketer, and a great captain for NSW and Australia. A case can be mounted that, by combining contributions on and off the field, he was New South Wales' most important cricketer. Bradman, of course, transferred to South Australia in 1934, two years before he became Australian captain. Only Richie Benaud, through his cricket and media work, and Bob Simpson, as cricketer, captain and coach, get near Noble for total contribution. He was a brilliant all-rounder, a revered leader of men, and later a highly respected administrator and commentator. This study is concerned only with on-field performances, but even with such a restriction Noble must be ranked highly.

To some of his friends he was Monty, to others Alf, occasionally 'Tommy'. He was tall, around 185cm (6ft 1in), and powerfully built, with huge feet to support that commanding physique, though still he was quick on his feet. With the bat in his hand, Noble could defend or attack, depending on his read of the situation, his bat close to his pad, his approach inevitably correct, befitting a student of the game. His only Test century was a vibrant, 133, made in four and a half hours on

MA Noble was probably the most influential figure in the first 100 years of NSW cricket.

225

the opening day of the 1903-04 Ashes series, after Australia had crashed to 3-12. Early on, Noble was understandably cautious as he and Warwick Armstrong sought to right the ship, but later in the day, when quick runs seemed necessary because an approaching storm was threatening to soak the pitch, Noble hit out brilliantly. In contrast, back in 1899 at Old Trafford he had batted more than three hours in the first innings for 60 not out and almost five and a half hours more in the second for 89 to save a game in which Australia was forced to follow on.

Noble had debuted in first-class cricket in 1894-95, as a specialist batsman after making an unbeaten 152 for a NSW Colts XVIII against Andrew Stoddart's Englishmen. However, he didn't establish himself in the NSW side until two years later, when he went on to top the season's batting averages. The following year, he was in the Test side, ostensibly as a batsman, but after he surprised by taking 6-49 when he was brought on third change in England's second innings, he announced himself as a genuine allrounder. In the next Test, he took another eight wickets, and by the end of the series he was batting six and bowling the opening over. His pace was slow-medium; in essence, he was a quickish off-spinner, of which there were plenty, but where he differed from others was that he had developed a 'swerve ball' that mesmerised the tourists. He developed it after seeing the way some American baseball pitchers touring Australia gripped the ball, and married his innovation to a lengthy run-up, perfect control and shrewd changes of pace. The future England captain, Charles Fry, faced Noble in four series in England, and once said that he believed Noble to be a better bowler than Sydney Barnes on good, hard wickets. At Lord's in 1909 Noble bowled Archie MacLaren with a vicious off-break that MacLaren's biographer Michael Down described as 'the only genuinely unplayable ball of the entire innings'.

Noble in England in 1909, when he led Australia to a 2-0 series win.

Noble's Sheffield Shield statistics are remarkable. His career batting average in the competition of 68.00 suggests he was a 19.64 runs per innings better batsman than Trumper, 15.72 runs per innings better than Clem Hill. His bowling record at Shield level is slightly inferior to Hugh Trumble's, but superior to just about anyone else from his time. At Test level, he was not as dominant, averaging 30.26 with the bat, with one century (but 16 fifties) from 42 Tests, and 25 with the ball, but still excellent. Revealingly, he was at his best the higher in the batting order he went in. As an opener, he averaged 38.45; as a No. 3, he averaged 34.80. From No. 4 to No. 9, however, he averaged only 28. It took Noble 27 Tests to reach the double of 1000 runs/100 wickets in Tests, the second man to do so after George Giffen (who took 30 Tests to complete the double). Three more runs in his final Test innings, 55 at The Oval in 1909 (when Australia, under Noble's captaincy, retained the Ashes his men had won decisively in 1907-08), would have made him the first from any country to score 2000 runs and take 100 wickets. Instead, Wilfred Rhodes became the first, in 1920, in his 48th Test. In 1950, four years after Keith Miller made his Test debut, Johnnie Moyes argued that Noble was 'the best all-rounder we have seen'.

Noble took 10 wickets in a Test twice, including a remarkable 13-77 at the MCG in 1901-02, when 25 wickets fell on the first day, seven of them to Noble for 17 runs. On days two and three, Test debutant Reggie Duff scored a hundred having been held back to No. 10 because of the wet pitch; when asked why Duff had been picked, Trumble said flatly, 'Because Alf Noble says he is a champion.'

Noble was a man of high principle, who in 1906 found himself involved in a bitter dispute with cricket administrators over how the game needed to be run, and though some relationships with officials were destroyed, he never lost the loyalty of his comrades or the respect of his opponents. Charlie Macartney called Noble 'the best captain it has been my pleasure to play under', a huge compliment considering that Macartney also scored centuries for Hill, Trumper, Armstrong and Bert Collins. Pelham Warner, England captain in 1903-04, thought Noble 'the wisest of all Australian captains'. Arthur Mailey described him as 'the most convincing captain to whom I ever listened' and 'the strongest personality I have met in cricket', while Don Bradman wrote of how a 'fleeting glimpse of Noble, long after his best years had passed, left me with a feeling of admiration for him'.

No wonder the SCG Trust named a grandstand after him. It was probably the least that they could do.

MONTY NOBLE (AUSTRALIA)

Test Cricket

Tests	Inn	NO	Runs	HS	Ave	100	50	Ct	Balls	Runs	Wkts	Ave	Best	5/	10/
42	73	7	1997	133	30.26	1	16	26	7159	3025	121	25.00	7-17	9	2

First-Class Cricket

Mat	Inn	NO	Runs	HS	Ave	100	50	Ct	Balls	Runs	Wkts	Ave	Best	5/	10/
248	377	34	13975	284	40.74	37	66	187	33112	14443	624	23.15	8-48	33	7

The 100 Greatest Cricketers

No. 71 & No. 72 Andy Roberts and Michael Holding

There have been a number of truly great fast bowling combinations over the years, but while some have worked their way into the centre of cricket's consciousness, never to be forgotten, others haven't quite received that same level of acceptance, where the surnames of the two bowlers become as one. A recent example is that of Australia's Glenn McGrath and Jason Gillespie — 'McGrath and Gillespie' hasn't quite got the same ring to it as 'Gregory and McDonald', 'Larwood and Voce', 'Lindwall and Miller', 'Trueman and Statham', 'Hall and Griffith', 'Lillee and Thomson', 'Waqar and Wasim'. McGrath and Gillespie had as many successful days as any dynamic duo, but McGrath has also forged a telling union with Shane Warne, so there wasn't that strong impression left that it was the two quicks who were working in partnership. Maybe, too, the value of the fast bowlers' teamwork was lost a little among all the outstanding players that made up the dominating Australian teams of the modern era.

Holding in England in 1976, demoralising England at The Oval.

In his autobiography, umpire 'Dickie' Bird remembered a conversation he once had with the late Peter Burge, the former Australian batsman of the 1950s and 1960s who was later an ICC match referee. Burge had seen all the great fast bowling duos since the war and he rated Wasim and Waqar as the best of them all. There are many across the cricket world, and especially in England, who share this view. In the 49 Tests they bowled in tandem between 1989 and 2001, Wasim and Waqar took 472 wickets, almost 10 wickets per match. Statistically, the partnership of Andy Roberts and Michael Holding isn't far behind.

In 30 Tests together, Roberts and Holding took 237 wickets, nearly eight wickets a Test. When you consider the other bowlers in the West Indies team of those days who were competing for wickets — including Keith Boyce, Bernard Julien, Vanburn Holder, Lance Gibbs, Joel Garner, Wayne Daniel, Colin Croft and Malcolm Marshall — this is quite an achievement, perhaps putting them on par with Wasim and Waqar. Further reflecting the quality of these two fast bowlers, in these 30 Tests only four times did another bowler open the West Indies attack. In the first innings of their second Test as a unit, at Perth in 1975-76, Boyce bowled the second over after Roberts, with Holding first change. And in their final three innings in Test cricket together, when Roberts came back into the team in India in December 1983, Marshall kept the new ball. Otherwise, it was usually Roberts then Holding, occasionally Holding then Roberts.

When Roberts made his debut against England at Bridgetown in 1974 he became the first man from Antigua

The Seventh XI

to play Test cricket. Eighteen months later, he was in Australia as a veteran of eight Tests and a successful World Cup campaign, while Holding, a former schoolboy track champion from Jamaica, was yet to make his Test debut. Despite his lack of Test time, Roberts' performance in India in 1974-75, when he took 32 wickets in five Tests (becoming the first West Indian to take 12 wickets in one Test in Madras), had established him as a quick of the highest class, and when Holding quickly showed enormous promise, sliding gracefully in off a long run to bowl almost as quickly as Jeff Thomson, the media were quick to promote the upcoming series as a battle of the fast men. In the end, though, it was no contest, Australia winning 5-1, but the experience toughened the men from the Caribbean, and when they arrived in England in 1976 they were ready to demonstrate just what an outstanding cricket team they could be. Roberts and Holding both took 28 wickets in the series, and Holding was irresistible at The Oval, when he took 14 wickets in the match, twice bowling the England captain Tony Greig through sheer speed. Dickie Bird called it 'one of the best spells of sustained fast bowling I have ever witnessed'. Later, in his autobiography, Greig described Holding as 'the fastest bowler I have ever faced'.

Roberts, the first Test cricketer to come from Antigua.

This might have been true, but many also thought Roberts was the more dangerous. In 1984, Lillee called him 'the most complete fast bowler I have seen', using an adjective that was often used later to describe Malcolm Marshall. At around 183cm (6ft), Roberts looked almost diminutive next to taller teammates such as Holding and especially 'Big Bird' Garner. He had two bouncers, one that you could hook, the other you wouldn't dare. In the space of a few months, in 1977-78, he broke David Hookes' jaw in a match at the Sydney Showground and then flattened another Australian, Peter Toohey, in a Test at Port-of-Spain. Both batsmen appeared to be seduced by a slower short ball that was dispatched for four, before the much quicker ball, delivered with no discernible change in action, struck like a cobra. From a relatively short run to wicket, Roberts built momentum quickly until as he neared the umpire he leant back and half slung the ball at the always wary batsman.

Holding's run-up was much longer, a glorious approach that earned him the nickname 'Whispering Death' from umpires who could hardly hear him as he approached the wickets but saw first-hand the carnage he wrought at the other end. Roberts might have swung and seamed the ball more; both knew the value of the yorker as well as the riser. The two became synonymous with the pace barrage that was a feature of World Series Cricket, and afterwards were as important as any of their famous teammates as the West Indies established themselves as one of cricket's greatest ever teams. Whereas before WSC, Roberts was invariably regarded as the better bowler, afterwards Holding was more damaging. This was especially true in Australia, where he was devastating in consecutive series in 1981-82 and 1984-85. And as Roberts had been nearly a decade before, Holding was magnificent in India, especially when he and Marshall were too much for most of the locals, even Sunil Gavaskar at times, in late 1983.

Through their careers, Holding looked the superior batsman, but Roberts was the man who played more key late-order innings.

The two, with Garner, were also magnificent in one-day cricket. A study of the bowling averages of all those to play at least 50 ODIs reveals Garner with the lowest average, at 18.85, then New Zealand's Shane Bond (19.33), Roberts (20.36), Lillee (20.83), Holding (21.37) and Richard Hadlee (21.56). Roberts was an especially crafty one-day bowler, and also a shrewd late-order batsman in both forms of the game. His most famous effort with the bat came during the 1975 World Cup, when with Deryck Murray he added an unbeaten 64 for the last wicket to win a match against Pakistan with two balls to spare. Holding was perhaps a better batsmen, but much less likely to hang around. At Headingley in 1984, in the same match he took his 200th Test wicket (the fourth West Indies bowler to do so, after Sobers, Gibbs and Roberts), he smashed five sixes in a innings of 59 that helped Larry Gomes to a century and gave his team a crucial first-innings lead.

ANDY ROBERTS (WEST INDIES)

Test Cricket

Tests	Inn	NO	Runs	HS	Ave	100	50	Ct	Balls	Runs	Wkts	Ave	Best	5/	10/
47	62	11	762	68	14.94	–	3	9	11135	5174	202	25.61	7-54	11	2

One-Day International Cricket

ODIs	Inn	NO	Runs	HS	Ave	100	50	Ct	Balls	Runs	Wkts	Ave	Best	4/
56	32	9	231	37*	10.04	–	–	6	3123	1771	87	20.36	5-22	3

The Seventh XI

Of all the overs Holding bowled in bigtime cricket, none is more famous than the six balls fired at Geoff Boycott at the start of England's first innings at Bridgetown in 1981. The pitch was hard and covered in grass, but quickly poor Boycott was jumping about as if it was on fire. Rarely has a bowler made an excellent batsman look so ruffled, yet in truth Boycott was exceptionally brave. First, he gloved down a riser, then he played and missed, was struck on the thigh, twice prodded 'throat balls' to the gully, and finally his off-stump was sent cartwheeling. The atmosphere was electric, closer to a bullfight than a cricket match, the fans exuberant while the batsman stumbled off as if he had seen a ghost. 'Six good reasons why I would never advise anyone to become a Test opening batsman,' Boycott wrote grimly afterwards.

Amazingly, Holding was bowling into the breeze, after Roberts had started with a superb over at Graham Gooch. There was really no escape; neither could the batsmen have looked forward to Garner and in this case Croft coming on first and second change. The atmosphere of intimidation was deep and relentless — a step or two beyond that established by Wes Hall and Charlie Griffith in the 1960s — and it continued on for another decade, having started from the time Roberts and Holding came together. Very few fast bowlers have been more electrifying; fewer still have worked better as a partnership or had a greater impact on the way the game was played, both in their day and in the years that followed their time at the top.

Above left: The Windies' pace quartet in 1981: (from left) Roberts, Holding, Colin Croft and Joel Garner.

Above: Few nicknames in cricket have seemed more appropriate than Holding's 'Whispering Death'.

MICHAEL HOLDING (WEST INDIES)

Test Cricket

Tests	Inn	NO	Runs	HS	Ave	100	50	Ct	Balls	Runs	Wkts	Ave	Best	5/	10/
60	76	10	910	73	13.79	–	6	22	12680	5898	249	23.69	8-92	13	2

One-Day International Cricket

ODIs	Inn	NO	Runs	HS	Ave	100	50	Ct	Balls	Runs	Wkts	Ave	Best	4/
102	42	11	282	64	9.10	–	2	30	5473	3034	142	21.37	5-26	6

The 100 Greatest Cricketers

No. 73 Bob Simpson

Bob Simpson made his first-class debut for New South Wales in 1953 as a 16-year-old middle-order batsman and occasional leg-spin bowler. He won his initial Test cap in 1957, as one of a group of promising young players sent to South Africa in the wake of Australia's disappointing displays in England in 1956. By 1960, he was an opening batsman, and in 1963 also captain of his country, appointed to the top job after Richie Benaud relinquished the leadership in the season after Neil Harvey and Alan Davidson retired. The following year, Simpson scored his first Test century: 311 in 762 minutes at Old Trafford in a drawn Test that allowed Australia to retain the Ashes.

From 1957 to 1996, Simpson was involved with the Australian team, as cricketer, captain and coach.

Spectators who saw Simpson in his first two Sheffield Shield games could hardly have believed that it would be more than 11 years before he'd make a Test hundred. His debut Shield innings came on January 26, Australia Day, when he made 44 not out against Victoria at the Sydney Cricket Ground. At the time, he had not even scored a century in first-grade cricket. He followed up with an unbeaten 8 in the second innings and then 69 against South Australia, giving him a first-class career average to that point of 121. The following year, he struggled with the bat, usually batting seven, eight or even No. 9, but did take 5-37 against Western Australia in Sydney after captain Keith Miller surprised by bringing him on second change. Miller also quickly recognised the teenager's remarkable catching ability, which was highlighted in a match between NSW and Len Hutton's English team in January 1955, when Hutton himself fell to two wonderful slip catches, the first off the spinner Jack Treanor, the second off Jim Burke. At season's end, Johnnie Moyes described Simpson as 'a lad who has no superior as a slip fielder in Australian cricket'.

Simpson could have been picked for Australia's tours of the Caribbean in 1955 and England in 1956 but it would only have been on potential, as he really hadn't scored enough runs. Feeling somewhat hamstrung among the star-studded NSW line-up, he made the bold decision to transfer to Western Australia for the 1956-57 season, where he batted three and quickly found comfort in being a key player

The Seventh XI

rather than just another cog in the wheel. In South Africa in 1957-58, his fielding was superb — 13 catches in five Tests — but though he was excellent in the tour games he struggled for runs in the biggest games. An impression was being established that Simpson was struggling with the expectations that had been placed upon him. Back in Perth in 1958-59, he had a moderate season and lost his Test place, but then, while Benaud's Australian team was touring the subcontinent, he made the decision to move to the top of the order, on the basis that such a move offered the best chance of him returning to the Australian side. The result was an extraordinary season in Australia, when he averaged 300.67 with the bat in five matches for WA and he was selected for the first Test of the 1960-61 home series against the West Indies.

Simpson hooks Garry Sobers during the 1960-61 'Calypso Summer'.

There is a perception today that Simpson was a fixture of the Australian team for this famous 'Calypso Summer', but this was hardly the case. He needed runs to ensure his place for the 1961 Ashes tour, but scores of 92, 0, 49, 27 not out, 10 and 12 hardly cemented his position. For the fourth Test in Adelaide, he swapped places in the batting order with Les Favell, who was used to opening in Adelaide, and though Simpson was scoring a stack of runs outside the Tests it is very possible that had Favell succeeded and Simpson failed, it would have been the South Australian captain on the boat to England. Instead, Favell made 1 and 4 in what proved to be his final Test. Restored to open for the final match of the series at the MCG, Simpson scored 75 and 92, dramatically taking 18 runs from Wes Hall's opening over of the second innings and nine from the second, and his place in the Australian XI was never seriously questioned again.

Geoff Boycott edges the ball to Simpson at first slip during the 1964 Ashes series.

Moyes thought that during that series Simpson 'proved conclusively that against the turning ball he was the best equipped player in the side'. He also believed that the display against Hall at Melbourne showed that Simpson 'had not lost his brilliance, but had simply stored it away until he felt it was required'. A criticism in later years was that it was stored away much too often, but at the same time — usually in tandem with fellow opener Bill Lawry — he gave the Australian batting order both a platform

233

The 100 Greatest Cricketers

Simpson is inducted into the Australian Cricket Hall of Fame in 2006.

and a backbone it vitally needed. As a Test opener, Simpson averaged 55.52. As Australian captain between 1963 and 1968, he averaged 60.10, scoring eight hundreds and 19 fifties in 52 innings. He made big hundreds at home, and in England, Pakistan, the West Indies and South Africa. In Karachi in 1964 he became the first batsman to score a century in each innings of a Test in Pakistan. He and Lawry added 382 against Hall and Griffith at Bridgetown in 1965, and in 1965-66 they put on 244 at almost a run a minute after England had been bowled out for 241 at the Adelaide Oval. In Cape Town in 1966-67, he played an innings of 153 that RS Whitington described as 'the nearest thing to the defensive side of Bradman I have watched'. Years later, when Simpson came back into the Australian team at 41 years of age during the World Series Cricket imbroglio, he made two hundreds against Bedi and Chandrasekhar.

In *Willow Patterns* (1969), Richie Benaud related how Simpson turned himself into a 'technique player', describing him as 'the best Australian player of the bat and pad technique I have ever seen'. Benaud attributed this to the season Simpson played in the Lancashire League in 1959. 'In many ways he is a remarkable batsman, giving the bowler less chance than most other players I have seen in modern day cricket,' was the former Australian captain's verdict.

In 1986, Simpson became the Australian team's coach and over the next decade helped turn the team from a poor side into the best in the world. Steve Waugh, who made his Test debut as a 20-year-old in December 1985, became a special project for him, especially when Waugh failed to live up to his early promise, struggled for years to make his maiden Test century, and was eventually dropped from the side. 'What he had to come to turns with,' Simpson wrote of Waugh in 1996, 'is that style isn't everything.' It was a lesson the coach himself had learnt the hard way 30 years before — that when it comes to runs, it's not how, but how many. It was only when he did so that he became one of the most effective batsman in the world.

BOB SIMPSON (AUSTRALIA)

Test Cricket

Tests	Inn	NO	Runs	HS	Ave	100	50	Ct	Balls	Runs	Wkts	Ave	Best	5/	10/
62	111	7	4869	311	46.82	10	27	110	6881	3001	71	42.27	5-57	2	–

First-Class Cricket

Mat	Inn	NO	Runs	HS	Ave	100	50	Ct	Balls	Runs	Wkts	Ave	Best	5/	10/
257	436	62	21029	359	56.23	60	100	383	28088	13288	349	38.07	5-33	6	–

Johnny Briggs

No.74

The first man to take 100 wickets in Test cricket was Johnny Briggs, of Lancashire and England. He did so on February 1, 1895, the opening day of the fourth Ashes Test of 1894-95. At the time, Briggs' bowling average in Tests was 13.50. Had he retired then, he would have the third best average of all to take 50 or more Test wickets, behind only George Lohmann and Jack Ferris.

Instead, Briggs' Test career would go on until 1899, his career average rising to 17.75, and end in desperate circumstances. On the first night of the third Test of 1899, while he was at the theatre, Briggs suffered a severe epileptic fit and was quickly transferred to Cheadle Asylum. He didn't play any cricket at all until the following year (when despite being patently ill he took 127 first-class wickets, including 10-55 in one innings against Worcestershire). He never bowled another over in Test cricket, and died, aged 39, at the asylum in January 1902. He spent his last few months in a world of his own, bowling at imaginary batsmen in Test matches along the corridor. Briggs' Test aggregate record of 118 wickets outlived him by nearly two years, when Australia's Hugh Trumble went past him.

In his *Complete Who's Who of Test Cricketers*, Christopher Martin-Jenkins described Briggs as 'one of the best-loved of Lancashire's characters, a little skipjack of a man and a magnificent allrounder'. He was tiny fellow, just 165cm (5ft 5in) short, who made his debut in county cricket in 1879, a few months before his 17th birthday. It was said that he was first chosen primarily for his fielding, and his speed to the ball and vitality quickly made him a popular figure at Old Trafford. Next, his aggressive batting began to have an impact, but it wasn't until 1885 that his name appeared near the top of the first-class bowling averages. By then he'd already made his Test debut, having accepted an invitation the previous year to join Arthur Shrewsbury's team of professionals that toured Australia. He played in all five Tests, scored 121 in the second Test at the MCG, but bowled just eight overs for 13 runs. The hundred was made in around 150 minutes, and included more fours (16) than singles (11). With keeper Joe Hunter, Briggs added 98 for the last wicket in an hour.

The first man to take 100 wickets in Test cricket.

In its summary of the 1885 season, Lillywhite's *Cricketers' Annual* had this to say: 'The most notable feature of 1885 was the marked advance of Briggs as a bowler. Until his Australian trip, Briggs had hardly been tried at all in the department, and even then his success was only partial. Last summer, though, he proved himself to be a bowler of really great merit, and possessed of considerable judgment, as well as the ability to get a lot of work on the ball, he is sure to rank very high among the best trundlers of the day.' His batting skills had also been on display, most notably against Surrey at Liverpool, when Briggs and Richard Pilling put on 173 for the last wicket in 100 minutes after coming together at 9-191. Briggs, contribution was 186; his marriage 48 hours earlier had clearly not done him any harm.

Within 12 months, he was, next to George Lohmann, the best bowler in the country. Having not bowled a ball in the first Test of 1886 (when he batted eight and scored 1 and 2 not out), he came on first change at Lord's, with Australia 0-45 in reply to 353, and promptly took 5-29 as the visitors crashed to 121 all out. After the follow-on was enforced, Briggs took a further 6-45, this time opening the bowling. In the final Test, he took 3-28 and 3-30 and England swept the series. The following year, a young Pelham Warner went to Lord's to watch a match between the MCC and an England XI, staged to celebrate the centenary of the famous ground. In his book *Lord's 1787–1945*, Warner wrote fondly, 'I can recall, too, AE Stoddart's and Shrewsbury's great first-wicket partnership of 266; Ulyett's powerful hits over deep extra cover's head off Barnes of Nottinghamshire, scattering the spectators in Block A; George Lohmann's artistic and cleverly flighted bowling; and Johnny Briggs at cover.' Briggs took seven wickets in the match, equal with Lohmann as the game's top wicket-taker, yet it was his fielding and his presence that stuck in Warner's memory.

Briggs toured South Africa in 1888-89, producing an astonishing performance in the second Test at Cape Town. On day two, after England had been dismissed for 292, the home team were bowled out for 47 and 43. Briggs, coming on first change in the first innings but then bowling for the rest of the match, took 7-17 and 8-11 — 15 wickets in one day. All but one of his victims were bowled, the other lbw.

In all, he toured Australia six times, perhaps his most notable cricket adventure coming under WG Grace's captaincy in 1891-92, when he snared a hat-trick in the second Test in Sydney and then took 12 wickets in the third as England won by an innings and 230 runs. He remained the only man to complete both a Test century and a Test hat-trick until Wasim Akram took his first Test hat-trick in 1999 (Pakistan's Abdul Razzaq achieved this double in 2000, New Zealand's James Franklin in 2006 and India's Irfan Pathan in 2007). Three years later, Briggs had a considerable role in England's famous victory at the SCG after they'd been forced to follow on. With the wicket wrecked after an overnight storm, but Australia needing just 64 runs with eight wickets in hand, Briggs and Yorkshire's Bobby Peel spun the visitors to an astonishing victory.

In 1899, Grace described Briggs' bowling this way: 'He bowls left handed at a medium or slow pace, breaking both ways at will and capable of perplexing the most confident of batsmen on a sticky wicket.' Tellingly, WG went on to say, 'Briggs is one of the best head bowlers we have ever had.' Given that tribute, and that he evolved into a great bowler after observing others during his first five years as a first-class cricketer, it is easy to believe that Briggs was one 19th century bowler who would have adapted to the game of any era. His blazing batting and sure, exciting fielding would have complemented his bowling beautifully in one-day cricket. Add this to his considerable record, and you have a cricketer fully entitled to be ranked among any all-time top 100.

JOHNNY BRIGGS (ENGLAND)

Test Cricket

Tests	Inn	NO	Runs	HS	Ave	100	50	Ct	Balls	Runs	Wkts	Ave	Best	5/	10/
33	50	5	815	121	18.11	1	2	12	5332	2095	118	17.75	8-11	9	4

First-Class Cricket

Mat	Inn	NO	Runs	HS	Ave	100	50	Ct	Balls	Runs	Wkts	Ave	Best	5/	10/
535	826	55	14092	186	18.28	10	58	258	100119	35430	2221	15.95	10-55	200	52

The Seventh XI

Rohan Kanhai

No. 75

Rohan Kanhai was one of the finest No. 3 batsmen of them all. As was pointed out in the Ken Barrington chapter, of all cricketers to play Test cricket in the 1960s, only three — Barrington, Garry Sobers and Graeme Pollock — averaged more than 50 for their career. Kanhai played most of his Test cricket during the '60s, almost always batting at the fall of the first wicket. As a Test No. 3, the position that for most of the first 100 years of Test cricket was considered to be where a captain always put his best batsman, Kanhai averaged 52.69.

Kanhai batted 'first drop' three times in his first 22 innings in Test matches, five times in his last 20. In between, from December 1958 to February 1973, more than 14 years, he batted 95 times and on only 13 occasions — whether it be because of a captain's decision, the use of a nightwatchman, illness or injury — did Kanhai not go in at three. He did so through a time when the main weakness in the West Indies team was its opening partnership. Conrad Hunte could never find a regular partner during the first half of Kanhai's life as Test No. 3, and for the seven years after Hunte retired in early 1967 only Roy Fredericks kept his place at the top of the Windies' batting order for long.

In West Indies domestic cricket, Kanhai was known to score flashing hundreds for Guyana against Barbados at a time when the Barbados attack featured Wes Hall and Charlie Griffith. Few little men have hit the ball harder. Denis Compton thought Kanhai was to the square cut as Wally Hammond was to the cover drive. Kanhai's technique was excellent, but with it came a flair that allowed him to deposit medium pacers over wide long on, and left him flat on his back against the spinners after he put everything into a cross between a pull and a sweep shot. Later, he became a little more defensive, leaving the blazing to the younger fellows. In Tests, he made runs against Fred Trueman, Brian Statham and John Snow, Alan Davidson and Graham McKenzie. In Australia in 1971-72, playing for a World XI, he made two hundreds against an attack led by Dennis Lillee, including 118 in the second innings of the international in Perth, after coming to the wicket at 1-9. Earlier that day, Lillee had sensationally taken 8-29 in the World XI's first innings of 59, but he didn't dismiss Kanhai, who was McKenzie's only wicket.

Through the 1960s, Kanhai was almost always the West Indies No. 3.

Kanhai's first tour of Australia was in 1960-61, the Tied Test series. Before the series started, he scored 252 against Victoria, but he was fairly quiet in the first three Tests. Then in Adelaide he was magnificent, scoring a century in each innings — the first in 126 minutes, the second in 150. Johnnie Moyes was captivated, arguing that he

237

'certainly a finer batsman and a greater menace than his left-handed colleague'. That 'left-handed colleague' was Sobers, no less, who had scored that brilliant 132 on the opening day of the Tied Test, and 168 in the third Test in Sydney. 'Kanhai will long be remembered in Australia,' Moyes wrote. 'When he arrived he had nothing like the reputation of Sobers, but, by the time he left these shores he had firmly established himself in the hearts of all who love scintillating batsmanship. This little man who sometimes reminded us of Macartney — that is no light praise — had such superb natural skill.'

Garry Sobers congratulates Kanhai on reaching his century in the fifth Test against England in 1967-68, at Georgetown. The pair added 250 for the fourth wicket.

Kanhai was a small, slightly built man who began his Test career as a wicket-keeper/batsman, but made little impact with the bat or gloves in his first 12 Tests, which featured just three fifties in 23 innings. It wasn't until he turned his first Test century into 256 against India at Calcutta on New Year's Day 1959 that he found the confidence to score regularly at the highest level. In his next Test innings he was run out for 99, and later in the tour he made his second Test ton another big one: 217 against Pakistan at Lahore. In all, Kanhai would make 15 Test-match hundreds, the last two of them, against Australia and then England, when he was West Indian captain, a post he held for 13 Tests in 1973-74. His captaincy was criticised as too conservative, but in truth he never had the talent his successor Clive Lloyd would enjoy utilising. Andy Roberts made his Test debut in Kanhai's 11th Test as skipper; Gordon Greenidge and Viv Richards debuted one match after he retired.

For so long he was remarkably consistent. From 1958 to 1973 he played in 14 series and scored a century in all but three of them, with a highest average for one series of 70.71 (at home against India in 1961-62) and a lowest average for one series of 37.10 (in Australia in 1968-69). His highest series aggregate was 538, in India in 1958-59, but he scored more than 400 runs in a series seven times. After struggling in those first two series, before he scored a Test hundred, he never had a genuinely mediocre series until his final rubber, when he only averaged 26.17 against England at home in early 1974. There have been some defensively minded batsmen in the game's history who have remained consistent over long periods, but few who batted in the style of Kanhai.

In 1966, the renowned West Indian cricket historian CLR James wrote an essay in which he compared Kanhai favourably to Don Bradman. He based this assessment on an innings of 170 in three hours James had seen Kanhai make for a West Indian XI against an England XI at Edgbaston in September 1964. The England XI attack that day was just below Test class, and they had knocked their opponents over for just 137 in the first innings. James wrote: 'Kanhai had found his way into

The Seventh XI

regions Bradman never knew. It was not only the technical skill and strategic generalship that made the innings the most noteworthy I have seen. There was more to it, to be seen as well as felt. Bradman was a ruthless executioner of bowlers. All through this demanding innings, Kanhai grinned with a grin that could be seen a mile away.'

Nine years later, the 39-year-old Kanhai came back to demonstrate what an adaptable batsman he could be, by playing a critical sheet-anchor role to Lloyd's brilliance in the inaugural World Cup final. He scored 55, batting five, after his team had slumped to 3-50 but recovered to 8-291. Later, he held an important pressure catch to dismiss Australia's Gary Gilmour as the West Indies closed in on their historic victory. The Windies were now on the verge of the greatest era in its cricket history; for Rohan Kanhai that famous day at Lord's became a glorious farewell.

The famous finish to cricket's first Tied Test. Kanhai is leaping high at the far, striker's end; Sobers is near him with arms outstretched; Frank Worrell (at the bowler's end) is the calmest man on the field.

ROHAN KANHAI (WEST INDIES)

Test Cricket

Tests	Inn	NO	Runs	HS	Ave	100	50	Ct	Balls	Runs	Wkts	Ave	Best	5/	10/
79	137	6	6227	256	47.53	15	28	50	183	85	—	—	0-1	—	—

First-Class Cricket

Mat	Inn	NO	Runs	HS	Ave	100	50	Ct	St	Balls	Runs	Wkts	Ave	Best	5/	10/
416	669	82	28774	256	49.02	83	120	320	7	1505	1009	18	56.06	2-5	—	—

No. 76 Wasim Bari

The Pakistan team that toured Australia in 1972-73 was not expected — at least in Australia — to be competitive. Ian Chappell's men had just returned from a surprisingly successful Ashes series, and despite the reputations of batsmen such as Zaheer Abbas, Majid Khan and Mushtaq Mohammad, most believed that the new ball attack of Dennis Lillee and Bob Massie would be too much for them. Furthermore, the visitors' bowling looked mediocre. A 3-0 cleansweep was expected, and duly occurred, though not with anything like the ease that had been predicted. Pakistan actually declared their first innings closed in Melbourne, at 8-574, but their bowlers couldn't break a key Paul Sheahan-John Benaud second-innings partnership and then there were three critical run outs on the final day. In Sydney, they needed only 159 to win but lost their last seven wickets for 23 to lose by 52.

Wasim Bari is undoubtedly the most accomplished gloveman Pakistan has produced.

At different times, all of Zaheer, Majid, Mushtaq, Sadiq Mohammad and Asif Iqbal looked good with the bat, while the first-change bowler Sarfraz Nawaz took eight wickets in Sydney and captain Intikhab Alam was as wily with his leg breaks as he had been the year before when he and Zaheer had been members of the World XI that toured Australia. However, of all the Pakistanis to make an impact, none was more impressive than wicketkeeper Wasim Bari. He more than matched the Australian custodian Rod Marsh, especially up at the stumps for the spin bowlers, and even lost little in comparisons with England's Alan Knott, who had left such a big impression through his displays in the 1970-71 Ashes series.

Perhaps Wasim did not cover quite as much ground down the legside as did Knott and Marsh, but he had a sense of timing when he gloved the ball that few wicketkeepers have ever matched. His talent had been recognised as early as 1967, when members of an England under-25 team reported that they had seen the best keeper ever to emerge from the subcontinent. Later that year, Wasim was in England with Hanif Mohammad's senior squad, playing in all three Tests and completing his first Test dismissal within minutes of his career beginning, when Colin Milburn edged a catch off Asif. At series end, *Wisden* reported, 'As a wicketkeeper, Wasim Bari was almost infallible, taking his chances without fuss.' For most of the next 17 years, Wasim was his country's keeper. When he retired in 1984, following his fifth tour of Australia, no other Pakistani had played as many as his 81 Tests.

The Seventh XI

In his book *The Cricket Revolution* (1981), England fast bowler Bob Willis recalled Knott saying more than once that Wasim was 'the best he had ever seen behind the stumps'. Willis described Wasim as 'a neat, unobtrusive performer, with the ability to dive in front of slip for low catches and to take throws from the outfield with that "give" of the gloves that stems from sheer class'. The great allrounder Imran Khan wrote of the difference having a keeper of Wasim's calibre made to his fast bowling, but like most of the great keepers Wasim was at his absolute best when up to the stumps. This was particularly evident late in his career, when he might have lost a step standing back but was still superb when working with the unpredictable, big spinning Abdul Qadir. Wasim was the first keeper to have to come to terms with the concept of 'reverse swing', as pioneered by Imran and Sarfraz, who worked on the old ball so that they could swing it the opposite way to what the batsman expected. Imran was especially clever at bowling big, late inswingers, and with the ball softer and subcontinent pitches rarely offering bounce this provided a real challenge for the keeper — who not only had to be soft of glove and quick of foot, but also brave whenever the ball bounced unpredictably in front of him.

At Leeds in 1971, Wasim equalled the then world record by holding eight catches in a Test, but the party was spoiled when Pakistan lost their last six wickets for 45 to surrender the match, and the series, by 25 runs. In Australia in 1976-77 he completed four stumpings in one Test, and was so consistent that Imran later claimed that for all the quality of Knott and Marsh, Wasim had become the best keeper in the world. At Auckland in February 1979, Wasim caught seven of the first eight New Zealand wickets to fall, establishing a new record for catches in an innings that has been equalled three times (by England's Bob Taylor, New Zealand's Ian Smith and the West Indies' Ridley Jacobs) but never bettered. Later that year he became the first (and as at June 30, 2009, still the only) Pakistani keeper to complete 150 Test-match dismissals.

Unlike most of the outstanding Pakistani players of the 1970s — Imran, Majid, Asif, Zaheer, Mushtaq, Intikhab, Sarfraz, Sadiq and Javed Miandad — who played in the English county championship, Wasim developed his game in Pakistani domestic cricket. This achievement of being a 'home grown' Pakistani star should not be underrated. As he told David Lemmon for *The Great Wicketkeepers*, he believed he

Wasim Bari and Imran Khan formed a superb keeper/bowler combination in the late '70s and early '80s.

was born to keep, explaining, 'Since I first kept wicket I have never wanted to do anything else. I do not mind where I bat, or if I bat, as long as they allow me to keep wicket.'

England's David Gower off-drives during the 1978 England-Pakistan series. Wasim Bari, the tourists' captain, is behind the stumps.

Given his love affair with the keeping gloves, perhaps it is not surprising that Wasim's final Test batting average was only 15.88, well below that of his famous rivals: Knott, Marsh and India's Syed Kirmani. He could glean runs in Tests, making half-centuries at different times against attacks led by Dennis Lillee, Andy Roberts and Kapil Dev, but he failed too often, sometimes playing silly shots, to be considered a likely threat. At Bridgetown in 1976 he made 60 not out after dropping down to No. 11, adding a then Test record 133 with Wasim Raja, following a harrowing incident on the rest day when he had to be dragged from the sea by lifeguards after getting himself into difficulties. Nowadays, with such a meagre average, he might have even struggled to hold his place, and one-day cricket might not have been for him, but he was such a professional most likely he would have worked harder on his runs, instead of focusing purely on his art. Certainly, in the years since he retired Pakistan have never had a gloveman of anything like his quality.

If any keeper could justify the old adage that you should always pick your best keeper regardless of his batting ability, Wasim Bari would be your man.

WASIM BARI (PAKISTAN)
Test Cricket

Tests	Inn	NO	Runs	HS	Ave	100	50	Ct	St	Balls	Runs	Wkts	Ave	Best	5/	10/
81	112	26	1366	85	15.88	–	6	201	27	8	2	–	–	0-2	–	–

First-Class Cricket

Mat	Inn	NO	Runs	HS	Ave	100	50	Ct	St	Balls	Runs	Wkts	Ave	Best	5/	10/
286	358	93	5799	177	21.88	2	21	683	144	66	30	1	30.00	1-11	–	–

The Seventh XI

Matthew Hayden

No. 77

The choice of Bob Simpson's opening partner in this seventh XI is a tricky one. There is a temptation — because the most effective opening bats work as a team — to choose his long-time partner Bill Lawry, something Simpson himself did when choosing an all-time Australian XI in 2005. 'While Lawry and I may have been a little unfashionable in our style and method,' he wrote, 'we had the most important asset for opening batsmen: the ability to rotate the strike and thus deprive new-ball bowlers the opportunity to contain either of us or put us under pressure.'

Hayden against the West Indies in Adelaide in 1996-97, during his maiden Test century.

Selecting Lawry, who averaged 47.15 in 67 Tests with 13 hundreds, is quite feasible, except for the problem that, for all his quality, it is very difficult to argue that he is Australia's greatest left-handed opener. Five other men also have claims to this title. In the 21st century, the left-handed pair of Matthew Hayden and Justin Langer established a number of records, not least the most number of double-century partnerships for the first wicket, while providing a springboard that men such as Steve Waugh, Ricky Ponting and Adam Gilchrist were delighted to exploit. Preceding them in the Australian team was Mark Taylor, who had some sensational seasons, especially early in his Test career, but ended with a Test average of 43.50. Sir Donald Bradman was just one of a number of experts who argued strongly that Arthur Morris was the best left-handed opener he saw, but veterans who watched Morris in his prime never conceded that he was superior to Warren Bardsley, who went in first for Australia from 1909 to 1926.

World War II meant Morris' Test career began later than it should have, and he was prolific in his first four series, between 1946 and 1950, averaging 67.78. But after that, he was really no more than an average batsman at the highest level, averaging 34.76 in 27 Tests against better bowling than he faced at the beginning of his international career. Similarly, Bardsley was hardly prolific in his later Tests, making just one score over 50 in the 17 innings he played after 1921 (that was, though, a magnificent knock: batting through the innings for 193 not out at Lord's in 1926, when he was 43 years old). He, too, was handicapped by seasons lost to war, but he also made many of his biggest scores against ordinary attacks. His batting average against South Africa was 61.38, against England 33.04.

Hayden in the WACA dressing room with his teammates after hitting a new Test record score of 380, against Zimbabwe in October 2003.

Hayden and Langer came together as an opening partnership at The Oval in 2001. Each man had made his Test debut long before that — Langer in January 1993, Hayden a year later — but neither yet was truly established in the Australian XI. Langer was playing his first Test since being dropped at the start of the series, and hadn't opened the batting at the highest level in more than eight years. Hayden had batted superbly in India earlier in 2001, his first great series, but in seven innings in this Ashes series had scored just 166 runs at 27.67. The rookie pair were great mates and now they added 158 on a flat wicket, enough to keep them together for the first Test of the following Australian summer. And the rest, as they say, is history. For a season, Hayden and Langer were as dominant as Hobbs and Sutcliffe had been during the 1924-25 Ashes series, averaging more than a 100 for the first wicket; from then until Langer's retirement from international at the end of the 2006-07 Ashes series, the Australian pair were merely superb. Significantly, when they struggled for the first four Tests in England in 2005, the remainder of the batting order, Ricky Ponting apart, tended to struggle, too.

Langer averaged almost 50 as an opener in Test cricket, but for all his quality he never had the assertive presence of his partner. Neither did he have the opportunities in one-day cricket that Hayden enjoyed, in part because the selectors strangely ruled that he was not suited to the abbreviated form of the game. Hayden is a big man, but though the bat looked small in his hands as he strode to the wicket to bat, at the top of his form it quickly looked imposingly wide. No batsmen has had more faith in his ability to hit straight through the line and over the top, or to punish bowlers who drifted into his pads. A plunderer of bad bowling, his judgment of which ball to hit and which to let go was usually impeccable, so when a bowler was carved through the offside field it was usually safe to assume the ball was an ordinary one. Against the spinners, he swept hard and often.

In his first 21 Tests (1994 to 2001), Hayden scored three centuries; in 82 Tests from the start of the 2001-02 Australian season to his retirement in January 2009, he hit another 27, including a then world record score of 380 against Zimbabwe at the WACA in October 2003. Only Ricky Ponting and Steve Waugh among Australians have scored more centuries; only Don Bradman and Ponting have a superior innings-to-century ratio. Hayden, Bradman and India's Mohammad Azharuddin are the only three batsmen with 6000 Test runs to have scored more centuries than half centuries.

The Seventh XI

At his peak, his appetite seemed never satisfied. Twice, he scored a century in each innings of a Test — both times in his home state of Queensland, once at the Gabba and once in Cairns. In the Test after he broke the world record against Zimbabwe, he scored another century, this time unbeaten, to give him a 250 average for the rubber. Australia played six Tests against South Africa in 2001-02, three at home and three away, and Hayden scored hundreds in each of the first four matches, and then 96 in the fifth. In 2005, after failing to meet his own high standards in the first four Ashes Tests, there was talk that his days were numbered, but he responded with centuries not just in the first Test at The Oval, but also in the first three Tests at home during the following season. At the 2007 World Cup, having forced his way back into the Australian one-day team after being omitted after the 2005 England tour, he scored three centuries, including 101 from 68 balls against South Africa at St Kitts. In the ODI immediately before that World Cup, he scored 181 not out against New Zealand at Hamilton, the highest score by an Australian in ODI cricket.

Hayden in South Africa in September 2007, as belligerent as ever during the inaugural World Twenty20 championship.

'He has worked very hard on his game and knows it very well,' Steve Waugh wrote about Hayden in 2003. No doubt, the years out of the Australian XI toughened him, and taught him to value the opportunity when it finally came. During the 2005 Ashes series, he went out to the middle with the message 'This is Worth Fighting For' penned on his bat, a reminder, perhaps, of the bad old days when he and his opening partner were on the reserves bench. The fact that he had to battle hard for everything he achieved is reason enough to rate Matthew Hayden as Australia's greatest left-handed opener, at the head of a small and elite field.

MATTHEW HAYDEN (AUSTRALIA)
Test Cricket

Tests	Inn	NO	Runs	HS	Ave	100	50	Ct	Balls	Runs	Wkts	Ave	Best	5/	10/
103	184	14	8625	380	50.74	30	29	128	54	40	—	—	0-7	—	—

One-Day International Cricket

ODIs	Inn	NO	Runs	HS	Ave	100	50	Ct	Balls	Runs	Wkts	Ave	Best	4/
161	155	15	6133	181*	43.81	10	36	68	6	18	—	—	0-18	—

The 100 Greatest Cricketers

John Snow

Clem Hill

The Eighth

Jacques Kallis

Fazal Mahmood

The Eighth XI

Ian Healy

Waqar Younis

Dudley Nourse

Graham Gooch

Billy Murdoch

Peter May

Hugh Trumble

No. 78 John Snow

There have been few Test series where one bowler has dominated as John Snow dominated the Ashes matches of 1970-71. This was a summer of often tedious cricket, where the run rates were slow yet the bowling usually struggled to break through. For Australia, Graham McKenzie and Alan Connolly were past their best, Dennis Lillee was raw and didn't come into the team until the second-last Test, the other pace bowlers were ordinary, the spinners lacked guile. Snow apart, the English fast bowlers rarely broke through. Derek Underwood and Ray Illingworth averaged a wicket every 100 balls.

Snow was a cricketer who revelled in the big occasion.

Snow was different. When he bowled, something was always likely to happen. Despondent Australian commentators resorted to lampooning some of the Australian batsmen for the manner in which they tried to counter him. During his career, 26 of Snow's 202 Test wickets were lbw decisions, but not once during this series could he get an umpire to rule in his favour. Neither could any of his colleagues. Yet despite not having the umps on side, he still managed to take 31 wickets in the six Tests, at 22.84, with a strike rate of 57.29. In an article for the *Australian Cricket Yearbook 1971*, Australian vice-captain Ian Chappell commented about his team's last two Test series — in South Africa in 1970 and against England in 1970-71 — which had both resulted in discouraging losses. 'In our last major international encounters, Australia has been on the run due to two outstanding pace bowlers with the great ability to break the back of a side before it can make any sort of start,' Chappell wrote. 'I refer to Mike Procter and John Snow, who probably stand on their own above the current batch of speedsters ... Snow conserves his energy into bursts but has a stylish approach and delivery. Both have that power to get the ball to lift when the batsman least suspects it.'

Snow would dismiss Chappell 10 times during his Test career, his most popular victim. In fact, 155 of his wickets were either Australians or West Indians; he played in 15 Tests against other nations (five against India, six against New Zealand, three against Pakistan and one against South Africa) but strangely had little success, never once taking five wickets in an innings against them. It was as if only the big international occasions could inspire him. As well as being a superb bowler, he was also enigmatic and strong-willed, which some administrators misinterpreted as uncaring. From his first Test to his last, 1965 to 1976, England played 103 Tests. Snow appeared in just 49 of them.

The Eighth XI

He went on only three Test tours, but on two of them — to the West Indies in 1968 (when he was dropped for the first Test but took 27 wickets in the other four) and to Australia and New Zealand in 1970-71 — he was magnificent. On the other, in early 1969, he was sacked for a Test after bowling bouncers at vice-captain Tom Graveney on a dodgy pitch in the nets at Lahore. Against India at Lord's in 1971, he was banned for a Test after he knocked down Sunil Gavaskar while the little opener went for a single after the ball had been hit towards mid-on. Not everyone agreed with the authorities that the collision had been deliberate. Some journalists thought he was unapproachable, but the truth was that this moody man with an independent heart didn't always enjoy the constant demands of life as a professional cricketer, and couldn't comprehend how many officials seemed to have little regard for the players' welfare.

The face of a supposed 'cricket rebel'.

So he was prejudged as difficult in more ways than one. In the final Test of the 1970-71 series, at the SCG, Snow had hit Terry Jenner in the head after the Australian No. 9 misjudged a delivery and ducked into it. Then he was accosted by a drunken spectator while fielding on the fence in front of the 'Paddo Hill'. Somehow, he became the villain in these episodes, which must have confused him given that in neither instance was he at fault. He did know he was a great bowler and thought it should count for something. He allowed his autobiography to be called 'Cricket Rebel' and was quick to sign for World Series Cricket when given the chance. The two England captains he most enjoyed playing for were Ray Illingworth and Tony Greig, strong men who were always ready to back their players.

'His true value lay in his ability to turn the course of a match, to pin down, or even defeat, batsmen who seemed in control,' wrote John Arlott of Snow in *The Ashes 1972*. 'He had the true fast bowler's ability to cut into the start of an innings and to destroy the tail.' Snow took 24 wickets in that series, having in Arlott's view, 'reached his technical and temperamental peak'. Australia's leading run-scorer in the Tests, Keith Stackpole, thought Snow to be a 'particularly fine bowler, because his first ball could be as dangerous as his last; both could be unplayable'. Like most of the great fast men, Snow did not bowl fast all the time, and when on song there was a smooth acceleration in his approach to the wicket, a full use of the shoulder and always a pronounced follow-through. His style was not classical, which explained why he couldn't get the late swing of a Trueman or a Lindwall, but when he got his rhythm right it was the movement off the pitch, and that steep lift from just short of a length, which made him lethal. As a batsman, Snow had a tailender's average but sometimes belied that to hold

The 100 Greatest Cricketers

Australian No. 9 Terry Jenner ducks into a Snow riser at Sydney in 1970-71. The angry reaction from the crowd prompted England captain Ray Illingworth to take his team from the field.

up an end or even score important runs, such as at The Oval in 1966, when he and Ken Higgs added 128 for the last wicket against Garry Sobers, Wes Hall, Charlie Griffith and Lance Gibbs. At Dacca in 1969, he defended grimly while Basil D'Oliveira went to a critical century, and against the Indian spinners at Lord's in 1971, he top-scored with 73 in a low-scoring match that England might have lost but for his runs. At Headingley in 1972, he and Ray Illingworth put on 104 for the eighth wicket, the only substantial stand of the Test that decided the fate of the Ashes.

It might have been interesting if Snow had gone out to Australia to take on Lillee and Thomson in 1974-75, but the selectors chose otherwise. However, he was back for the 1975 World Cup, and then the Tests against Australia that followed, 33 years old and thought to be past his best. Tony Greig gave him the first over at Lord's and he responded by getting Alan Turner and the Chappell brothers in his first spell. 'Each of these three batsmen was well beaten by a good delivery, two out leg before and Ian Chappell caught behind,' Snow recounted in *Cricket Rebel*, 'Down at fine leg after that opening spell I bloody nearly cried.'

JOHN SNOW (ENGLAND)

Test Cricket

Tests	Inn	NO	Runs	HS	Ave	100	50	Ct	Balls	Runs	Wkts	Ave	Best	5/	10/
49	71	14	772	73	13.54	–	2	16	12021	5387	202	26.67	7-40	8	1

First-Class Cricket

Mat	Inn	NO	Runs	HS	Ave	100	50	Ct	Balls	Runs	Wkts	Ave	Best	5/	10/
346	451	110	4832	73*	14.17	–	11	125	60958	26695	1174	22.74	8-87	56	9

The Eighth XI

Clem Hill   No. 79

It is remarkable, given the number of outstanding left-handed batsmen around today (Lara, Gilchrist, Hayden, Langer, Jayasuriya, Strauss, et al), to think that it took nearly 20 years before Test cricket's first great left-hander emerged. Clem Hill was born while cricket's first ever Test match was being played in March 1877, and first came to attention in his home town Adelaide when he scored 360 for Prince Alfred College in their annual encounter with St Peters College in 1893. Hill was from good cricketing stock. His father John (who sired 16 children!) had scored the first ever century on the Adelaide Oval, but that feat was overwhelmed by Clem, who finished his career with 45 first-class centuries, seven of them in Tests.

Hill was famous for his hook shot, but his brand of the stroke might never have been seen by the Australian public, had it not been for the intervention of the famous allrounder George Giffen. The story goes that when Hill was 13 his sportsmaster warned the precocious left-hander that he would be left out of any future school elevens if he persisted in blazing across the line. Giffen was coaching at the school and was amazed at the talents of this youngster who was hooking his best deliveries. 'Sonny, you're going to be a world's batsman,' Giffen is reputed to have said. 'That's the shot of a champion.' He then went over to the sportsmaster to ensure Hill remained in the side.

Hill was short, powerfully built, and light on his feet. He gripped the bat lower on the handle than most, and stood at the crease with his feet wide apart, the bat between them, body crouching. He could cut and cover drive and jump down the wicket to the spinners, but loved to score his runs on the legside, making a habit of turning deliveries aimed at middle and off to mid-wicket and even behind square. Yet he was only once out lbw in 89 Test innings. The fastest bowling scarcely worried him and, in the manner of all great players, he was at his best in a crisis. All four of his hundreds against England led to important victories. Perhaps his most celebrated performance came early in his career — a defiant 188 against England in the fourth Test of the 1897-98 series, his first home rubber, when he led an Australian fightback after six more experienced wickets had fallen for 58.

The mighty Clem, Australia's first truly great left-handed batsman.

The 100 Greatest Cricketers

By the end of Australia's 1902 tour of England and South Africa, Hill had a Test batting average of 47.23, good by any standards, remarkable for those days of uncovered wickets. He had scored a hundred in the third Test at Sheffield and another in Johannesburg, and in the fourth Test at Old Trafford ran 25 metres from deep mid-wicket to deep square-leg before diving full-length to catch 'Dick' Lilley one-handed when England needed eight runs to win with two wickets in hand. This might just have been the greatest catch in Test-match history. Four runs later, Fred Tate was bowled by Jack Saunders and Australia retained the Ashes.

The Australian team that retained the Ashes in England in 1899. Hill is sitting on the ground, front left. Also in the photograph are Victor Trumper (back, far left), Hugh Trumble (back, third from left) and Monty Noble (back, far right).

One of Hill's most famous quotes came after he was asked how he compared to Victor Trumper. 'I wasn't fit to lick Vic's boots,' he replied. In the 'smoking room' of his Adelaide home, Hill had hanging in the most prominent position a large photograph of Trumper jumping out to drive. Yet a study of these two great batsmen shows that, based on their statistics at least, there was very little between them. Hill scored 3412 runs at 39.32 in 49 Test matches; Trumper finished with 3163 runs at 39.05 in 48 Tests. Trumper scored one more century than Hill, but six less fifties. (Hill actually became renowned for just missing Test hundreds, making 11 scores between 80 and 99, including one run of 99, 98 and 97 in successive innings in 1901-02.) Sydney Barnes was one who thought Hill might actually have been superior. 'Trumper was always giving you a chance,' explained Barnes when asked to compare the two, the implication being that Hill rarely did. While Trumper played a majority of his innings as an opener, Hill was usually the No. 3, from where he scored five of his seven Test hundreds.

His last hundred, scored as captain against South Africa at the MCG in 1910-11, was made as a No. 5 after he rearranged the batting order for Australia's second innings. His final century against England, a knock of 160 at the Adelaide Oval in the second week of January 1908, was made as a No. 9, might have been his bravest and was certainly one of his most important. He was suffering from influenza so badly that he had batted seven on the opening day and then not fielded as the tourists built a first-innings lead of 78 (his brother Roy taking his place). Monty Noble held him back as long as he dared on day four, and when he finally came out Australia was 7-180, a lead of just 102.

Hill's partner, Roger Hartigan, was making his Test debut, the temperature reached 42°C in the shade, and the next day the *South Australian Register* reported that the local hero was sick on the field at least twice and seemed 'on the verge of collapse'. More than once, he had to make a dash for the dressing room, and critically, he was dropped at mid-off when 22. But from there he was supreme — in the words of Johnnie Moyes, 'a triumph of mind over both matter and bowlers' — batting through to stumps when he was 106, Hartigan 105, and the game in Australian hands. The next day, the eighth-wicket stand ran to 243 and Hill went all the way to 160, setting up a home win by 245 runs.

He was an unlucky Test captain, beating South Africa easily in 1910-11 but losing to an outstanding English team a season later, at a time when he and other leading Australian players were in dispute with cricket authorities. An argument in Sydney over team selections and the captaincy ended with Hill punching Peter McAlister, a former teammate and fellow selector, while a disagreement over who should manage the 1912 Australian team in England led to he and five of his comrades missing the tour. He always believed in fighting for a worthy cause, and became an icon among his fellow players. 'It was a thrill to see his name go on the scoreboard, a joy and a privilege to take the field under his leadership,' remembered AG Moyes, who played with Hill for South Australia. 'As long as he was there, we felt that everything would turn out all right.'

Straight after the war, Hill came back to captain South Australia briefly, for the good of the team and the game, and then returned for one last Shield game in February 1923, because the match against Victoria was doubling as a benefit game for George Giffen. He scored 66 and 39. You could never keep the mighty Clem down, not even a month shy of his 46th birthday.

CLEM HILL (AUSTRALIA)
Test Cricket

Tests	Inn	NO	Runs	HS	Ave	100	50	Ct	Balls	Runs	Wkts	Ave	Best	5/	10/
49	89	2	3412	191	39.22	7	19	33	—	—	—	—	—	—	—

First-Class Cricket

Mat	Inn	NO	Runs	HS	Ave	100	50	Ct	St	Balls	Runs	Wkts	Ave	Best	5/	10/
252	416	21	17213	365*	43.58	45	83	168	1	510	323	10	32.30	2-6	—	—

No. 80 Ian Healy

The most important thing to happen to Ian Healy's international cricket career was the emergence of a young leg spinner named Shane Warne. Healy made his Test debut for Australia in Pakistan in September 1988; Warne started against India in Sydney in the first week of 1992. When the pair arrived in England for the 1993 Ashes tour, Healy was hardly confident of retaining his place after a sometimes controversial season in Australia and the fact that his Test batting average was just 21.73. Warne was something of an unknown quantity, at least to the Englishmen.

Healy celebrates the wonder ball from Shane Warne that bowled England's Mike Gatting at Old Trafford in 1993.

The first Test changed all this. First came the 'Gatting ball', when Warne started his Ashes career with that vicious leg break that spun past Mike Gatting to hit the top of the off stump. Then, on the fourth day, Healy hit his maiden first-class century. In his diary, he wrote, 'Amazing joy.' But perhaps more significantly, after the final day, following Australia's 179-run victory, he wrote, 'Great day of my life ... kept brilliantly all day.' He was always a keeper first, batsman second. After that first Test, he was sure of his role in the side, and while Warne took 34 wickets in the series, the most by an Australian spinner in an Ashes rubber since Arthur Mailey took 36 in 1920-21, Healy finished with 21 catches and five stumpings — a new record for most dismissals by an Aussie keeper in an Ashes series in England.

Six years later, when Healy's career ended, he had completed more Test dismissals than any other wicketkeeper, and was regarded in many quarters, not least by the panel who selected Australia's official 'Team of the Century' in 2000, as his country's greatest ever keeper. His Test batting average had climbed by nearly six runs per innings since 1993, but the thing that forged his reputation was the remarkable way he worked in tandem with Warne. Forty-nine of those dismissals (34 catches and 15 stumpings) had come from the leg-spinner's bowling, but more than that people were hard-pressed to recall many chances missed, or days of rampant byes, even though Warne's mode of operation was often to go around the wicket, and aim at the rough outside the batsmen's leg stump.

Behind the stumps, Healy had an innate ability to be in the right place at the right time, and was never flustered by the thought that the ball might leap off a crack in the pitch, or scuttle out of the rough. A classic example came in Manchester in

The Eighth XI

1997, when the quick, part-time Chinaman bowler Michael Bevan speared a full-pitched delivery down the legside to Mark Butcher. Healy could hardly have had a view of the ball, but he collected it on the half-volley as Butcher fell slightly forward, and knocked the bails off while the batsman was momentarily out of his crease. 'It was a moment of pure wicketkeeping brilliance that swung the momentum our way,' Steve Waugh remembered in 1999, before adding, 'as "Heals" so often did.'

Healy has just hit the six that won the second Test against South Africa at Port Elizabeth in 1997.

Healy was equally proficient standing back to the fast bowlers. Perhaps he didn't cover quite as much ground as had his predecessor from the 1970s, Rod Marsh, but quicks such as Craig McDermott (55 dismissals in 28 Tests), Merv Hughes (46 in 30) and Glenn McGrath (58 in 33) came to rely on him. Healy also added a sense of 'mongrel' to the Australian team, combining with other tough characters such as Hughes, Warne, Allan Border, Steve Waugh and David Boon to provide the starch that the Aussie sides of the mid '80s had lacked. When Boon retired, Healy took over as the leader of the team when they roared their victory song. One of his few mishaps was to muff a stumping chance in Karachi in 1994 when Pakistan were nine wickets down and needed three to win, but a little less than three years later he made up for it by hitting South African captain Hansie Cronje for six to win a Test at Port Elizabeth. In between, he'd responded to some media criticism by smashing 161 not out against the West Indies at his home track, the Gabba. It was the third and highest of his four Test centuries. Another 45 not out in the second innings made him the first Australian keeper to score 200 runs in a Test.

Arguably Healy's great strength as a keeper was that he came to understand what it took to be outstanding, appreciating the art of keeping in the same way a great bowler such as Dennis Lillee came to understand the art of fast bowling. He was a disciple of technique, who used the simple game of catching a golf ball bounced off a wall over and over to hone his catching skills and to make sure he was always watching the ball. Many of his teammates have paid tribute to the advice he gave, and for three years, 1994 to 1997, he was a proud and effective Australian vice-captain. He was also extraordinarily tough, missing just one Test out of 120 from his debut to his farewell. If he played with injuries, which he must have given the job he always did, no one other than the team physio ever knew. He was the first keeper to appear in 100 Test matches, as well as playing 168 ODIs, where he scored his runs at a rate of 83.84 runs per 100 balls and often played crucial hands that helped win games with just a few balls to spare.

Healy celebrates stumping England's Mark Butcher at Old Trafford in 1997.

'Quite simply,' Waugh wrote, 'Heals is now the benchmark for other keepers to aspire to.' He might actually have been even more than that — the last great keeper, as distinct from a great keeper-batsman. In the modern era, keepers such as Adam Gilchrist, Sri Lanka's Kumar Sangakkara, Zimbabwe's Andy Flower and South Africa's Mark Boucher might have outdone Healy for runs scored, but none of these or others have matched him for pure wicketkeeping excellence. If Gilchrist and co. have changed the game, and batting averages of 40-plus are essential if you want to be a regular Test keeper, then Ian Healy may well have been the last of his kind.

IAN HEALY (AUSTRALIA)

Test Cricket

Tests	Inn	NO	Runs	HS	Ave	100	50	Ct	St
119	182	23	4356	161*	27.40	4	22	366	29

One-Day International Cricket

ODIs	Inn	NO	Runs	HS	Ave	100	50	Ct	St
168	120	36	1764	56	21.00	–	4	194	39

The Eighth XI

Waqar Younis

No. 81

If a cricketer's career record was the sole measure of his place in history, Waqar Younis must be ranked very highly indeed. In 87 Tests between 1989 and 2003 he took 373 wickets — which at the time of his final Test put him 11th highest — at 23.56. Most impressively, he had a strike rate of 43.50, easily the best of all bowlers with 200 Test wickets. Next best, more than three runs per wicket behind him, is Malcolm Marshall (376 wickets at 46.77 balls per wicket). In one-day cricket, Waqar took 416 wickets in 262 matches, with a strike rate of 30.52, fourth best of all those with at least 200 wickets, behind Australia's Brett Lee and Pakistan's Saqlain Mushtaq and Shoaib Akhtar. As at June 30, 2009, only Muttiah Muralitharan (505 wickets) and Wasim Akram (502) had taken more ODI wickets than Waqar. In all, Wasim and Waqar took 1705 international wickets, 787 in Tests and 918 in ODIs.

The style of one of the most prolific wicket-takers in modern international cricket.

When Waqar first came into the Pakistani squad in the late '80s, his cricket was raw, but he was strong, bowled fast and was very ambitious and determined. Imran Khan set about removing the rough edges, and the new paceman made his Test debut in late 1989. He opened the bowling ahead of Imran, and started by taking four wickets, including fellow Test debutant Sachin Tendulkar. In 1990, he made a stunning debut for Surrey in the county championship, to the point that a new expression, to be 'Waqared' — as in bowled or hit on the toe by a pacy in-swinging yorker — was freely used. As a contrast to the bouncers that had been the basis of many fast-bowling strategies for the previous 15 years he was a revelation; his penchant for attacking the stumps at high speed explains his prodigious strike rate, especially in the first five years when he was lightning quick.

Waqar didn't so much run as hurtle to the wicket, and when he finally reached the bowling crease the ball was more catapulted at than delivered to the batsman. Michael Atherton remembered his Lancashire teammate Paul Allott dismissing the length of Waqar's approach, suggesting that a season in county cricket would soon curtail it, but that didn't happen. Instead, Waqar was a warrior who kept charging in for the next decade and beyond, more and more having to recover from injury, but never surrendering. 'He was a magnificent competitor and there are few more glorious sights in cricket than Waqar steaming in at full tilt,' Atherton wrote in 2002.

The 100 Greatest Cricketers

If fans of county cricket were well aware of Waqar's ability by the end of the 1990 season, Test followers were soon in the picture, too, as he ran through New Zealand in a series at home later in that year. He managed 'only' seven wickets (for 79 runs) in the first Test, followed by 10-106 in the second and 12-130 in the third. Martin Crowe, the New Zealand captain, stated that he had never faced better pace and swing bowling. Waqar even forced Crowe into using a grille on his helmet, something the West Indian quicks could never do. Two and a half years later, in his 20th Test, Waqar took his 100th Test wicket during a spell of 5-22 that destroyed New Zealand in astonishing fashion in Hamilton. The Kiwis needed only 127 to win, and reached 3-65, but Waqar and Wasim were too dynamic for them. Waqar took another six Test five-fours in 1993, five more in 1994, but then only three for the rest of his career, as he lost that explosive edge that made him so special. After confronting Australia at Rawalpindi in October 1994, his last Test for 11 months as he battled a back ailment, he had taken 190 wickets at 19.16 in 33 Tests. 'Waqar was a guy we all respected for always putting in, never shirking any task,' wrote Steve Waugh as he remembered his 98 in that Rawalpindi Test that left him bruised, battered and proud. 'This combined with his blistering pace and wicked reverse swing made him the complete package.' He may have continued to take Test wickets, and to be especially effective in one-day cricket, but it is the Waqar Younis of 1990 to 1994 who makes this top 100.

An image England fans became used to in 1992: Waqar on the rampage.

The development of reverse swing reached a climax in England in 1992, when Waqar and Wasim had some famous days. At Lord's, Headingley and The Oval, the home side made good starts to their innings but were then blown away when the two fast men came back with the old ball, and made it bend prodigiously. So startling was this bowling, accusations were made that the cricket balls were being

The Eighth XI

tampered with, but eventually the rest of the world caught up and by 2005 the reverse swing generated by Simon Jones and Andrew Flintoff was an important factor in England's triumph over Australia. 'Beyond doubt Waqar is an outstanding bowler,' *Wisden* wrote after naming him one of the cricketers of the year for 1992, 'probably the finest to emerge from Pakistan since Fazal Mahmood.' Later in the tribute, the Almanack added, 'This is a bowler of brilliance and élan, a bowler as entertaining in his way as any batsman, as enthralling as any spinner, a bowler who could become, as Imran predicted, the greatest of them all.'

In the end, his career did not quite work out that way. More than once after 1995, he and Wasim seemed in dispute, which inevitably hurt the team, and when Waqar took on the captaincy he was not particularly inspiring or successful. Waqar made surprisingly few breakthroughs in Tests against Australia (30 wickets at 33.80 in 12 matches), while his Test average against England blew out somewhat as well (50 wickets at 27.04). He took nearly half his Test wickets against New Zealand, Zimbabwe and Sri Lanka, at small cost, but in his four Tests against India (two in 1989, two in 1999) he never had a major impact after his first innings. His international career finished at the 2003 World Cup — which he went into as Pakistan captain hoping to make up for his personal disappointment of missing the 1992 Cup triumph because of injury — when his team was mediocre at best, and failed to make the final six. Waqar took seven wickets in six matches, a sad farewell.

By 1990, with the excellence of Wasim Akram and the rise of Waqar, the great Imran was not always required to open the Pakistani bowling.

Much better to remember the great fast bowler who, in the words of his bowling partner Wasim Akram, was 'one of the most devastating bowlers I have seen', and to also recall that the two of them, Waqar and Wasim, were such a lethal partnership. When they were at their peak, Pakistan could more than match it with any other team in the world.

WAQAR YOUNIS (PAKISTAN)
Test Cricket

Tests	Inn	NO	Runs	HS	Ave	100	50	Ct	Balls	Runs	Wkts	Ave	Best	5/	10/
87	120	21	1010	45	10.20	–	–	18	16224	8788	373	23.56	7-76	22	5

One-Day International Cricket

ODIs	Inn	NO	Runs	HS	Ave	100	50	Ct	Balls	Runs	Wkts	Ave	Best	4/
262	139	45	969	37	10.31	–	–	35	12698	9919	416	23.84	7-36	27

No. 82 Dudley Nourse

Dudley Nourse is one of the few Test cricketers whose father was also a Test cricketer. AW 'Dave' Nourse made 45 consecutive appearances for South Africa between 1902 and 1924, making 2234 runs at 29.78, including 111 against Jack Gregory, Ted McDonald and Arthur Mailey at Johannesburg in 1921, when he was 42 years old. No wonder he was known as the 'Grand Old Man' of South African cricket (or, as *Wisden* simply described him while naming Dudley as one its cricketers of the year for 1947, 'G.O.M.'). Dave also took 41 wickets at 37.87, and was remembered in 1926 by Pelham Warner in a letter to *The Cricketer* as having unusually large hands, which, no doubt, helped him turn his left-arm spinners. As excellent a player as Dave undoubtedly was, though, his son Dudley was better.

Nourse in England in 1951, when he scored 208 in the first Test despite batting with a broken thumb.

He was named 'Dudley' after the Earl of Dudley, Governor of South Australia. As the story goes, the governor was present when Dave make 201 not out for the touring South Africans against South Australia in Adelaide in November 1910, and then four days later a cable arrived from home saying that a boy had been born. Dudley Nourse played his first Test at Trent Bridge in 1935, his 34th and last at The Oval 16 seasons later. His aggregate of 2960 runs, at the impressive average of 53.81, established him as South Africa's greatest batsman to that point. On his farewell from Test cricket, only 11 men — England's Wally Hammond, Jack Hobbs, Herbert Sutcliffe, 'Patsy' Hendren, Frank Woolley, Len Hutton and Denis Compton; Australia's Don Bradman, Clem Hill and Victor Trumper; and South Africa's Bruce Mitchell — had scored more runs. Of this illustrious group, only Hammond, Hobbs, Sutcliffe, Hutton and Bradman had a better average. Now being clearly the best batsman in the side has its advantages and disadvantages. Inevitably, there will be times when the opposition will target you, because, after all, you're the key wicket. At other times, though, they'll probably leave you alone, and focus on getting everyone else out. Either way, you have to be a damn good player to warrant such respect.

Dudley Nourse averaged more than 50 against both England and Australia, and though his figures were better at home than away (he never toured Australia, so his Test experience was limited to his homeland and England), the 46.91 Test average he gleaned from 14 Tests in three tours to the UK is excellent. He certainly had the handicap of almost always having to play from behind, for South Africa won only twice during his career, and lost 17 times. Crazily, the one series South Africa won during his career, in England in 1935 when four Tests were drawn and

The Eighth XI

the tourists won at Lord's, was from a run-making perspective easily his worst. He averaged 26.17, after making just nine runs in his first three innings and being dropped for the third Test. In its tribute to Nourse on his death in 1981, Wisden described him as 'a fighting batsman, defensive when need be but ever ready to punch the ball with all the strength of his beefy forearms'. If he wasn't a fighter, one suspects he wouldn't have lasted very long.

Nourse made two double centuries in Test cricket: 231 in less than five hours (featuring 36 fours) against Australia at Johannesburg at the end of 1935 and 208 in the Nottingham Test of 1951. The Australian attack he mastered included Bill O'Reilly and Clarrie Grimmett, after he'd come to the wicket with the score 3-90, meaning South Africa needed three more runs to wipe off a first-innings deficit. Having made a duck in the first innings, he needed 20 minutes to avoid a pair, but in the words of O'Reilly was 'unflappable' and a 'genius', and eventually Australia needed all of 399 to win the Test. One shot in particular caught the eye of the 'Tiger': 'It was the accuracy and power of that drive of his wide of mid-on that impressed me most,' he explained. 'Excellence in this stroke is the criterion of the truly great batsman.' Because Stan McCabe (189 not out) played one of immortal innings, the tourists might have won, but then the rains came and they were left 125 runs short, with eight wickets in hand.

By 1951, Nourse was 40 years old. A pin had been put in his right thumb after it was broken three weeks earlier, but he batted for nine hours and 10 minutes to score South Africa's first double century against England. He took no further part in the match after he was run out, but his gallant effort set up South Africa's first Test win in 16 years. For courage, this innings was probably his greatest, but most observers felt that technically he'd been at his best four years earlier at Old Trafford, when he made 115 on a pitch softened by overnight rain. For a period before the surface dried, the ball was kicking nastily, but Nourse stood firm, hitting 13 fours and two sixes. His century that day came in 110 minutes, the second fifty in just 35. 'In face of this punishment,' recalled the 1948 Wisden, '[England captain Norman] Yardley was compelled to take off his slow bowlers and place a defensive field — on a bowler's wicket.'

Nourse and England captain George Mann toss before the third Test at Cape Town in 1948-49. Mann won the right to bat first, but it was the South African skipper who went on to score a century.

The Almanack continued: 'That was Nourse at his best. This stocky batsman with broad shoulders and blacksmith forearms seldom goes right forward except when moving out to drive the slow bowlers; off his back foot he hits exceedingly hard, particularly when hooking, driving to the off or cutting square. In executing these, he strikes as with a bludgeon.' Nourse's nine Test centuries came in six series; there was never a rubber he was involved in, except for his debut, in which he did not make at least one hundred. He could score quickly, as his blazing batting against Grimmett and O'Reilly in 1935-36 demonstrated, or grimly, such as when he persisted for six hours for 103 against Wally Hammond's Englishmen at Durban in 1939.

Dudley Nourse's father 'Dave' played 45 Tests for South Africa between 1902 and 1924.

Below: England's Alec Bedser greets Nourse at the start of South Africa's 1951 tour of England.

Dudley Nourse's tally of nine Test centuries (seven against England) remained a South African Test record until Daryll Cullinan scored his 10th in January 2000, in his 54th Test. In 1983, the veteran cricket journalist EW Swanton described Herbie Taylor and Dudley Nourse as 'perhaps the two finest (South African) batsmen prior to their country's departure from the ICC'. One presumes Swanton was leaving out Graeme Pollock and Barry Richards, whose Test careers were abbreviated by the apartheid ban, but he did not say so. It is difficult, though, to name a batsman who has played Test cricket for South Africa since 1992 who could be ranked above Nourse. But this is not a sledge on the current-day players, just the reality that the son of the Grand Old Man was a very fine player indeed.

DUDLEY NOURSE (SOUTH AFRICA)

Test Cricket

Tests	Inn	NO	Runs	HS	Ave	100	50	Ct	Balls	Runs	Wkts	Ave	Best	5/	10/
34	62	7	2960	231	53.82	9	14	12	20	9	–	–	0-9	–	–

First-Class Cricket

Mat	Inn	NO	Runs	HS	Ave	100	50	Ct	Balls	Runs	Wkts	Ave	Best	5/	10/
175	269	27	12472	260*	51.54	41	54	135	246	124	–	–	0-0	–	–

The Eighth XI

Graham Gooch

No. 83

An Australian cricket fan from the 1980s and early '90s would have a good deal of difficulty including Graham Gooch in an all-time top 100. Gooch started his career by making a pair against Dennis Lillee and Jeff Thomson at Edgbaston in 1975, and finished with a Test average against Australia of just 33.32. In Tests against other teams, Gooch scored 16 hundreds and 30 fifties in 136 innings, but against Australia he managed just four centuries and 16 fifties in 79 innings. In the Caribbean in 1981, in the most agitated of atmospheres facing Andy Roberts, Michael Holding, Joel Garner and Malcolm Marshall, he hit two fearless centuries and averaged 57.50. Against India at Lord's in 1990, he totalled a record 752 runs for a three-match series, including 333 and 123 at Lord's, the most runs ever scored by one batsman in a Test. But during the 1989 Ashes series, the tactics devised by Allan Border and put into practice by Terry Alderman made such a mess of him that he asked to be dropped. At other times in Ashes contests, his body language reflected the negativity that engulfed him.

Gooch at Bridgetown in 1981, bravely counter-attacking against Roberts, Holding, Garner and Croft.

During the 1980s, a decade of truly great opening bowlers — the above mentioned Windies' quicks, Curtly Ambrose, Courtney Walsh, Wasim Akram and Waqar Younis, Kapil Dev, Richard Hadlee — Gooch was often quite superb. He amassed a mountain of Test-match runs, scoring more Test hundreds in England (15) than any other player in the game's history, and by adding 'first-class' one-day runs to those scored in genuine first-class cricket, became, in one sense, the heaviest run-scorer of all time. When he first emerged in county cricket, he was an unrestrained hitter but with experience came inhibitions that may not have helped his game. He was banned from international cricket for three years during the 1980s after captaining a rebel tour to South Africa, and occasionally was reluctant to go on yet another Test and one-day tour, but he still built a reputation as a thorough professional.

The 100 Greatest Cricketers

Gooch came into Test cricket as a middle-order batsman, but seemed a better cricketer from the day he started opening the innings for Essex in the county championship in 1978. Soon enough, he'd earned a Test recall and though in the following year he would sometimes be pushed down to No. 3 or No. 4, from 1980 to 1993 whenever he batted for England he always faced the first ball of the innings. 'He was a magnificent sight in full sail,' remembered Christopher Martin-Jenkins in 1998. 'This was no dabber of singles, no delicate leg-glancer or specialist in the smooth caress of a half-volley through extra cover. On the contrary, he was a bold, imposing player, a mighty driver and fierce square cutter.' Gooch's greatest innings were against high-quality pace bowling, yet as good a judge as Richie Benaud reckoned he played Shane Warne 'as well as anyone I have seen'.

Three memorable hundreds — all against the West Indies, the first two made 10 years before the third — sealed Gooch's reputation. The first, at Bridgetown in 1981, was made despite a bruised hand and just two days after manager Ken Barrington collapsed and died after suffering a heart attack. Teammate Mike Gatting called the innings 'a truly lion-hearted knock ... it was quite magnificent to see him standing there in the line of the fastest attack in the world, and taking it apart.' Four weeks later, on the opening day of the final Test of the same series, in Kingston, Gooch was similarly belligerent. Colin Croft, who'd taken 21 wickets in the first three Tests at 13.57, was sliced over third man for six. Marshall was hooked into the crowd. He reached his hundred in the 40th over, out of a score of 155, and was fifth out for 153 when the total was 249.

Gooch at the 1987 World Cup, when his stunning century was too much for the hosts, India, in the semi-final.

Gooch at Lord's in 1991, smashing 333 and 123 against India.

The Eighth XI

At Leeds in 1991, this time against Marshall, Curtly Ambrose, Courtney Walsh and Patrick Patterson, Gooch played what Michael Atherton called 'the ultimate captain's knock', and what Gooch himself considered to be his greatest innings. Both teams had been dismissed for less than 200 in their first innings, in conditions ideal for swing and seam bowling, but when England batted again Gooch was resolute and magnificent, becoming the first opener to bat through an innings against the West Indies since Roberts and Holding emerged in the mid '70s. He did so against Ambrose at his finest, the great Antiguan taking the first six wickets to fall in the innings, including Allan Lamb and Robin Smith for first-ball ducks. Gooch finished unbeaten on 154, out of 252 all out, setting up England's first home victory against the Windies since 1969. In 2001, Wisden rated this the greatest Test innings ever played by an Englishman, ahead of Ian Botham's 149 not out against Australia in 1981 and Reg Foster's 287 at Sydney in 1903-04.

'I can't think of another batsman who got more out of himself than he did,' wrote Lamb in his autobiography. 'And, other than Allan Border, no batsman ever gave a better example to his teammates.'

As a one-day cricketer, Gooch made a habit of starring for Essex in major matches at home, and also played in three World Cup finals, though on the losing side each time. Christopher Martin-Jenkins believed his 129 not out at Port-of-Spain in early 1986 was 'the most exciting, sustained one-day innings I have ever seen', though it was not as important as the 115 he made in Bombay in 1987 that knocked India out of the World Cup. During that tournament, Gooch averaged 58.88 with the bat, and won the man-of-the-match award in three straight games. He is one of four Englishmen to have scored 4000 runs in ODIs (with Lamb, Alec Stewart and Marcus Trescothick). Only Trescothick has scored more ODI hundreds for England.

Gooch's Test debut ended in disaster when England was thrashed by an innings and 85 runs and he was dismissed for a pair.

In 1998, Wasim Akram recalled the Old Trafford Test of six years before. 'Waqar and I really bent our backs on the Saturday night, trying to dismiss Gooch,' he wrote. 'We knew that if he went that evening, we'd have a great chance of enforcing the follow-on. He never buckled. It was a great duel on a quick wicket and Gooch was too good for us.' In the following match, at Leeds, Gooch made 137 and 35 in a match in which Pakistan was bowled out for 197 and 221, setting up England's only Test win of the season. Australians might be a little confused, but if you study Gooch's overall record it really isn't that hard to understand why Wasim would describe him as 'definitely the kind of batsman to play for your life'.

GRAHAM GOOCH (ENGLAND)
Test Cricket

Tests	Inn	NO	Runs	HS	Ave	100	50	Ct	Balls	Runs	Wkts	Ave	Best	5/	10/
118	215	6	8900	333	42.58	20	46	103	2655	1069	23	46.48	3-39	–	–

One-Day International Cricket

ODIs	Inn	NO	Runs	HS	Ave	100	50	Ct	Balls	Runs	Wkts	Ave	Best	4/
125	122	6	4290	142	36.98	8	23	45	2066	1516	36	42.11	3-19	–

No. 84 Hugh Trumble

From the final Test of the 1896 Ashes series to his farewell from international cricket in March 1904, Victoria's Hugh Trumble was Australia's leading bowler. He was one of a number of off-spinners who bowled at somewhere between slow-medium and medium pace and whose style of bowling dominated cricket in this era of uncovered pitches. However, few of these men utilised their height to greater advantage, had superior control, or possessed a shrewder cricket brain. Charles Fry remembered Trumble 'had the subtle knack of getting one out off one's best stroke'. He used swerve, flight, change of pace and sufficient off-spin to trouble all batsmen on good wickets, and on a wet deck he could make the ball grip and spit nastily.

Trumble was the first man to take two hat-tricks in Tests (Australia's 'Jimmy' Matthews and Pakistan's Wasim Akram have done so since), and from 1904 to 1913 was Test cricket's leading wicket-taker

Trumble was a reasonable batsman, good enough to open the batting and score 1000 first-class runs on the 1899 Ashes tour, an excellent catcher, especially in the slips, and a bowler of the highest class. At The Oval in 1902, the Test that England won by one wicket after Gilbert Jessop, the 'Croucher', blazed a memorable century in 85 minutes, Trumble scored 64 not out in Australia's first innings and then took 8-65 and 4-108. Australian captain Joe Darling was criticised for over-bowling Trumble on that thrilling last day, and a study of the scorecard suggests in this case the critics might have been right — he bowled unchanged through an innings that lasted 66.5 overs, while Monty Noble and Warwick Armstrong sent down just nine overs between them. But in a way the skipper's unflinching faith in his star bowler was further proof of Trumble's greatness.

Trumble's first tour of England was in 1890, as a support bowler to Charlie Turner and Jack Ferris. *Wisden* noted that English batsmen thought his bowling lacked 'sting and variety', but by the time he returned in 1893, having not played a Test match in the meantime, he was a much improved cricketer, now batting at No. 8 instead of last man in and reasonably sure of his place as part of the Australian attack. However, in the Tests he was hardly successful, and then in 1894-95 he played in only the second Test, when Andrew Stoddart was too good for him and captain George Giffen seemed happier when he was bowling himself and Trumble was in the outfield. Even when Turner dropped out of the third Test because of illness, Trumble was not considered. Yet when Giffen released his autobiography in 1898 he suggested Trumble 'vies with Harry Trott for the title of Victorian champion'.

Giffen conceded that 'there were excellent judges who thought a mistake was made in taking him to England in 1896', but by tour's end Trumble was 'the most reliable bowler in the team'. The turning point was the final Test of the season, at The Oval. In the first Test, Trumble had bowled third change and took one wicket in each innings; in the second he bowled second change and took two wickets in each innings. The weather that English summer was fine and warm through May to July, and though Trumble's record did not look much better than it had been in 1893, keen observers recognised that his control and variety on the good batting wickets was outstanding. Then the rains came in August, and on wet surfaces Trumble was irresistible. In the final Test, he took 6-59 and 6-30 on a pitch that deteriorated from poor to horrible, but Australia disintegrated on the final afternoon, being bowled out for 44 when 111 would have regained the Ashes. So dire was the collapse, Australia was 9-25 before Trumble (7 not out) and Tom McKibbin (16) added 19 for the 10th wicket.

The Eighth XI

In the next four Ashes series — from 1897-98 to 1902 — Trumble took 19, 15, 28 and 26 wickets, playing all five Tests in the first three of these seasons (the last two of 1901-02 as captain, for two wins), but only three in the fourth, when a dislocated finger and then influenza kept him out of the opening two Tests. He actually announced his retirement after that tour, to focus on his career in banking, but kept in trim and during the 1903-04 Australian summer was persuaded to return after missing the first Test. In its preview of the series opener, the *Sydney Morning Herald*'s correspondent wrote, 'With regard to our bowling, we will have to find someone to fill the vacancy caused by the absence of Hugh Trumble. A Test without the tall Victorian will be difficult to understand.' The fact that the English batsmen went out and ran up a huge total 577, with Reg Foster making a record 287 in his maiden Test-match innings, accelerated the push for the 36-year-old Trumble's comeback.

Leave was granted, and immediately he took nine wickets in the second Test. However, he was unable to prevent another victory for Pelham Warner's team. One interesting piece of trivia from this game was that Trumble dismissed Wilfred Rhodes lbw with the third ball of the final over of the day on both the Saturday (to make England 6-306 in their first innings) and the Monday (to make England 5-74 in their second). Australia won the third Test, but lost the fourth, despite a glorious exhibition of bowling on the opening day from Trumble and Monty Noble, when the pitch was dry and flat. 'Probably no finer nor more "heady" bowling on such a wicket was ever witnessed as that by the Australian and the ex-Australian captains,' wrote the *Herald*. 'Noble and Trumble never looked like sending a loose ball down, nor did they, unless there was a trap underlying it.' Later in his story, the reporter added gloomily, 'When one saw the veteran Trumble bowling at the very top of his form it was regretted that, as he himself says, this is to be his last Test and, perhaps, his last first-class match.' Sadly for the Australians, for the third Test out of four they had the worst of the batting conditions, and despite their leading bowlers' heroics England took an unassailable 3-1 series lead.

Fortunately for Trumble, he would find the time to play one more first-class game, the fifth Test on his home ground, and he crowned his career by taking the last seven wickets to fall in the match, the first six of them for just 11 runs, including a hat-trick. This was the seventh hat-trick taken in Tests, and the fourth, including Trumble's two, to occur at the MCG. The next Test hat-trick to be completed in Melbourne would also be taken by another champion Victorian, Shane Warne, all of 91 years later. Unfortunately, Hugh Trumble's final great performance in cricket came too late to save the Ashes, but that aside it was just about the perfect farewell.

HUGH TRUMBLE (AUSTRALIA)

Test Cricket

Tests	Inn	NO	Runs	HS	Ave	100	50	Ct	Balls	Runs	Wkts	Ave	Best	5/	10/
32	57	14	851	70	19.79	–	4	45	8099	3072	141	21.79	8-65	9	3

First-Class Cricket

Mat	Inn	NO	Runs	HS	Ave	100	50	Ct	Balls	Runs	Wkts	Ave	Best	5/	10/
213	344	67	5395	107	19.48	3	20	329	44060	17134	929	18.44	9-39	69	25

The 100 Greatest Cricketers

No. 85 Peter May

As we move towards the end of this Top 100, there is room for only one more English middle-order batsmen. The choice came down to one of Gilbert Jessop, Peter May, Ted Dexter, David Gower or perhaps Kevin Pietersen.

HS Altham's opinion of Jessop, repeated in Wisden in 1955, was that 'no cricketer that has ever lived hit the ball so often, so fast and with such a bewildering variety of strokes'. In 1902, he played one of cricket's most fantastic innings — 104 in 85 minutes against an outstanding Australian bowling attack after England had been reduced to 5-48 chasing 263 — to win a Test match. But that was his one century at the highest level. Otherwise, he averaged 18.60 in Tests, a poor return for such a reputedly fine player.

Dexter was one of the best batsmen of the 1960s, whom John Woodcock ranked as high as No. 24 when he nominated his top 100 all-time cricketers in 1998. Dexter hit two of the most famous seventies in Test cricket — 76 against Australia at Old Trafford in 1961 and 70 from 73 balls against Wes Hall and Charlie Griffith at Lord's in 1963 — in both cases retaliating first against impressive bowling line-ups. However, neither of these innings led to a victory. Nor could he lead England to a series win against Australia during his career. Overall, Dexter averaged 47.89 with the bat while England was winning 23 of the 62 Tests in which he played; against Australia, he averaged only 38.80 while just three Tests were won out of 19.

David Gower provided some of the most attractive innings played in international cricket between 1978 and 1991, without ever quite convincing critics that he was entitled to be ranked with the very best of batsmen. At times, such as when he hit 732 runs during the Ashes series of 1985, or when he made 154 not out against Marshall, Holding and Garner at Sabina Park in 1981, or 173 not out against Abdul Qadir at Lahore in 1984, he was magnificent. Elsewhere, he could be cruelly frustrating. At Sydney in 1990-91, he compiled one of the most beautiful centuries ever made; in the very next Test, he was caught in the deep last ball before lunch, a ridiculous lapse of concentration. His final Test average of 44.25 is ordinary for a batsman of his skill, and reflects his daring. The noted cricket historian David Frith got it right when he said of Gower in Rob Steen's book *David Gower: A Man Out of Time*, 'To me, he is Great with a capital G for aesthetic appeal, and a small g in terms of the practical, the effectiveness.'

May and Colin Cowdrey during their 411-run partnership against the West Indies at Edgbaston in 1957.

The Eighth XI

Romantics might like to include Gower, but the straight fact is that if you needed someone to score a Test hundred for you, Peter May would be a better choice. Gower scored 18 Test centuries in 204 innings; May managed 13 in 106. In the 1950s, May succeeded Len Hutton and Denis Compton as England's premier batsman. 'He was tall and handsome with a batting style that was close to classical, and he was the hero of a generation of schoolboys,' recalled *Wisden* following his death in 1994. Back in 1951, he had made his debut as a 21 year old, going in at No. 3 against South Africa and sharing a stand of 198 with Hutton. He went on to 138, the seventh Englishman to score a hundred in his first Test innings. Two years later, he had to suffer the indignity of being dropped during the 1953 Ashes series (though he came back to play two important innings in the final Test), before earning his stripes with a dogged 135 on the mat at Port-of-Spain during the following March.

May had been a champion schoolboy cricketer and remained an amateur as the concept drifted out of fashion. He was vice-captain in Australia in 1954-55, when in a low-scoring series he was arguably the most important batsman on either side, and inherited the leadership upon Hutton's retirement. From there, he led England in every Test he played, bar Lord's in 1961 when he came back to play in the final four matches of that year's Ashes series, and was captain in the last three. Being bowled behind his legs by Richie Benaud on the last day of the fourth Test at Old Trafford, when England lost a game it should have won, was not how he would have liked to have left the international game.

England won 20 of the 41 Tests in which May was captain and lost 10, four of them in the one Ashes series, in Australia in 1958-59. Forgotten amid all the controversy of 1956, when Jim Laker spun his magic, was that captain May averaged 90.60 for the series, with a century and four fifties from seven innings. At Leeds, with England one down after losing at Lord's, he scored 101 to rescue his team from a 3-17 start on the first morning. The following year at Edgbaston he scored 285 not out, after Sonny Ramadhin had taken 7-49 during England's first innings and the West Indies had then built a first-innings lead of 288. With Colin Cowdrey, May added 411 for the third wicket, blunting Ramadhin's impact and setting the tone for the rest of the series. In 1958, he scored two Test centuries against New Zealand and for the first-class season averaged 63.74; in a season of awkward wickets this was an amazing 17.12 runs per innings more than anyone else.

The finest English batsman in the years between Len Hutton and Geoffrey Boycott.

The last three years of May's career were disappointing by his standards, starting with his trip down under in 1958-59. It seemed he lost some enthusiasm for the game, and the controversy over the actions of some of the local bowlers overshadowed the fact that May was England's leading runscorer for the third straight Ashes series. His 113 at the MCG was the first Test century by an England captain in Australia since Archie MacLaren scored 116 in the first Test of 1901-02, and came after Alan Davidson took three wickets in his second over. At one point on tour he was heard to say, 'This kind of thing isn't exactly fun, you know.' Because of illness, he was forced to leave England's tour of the Caribbean in 1959-60 early, and didn't play any more Tests until those Ashes Tests of 1961.

Len Hutton always thought that May would make an ideal opening batsman. 'This footwork was excellent, going right back or down the pitch,' wrote Benaud about May in *The Appeal of Cricket* (1995). 'He was predominantly an onside player but very strong on the offside as well.' Benaud also thought May to be the best England captain he faced. 'There was not the laughter of Compton in his batting, nor the grace of Hutton, but the authoritative power of his play was very impressive,' recalled Trevor Bailey in *The Greatest of My Time*. There are many people who agree with Benaud that Peter May was 'the finest batsman produced by England in the fifty years since the end of the Second World War.'

May flays the Australian attack (above) on day two of the fourth Ashes Test of 1961, at Manchester. In the second innings (right), the England captain was bowled behind his legs by Richie Benaud.

PETER MAY (ENGLAND)

Test Cricket

Tests	Inn	NO	Runs	HS	Ave	100	50	Ct	Balls	Runs	Wkts	Ave	Best	5/	10/
66	106	9	4537	285*	46.77	13	22	42	–	–	–	–	–	–	–

First-Class Cricket

Mat	Inn	NO	Runs	HS	Ave	100	50	Ct	Balls	Runs	Wkts	Ave	Best	5/	10/
388	618	77	27592	285*	51.00	85	127	282	102	49	–	–	0-0	–	–

The Eighth XI

Billy Murdoch
No.86

For more than 50 years, from the 1880s to the 1930s, JC Davis was one of Australia's most respected sporting journalists. He was the long-time editor of Sydney's finest ever sporting publication, *The Referee*, and wrote about all sports, while focusing on cricket and the two rugby codes, union and (from when it was formed in 1908) league. In November 1935, while writing of a famous cricketer from his early days of reporting cricket, Davis commented, 'His Australian contemporaries who lived to see Victor Trumper were loathe to agree that Victor was greater.'

Some who saw Victor Trumper and Clem Hill bat still thought Murdoch was their superior.

He was writing about Billy Murdoch, Australian captain from 1880 to 1884 and again in 1890, a man whom WG Grace described in 1899, the year of Victor Trumper's Test debut, as being Australia finest batsman to that point. WG was not alone in rating Murdoch highly. George Bonnor, the Australian hitter, was once asked who was the world's best batsman. 'Grace must be first and Murdoch second,' he replied. Johnnie Moyes called Murdoch the 'Bradman of the 19th century.'

Murdoch held the record for the highest score made in Test cricket from 1884, when he made 211 at The Oval, until December 1903, when Reg Foster scored 287 at the Sydney Cricket Ground. Seven years before he made that double century, Fred Spofforth famously refused to play in cricket's first ever Test match because Victoria's Jack Blackham was picked in the Australian XI ahead of the NSW keeper, Murdoch. History shows that Spofforth was wrong, because Blackham was actually the best wicketkeeper in the world, but Murdoch responded in his own way, developing during the Australians' 1878 tour of England into a specialist batsman of the highest order. He failed in the only Test of the 1878-79 Australian summer, but was a pivotal figure in the riot that marred the second encounter of the season between NSW v an England XI captain by Lord Harris. Murdoch had scored 70 and 49 in the first game, and in the return fixture a fortnight later had batted through the first innings for 82 not out, before being ruled run out for 10 in the second.

The decision that ended Murdoch's innings was given by a Victorian umpire, George Coulthard, who was accompanying the tourists at the invitation of the England captain. (Coulthard is an interesting figure, a champion Australian Rules footballer who later in 1879 would be described by the *Australasian's* football correspondent as the 'grandest player of his day', and a man who played in a cricket Test match in 1881-82 three years *after* he umpired a Test.) Murdoch was stunned by the verdict against him, a reaction which aroused the passion of the NSW captain Dave Gregory, who wanted to complain about the umpire before the innings continued. Murdoch's many fans were similarly enraged by the demise of their hero, while the punters in the crowd, who knew with Murdoch's dismissal that they'd backed the wrong team, opted to invade the field of play. During the fracas, some rioters managed to assault some of the English cricketers as well as threaten Coulthard, and when the ground couldn't be cleared play was abandoned for the afternoon, a good result for the visitors as it turned out because it rained overnight and NSW lost 9-30 when play resumed the next day.

WG Grace at London's Crystal Palace field in London in the early 1900s, with his former rival and still great friend Murdoch (wearing a cap, to Grace's left).

Murdoch was the first batsman outside of England to consistently make big scores. He became the first Australian to score a Test century in England when he made 153 not out at The Oval in 1880. In the first innings of the match, WG Grace had scored 152, after which Murdoch bet him a sovereign he'd do even better. However, he was out immediately for a duck, and though he shaped up well after Australia was forced to follow on, it soon seemed likely that he'd run out of partners well before he got anywhere near WG's total. He was not yet even 100 when the eighth wicket fell, but 140 runs were added for the final two wickets to allow Murdoch to win his wager. Grace called the innings 'one of the most heroic performances that has ever been achieved by a batsman in a thoroughly first-class match'. Eighteen months later, Murdoch also made the first triple century in Australian first-class cricket: 321 for NSW against Victoria at the SCG. A few months after that, back in England, he scored 286 against Sussex.

That knock remained the highest by an Australian on tour until Victor Trumper scored 300 not out in 1899. However, as well as he batted, most likely the thing that gave Murdoch the most satisfaction from that 1882 tour was his captaincy at

The Eighth XI

the death during the thrilling Test at The Oval that Australia won by seven runs. England reached 2-51 chasing 85 in that Test, but Murdoch kept his nerve, backing Spofforth and Harry Boyle to get the wickets. At one point, there was a succession of maiden overs, but all the captain said to Boyle was, 'Keep 'em on the spot, Harry, old chap.' With the score at 4-65, he approved a deliberate misfield, conceding a single, so the Demon could get at Alfred Lyttelton. Four overs later, Lyttelton was bowled and then the last five wickets crashed for seven dramatic runs.

In the first week of 1884, Murdoch hit 279 not out in what was essentially a trial for another upcoming tour of England, the opposing captain Tom Horan later describing the innings as 'an exhibition of true, scientific cricket, elegant and vigorous in attack, graceful and impregnable in defence'. That reliable defensive technique gave him something to fall back on, even when he was struggling for his best form. Most critics agreed that Murdoch was disappointing when he returned to big-time cricket to captain the Australian team in 1890, after more than five years out of Tests, yet he still topped the tour batting averages and scored two of the four hundreds made by members of the touring team during that English season. As late as 1904, when living in England in his 50th year, he scored 140 for the Gentlemen against the Players at The Oval.

The Australians of 1884. Murdoch, the captain, is most prominent in the front row, with the Demon Spofforth to his left. Jack Blackham is in the middle row, far left.

Of the 'old time' champions, Murdoch would have had to adapt to the modern game more than most. Whereas Grace was equally adept on the front and back foot, and was hence a champion on all wickets, wet or dry, Murdoch was much more of a front foot player, renowned for his straight bat and the way he could get down the pitch to drive. 'The daring pulls and hooks by which bowlers are now so often demoralised were not within his range,' *Wisden* commented in its obituary of Murdoch in 1912 (he had died while watching an Australia-South Africa Test at the MCG), 'and when the ball turned a great deal he was reduced to defence. To be seen at his best, he needed sunshine and a lively pitch. Then he could be great indeed.'

BILLY MURDOCH (AUSTRALIA)
Test Cricket#

Tests	Inn	NO	Runs	HS	Ave	100	50	Ct	St	Balls	Runs	Wkts	Ave	Best	5/	10/
19	34	5	908	211	31.31	2	1	14	1	–	–	–	–	–	–	–

First-Class Cricket

Mat	Inn	NO	Runs	HS	Ave	100	50	Ct	St	Balls	Runs	Wkts	Ave	Best	5/	10/
391	679	48	16953	321	26.87	19	85	218	24	764	430	10	43.00	2-11	–	–

No. 87 Fazal Mahmood

It was 25-year-old Fazal Mahmood, along with the teenage opening batsman, Hanif Mohammad, who gave the fledgling Pakistani team genuine Test class from the moment they began in international cricket in 1952. Both Fazal and Hanif were in the Pakistan line-up that faced India at Delhi in their nation's inaugural Test match — Fazal taking 2-92 from 40 overs, Hanif scoring 51 and 1 in a match dominated by the left-arm spin of India's Vinoo Mankad. Most cricket in Pakistan at this time was played 'on the mat', and for the second Test the Indian authorities generously decided to provide such a wicket, hence the unusual choice of the University Ground at Lucknow as the venue. No one was more grateful for this than Fazal, who on his favourite surface took 12-94 as Pakistan won by an innings and 43 runs. Back on turf, he took only six wickets in the final three Tests, and a suspicion arose that he might be a matting specialist.

Pakistan's first outstanding Test-match bowler.

Fazal was actually the 'Alec Bedser of Pakistan', a title given to him by *Wisden* after the Almanack named him one of its cricketers of the year for the 1954 season. 'In build, run-up and bowling action, Fazal does not resemble Bedser,' was *Wisden's* view. 'But their bowling methods bear a distinct similarity. Both concentrate on varied swing and a mixture of leg-cutters and break-backs at just above medium-pace; both are masters of length.' In first-class matches on tour, Fazal captured 77 wickets at 17.53; in the four Tests, two of which were rain-interrupted, he took 20 wickets at 20.40. The two times he bowled at Len Hutton, he got him out, for 14 and 5, both times inducing the great batsman to edge leg-cutters to keeper Imitiaz Ahmed in the fourth Test, at The Oval. In all, Fazal took 12 wickets in this Test (6-53 and 6-46) as Pakistan won an exciting game by 24 runs, the last eight English wickets collapsing for just 34. Hutton, who missed the second and third Tests of this series, was so transfixed by Fazal that when he wrote his life story two years later he also gave him credit for the golden duck he suffered in England's only innings at Lord's. 'Fazal Mahmood, a splendid opening bowler at all times, bowled me with a lovely inswinger the first ball he sent down to me,' Hutton wrote. In fact, the bowler was Khan Mohammad.

The respected West Indian commentator CLR James was impressed from the opening game of the tour, against Worcestershire, when Fazal took 11-102 for the match, having already scored 67 in the Pakistanis' first innings. 'At half-past three, this well-built and powerful man, whose every step both running up to bowl and walking back is charged with energy, was bowling as strongly as he had been doing at eleven in the morning,' James wrote in the *Manchester Guardian*.

The Eighth XI

Born in Lahore, Fazal played for Northern India in the Ranji Trophy before the Partition. As a boy, he could control a fast leg-break but as he grew older he found through constant practise in the nets that by eliminating the wrist action he could better deceive batsmen by combining a leg cutter with a variety of quickish off-spinners and breakbacks. He might have made the Indian team that toured England in 1946, and was chosen for the tour of Australia in 1947-48, but the division of India and Pakistan in August 1947 meant that, for him at least, the journey 'down under' did not happen. Over the next four years, he did well in matches against a West Indies side, Ceylon and the MCC team that drew four and lost one of its five matches in Pakistan as part of its subcontinent tour of 1951-52. So his early successes in Test cricket were no real surprise.

The Pakistanis in England in 1954. Fazal is in the front row, second from left.

Fazal followed up his triumph at The Oval with a stunning performance in Pakistan's first Test against Australia, on matting in Karachi. At the start, batsmen could do no more than survive, as only 95 runs were scored on the opening day — 80 by Australia and 1-15 by Pakistan. Fazal had taken 6-34 from 27 overs, Khan 4-43 from 26.1. When Australia batted again, he took 7-80 from 48 overs, setting up a nine-wicket victory. Richie Benaud made 56 in the second innings, facing more than 300 deliveries. He estimated later that he'd hit about a third of them, the rest whipping past the inside or outside edge. Referring to the two Pakistani bowlers, he said, 'This pair cut the ball further than I could turn it off the matting.' Alan Davidson remembered that the Australians were 'mesmerised', and called Fazal 'the greatest bowler of all time on matting wickets'. Of course, not all the great bowlers had the chance to play on this surface, but of those that did it would seemed that Fazal and Sydney Barnes, who routed South Africa in 1913-14, were the most effective.

Fazal strides up to the away team dressing-room at The Oval in 1954. He took six wickets in each innings of this Test, which Pakistan won by 24 runs, their first ever victory over England.

Between Pakistan's tour of England in 1954 and 1962, Fazal played only two series away from the matting — in the Caribbean in 1957-58, when Garry Sobers, Conrad Hunte, Clyde Walcott and Everton Weekes all scored heavily, and against India in 1960-61, when all five Tests were drawn and he took nine wickets, albeit at the acceptable average of 26.56. Against the West Indies in 1958-59, Fazal took seven wickets in the first Test at Karachi and 12 in the second at Dacca, but when a Test was played on a turf pitch in Lahore he could do no better than 2-109 from 40 overs as Pakistan lost a Test at home for the first time, by an innings and 156 runs. We are thus left with a paucity of evidence as to whether Fazal could have consistently wreaked the same havoc on grass pitches that he achieved so often on mats. Perhaps he would he have been a supremely accurate medium-pacer whose main forte was checking the scoring rate. More likely, given his skill, dedication and confidence, he would have adapted quickly to whatever circumstances were put in front of him, as he'd done in England in 1954.

As the story goes, after the Test at The Oval that year, he quietly said, 'Even though we were bowled out for 133, I did not think for a second we would lose.' On Fazal's death 51 years later, Hanif paid tribute, 'He was the doyen of Pakistan bowlers in the formative years and all our wins since we started playing Test cricket were indebted to him.' The current fast-bowling star, Shoaib Akhtar, called him 'the torch bearer'. Fazal Mahmood's role in building Pakistan into a Test team worthy of that status, so soon after the country itself was so traumatically born, was a mighty one. For that reason alone, he is entitled to be included among cricket's top 100.

FAZAL MAHMOOD (PAKISTAN)

Test Cricket

Tests	Inn	NO	Runs	HS	Ave	100	50	Ct	Balls	Runs	Wkts	Ave	Best	5/	10/
34	50	6	620	60	14.09	–	1	11	9834	3434	139	24.71	7-42	13	4

First-Class Cricket

Mat	Inn	NO	Runs	HS	Ave	100	50	Ct	Balls	Runs	Wkts	Ave	Best	5/	10/
112	147	33	2662	100*	23.35	1	13	39	25932	8837	466	18.96	9-43	38	8

Jacques Kallis

No. 88

South African cricket has produced a number of high-quality allrounders. It began in the first decade of the 20th century, when Aubrey Faulkner compiled some impressive statistics while his country was winning Test matches for the first time. Through the '60s, Trevor Goddard and Eddie Barlow complemented their outstanding opening partnership (average of 48.47 in 34 Tests) by taking vital wickets at important times. Then, after South Africa returned to international cricket in 1992, Jacques Kallis and Shaun Pollock built statistically impressive records while each playing more than 100 Tests.

If a South African allrounder is to make this top 100, it has to be either Faulkner or Kallis. With the bat, Faulkner was inelegant but technically correct, a man who understood his game and could hit big scores. In Australia in 1910-11, by compiling 732 runs in the five Tests (including 204 in 315 minutes, with 26 fours, in Melbourne) he outscored Victor Trumper even though the great batsman was in peak form. Faulkner was also one of the earliest exponents of the googly, complementing a variety of wrist spinners with a fast ball that often stunned well-set batsmen. At Headingley in 1907, he came on first change and took 6-17 as England was bowled out for 76. In 1909-10, he took 29 English wickets in five Tests while also scoring 545 runs at 60.56, the personal highlight coming at Johannesburg when he scored 78 and 123 and took 5-120 and 3-40.

Of the 24 Tests Faulkner played between 1905 and 1912 (he made one ill-fated appearance in 1924), South Africa won eight times. From 1913 to 1950, South Africa played 70 Tests and won seven of them. In an interview with Jack Hobbs in 1930, just days before Faulkner died, he said, 'These young fellows today don't know how marvellous it is to be young enough to get on with things.' That phrase, to get on with things, captured the positive attitude he brought to his cricket.

From 1992 to June 2009, South Africa has won more than half of its Test matches and more than 60 per cent of its ODIs. Yet it has never stamped itself as a brilliant cricket team, being dominated by Australia and losing critical Tests to other teams, while also falling short in major one-day tournaments. Kallis, as his country's most gifted cricketer, has in a way come to personify this lack of major achievement. In February 2009, he became the first man to complete the 10,000 runs/250 wickets Test double. For a No. 4 batsman, Kallis has a remarkable number of not outs (33 in 221 innings; Brian Lara, by com-

Kallis, the bowler, is an accumulator of wickets rather than a prolific strike bowler.

parison, has six in 232) and he has proved especially proficient at scoring runs and staying unbeaten against weak bowling attacks. Tellingly, his batting averages against Australia, England and Sri Lanka are less than 41, as it was against Pakistan until 2007. Eleven of his 31 Test hundreds have come against the West Indies, Zimbabwe and Bangladesh.

Kallis is only the second man, after Garry Sobers, to score 8000 runs and take 200 wickets in Test cricket.

Statistically, it is impossible to leave Kallis out of this top 100. The number of Tests, runs, hundreds, wickets, at averages that are comparable to Sobers — they all add up to a distinguished record. At times, when batting, he has seemed impossible to dismiss. However, in Test cricket he has rarely managed to dominate with bat and ball at the same time, and while one should not be critical of him for that — cricket is not, after all, a one-man game — it stops him being ranked with the greatest allrounders.

In England in 1998, in a five-Test series, Kallis scored 294 runs, including 132 at Old Trafford, and took 11 wickets at 27.82. Immediately afterwards, at home against a West Indian attack led by Curtly Ambrose and Courtney Walsh, he averaged almost 70 in a series in which no other batsman averaged even fifty, and took 17 wickets at 17.58, as Brian Lara's disheartened team was swept 5-0. At Cape Town, in the fourth Test, he scored 110, took 2-34, scored 88 not out and then, with Allan Donald injured, heroically opened the bowling, sent down 27.4 overs and took 5-90. The only South African to previously hit a hundred, a fifty and take a five-for in the same Test was Aubrey Faulkner. However, in the 10 years since, Kallis has never taken 10 or more wickets and scored a century in the same Test series.

It's always been runs or wickets, usually runs. In the Caribbean in early 2001, he bowled nearly 200 overs while taking 20 wickets at 19.75, but scored only 267 runs with a highest score of 53. Straight after, he took three Zimbabwean wickets while scoring 388 runs without being dismissed. In England in 2003, he took 14 wickets at 25.86 but scored only 188 runs at 31.33. Six months later, against the West Indies, he amassed 712 runs at 178, with four centuries, but took five wickets at 64.20. In 2004-05, again versus the Windies, he averaged 98 with the bat while scoring his 21st and 22nd Test centuries, but averaged 140 with the ball. Against England in 2008, he took 10 wickets in the series, but scored only 104 runs, average 14.86. When South Africa finally won a Test series in Australia, in 2008-09, Kallis contributed, but was hardly a central figure, as Graeme Smith, AB de Villiers, JP Duminy and Dale Steyn all starred. Kallis' only century against Ricky Ponting's team that season came in the last of six Tests the two teams played, after the three-game series in South Africa had been lost. He has been man of the match in 19 Tests, but only five times for all-round achievement — that Test against the West Indies at Cape Town in early 1999, and then twice against Zimbabwe,

The Eighth XI

once against Bangladesh and once against Pakistan. Similarly, he has been man of the match 31 times in ODIs, but the only time he won the award for taking more than three wickets in the innings (5-38 v West Indies in 1998), he scored 37. He has hit 16 one-day centuries, but only twice has he taken even two wickets in a ODI in which he scored a century.

Shane Warne described Kallis as 'a solid, dependable batsman'. Steve Waugh called him 'an outstanding technical batsman with an impressive shot-making ability'. A cricinfo study in early 2006 noted that during his first 23 Test centuries, Kallis

Kallis in England in 1997, playing for Middlesex.

scored at 48 runs per 100 balls, 'nowhere near the rates of Sachin Tendulkar (59.5), Inzamam-ul-Haq (61.5), Ricky Ponting (63) or Brian Lara (70)'. At Sydney at the start of 2006, South Africa needed a win to square the series and captain Graeme Smith was desperate for quick runs so he could set the home team a decent target. But Kallis could do no better than 50 from 96 balls, with three fours. Ponting then came out and hit 143 not out from 159 balls to win the match. We can be hard markers when it comes to the great players, but this match was something of a microcosm of Kallis' career. If only he could have followed Aubrey Faulkner's advice to young players and got on with things, the end result might have been so much greater.

JACQUES KALLIS (SOUTH AFRICA)
Test Cricket

Tests	Inn	NO	Runs	HS	Ave	100	50	Ct	Balls	Runs	Wkts	Ave	Best	5/	10/
131	221	33	10277	189*	54.66	31	51	147	17040	8021	258	31.09	6-54	5	–

One-Day International Cricket

ODIs	Inn	NO	Runs	HS	Ave	100	50	Ct	Balls	Runs	Wkts	Ave	Best	4/
291	277	51	10239	139	45.31	16	73	105	9790	7881	247	31.91	5-30	4

The 100 Greatest Cricketers

Stan McCabe

Clive Lloyd

The Ninth

Arthur Mailey

Kumar Sangakkara

The Ninth XI

Bill Lockwood

Tom Richardson

Vijay Hazare

XI

Jeff Thomson

Andy Flower

Graeme Smith

Andrew Flintoff

No. 89 Stan McCabe

For the purpose of this top 100, Stan McCabe is selected as an opening bat even though going in first was not his caper during his Test career. McCabe is universally recognised to have been a superb player of fast bowling, yet he never once opened the batting in a Test match. The reason for that is simple: from 1932 to 1938 he was clearly Australia's second-best batsman, so invariably he was at No. 4 in the batting order, straight after The Don.

McCabe was responsible for three of cricket's greatest ever innings: 187 not out against bodyline in 1932-33; 189 not out against South Africa in 1935-36; and 232 at Trent Bridge in 1938.

It needs only one innings — arguably the greatest knock by an Australian batsman in Test cricket — to prove that McCabe would have been an outstanding man against the new ball. In December 1932, in the first bodyline Test at Sydney, McCabe launched a classic counterattack against Harold Larwood at his fastest, at a time when Australia could have been overwhelmed by England's shock tactics. He was in soon after lunch on the opening day, after Bill Ponsford left his leg stump exposed and Jack Fingleton popped up a riser to short leg, with the score at 3-82 and just in time to see his partner, Alan Kippax, struck a glancing blow to the head. Straight after, Kippax was overwhelmed by Larwood's speed, but McCabe and Vic Richardson (who would open the Australian innings later in the series) mounted a revival. They added 129, Richardson making 49, but Australia then struggled to 9-305 before McCabe and Tim Wall added 55 for the last wicket in 33 minutes, Wall getting four of them.

Going into this Test, the 22-year-old McCabe had scored only 607 runs at 33.72 in 15 Tests, many of them against poor bowling. With Archie Jackson desperately ill and Don Bradman (who missed this first Test through sickness) established as a superstar, McCabe was considered the country's most promising batsman, but as with all young cricketers struggling with high expectations there was some conjecture about his temperament. Now he set the record straight, finishing with 187 not out. 'This innings stamped Stan as one of the world's greatest batsmen,' wrote umpire George Hele in 1974. 'He stepped into the bowling, he hooked, pulled, and did what he liked with it. The faster they bowled the more he seemed to enjoy it.' Reports suggest that most of the hook shots were actually hit forward of square, away from the two deep fieldsmen England captain Douglas Jardine placed behind the leg slips and short legs. 'Though McCabe was taking many chances,' Jardine wrote in his tour diary, 'there seemed no particular reason why he should ever get out.'

Australia eventually lost the Test by 10 wickets, and McCabe had surprisingly little impact on the rest of the series. In England in 1934 he was the key batsman in Australia's victory in the opening Test, and then made an important hundred at Manchester. In South Africa in 1935-36, he played another famous innings, this

The Ninth XI

time 189 not out as Australia made a thrilling chase for 399 on the final day of the third Test at Johannesburg. Legend has it that the home captain Herbie Wade successfully appealed against the light on the basis that McCabe's shots were endangering his fieldsmen. Soon after the rain came and the Test was drawn. McCabe's biographer Jack McHarg told of another time during this tour when the Australians agreed to play in a charity baseball match against a team from Transvaal. A number of the tourists had never played the game before, but McCabe for one was not concerned. After another hit, his teammate Len Darling asked for his secret. 'How can you miss?' McCabe replied. 'They're all full tosses!'

He averaged 84 in the Tests on that tour, and then scored five fifties and finally 112 in the 1936-37 Ashes series. By now his Test average was up to 48.69 and in England in 1938 he immediately took it well over 50, by scoring 232 in the first Test at Trent Bridge. Some observers, chief among them Bradman, believed this to be the greatest innings ever played. England had made 8-658 (declared) and Australia were 6-194 before McCabe went on the attack. Again, he was involved in a dynamic last-wicket stand, this time adding 77 in 28 minutes with Chuck Fleetwood-Smith, the No. 11 finishing unbeaten on 5. 'I doubt whether I have ever been so punished as a fielder as I was for four hours during that majestic innings,' Denis Compton remembered.

Match descriptions from McCabe's day suggest he was a batsman with all the shots. Photographs show that technically he was outstanding, especially on the back foot. Because of that famous innings against bodyline, he is remembered instantly for his hook and pull shots, but in his autobiography Bill O'Reilly recalled most fondly something else from his great friend's repertoire. 'McCabe lived at a time when the late cut was looked upon as undeniable evidence of batting skill,' wrote the Tiger, 'and he completely mastered it.'

Some will be surprised at McCabe's selection here ahead of Victoria's Bill Ponsford, who was a teammate on the 1930 and 1934 Ashes tours. Yet a close study of Ponsford's Test career strongly suggests that he was not quite the player many of his strongest supporters in Melbourne make him out to be. He did score hundreds in his first two Tests, in 1924-25, and also in his final two Tests, in England in 1934, when he was involved in two colossal partnerships with Bradman. In between, though, Ponsford played in 27 Tests and scored 1384 runs at 37.40, including three centuries. That's a rate of one hundred every 13.67 innings, which is hardly prolific. Those three hundreds actually came in a run of four Tests from the final Test of the 1930 Ashes series to the third Test against an ordinary West Indies team in 1930-31.

McCabe and Don Bradman go out to bat during the 1936-37 Ashes series.

Just as Clarrie Grimmett took plenty of wickets in the Sheffield Shield, Ponsford accumulated a mountain of runs on flat wickets at first-class level, but he was dropped more than once during his Test career and was considered by some to have been lucky to make the 1930 tour of England. *The Sydney Morning Herald* for one, referring to the controversy over the omission of Jack Ryder, thought the final batting place had come down to a choice between Ryder and Ponsford.

Question marks also existed over Ponsford's ability against very quick bowling. Footage of him batting against Larwood in Brisbane during the 1928-29 series — where the tourists made 521 in their first innings — shows him backing away as he faces the great English fast man. This seems more a problem of technique than courage, for four years later, Ponsford was very brave, most notably in Adelaide when he made 85 and took a series of blows on the body. However, he was dropped twice during that summer, for the second and fifth Tests, as his footwork was consistently shown up by the speed and skill of Larwood and Voce. Compared to the way McCabe used his bat as D'Artagnan had used his sword, Ponsford looked very ponderous indeed.

McCabe leaves the field at Trent Bridge in 1938, after his famous 232 in the first Test.

STAN McCABE (AUSTRALIA)

Test Cricket

Tests	Inn	NO	Runs	HS	Ave	100	50	Ct	Balls	Runs	Wkts	Ave	Best	5/	10/
39	62	5	2748	232	48.21	6	13	41	3746	1543	36	42.86	4-13	—	—

First-Class Cricket

Mat	Inn	NO	Runs	HS	Ave	100	50	Ct	Balls	Runs	Wkts	Ave	Best	5/	10/
182	262	20	11951	240	49.38	29	68	138	13440	5362	159	33.72	5-36	1	—

The Ninth XI

Clive Lloyd — No. 90

There is room for another West Indian middle-order batsman, and the choice comes down to one of three: Richie Richardson, Alvin Kallicharran or Clive Lloyd. Richardson almost always batted first wicket down in Test cricket from 1983 to 1996. He seemed to revel in matches against Australia, scoring nine of his 16 Test centuries against them, including two in each of three series: 1984, 1988-89 and 1991. His 182 at Georgetown in 1991 was a stunning innings that set the mood for the series. David Boon remembered how the Australians set a square gully, a deep point and a third man and Richardson kept cutting fours. When Merv Hughes, who took 0-93 that day, sat down in 1997 to pick a best XI from the men he played against the No. 3 position was easy. 'Richie was completely unflappable as a batsman and nothing you ever did would ever seem to worry him,' Hughes explained. 'My weapon is obviously the short ball, but he loved that and would take you on and take you down. Richie scored at a good pace and when he got going, he was just about impossible to put the brakes on.'

Kallicharran is something of a forgotten figure today, but for a time in the mid 1970s he was one of the best batsmen in the world. 'In the selection of any World XI, it is difficult to see how he could be omitted at present,' wrote Tony Cozier in *The Cricketer* in 1976. Kallicharran scored a hundred in each of his first two Test innings, against New Zealand in 1972, and sustained a Test average of above or about 50 for the next seven years. After 23 Tests, he was averaging 56.82 in Test cricket, had scored a century against each of the then Test-playing nations and Wes Hall was confidently predicting he would break Garry Sobers' Test run-getting record. However, the pressure of being one of the few players of Indian descent in the side gradually wore at him, and then he was the only major West Indian player not to go to World Series Cricket. From the moment the WSC men came back in 1979, Kallicharran was on the outer, and his form deteriorated to the point that he only scored 530 runs in his last 21 Test innings, with one century and one fifty.

Kallicharran's dramatic assault on Dennis Lillee at The Oval during the 1975 World Cup — the faster Lillee bowled, the further Kallicharran hit him — was one of the highlights of the tournament. The Australians' reaction when they dismissed him for 12 in the final reflected the impact the earlier innings had made. It was as if, with Kallicharran gone, that they suddenly had a chance. Hardly. Clive Lloyd then strode out to play one of one-day cricket's most famous innings, blasting a century from 82 deliveries. This would be his only ODI century, but he

Lloyd during the 1975 World Cup final at Lord's.

The 100 Greatest Cricketers

Lloyd was an explosive hitter from his international debut in 1966 until his final Test appearance almost 20 years later.

still managed to average more than 40 in the abbreviated form of the game, an excellent effort for a batsman who was often required to bat in the innings' final 15-over flurry. It was believed the World Cup triumph would establish the West Indies as the new powerhouse in world cricket, but instead they were promptly thrashed in Australia a few months later. From there, though, the men from the Caribbean regrouped under the Lloyd captaincy, and in WSC and beyond they established a supremacy that wasn't challenged until the early '90s.

When Lloyd first came into big-time cricket he was tagged as a big hitter with a loose technique. He was also a fantastic cover fieldsman until he injured his back while attempting to take a spectacular catch in Adelaide in December 1968. He scored 82 and 78 not out in his maiden Test, against India at Bombay two years before that accident, and then scored a hundred at the earliest opportunity against both England and Australia. But having batted so beautifully at the Gabba in December 1968, he didn't score another century at the highest level until April 1973. He was hardly a unanimous choice as West Indies captain in 1974, not least because his Test batting average was only 38.68, but he started his time in charge with an important second-innings 163, the first hundred coming from 85 balls, which allowed him to make his first declaration and start his Test captaincy career with a win. India fought back from 2-0 down to square the series, but in the decider in

Lloyd in Barbados in 1981, scoring a crucial first-day hundred against England.

The Ninth XI

Bombay, Lloyd made 242 not out to set up a 201-run triumph. Even after the debacle in Australia the following year, his place as captain was never seriously threatened until he retired in 1985. He won 36 of his 74 Tests as captain, and lost only 12.

In a batting order that at different times over the decade featured names such as Richardson, Kallicharran, Gordon Greenidge, Roy Fredericks, Viv Richards, Lawrence Rowe, Desmond Haynes and Larry Gomes, the captain's batting ability was often overlooked. But he averaged 51.30 with the bat while skipper and often made his runs when they were most needed. Against England at Manchester in 1980 and Bridgetown in 1981, and against India at Port-of-Spain in 1983, he scored hundreds after coming to the wicket at three for less than 50. In the latter match, he was in at 3-1 to add 237 for the fourth wicket with Gomes. In India in late 1983, his 109 rescued the Test at Delhi and then a superb unbeaten 161 at Calcutta, which took more than eight hours, was the crucial innings in a game in which the hosts were bowled out for 241 and 90.

In a profile for *The Cricketer* in 1971, Mike Stevenson told of a county game in which a couple of medium-pacers set out to exploit a so-called weakness Lloyd had against the short ball. 'The first time a ball was bounced at him, its next bounce occurred around 40 yards over the long-leg boundary,' Stevenson wrote. 'You can't kill tigers with a toothpick.' With the captaincy came a sense of responsibility but Lloyd never lost that ability to make the bat in his hands and the bowlers opposing him look mighty small as he slashed the ball past point, or clouted it away to the mid-wicket boundary with a hefty swing of the bat.

Throughout this study leadership skills have been largely ignored when ranking players, on the basis that it is unfair to do so when some players had better chances as captains than did others. Some, of course, had no opportunities at all. The exceptions are Imran Khan, Frank Worrell, Steve Waugh, Archie MacLaren, Richie Benaud and Monty Noble, all of whom might have been ranked slightly lower but for their contributions as leaders. Certainly, Lloyd captained more talented teams than did Kallicharran (1978-1979) and Richardson (1992-1996), but even so the manner in which he brought his group of wonderful players together, and then kept them together, is what ensures his selection in this ninth XI. Clive Lloyd was a winner. The West Indies have never been quite the same since he retired.

Lloyd with Michael Holding in Australia during the one-day series of 1984-85.

CLIVE LLOYD (WEST INDIES)

Test Cricket

Tests	Inn	NO	Runs	HS	Ave	100	50	Ct	Balls	Runs	Wkts	Ave	Best	5/	10/
110	175	14	7515	242*	46.68	19	39	90	1716	622	10	62.20	2-13	–	–

One-Day International Cricket

ODIs	Inn	NO	Runs	HS	Ave	100	50	Ct	Balls	Runs	Wkts	Ave	Best	4/
87	70	20	2027	102	40.54	1	12	39	358	210	8	26.25	2-4	–

The 100 Greatest Cricketers

No. 91 & No. 92 Bill Lockwood and Tom Richardson

His Test record might not have been that of an out-and-out champion, but according to many of Bill Lockwood's contemporaries, that's exactly what he was. Ranji and Billy Murdoch were two who thought Lockwood was the most difficult bowler they ever faced. As was described in the chapter on Les Ames, in 1932, some members of the English cricket team in Australia, 'chaired' by Sir Pelham Warner, picked their best ever England XI, and they selected Lockwood alongside Sydney Barnes, the left-armer Frank Foster and George Lohmann as their bowlers. WG Grace described Lockwood in 1899 as 'one of the very best of living cricketers'.

Lockwood (left) with a renowned England teammate, the left-arm spinner Bobby Peel.

In 1893, 25-year-old Lockwood and the two-years-younger Tom Richardson formed a sensational bowling partnership for Surrey in the county championship. This was Richardson's first great season, and Lockwood's second, and between them they took 324 wickets for the season. Strangely, though, they did not bowl together during that year's Ashes series. Lockwood was superb in the first two Tests, opening the bowling with Lancashire's Arthur Mold, but then an injury allowed Richardson to make his Test debut at Old Trafford, where he made an immediate impact by taking five wickets in each innings.

'The secret of the deadliness of his bowling is his combination of pace and break,' wrote WG of Lockwood, 'with a faculty for deceiving the batsmen by sending down slower balls without perceptible change of action.' During the previous season, the Gentlemen v Players match had ended in thrilling fashion — Grace was batting for the Gentlemen with an injured hand, but after his team crashed to 9-80 he and Charles Kortright added 78 for the final wicket to get within four minutes of an honourable draw. However, Players captain Arthur Shrewsbury brought back Lockwood in fading light, and third ball Kortright (who was four short of a rare first-class fifty) had an impulse to swing away. Unfortunately for the batsmen, it was Lockwood's much-feared slower ball, and it speared off the leading edge to deepish cover, where Schofield Haigh took the catch.

The natural ally to that well-disguised delivery was a big off-cutter that Lockwood could bowl at rare pace, which gave many a batsmen a nasty crack on the fleshy part of the back thigh. Further, from a high action and with a distinct surge of the shoulder at delivery, he could make the ball fizz off the wicket, and also get it to

The Ninth XI

lift from short of a length, an asset that set him apart from most other English bowlers of the 19th century. At times, he could be scary. Charles Fry once told HS Altham that, 'I never knew when the beggar wasn't going to bowl me out neck and crop, however well I was playing.' Lockwood made a habit of getting good batsmen out caught behind (10 of his 43 Test wickets came in this way), which suggested that at least one or two weren't always keen to get behind the line. And he was a reasonable batsman, capable of scoring 15 first-class centuries. Indeed, it was his batting that had first got him into the Surrey team, in the days when Lohmann bowled most of their overs.

Lockwood's Test career was confined to just four series in nine years, and one of those — in Australia in 1894-95 — was a disaster. He was often superb in the other three, taking 38 Australian wickets in seven Tests at 14.31. In normal circumstances, such a small sample of matches would not be enough to get a cricketer into this top 100, but Lockwood's was a peculiar career, wrecked in the middle by that Australian tour and its immediate aftermath.

He'd departed England with a colossal reputation, built in part on the 14 wickets he took in those two Tests of 1893, and also through the 451 first-class wickets he'd accumulated over the previous three English seasons. However, while on a cruise on Sydney Harbour before the first Test, the fast bowler dived in for a swim and nearly drowned. Later, he hurt a shoulder and then on the first day of the fourth he was sitting next to teammate Bobby Peel when a soda bottle Peel was holding suddenly exploded. The result was a severely cut hand for Lockwood that meant he could hardly bowl in the Test and was still hurting him when the fifth Test was played out four weeks later.

There were also suspicions that Lockwood might have enjoyed touring just a little too well, and comparisons with Richardson, who persevered on the often flat Australian pitches so well that he took 32 wickets in the Tests to Lockwood's five, were hardly kind. However, none of this meant anything when during 1895 both his wife and one of his daughters died. The poor man was shattered, took solace in the grog and let his cricket career slide away. In 1897, he took a solitary wicket from two matches, and then disappeared, apparently for good. If anyone at this stage had suggested that he was a better bowler than Richardson, who would work all day, every day, and had taken no less than 809 wickets in the past three seasons, they'd have been

Richardson, a great bowler who gained fame for his rare skill and even rarer courage and tenacity.

ridiculed, even if there'd always been a sneaking suspicion that Lockwood was the more gifted of the two. But then, during the 1897-98 winter, Lockwood was convinced to tackle his demons. In its way, his subsequent comeback was every bit as courageous as was Dennis Lillee's nearly 80 years later. In 1898, he took 134 wickets and was named one of *Wisden's* Cricketers of the Year, and in its tribute the Almanack wrote, 'A more remarkable cricketer than Lockwood, at his best, has rarely been seen on our cricket fields.'

Meanwhile, Tom Richardson had been taking an incredible 1340 wickets in six English first-class seasons (1893 to 1898), building a reputation for courage and endurance on top of skill that perhaps no player, let alone a fast bowler, has ever matched. On two tours of Australia, 1894-95 and 1897-98, he took another 122, impressing all with his constant energy under the blazing sun and once hitting Harry Trott so hard on the thigh that the batsman spent the next few overs stumbling around as if he'd been kicked by an angry colt. 'This man Richardson was the greatest cricketer that ever took to fast bowling,' wrote Neville Cardus. 'Richardson bowled from a natural impulse to bowl, and whether he bowled well or ill that impulse was always strong. His action moved one like music because it was so rhythmical. He ran to the wicket a long distance, and at the bowling crease his terminating leap made you catch breath. His break-back most cricketers of the day counted among the seven wonders of the world ...'

For Cardus, Richardson's greatest day came at Old Trafford in 1896, in a Test England lost, where he 'did bowl and bowl and bowl, and his fury diminished not a jot'. The Surrey champion had already taken 11-173 in the first Test, and now, in Australia's first innings, on the most benign of pitches, he bowled 68 overs and finished with 7-168. England then stumbled to 231, and had to follow on, doing well enough the second time to set Australia an awkward 125 to win. In the end, it took them 84.3 five-ball overs and seven wickets to get them, the tension being so cruel that Trott, now the Australian captain, opted to circle the ground in a hansom cab rather than try to sit and watch. Richardson bowled throughout the innings without a break to take 6-76. After the winning run was hit, the players dashed from the field ... except Richardson, who stood wearily at the bowling crease, dazed and shattered that his Herculean effort had not quite been enough. In their classic book *Test Cricket: England v Australia*, the eminent cricket historians Ralph Barker and Irving Rosenwater called it 'perhaps the greatest sustained effort ever accomplished by a fast bowler'.

Richardson only played in 14 Tests, all against Australia, but in those matches he took five wickets in an innings 11 times and 10 wickets in a match four times. Sadly, from 1898 his impact began to fade, perhaps a burnout, possibly, too because he lost the fitness edge that had been such an asset in his prime. WG

BILL LOCKWOOD (ENGLAND)

Test Cricket

Tests	Inn	NO	Runs	HS	Ave	100	50	Ct	Balls	Runs	Wkts	Ave	Best	5/	10/
12	16	3	231	52*	17.77	–	1	4	1970	883	43	20.53	7-71	5	1

First-Class Cricket

Mat	Inn	NO	Runs	HS	Ave	100	50	Ct	Balls	Runs	Wkts	Ave	Best	5/	10/
363	531	45	10673	165	21.96	15	48	140	52121	25246	1376	18.35	9-59	121	29

recorded that Richardson's bowling appeared to have 'lost most of its sting' and he never played another Test after his second Australian tour. However, his guts and spirit still ensured that he took more than 100 first-class wickets in each season from 1900 to 1903, albeit at a higher average than he achieved in his glory days.

Ironically, the man who eventually filled the breach at Test level left by his decline was Lockwood, who returned to Test cricket in 1899 in spectacular style, taking 7-71 in the first innings of the final drawn match of the Ashes series. Until then, a leg strain had hindered him, but when fit, according to Lillywhite's *Cricketer's Annual*, he 'bowled with all his old devil'. In 1902 he played in four of the five Tests, but England didn't bowl at Lord's because of the rain, leaving him only three games to take 17 wickets at 12.12, including 6-48 and 5-28 in the famous match at Old Trafford that Australia won by three runs.

On the opening morning of that Test, Victor Trumper scored his famous century before lunch, in part because of Lockwood's influence. The run-ups were so wet that the pace man couldn't use them, and Trumper flailed away before he came on. When Lockwood finally took his first over, after 75 minutes, the score was 0-129. Immediately, the tone of the game changed, but enough damage had been done, and his Richardson-like effort of class and endurance — during which he outbowled acclaimed figures such as Wilfred Rhodes and Hugh Trumble — was largely overshadowed by the remarkable drama of the finish, when England lost their last seven wickets for 28 and the Test by three runs.

A straw poll of the great players of the era would probably rank Lockwood fractionally ahead of Richardson, but only because Lockwood's uniqueness and unpredictably made him more dangerous. 'It is possible to be 120 not out on a plumb wicket,' Ranji wrote, 'and then to be clean bowled by Lockwood and walk away to the pavilion not knowing what one would have done if one had another chance at the ball.' However, Richardson still had his supporters, including Gilbert Jessop, George Lohmann and long-time England keeper 'Dick' Lilley. In 1939, Australia's Clem Hill described Richardson as 'the greatest fast bowler England ever had', which would make him superior to Harold Larwood. Then Hill added, 'For the young man of today who thinks he knows all about fast bowling I would recommend a session against Tom Richardson or Ernest Jones, our own express. Our greatest batsmen today would wonder what has struck them.'

Especially, you would think, if Bill Lockwood was coming at them from the other end.

TOM RICHARDSON (ENGLAND)

Test Cricket

Tests	Inn	NO	Runs	HS	Ave	100	50	Ct	Balls	Runs	Wkts	Ave	Best	5/	10/
14	24	8	177	25*	11.06	–	–	5	4498	2220	88	25.23	8-94	11	4

First-Class Cricket

Mat	Inn	NO	Runs	HS	Ave	100	50	Ct	Balls	Runs	Wkts	Ave	Best	5/	10/
358	479	124	3424	69	9.65	–	2	126	78992	38793	2104	18.44	10-45	200	72

No. 93 Vijay Hazare

The scene was the first Test against England at Leeds in 1952, on the Saturday, the third day. Vijay Hazare had made 89 in India's first innings, sharing a stand of 222 with Vijay Manjrekar (133), but the rest of the Indian batting line-up had looked extremely fragile as they were bowled out for 293.

England had earned a first-innings lead of 41 in reply, with Hazare taking 1-22 from 20 overs. Now Len Hutton, the first professional to be appointed captain of England, threw the ball to his debutant, 21-year-old fast bowler Fred Trueman, and asked him to bowl down breeze from the Kirkstall Lane end. Fourteen balls later, India were four wickets down for nought. Hazare was left to survey the wreckage, and get India off the mark.

Hazare was only small of stature, but he amassed some colossal scores in first-class cricket and averaged almost 50 in Tests.

In his autobiography, *As It Was*, Trueman rated Hazare (and Manjrekar) as being among the best players of fast bowling in the game at that time. He was on a hat-trick and described his next delivery this way: 'Hazare moved into line, bat close to pad, and the ball missed the edge by a fag paper's width.' Many of the Indian batsmen would be criticised later for not showing enough courage against Trueman's pace, but not Hazare. Polly Umrigar was out with the score on 26, and then the captain and Dattu Phadkar added 95 for the sixth wicket before Trueman finally knocked over Hazare's off stump.

Hazare was 37 years old when this battle took place and past his prime. Because of World War II, he had not made his Test debut until 1946, but he was still averaging 51.50 with the bat in Test cricket going into that clash with Trueman (in 16 matches), even though he had scored just 28 runs in his previous five Test innings. His greatest claim to fame in international cricket was that he had scored a century in each innings against Bradman's Australians in 1947-48. At home, however, he was better known for the incredible run-making duels he had been involved in with Vijay Merchant in the early 1940s, the war years, when the two sustained interest in local cricket in the most astonishing way.

For much of the 1930s, Merchant had been India's No. 1 batsman, firmly establishing his reputation in England in 1936 when he scored 114 at Old Trafford and was later named one of *Wisden*'s cricketers of the year. But in 1940, Hazare established a new Ranji Trophy record when he scored 316 not out for Maharashtra against Baroda, and in the process announced himself as Merchant's new rival in Indian cricket. In 1943-44, Hazare made consecutive scores of 248, 59, 309, 101, 223 and 87, becoming the first man to total 1000 runs in an Indian first-class season — in six innings! The first double century was made for 'The Rest' against the 'Muslims' in the Pentangular, at that time Bombay's (and arguably India's) biggest cricket tournament, and broke Merchant's previous record score for the event, 243 not out,

The Ninth XI

which had been achieved in 1941-42. Within a week, The Rest played the 'Hindus' and in the Hindus' first innings Merchant went to 250 before he declared. After The Rest was bowled out for just 133, they had to follow-on and had collapsed to 5-60 when Hazare was joined by his brother Vivek. They added 300, of which Vivek scored 21. When Vijay Hazare's own score reached 295 he hit the first six of his life at Brabourne Stadium. When he was finally caught and bowled, the innings total was 387 and he had scored almost 80 per cent of his team's runs. Then, in late December, Merchant broke Hazare's Ranji Trophy record when he scored 359 not out for Bombay against Maharashtra.

Through the 1930s, Merchant had shown the next generation of Indian batsmen the virtues of defence, and as his aura grew so lofted shots disappeared from the game. Hazare was not his disciple; it was more a case of the younger man taking batting to a new level. 'Hazare was not quite as defensive as Merchant' wrote Mihir Bose in *A History of Indian Cricket*. 'The cover drive, always a flowing cricket stroke, was his great stroke, along with his on drive.' Hazare gripped the bat handle with his hands well apart, and stood awkwardly at the crease with his bat between his pads, but in 1947, on a matting pitch, he and Gul Mohammed compiled a world record 577 partnership in the Ranji Trophy final against Holkar. He started slowly in Test cricket, scoring just 207 runs in his first 11 innings, but in Adelaide in late January 1948 he scored 116 out of 381 and then 145 of 277 against Ray Lindwall and Keith Miller in a match India lost by an innings and 16 runs. AG Moyes wrote of his style, timing, and 'gift of placement (that) helped him to many boundaries'. Earlier in the Test, Hazare had bowled Bradman for the second time in the series, a good trick for a man who only managed 20 wickets in his Test career. The only other bowlers to hit Bradman's stumps more than once in Test cricket were Bill Bowes (four times), Hedley Verity (three times) and Harold Larwood (twice).

Hazare and Len Hutton toss before the fourth Test at The Oval in 1952.

Hazare averaged 50 or more in each of his next four Test series after the Australian adventure (including the 1952 series in England, when he scored 333 runs at 55.50), before struggling on India's first ever tour of the Caribbean, in 1952-53. His final Test batting average of 47.65 is fractionally below that of Merchant (47.72), but he played in 30 Tests to Merchant's 10, and in men such as Lindwall, Miller,

293

Trueman and Fazal Mahmood faced superior bowlers to those Merchant saw in the 1930s. Hazare did captain India, but not very well, while Merchant never had the opportunity (he could have led the team to Australia, but declined, purportedly because of injury). Both Hazare and Merchant compiled outstanding first-class figures: Hazare, 18,740 runs at 58.38; Merchant, 13,470 runs at 71.64. Yes, Merchant did have much more success in England in 1946, and he made most of his runs as an opener, but after much consideration, Hazare is the man included in this top 100, by a narrow margin.

Hazare on the defensive in England in 1952, when he was the only Indian batsman who ever looked like consistently coping with the danger posed by Alec Bedser and Fred Trueman.

In his autobiography, *Farewell to Cricket*, Don Bradman wrote that he 'had been very impressed by the soundness of Hazare and the correctness of his stroke production'. The Don thought he was a 'great player', but added that Hazare's only failing was 'a lack of aggression which prevented him taking charge of an attack and tearing it to pieces'. The implication is that Bradman thought Hazare was quite capable of doing this. Had he been part of a more successful Test batting line-up rather than one that could lose its first four wickets for nought, Vijay Hazare may well have been a very great player indeed.

VIJAY HAZARE (PAKISTAN)

Test Cricket

Tests	Inn	NO	Runs	HS	Ave	100	50	Ct	Balls	Runs	Wkts	Ave	Best	5/	10/
30	52	6	2192	164*	47.65	7	9	11	2840	1220	20	61.00	4-29	–	–

First-Class Cricket

Mat	Inn	NO	Runs	HS	Ave	100	50	Ct	Balls	Runs	Wkts	Ave	Best	5/	10/
238	367	46	18740	316*	58.38	60	73	166	38628	14645	595	24.61	8-90	27	3

Jeff Thomson

No. 94

As good a judge as Sir Donald Bradman wrote in 1986 that the three fastest bowlers he saw were Harold Larwood, Frank Tyson and Malcolm Marshall. Perhaps Sir Donald was keen not be viewed as being biased towards his homeland. Because it is this author's view that in the last 40 years at least no man has ever bowled faster than Jeff Thomson. For a little more than two Australian seasons, from the start of the 1974-75 Ashes season to the first Test against Pakistan in 1976-77, when he badly damaged his shoulder in a fielding accident, 'Thommo' made not just batsmen but also his keeper, Rod Marsh, jump in a manner that strongly suggested he was lightning.

Thomson's action set him apart. Having used it to such intimidating effect, one would have thought a succession of imitators would have quickly emerged, but instead in the three decades since no one has really come to close to his slinging style. 'When I first saw Thomson bowl in the Queensland match in 1974,' England's Bob Willis wrote in 1981, 'I immediately thought: "What a sensible way to bowl." He seemed to take very little out of himself with his javelin thrower's action: no strain on the joints, no pounding down on the left foot, and little pressure on the hips or left knee. It was the first time I had faced a bowler and been frightened because I could not pick up the length of the ball.'

Tyson, working as a TV commentator and journalist during the 1974-75 series, wrote in Brisbane during the first Test of Thomson's 'strong, backward rock in the split second before delivery, and an overall whippiness in his action which time and time again had the agile keeper Marsh skipping like a monkey to clutch the ball above his head'. The writer and commentator Christopher Martin-Jenkins, who was travelling with the England team, couldn't think of any other great fast bowler whose action even resembled Thomson.

Thommo is the mid '70s, when he was the fastest bowler in the world.

The new fast man jogged up to the wicket, slowly but rhythmically accelerating, and as he approached the stumps, he crossed his feet and moved his body totally side-on, his bowling arm disappearing away from the batsman, the right hand now down by his right (back) buttock, left arm straight and pointing skywards. Then, with a mighty thrust of the shoulder, the ball was propelled down the pitch with maximum force. At the other end, Dennis Lillee was fast-medium by comparison. In the first innings, both English openers were caught off the glove; in the second, Tony Greig was bowled by a bullet-like yorker that was quickly and in Australia very popularly christened the 'sandshoe crusher'.

The classic side-on slinging action, which seems such a sensible way to bowl, but which no one has ever matched with anything like the same effectiveness.

Thomson had actually made his Test debut two seasons earlier, but playing with a broken foot he took 0-100 and 0-10 and was quickly discarded. For a while he couldn't even make the New South Wales Sheffield Shield team, until he was recalled for the final match of 1973-74 and promptly wrecked Queensland's hopes of a first Shield title, taking 7-85. Bill O'Reilly, watching in the press box, described him as 'the most lethal bowler in Australian cricket'. In the off-season, Thomson signed to play for Queensland and also gave an infamous interview to Phil Wilkins of Cricketer magazine, in which he said, among other things, that he preferred to hit batsmen rather than get them out. 'It doesn't worry me in the least to see a batsman hurt, rolling around screaming and blood on the pitch,' he explained.

Against England in 1974-75, he took 33 wickets in four and a half Tests before he hurt his shoulder playing tennis during the rest day of the Adelaide Test. The rhyme 'Ashes to Ashes, Dust to Dust. If Lillee don't get you, Thommo must!' became a catch phrase of the summer. He took another 16 wickets in four Tests against England in 1975 (when he also bowled beautifully in the World Cup final, but early on was beset by no-ball problems), then 29 in six Tests at home against the West Indies, when he and Lillee clearly outbowled Andy Roberts and Michael Holding to inspire a 5-1 thrashing of their highly touted opponents. The following

The Ninth XI

year, against Pakistan in Adelaide, Thomson was in the middle of a magnificent spell, making as outstanding a batsman as Zaheer Abbas look awful with both pace and movement off the pitch. Into his ninth over, he already had two wickets when Zaheer wafted at a riser and top-edged it to wide mid-on. Showing amazing agility, the bowler changed direction in his follow through and sprinted after the catch, but sadly his dive for the ball was cruelly interrupted by a clash with Alan Turner, who had run for the catch from mid-wicket. Turner's head smashed into Thomson's collarbone. Not only was he out for the season; rarely would he ever bowl with quite the dynamic skill he provided for the 8.5 overs before the sickening collision.

He did come back to play first-class cricket for another decade, and having taken 80 wickets in 17 Tests before the accident, he took another 120 in 34 afterwards. There was the occasional throwback to the glory days, such as at Bridgetown in 1978, when in a dynamic spell of 6.5 overs he was simply too quick for the West Indies top order. The English journalist Henry Blofeld, who was on the scene, wrote how Viv Richards 'hooked and drove and flailed at Thomson in sheer desperation'. But mostly, Thommo was now that critical split second below lightning quick, and without the innate understanding of the art of fast bowling that made men such as Lillee and Marshall so superb, he was now a good rather than great paceman.

Thomson with the great Lillee in England in 1975, when they were the most intimidating opening pair in world cricket.

Still, for those two fantastic years, he was quicker and more frightening than anyone. Which is why he has made this ninth XI, and other outstanding fast men such as England's Brian Statham, South Africa's Allan Donald, the West Indies' Wes Hall and Courtney Walsh, and Australia's Jack Gregory and Graham McKenzie, have missed out.

JEFF THOMSON (AUSTRALIA)

Test Cricket

Tests	Inn	NO	Runs	HS	Ave	100	50	Ct	Balls	Runs	Wkts	Ave	Best	5/	10/
51	73	20	679	49	12.81	–	–	20	10535	5601	200	28.01	6-46	8	–

First-Class Cricket

Mat	Inn	NO	Runs	HS	Ave	100	50	Ct	Balls	Runs	Wkts	Ave	Best	5/	10/
187	216	64	2065	61	13.59	–	1	61	33318	17864	675	26.47	7-27	28	3

The 100 Greatest Cricketers

No. 95 Andrew Flintoff

Two of the finest all-round performances from Englishmen in Ashes cricket came exactly 100 years apart. One came from a Yorkshireman, the other from a Lancastrian. One was a soldier, politician and, statesman as well as an exceptional cricketer; the other became something of a statesman of his own kind, a man of the people who gave the game a buzz and a profile in England it had not enjoyed since Ian Botham was running the show.

Flintoff in the England one-day colours in 1999, before he evolved into the best allrounder of the early 21st century.

In 1905, England captain FS Jackson, Stanley or 'Jacker' to his friends, later to become 'Colonel the Hon. Sir Stanley Jackson' topped the batting and bowling averages (70.28 with the bat, 15.46 with the ball) while the Ashes were won 2-0. During the series, Jackson scored two centuries, 82 not out and 76, and at a crucial moment in the first Test took three big wickets — Clem Hill, Monty Noble and Joe Darling — in one over. He also won all five tosses. The way Jackson motivated his troops, his tactical acumen which proved especially crucial on the final day of the opening Test when he got his declaration just right, and the way he worked with Archie MacLaren, a great player who could be disruptive if he didn't get his own way, was inspired.

Jackson only played Test cricket at home, five series from 1893 to 1905, and in that time scored five hundreds in 20 Tests. His bowling, though, was less penetrative — only five wickets in his first 11 Tests, 11 in his first 15 — but he did take four wickets in five balls for Yorkshire in 1902, when he and George Hirst bowled out the Australians, of all teams, for 23. 'It was a pity he never toured Australia,' Wilfred Rhodes said after Jackson died in 1947, 'as I think he would have been very successful with his style of play on their fast wickets.'

As good as Jackson was in 1905, as a player he was no more influential to the fate of the Ashes that year than was Andrew Flintoff 100 years later. Flintoff went into the 2005 series as a cricketer on the rise — he had made his Test debut in 1998, but it wasn't until 2003 that he began to make his mark. At the end of 2002, the often injured Flintoff had played 21 Tests and was averaging 19.48 with the bat and 47.15 with the ball. However, from the home series against South Africa in 2003 to the tour of Pakistan at the end of 2005, his batting average was 40.24, his bowling average 27.54. Four of his five Test centuries came during this period. As a batsman, he hit hard and often, with enough faith in his eye and technique to

The Ninth XI

stay aggressive whatever the circumstances. In an article in *The Sportstar* in September 2004, Bob Simpson, who coached Flintoff at Lancashire, identified 'his great power and the correctness of his technique' as his biggest strength as a batsman, before adding, 'While he hits the ball as hard as anyone I have seen, he is very clever in picking up singles and is very quick between the wickets.' Using a front-on bowling action, Flintoff's pace could change from just over medium to not far from express, but perhaps his greatest asset was his ability to get the old ball to swing both ways. And there was his sheer persistence and combative spirit, which suggested that no cause was ever completely lost.

This was amply demonstrated against Ricky Ponting's 2005 Australians. Flintoff's statistics for the series were fine enough: 403 runs at 40.30; 24 wickets at 27.29. But it was the manner in which he 'took it up' to a team that had been totally dominant in Ashes cricket for 16 years that really mattered. In the second Test, at Edgbaston, when England won by two runs to level the series, he scored 68 and 73 and took four wickets in Australia's second innings, including Justin Langer and Ponting from successive balls. In the second innings, he'd come in to a mini-crisis at 5-72, after England had won a first-innings lead of 99. Soon it was 6-75, then 9-131, but Flintoff and Simon Jones (who made 12) added 51 for the last wicket. No other England batsman scored more than 21. As his sixes off the legendary Warne sailed into the crowd, the excitement was everywhere. Cricket pushed football off the back pages, while the image of Flintoff, the hero, commiserating with Australian batsman Brett Lee after the last wicket fell captured the hard-but-fair spirit in which the series was played.

Flintoff takes to Shane Warne at Trent Bridge during the 2005 Ashes series.

A crucial battle was the one between Flintoff and Adam Gilchrist. It seemed as if every time Gilchrist came out to bat, Flintoff went around the wicket and attacked him relentlessly just outside the off-stump. He only dismissed the great keeper/batsman three times in the series, but the way Gilchrist appeared nonplussed by the method of attack took away one of Australia's most lethal weapons. In the fourth Test at Trent

Flintoff in India in early 2006, by now the England captain in the absence of the injured Michael Vaughan.

299

The 100 Greatest Cricketers

Bridge, Flintoff — now known across the country by his nickname 'Freddie' — hit 102 from 132 deliveries as England took control of the Australian bowling in a manner their fans hadn't enjoyed for 20 years. Finally, at The Oval, Flintoff made 72 on the opening day, with Andrew Strauss restoring England's first innings after it had slumped to 4-131. Then he took his first five-for of the series as the match progressed towards the draw that saw the Ashes finally change hands.

Flintoff gave England a certain swagger that stated unequivocally that they would not be intimidated by more celebrated opponents. Even though he finished his test career in some style in the 2009 Ashes series, if, during the three years from 2006 to 2009, another allrounder had stepped forward, Andrew Flintoff would have been dropped from this top 100. But no such cricketer has emerged, He led England in Australia in 2006-07, when the home team regained the Ashes in spectacularly emphatic fashion, and though he always tried hard and was clearly his team's best bowler, he was eventually overwhelmed by Ricky Ponting's vibrant team. It is true that when fit (which has not been often) Flintoff has bowled extremely well during this time, though usually with little luck, but he has also been involved in some off-field incidents that have tarnished his reputation. Still, he is one of only six men in Test history to score more than 3500 runs and take more than 200 wickets and 50 catches (the others being Jacques Kallis, Garry Sobers, Kapil Dev, Ian Botham and Shaun Pollock), and the big money the IPL's Chennai Super Kings paid for his services in early 2009 reflected the regard with which he is still held. However, an ankle injury quickly forced him out of the tournament, so he had no chance to justify the Super Kings' gamble. Before the Ashes Test at Lord's, he announced he would retire from Test cricket at the end of the series, and then he promptly bowled England to victory. It was a reminder of his glory days — why he deserves to be ranked as one of the game's most dynamic all-rounders.

Flintoff commiserates with Australia's Brett Lee after England won the second Test of the 2005 Ashes series in a thrilling finish by just two runs.

ANDREW FLINTOFF (ENGLAND)

Test Cricket

Tests	Inn	NO	Runs	HS	Ave	100	50	Ct	Balls	Runs	Wkts	Ave	Best	5/	10/
75	123	8	3645	167	31.69	5	25	51	14178	6993	218	32.07	5-58	2	—

One-Day International Cricket

ODIs	Inn	NO	Runs	HS	Ave	100	50	Ct	Balls	Runs	Wkts	Ave	Best	4/
141	122	16	3394	123	32.01	3	18	47	5624	4121	169	24.38	5-19	8

The Ninth XI

Graeme Smith No. 96

In the original edition of this book, one of the openers in our ninth XI was a South African. Herbie Taylor, undoubtedly his country's finest batsman of the early years of the 20th century, owed his selection primarily to his superb batting against the great Sydney Barnes in the series in South Africa in 1913–14 when Barnes took 49 wickets at 10.94. Of Taylor's batting during those Tests, the great cricket historian HS Altham wrote: 'The English cricketers were unanimous in saying that finer batting than his against Barnes at his best they never hoped to see. Based on superbly correct principles, his batting was above all remarkable for superb footwork, and he possessed that gift, common to only the greatest players, of being found in perfect position and balanced for his stroke well before the ball had reached him.'

For all the virtues of players that followed — such as Bruce Mitchell, 'Jackie' McGlew, Trevor Goddard and Eddie Barlow — Taylor remained the finest of all South African openers, at least until the emergence in 2002 of a left-handed batsman who quickly established a reputation for making big scores in a style that set him apart from those who had preceded him.

Graeme Smith at the World Twenty20 in England in 2009, only 28 years old but entrenched as South Africa's leader after six years in the job.

Graeme Smith made his Test debut in 2002, as a No. 3 batsman in a home series against the all-conquering Australians. He scored an impressive second-innings 68, but following the series earned the ire of some in Steve Waugh's team when he claimed he was sledged during that and subsequent innings. While the Aussies might have been disappointed by Smith's remarks (which he now regrets making), they also knew that South Africa had found themselves a highly competitive cricketer, and in the months that followed, as they observed Smith's prodigious run-scoring, they also realised he was a special batsman. For all the quality of Jacques Kallis, Smith became the key South African wicket. By 2009, upon the retirement of Matthew Hayden, he was clearly the best left-handed opener in the game.

Ironically, it took seven long years for Smith to finally win the total respect of the Australian cricket community. No one doubted his talent — that had been obvious from his first 18 months in Test cricket, when he compiled four big hundreds (200 against Bangladesh; 177 versus Pakistan; successive double centuries in England) — but until Smith could spearhead his team to victory over the No. 1 team in the world he was always seen as somewhat flawed, a terrific run-getter but not always a winner. That success finally came in 2008-09, when South Africa prevailed in dramatic circumstances in the first two Tests of a three-match series in Australia. Ironically, Smith broke a finger in his next Test innings, in Sydney, but won further kudos from his former critics by gallantly coming out to bat on the final day, despite his injury, to try to prevent a face-saving Aussie victory.

The 100 Greatest Cricketers

A little less than three years earlier, in South Africa during a southern hemisphere summer in which Australia won five Tests out of six, Smith had conceded that — at that time at least — playing six months' cricket against Australia was 'just too hard'. Ponting, in his *Captain's Diary 2006*, wrote that 'I learnt a lot from our Ashes defeat (in 2005), and came out of the experience a better captain. Maybe the same will happen to Graeme Smith after his battles with my Australian team.' Few could doubt that eventually this is what occurred, though it wasn't until the start of 2008 that Smith's Test batting average started climbing again — not least because of two more superb hundreds in England, the second of which, an unbeaten fourth-innings 154 at Edgbaston, won a match many thought lost.

The South African captain has been a prolific run-scorer in all forms of the modern game.

Smith had become South Africa's captain as long ago as March 2003, after South Africa failed to make it through the first stage of the World Cup. He was just 22, a 'veteran' of only eight Tests, his country's youngest ever leader. His feat in being awarded the captaincy of his country at such a young age and then retaining the job with a fair degree of success for six or more years — 33 wins in 69 Tests and 69 wins in 118 ODIs to June 1, 2009 — is unprecedented in cricket history.

Immediately upon gaining the leadership, Smith had English writers comparing his appetite for runs to that of Brian Lara and Sachin Tendulkar. In scoring 277, 85 and 259 in successive innings, he almost set a new record for most runs in three straight Test innings (behind only Don Bradman's 304, 244 and 77 against England in 1934 and Wally Hammond's 75, 227 and 336 in New Zealand in 1932-33). That 277 remains the highest Test score by a South African. Only Bradman had previously hit two

The Ninth XI

scores above 250 in successive Tests and the 259 broke by five runs The Don's record for the highest Test score by an 'overseas' batsman at Lord's. Smith's Test batting average after that knock was more than 78, and though in the years since it has declined to around 50, it remains an impressive statistic, not least because of the burdens of leadership he has carried so stoically. Of all the regular openers to have played more than 25 Tests, only four — Herbert Sutcliffe, Jack Hobbs, Len Hutton and Matthew Hayden — have a higher career Test average.

Like Hayden, Smith has managed to mimic his Test success in the 50-over game and more recently in Twenty20 cricket, though unlike the Australian he has not been able to turn those runs into major tournament victories. The highlight, inevitably, came in the encounter South Africans like to think of as the greatest ODI ever played, at Johannesburg in 2006, when Australia made 4-434 from their 50 overs, only to lose by one wicket with a ball to spare. Smith made 90 that day from 55 balls, a performance more than fit to compare with any of his seven one-day hundreds. Throughout his career he has been one of those batsmen who, when on song, can look impregnable, skilled at following up a bludgeoning drive with a deft, equally productive deflection. Again like Hayden, Smith's Test game plan often seems similar to his one-day approach; with other bold hitters such as India's Virender Sehwag, Sri Lanka's Sanath Jayasuriya and the West Indies' Chris Gayle, they have revolutionised the way Test-match openers go about their business.

Back in 2006, it was noted that the competition for the final opening batsman's spot in this top 100 was very tight. Chief among those considered were the two men who opened for most of the Windies' great days of the late 1970s and '80s, Gordon Greenidge and Desmond Haynes. However, the fact that both these players averaged less than 45 in Test cricket, even though they never had to face the bevy of fast bowlers who made West Indian cricket so strong from 1976 to 1991, counts against them.

In this study's view, there is nothing in the records of Greenidge or Haynes, or other famous openers such as Arthur Morris, Sid Barnes, Tom Hayward, Hanif Mohammad or Sanath Jayasuriya, to match the success Herbie Taylor enjoyed over a series against a bowler as great as Sydney Barnes at his most dangerous. And for all Taylor's success, spread over 42 Tests and 20 years, Graeme Smith's batting and leadership achievements to date are such that he deserves to be rated just ahead of him. As this edition goes to the printers, Smith is 28, almost 10 years younger than Hayden; in a decade's time, he could well be ranked even higher than the great Australian left-hander. As his team strives to become the No. 1 Test nation, achieving such a ranking is just one of the challenges the South African captain will face in the seasons to come.

GRAEME SMITH (SOUTH AFRICA)
Test Cricket

Tests	Inn	NO	Runs	HS	Ave	100	50	Ct	Balls	Runs	Wkts	Ave	Best	5/	10/
77	135	9	6342	277	50.33	18	25	104	1319	801	8	100.13	2-145	–	–

One-day International Cricket

Mat	Inn	NO	Runs	HS	Ave	100	50	Ct	Balls	Runs	Wkts	Ave	Best	5/	10/
141	139	9	5251	134*	40.39	7	38	72	1026	951	18	52.83	3-30	–	–

No. 97 Andy Flower

The choice of the final wicketkeeper in this top 100 was extremely difficult. It comes down, essentially, to deciding between one of a number of accomplished glovemen — such as England's Harold Strudwick, Bob Taylor or 'Jack' Russell, or Australia's Hanson Carter, Bert Oldfield, Wally Grout or Rod Marsh, or South Africa's world-record holder Mark Boucher — or a wicketkeeper/batsman such as India's Farokh Engineer, South Africa's Denis Lindsay, the West Indies' Jeffrey Dujon, Zimbabwe's Andy Flower, Sri Lanka's Kumar Sangakkara or India's super competitive and highly effective MS Dhoni. In the end, on the basis that of the eight keepers already nominated six were selected primarily for their wicketkeeping — even though in modern times the work of a keeper who doubles as a batting allrounder has been amply demonstrated — the choice was made to go with the man who has averaged the most in Test cricket with the bat while also donning the gloves.

The two best keeper-batsmen in modern Test history — Flower and Australia's Adam Gilchrist — playing in Australia in 2000-01.

That man is Andy Flower, who in 55 Test matches between 1992 and 2002 averaged 53.71 with the bat while also keeping, with 12 centuries. Strangely, in the eight Tests he did not start as keeper (one in 1993, three in 1994, and his final four matches) he averaged only 35.45. Of course, Flower's runs did not win matches in the way that Adam Gilchrist's quickfire scoring helped Australia on many occasions, but that is not a knock on Flower, rather a reflection of Zimbabwe's low ranking as a Test nation. As well as being the keeper and 20 times the captain, Flower was often his country's only batsman of genuine Test quality. In late 2000 and for most of 2001, he might have been the best batsman in the world. Yet he was always fighting from behind. Zimbabwe won only seven Tests and 54 ODIs during his career. Only three other Zimbabwean cricketers have averaged more than 40 in Test cricket, and one of those played in only four Tests. Only two players besides Flower — David Houghton (43.06 in 22 Tests) and Murray Goodwin (42.85 in 19 Tests) — have played in more than five Tests for Zimbabwe and averaged more than 30.

In Test cricket, Flower preferred to bat at five or six; in ODIs, he opened early in his career before moving into the middle order. His career average (35.34) and strike rate (74.60) in the shorter form of the game are more than acceptable, given again that Zimbabwe were usually on the back foot, but it was in Test matches that he made his reputation as a cricketer. It was, though, at the start of a limited-over tournament, the 2003 World Cup, that he made his bravest move — when he and his comrade Henry Olonga mounted a highly publicised protest against the way their country was being governed. 'We cannot in good conscience take to the field and ignore the fact that millions of our compatriots are starving, unemployed and oppressed,' a statement from the pair read in part. 'We have decided that we will

The Ninth XI

each wear a black armband for the duration of the World Cup. In doing so we are mourning the death of democracy in our beloved Zimbabwe. In doing so we are making a silent plea to those responsible to stop the abuse of human rights in Zimbabwe. In doing so we pray that our small action may help to restore sanity and dignity to our Nation.' Flower never played international cricket again, but his place in the game's history was guaranteed.

In his youth, Flower often opened the batting, so it was no surprise that he could handle himself against the best pace bowlers of his era. He had to work to become an accomplished player of spin, but did so to the point that Steve Waugh described him as the best exponent of the reverse sweep he had seen. In Zimbabwe's first eight years in international cricket, from the time he hit a 115 on his one-day debut during the 1992 World Cup, Flower built an incredible record of durability, playing in all of Zimbabwe's first 52 Tests and 172 ODIs until he damaged ligaments and dislocated a thumb in a Test against India in 2001. He had twice been captain, resigning in 1996 and being controversially sacked following a pay dispute in 2000. In Zimbabwe's maiden Test victory, against Pakistan at Harare in 1994-95, he'd scored 156 and shared a stand of 269 with his brother Grant, the highest between

Flower batting against Sri Lanka during the 2003 World Cup, when he and teammate Henry Olonga mounted a gallant protest against human-rights violations in their country.

brothers in Tests.

The great irony of Flower's career is that his batting blossomed as his team sank. At home against Sri Lanka in November 1999, he scored 74 and 129 but Zimbabwe lost by six wickets. At Port-of-Spain four months later, he hit 113 in the first innings, the only score of more than 50 in the match, but Zimbabwe was bowled on the last day for 63 when 99 were needed. In a run of 11 Tests from

The 100 Greatest Cricketers

November 2000 to November 2001, Flower scored 1466 runs at 133.27, with five centuries and seven fifties in 17 innings. He started by making 183 not out and 70 against India at Delhi, a new record for the most runs scored by a keeper in a Test, and then did even better in the second Test, at Nagpur, when he scored 55 and 232 not out (the highest individual Test innings by a keeper). He equalled Everton Weekes' record of seven consecutive fifties in Tests, the sequence ending with a run out. Against South Africa in Harare, he scored 142 and 199 not out, more than half Zimbabwe's runs, yet the Test was lost by nine wickets. No other keeper has scored a century in each innings of a Test. Adding to the achievement, South Africa's first innings score of 3-600 (declared) did not include a single bye. He finished the sequence by scoring 114 not out against Bangladesh, the first 'easy' Test century of his life. It was the second (and last) time an Andy Flower century came during a Zimbabwean victory.

Flower during his hundred in the inaugural Zimbabwe-England Test match, played at Bulawayo in December 1996.

In his final 12 months as a Test cricketer, Flower's career average dropped from 56.61 to its final 51.55, with just two fifties coming in his final 14 innings. It seemed the dual responsibilities of wicketkeeping and carrying the Zimbabwean batting order like George Headley carried the West Indies in the 1930s had finally taken its toll. While he was never a pure gloveman in the manner of an Alan Knott or a Syed Kirmani, Flower was an outstanding allrounder, scoring all those runs and managing to complete more than 150 dismissals in both Tests and ODIs despite seeing fewer edges than keepers from more successful nations. None of the great allrounders — not Sobers with his bowling (a Test average of 34.04); Botham (33.55), Kapil Dev (31.05) or Miller (36.98) with their batting — were phenomenal in every form of the game. And playing for a losing side all the time can't have always been invigorating. Had Zimbabwe been a more competitive outfit during his career, who knows what Andy Flower might have achieved?

ANDY FLOWER (ZIMBABWE)

Test Cricket

Tests	Inn	NO	Runs	HS	Ave	100	50	Ct	St	Balls	Runs	Wkts	Ave	Best	5/	10/
63	112	19	4794	232*	51.55	12	27	151	9	3	4	–	–	0-4	–	–

One-Day International Cricket

ODIs	Inn	NO	Runs	HS	Ave	100	50	Ct	St	Balls	Runs	Wkts	Ave	Best	4/
213	208	16	6786	145	35.34	4	55	141	32	30	23	–	–	0-9	–

The Ninth XI

Kumar Sangakkara — No. 98

The final batsman? Selectors choosing touring teams have faced this dilemma for as long as international cricket has been played. Do we go for youth or experience? Flair or stability? In the first edition of *The 100 Greatest Cricketers*, the choice for the last middle-order batting position came down to a choice between two Pakistanis — Zaheer Abbas and Inzamam-ul-Haq — with Inzamam narrowly prevailing. Since 2006, there have been a number of batsmen who have staked a claim for this position, among them a third Pakistani, Mohammad Yousuf. An irony is that the man who we have finally chosen to take Inzamam's spot could easily have made the ninth XI in 2006, but as the wicketkeeper.

A problem in assessing the finest 21st century batsmen is that the great measuring stick — a Test batting average greater than 50 — has become less precious in recent years. As at June 1, 2009, there were 38 men in Test history who had played at least 30 innings and had a career average of more than 50. No less than 18 of this group appeared in Test matches in the 21st century. Only six of the 38 played in the 1980s (Greg Chappell, Javed Miandad, Sunil Gavaskar, Steve Waugh, Allan Border and Viv Richards). Only three played in the 1960s (Graeme Pollock, Ken Barrington and Garry Sobers).

Through 2008 and the first half of 2009, Kumar Sangakkara was consistently ranked among the top two or three batsmen in Test cricket.

Among the 18 players from the 21st century are some who have already been featured in this book: Ricky Ponting, Jacques Kallis, Sachin Tendulkar, Brian Lara, Rahul Dravid, Andy Flower, Steve Waugh, Matthew Hayden, Graeme Smith and Virender Sehwag. The rest include some notable, and a couple of not quite so notable names: Pakistan's Mohammed Yousuf and Younis Khan; Australia's Michael Hussey; Sri Lanka's Kumar Sangakkara, Mahela Jayawardene and Thilan Samaraweera; India's Gautam Gambhir; England's Kevin Pietersen. A few of these players will probably see their career averages drop below the 50 benchmark before their time is done; some have undoubtedly benefitted from playing Tests against the weaker nations. Significantly, of the 14 non-Australians in this group of 18 only five — Tendulkar, Gambhir (in four Tests), Lara, Pietersen and Sehwag — have averaged more than 50 against the No. 1 side on the planet.

Mohammad Yousuf made his reputation in 2006, when he scored a remarkable 1788 runs in 11 Tests against India, Sri Lanka, England and the West Indies, averaging 99.33 and making nine centuries, including six in a run of five consecutive Tests. Take that year out, though, and his Test batting averages drops to 48. Against Australia, he averages less than 30, with just one hundred in 15 innings. A case can be made out that he is the equal of Zaheer, who in 1982 became the 20th batsman and third non-Englishman, after Don Bradman and New Zealand's Glenn Turner, to score 100 first-class centuries. However, it is this study's contention that he is still behind Inzamam,

307

The 100 Greatest Cricketers

a batsman who developed an amazing propensity to score runs during Pakistani victories, as if the two went together. Inzamam averaged more than 78 with the bat when Pakistan won, less than 30 when they lost. Seventeen of his 25 Test centuries helped his team to victory. Mohammad Yousuf, in contrast, has scored nearly as many centuries (seven) in Pakistani losses as he has (eight) in wins.

So the principal challengers for Inzamam's spot are two of the most gifted stroke-makers in the modern game: Kevin Pietersen and Kumar Sangakkara. Since he made his Test debut at the start of the 2005 Ashes series, the South African-born Pietersen has shown himself to be one of the most devastating hitters in the game's history. His effort against the Australians at the Oval in 2005, when he hit seven sixes on his way to 158, putting his adopted team into a series-winning position, was inspirational. He is a batsman incapable of playing a boring innings, and has shown in limited-over cricket that he has a skill for innovation few can match. Not content with just a reverse sweep, in 2008 he 'reverse slogged' (by taking guard as a right-hander but then switching to left) New Zealand's Scott Styris for two sixes, one forward of square and the other to wide long-on. However, as brilliant as Pietersen undoubtedly is, on the eve of the 2009 Ashes series he did not have as deep a resume as did the left-handed Sangakkara, who has moved past men such as Aravinda de Silva and Sanath Jayasuriya to be recognised, behind Muttiah Muralitharan, as Sri Lanka's second greatest ever player.

Though Sangakkara (seen here wicketkeeping against Pakistan's Younis Khan) is picked in this Top 100 for his run-scoring, he also ranks behind only Adam Gilchrist and Andy Flower among keeper-batsmen of the past 20 years.

As was noted in the chapter on Andy Flower, Sangakkara could have been selected as the keeper/batsman for this ninth XI. Of those men to keep regularly in Test matches during the past 20 years, Flower, Sangakkara and Adam Gilchrist are clearly the finest batsmen. The Sri Lankan's Test batting average at June 1, 2009 is 54.99, achieved in 80 matches dating back to July 2000. In 48 of those games he has been his team's designated keeper, and in those encounters his average has been 'only' 40.48, but what this means is that he has built an average of nearly 80 in Tests where he does not keep wicket. In the two Tests he has played against Australia as a non-keeper he has scored 389 runs at 97.25, with one century and three fifties. (In ODIs, where he has continued to wear the keeper's gloves, Sangakkara's averages are similar: 36.31 in 246 ODIs during his career; 38.32 in 204 games as the keeper.)

Sangakkara has hardly kept wicket in Tests since Sri Lanka's series in England in 2006 (in just two Tests out of 20), making it hard to justify now selecting him ahead of Flower as the ninth XI's keeper/batsman. However, since the decision was made that he would offer greatest value to the Sri Lankan Test team playing purely as a batsman his output has been remarkable: 2308 runs at 82.43, with nine centuries. In a run of nine Tests in 2006 and 2007 he produced scores of 287, 14 and 39, 4 and 100 not out, 156 not out and 8, 6, 200 not out, 222 not out, 57 and

The Ninth XI

192, 92 and 152. The 287 versus South Africa at Colombo was made as part of a world-record partnership of 624 with his captain Jayawardene (who scored 374), made after they came together at 2 for 14. After the 192, a spectacular innings made against Australia in Hobart that was ended by an appalling umpiring decision, Ricky Ponting said he'd never seen a better display by a batsman who was running out of partners. One delivery from the left-arm quick Mitchell Johnson was sent sailing over cover for six.

Two weeks later, he was back home, playing the first Test against England at Kandy, and in the second innings he went past 150 for the fifth time in six Tests. In doing so, he became the ninth batsman to score centuries against the other nine Test teams, after Gary Kirsten, Steve Waugh, Sachin Tendulkar, Rahul Dravid, Marvan Atapattu, Brian Lara, Adam Gilchrist and Ricky Ponting.

'Sangakkara's innings was littered with sumptuous drives, cuts and effortless clips off his legs,' wrote the former Test seamer Angus Fraser in his match report. 'But it was the 30-year-old's driving off Monty Panesar that stood out. To strike a spinning ball that lands in footholes that sweetly takes an enormous amount of skill.'

Two Tests later, Sangakkara became the fourth Sri Lankan to score 6000 Test runs, after de Silva, Jayasuriya and Jayawardene. It had taken him 116 innings, same as Len Hutton and Ken Barrington. Only Don Bradman, Garry Sobers and Wally Hammond have reached this landmark faster. Sunil Gavaskar, next fastest among batsmen from the subcontinent, took 117 innings.

Youth or experience? Sangakkara is just past 30 years of age, into his 10th year as an international cricketer but in all likelihood with plenty of top cricket left in him. Flair or stability? His performances since 2006 show a wonderful consistency, and he has done so in a manner that was often Lara-like, beautifully balanced, graceful and brilliant. He has the style to go with the statistics. And he is a cricketer of character, too, capable of digging in when needed. In the final of a Tri-Series tournament in Bangladesh in January 2009, he made a match-winning 59 from 133 balls against the home team after Sri Lanka collapsed to be 5-6 in the eighth over. In 2009, he was delivering a gallant unbeaten 64 from 52 balls while wickets fell around him against Pakistan in the ICC World Twenty20 final at Lord's, demonstrating how his game sits comfortably in the most frenetic form of the sport. Kumar Sangakkara has shown many times, especially in the past three years, that he deserves to be included in this top 100; how high he might rank two or three years from now, only time will tell.

KUMAR SANGAKKARA (SRI LANKA)

Test Cricket

Tests	Inn	NO	Runs	HS	Ave	100	50	Ct	St	Balls	Runs	Wkts	Ave	Best	5/	10/
81	134	9	6787	287	54.30	18	30	153	20	66	38	0	–	–	–	–

One-Day International Cricket

ODIs	Inn	NO	Runs	HS	Ave	100	50	Ct	St	Balls	Runs	Wkts	Ave	Best	5/	10/
246	229	25	7408	138*	36.31	10	48	227	64	–	–	–	–	–	–	–

No. 99 Arthur Mailey

From almost the day Arthur Mailey retired from big-time cricket, he set about maligning his own ability. His favourite stories all seemed to be about how he wasn't much good. There were the couple of days in 1926-27 when Victoria scored 1107 in a Shield match against NSW, and Mailey finished with the very unflattering figures of 4-362. At one stage, NSW captain Alan Kippax sarcastically asked his main bowler if he was ever going to get anyone out, to which Mailey replied, 'If that chap in the brown derby at the back of the grandstand had held his chances, I'd have had them out days ago.' He delighted in telling the yarn of how he tried to start a conversation at a function in England by saying, 'I'm a little stiff from bowling.' To which a woman replied, 'I was wondering where you came from.' Later, Mailey became a journalist, and then a butcher, which he explained this way: 'I bowled tripe, wrote tripe ... now I sell tripe.'

Australia's No. 1 spin bowler of the 1920s.

If you talk yourself down often enough you'll eventually get there. In contrast, backers of Clarrie Grimmett — Bill O'Reilly and Don Bradman prominent among them — have always sung their man's praises. Neither O'Reilly nor Bradman played first-class cricket with Mailey. Such has been the support for Grimmett, there would be very few judges today who would even think of him and Mailey as being in the same class. However, a close examination of the two leg-spinners' Test records suggest in fact there was at least very little between them. It could even be that Mailey was superior.

Had it not been for World War I, Mailey would have made his Test debut earlier than the 1920-21 Tests against England, when he was 34 years old. He marked his first series with 36 wickets, an Australian record for an Ashes series that stood for nearly 60 years, even though he didn't bowl a single over in the second Test (when he carried an injury into the game and shouldn't have played). His strike rate in that series was a wicket every 40.69 balls. In the England tour that followed straight after, Mailey played in three of the five Tests, but as these were just three-day games there were few chances for him (he finished with 12 wickets at 33.17). After that, he never missed a Test until his retirement after Australia lost the Ashes in 1926, explaining to Neville Cardus, 'If I ever bowl a maiden over, it's not my fault but the batsman's.'

The Ninth XI

Mailey finished with 99 wickets from 21 Tests, all but three of them against England, a record that at first glance is dwarfed by Grimmett's 216 wickets in 37 Tests. However, a closer study reveals that, at least when it comes to comparative strike rates, Mailey's record is not too bad. Grimmett bowled a lot of deliveries in Test cricket — 14,513 in to Mailey's 6119 — and 110 of his wickets came against the West Indies and South Africa. Grimmett bowled 736 maiden overs in Tests to Mailey's 115.

The 1921 Australians. Mailey is far right in the back row. Charlie Macartney is second from left in the middle row.

Grimmett took 11 wickets in his debut Test, the fifth against England in 1924-25 (when he was a surprise selection at age 33), coming on third change. After that, he bowled in five Ashes series, and was dropped from the side during two of them — in 1926 and 1932-33. During the bodyline summer, he took five wickets in the first three Tests, at 65.20. In 21 Ashes Tests between 1926 and 1934, Grimmett took 95 wickets from 1496.1 overs: a wicket every 94.49 deliveries. In two Ashes series in Australia (1928-29 and 1932-33) he took 28 wickets from 545.2 overs, a wicket every 116.85 balls (that's one every 19-and-a-half overs!). His best Ashes series was in England in 1930, when Bradman made so many runs so quickly that Grimmett could take his time spinning people out. Grimmett's best performance in that series was at Lord's, when he took 6-167 from 53 overs in England's second innings. In the deciding fifth Test at The Oval, a match with no time limit, he took 5-225 for the match from 109.2 six-ball overs. This is good bowling, especially on what were clearly batsmen-friendly wickets, but it is hardly the stuff of legend.

Leaving Grimmett out to fit Mailey in this top 100 is extremely difficult. But the fact Mailey took an English wicket every 60.48 deliveries, a better strike rate than not just Grimmett but also Jack Gregory and Ted McDonald, the outstanding Australian fast men of the 1920s, is a compelling argument in his favour. Mailey's strike rate is also better than a number of other exceptional spinners from different eras, such as South Africa's Hugh Tayfield (79.81), India's Subash Gupte (75.73), England's Derek Underwood (73.61), Pakistan's Abdul Qadir (72.57) and India's Anil Kumble (65.48). Of course, strike rates on their own are not conclusive proof of one bowler's value compared to another, but clearly Mailey was very good at spinning batsmen out.

He had seen England's Bernard Bosanquet bowl his new discovery, the bosie, googly or wrong 'un (depending on what you want to call it) — the one that looked like a leg break but spun the other way — at the Sydney Cricket Ground in 1903–04. Later, he told RS Whitington of how he used to practise his leg-breaks by bowling at a toilet-block wall in the Sydney Domain, and how a homeless man came up to him and volunteered to show him how to master the new delivery. Thus was developed the skill that would go on to dismiss Hobbs and Frank Woolley nine times in Tests, Herbert Sutcliffe eight times. In his biography of O'Reilly, *Time of the Tiger*, Whitington quoted the Victorian fast bowler Ernie McCormick as saying that 'no slow bowler I have seen got more weight into his delivery than Arthur'. McCormick played Tests with Grimmett and O'Reilly in South Africa in 1935-36. He thought only 'Chuck' Fleetwood-Smith spun the ball more than Mailey.

'Grimmett and I were not, as most people thought, identical,' Mailey explained in Whitington's book. 'It is true that we both bowled leg breaks and googlies. But there the similarity ended. My best leg break was a top spinner while Grimmett's spun half laterally and half horizontally. Clarrie's round-arm delivery was mainly responsible for the amount of sidespin he put on the ball and it was also the secret of his immaculate length ... While the side-spinning leg-break has the virtue of a good length, it also lacks the confusing trajectory of the top-spinner.'

In 1935, Jack Hobbs released his autobiography and in it he recalled how in the first decade of the 20th century the South African wrist-spinners, notably Reggie Schwarz, Ernie Vogler and Aubrey Faulkner, took Bosanquet's new delivery to a higher level. 'Faulkner will go down to history as South Africa's greatest allrounder,' Hobbs wrote. 'He was a really splendid googly bowler, keeping an immaculate length, much faster than Grimmett, and perhaps the best of the googly bowlers ...'

And then the legendary batsman added, 'With the exception of Arthur Mailey.'

ARTHUR MAILEY (AUSTRALIA)

Test Cricket

Tests	Inn	NO	Runs	HS	Ave	100	50	Ct	Balls	Runs	Wkts	Ave	Best	5/	10/
21	29	9	222	46*	11.10	–	–	14	6119	3358	99	33.92	9-121	6	2

First-Class Cricket

Mat	Inn	NO	Runs	HS	Ave	100	50	Ct	Balls	Runs	Wkts	Ave	Best	5/	10/
158	186	62	1530	66	12.34	–	3	157	36285	18772	779	24.10	10-66	61	16

The Hundreth Man

Doug Walters — No. 100

Doug Walters was my favourite player when I was a kid. I was hardly alone in this; for all the appeal of men such as Ian Chappell, Rod Marsh, Lillee and Thommo and Greg Chappell, for just about every young cricket fan in New South Wales, and many others across Australia during the 1970s, Dougie was No. 1. Since his retirement, there has been some extraordinary outpourings of support for players at different times, most notably for Steve Waugh when it seemed he was about to be sacked and then in his farewell Test match. But for all Waugh's greatness as a cricketer and good qualities as a person, and the way he gelled with his fan base by being no more than himself, his support was different — in part media driven, some of it almost trendy. A little ironically, Waugh was a keen Walters fan in his youth. But like the rest of us, he didn't revere Dougie because he had a Bradman-like career record or a Miller-like aura, but simply because of the way he played our game.

Walters in 1965-66, his first season of Test cricket, when he became the third Australian teenager after Archie Jackson and Neil Harvey to score a hundred on his Test debut.

Dougie won over all generations for different reasons, the one constant being that his cricket was thrilling and thus appealed to everyone. When it came to making runs there were lean times, so he demanded loyalty, but always, eventually, he paid you back with interest. There was that same sense of anticipation when he came out to bat that Viv Richards had and that Tendulkar, Ponting and Sehwag have. To the wise sages in the Members Stand who wanted 'another Bradman' but knew that no one could ever be that good, he was skilled enough to keep their attention and he seemed to respect the game in the way the old champions did. While the rowdy lot on the Sydney Hill were chanting his name and erecting huge banners proclaiming their territory as 'The Doug Walters Stand', Dougie would do nothing to encourage them, and only acknowledge them with a brief raising of the bat when he reached his 50 or his 100. Back in the '70s, that was what cricket fans preferred, more so than pretentious celebrations. Adults saw him as 'one of us', an uncomplicated bloke who liked a drink, a smoke and good times with his mates. To kids ... well, he was just our champion, a man who had a happy knack of coming through for us when we needed him to. When my Dad would gently rib me after a low score or a seemingly soft dismissal, I could take comfort in the fact that next time would be different. It always was. And anyway, I'd read enough cricket books to know that if a bloke was averaging 50 in Test cricket, he must be all right.

The first two cricket publications I owned had Dougie on the cover: the 1968 *ABC Cricket Book* and Jack Pollard's 1968 edition of *Cricket: the Australian Way*. Almost straightaway, he smashed the West Indies for 699 runs in six innings in the 1968-69 series in Australia, becoming in Sydney the first man to score a double century and a century (242 and 103) in the same Test, so he was my cricket hero. I discovered how he had scored centuries in his first two Tests, but then had to miss two years of big-time cricket because of national service (whatever that was), before having a disappointing tour of England in 1968. His Test batting average when he set off for India in October 1969 was 74.17, which according to the stats section of that now battered *ABC Cricket Book* was very good indeed.

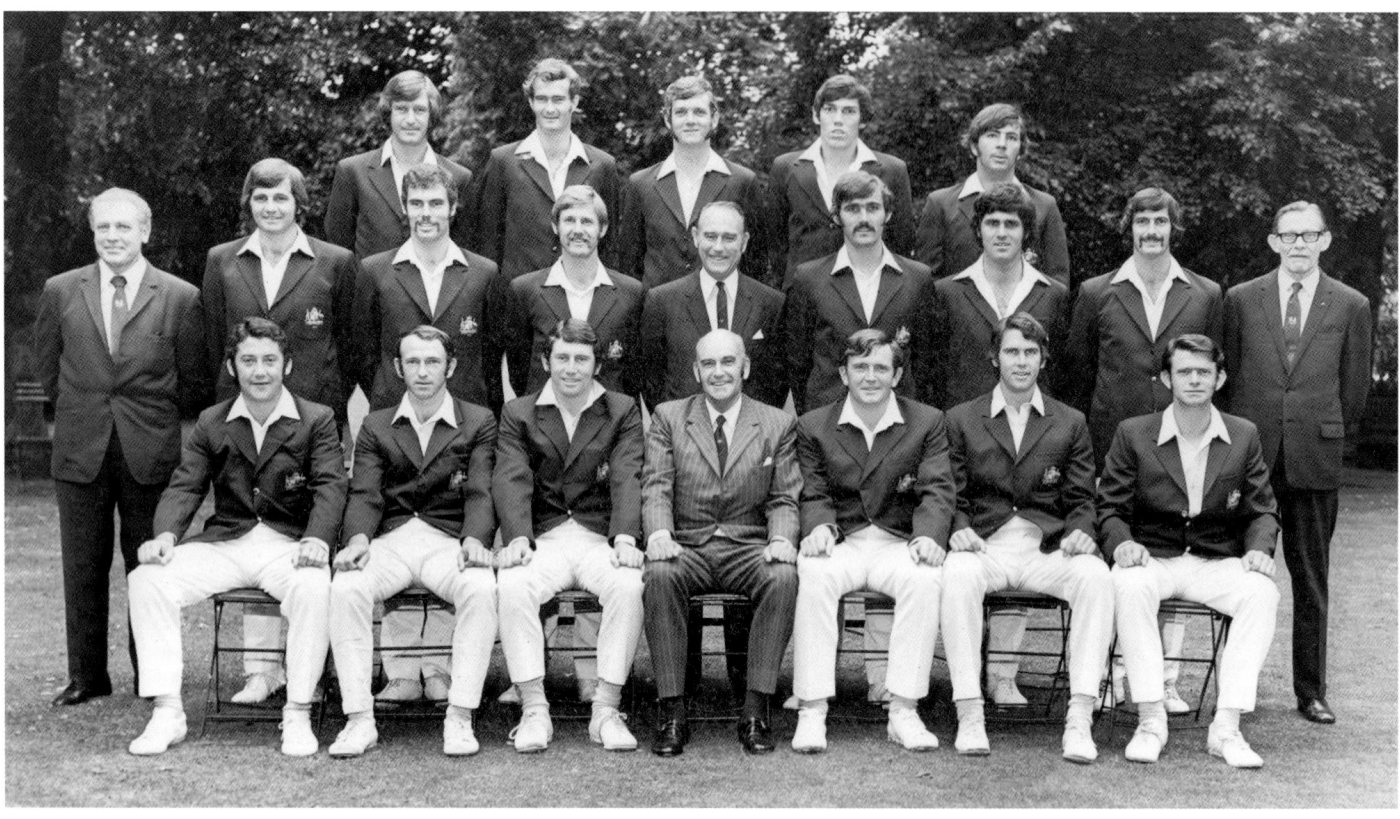

Ian Chappell's 1972 Australian team, which surprised by squaring that year's Ashes series. Walters is second from left in the front row, with Greg Chappell behind him and Dennis Lillee second from right in the middle row.

By the end of his career, that average had dropped to 48.26. Of all Australian batsmen who played in even one Test in the 1960s, only Neil Harvey (48.41) has a superior career average. Of cricketers from all countries to score 1000 Test runs against the West Indies, only Pakistan's Mohammad Yousuf has a better batting average (1214 runs against the Windies at 101.17, compared to the Australian's 1196 runs at 92.00, with six centuries). Dougie's 250 against New Zealand at Christchurch in 1977, made after Australia had slumped to 6-208, is the highest score ever made in Tests by a No. 6 batsman. Yet he was not about statistics so much as the games he won off his own bat, or the exhilarating moments such as when he hit Bob Willis for six from the final ball of the day in Perth in 1974-75, to reach not just his hundred but also make a hundred in a session. That gambler's instinct to go for it when everyone else would have played for time was another cog in the Walters legend; there was a bit of Dougie in that cover drive by Steve Waugh at the SCG in 2002-03, when the Australian captain reached one of the most important hundreds of his life with a last-ball-of-the-day four. The great players influence not just their own generation.

He could take important wickets, field brilliantly and play the spinners as well as just about anyone. Ian Chappell maintains that his mate's best Test hundred was made at Port-of-Spain in 1973. On a turning pitch, he started with a cover drive for four off Gibbs and, again, reached his hundred in a session. Chappell was particularly impressed with one sequence of play that started with a lofted pull for

The Hundreth Man

four. Rohan Kanhai, the West Indies captain, moved a man from the point to the mid-wicket boundary, so next ball Dougie gave himself room and cut the off-spinner through the vacant gap for four more. Kanhai went back to his original field, so the following delivery went flying over mid-wicket. 'The incredible thing about that piece of batting was that all three deliveries pitched within a circle of no more than nine inches in diameter,' Chappell wrote in the *Doug Walters Benefit Year Book*.

At times, he struggled when faced with high-quality pace bowling — against Mike Procter and John Snow, and then during World Series Cricket — and there was that matter of him not making a Test century in England in four tours there. These are the flaws that stop cynics rating him among the all-time greats. Maybe they're right, though I'd like to think that the joy he gave us would counteract such criticism. I often wonder if, a little like Arthur Mailey, the fact that Dougie's a knockabout kind of bloke has disguised a little of his true worth. People often seem quicker to yarn about his wonderful character than rave about his virtues as a cricketer.

If only he'd been chosen for the 1981 Ashes tour. He had made a sensational return to Test cricket in 1980-81, topping the Test averages after three years in the 'wilderness', but because of his poor record in England the selectors left him behind. But in Australia's most recent Test, against India at the MCG, when they had collapsed for 83 chasing 143, Dougie was the one batsman who'd refused to yield. He might have changed cricket history if he'd been there for the third Test at Headingley and the fourth at Edgbaston, when Kim Hughes' team buckled chasing small targets. Instead of 'Botham's Ashes', it might have been Dougie's. Maybe then his place among the game's elite would have been assured.

Walters at Old Trafford in 1968, when he scored 81 and 86 in a low-scoring first Ashes Test, and spearheaded Australia to a crucial victory.

DOUG WALTERS (AUSTRALIA)

Test Cricket

Tests	Inn	NO	Runs	HS	Ave	100	50	Ct	Balls	Runs	Wkts	Ave	Best	5/	10/
74	125	14	5357	250	48.26	15	33	43	3295	1425	49	29.08	5-66	1	—

First-Class Cricket

Mat	Inn	NO	Runs	HS	Ave	100	50	Ct	Balls	Runs	Wkts	Ave	Best	5/	10/
258	426	57	16180	253	43.85	45	81	149	14756	6782	190	35.69	7-63	6	—

Further Reading

Autobiographies & Biographies

John Arlott, Fred: Portrait of a Fast Bowler; Eyre & Spottiswoode; London, 1971
Mike Atherton, Opening Up; Hodder & Stoughton, London, 2002
Richie Benaud, On Reflection; Collins, Sydney, 1984
Richie Benaud, The Appeal of Cricket; Hodder & Stoughton, London, 1995
Richie Benaud, Anything But ... An Autobiography; Hodder & Stoughton, London, 1998
Dickie Bird, My Autobiography; Hodder & Stoughton, London, 1997
David Boon, Under the Southern Cross; HarperSports, Sydney, 1996
Ian Botham, My Autobiography; Collins Willow, London, 1994
Geoff Boycott, The Autobiography; Macmillan, London, 1987
Don Bradman, Farewell to Cricket; Hodder & Stoughton, London, 1950
Richard Cashman, The Demon Spofforth; NSW University Press, Sydney, 1990
Ian Chappell, Chappelli; Hutchinson, Melbourne, 1976
Denis Compton, Playing For England; Sampson, Low, Marston & Co., London, 1948
Alan Davidson, Fifteen Paces; Souvenir Press, London, 1963
Michael Down, Archie: A Biography of AC MacLaren; George Allen & Unwin, London, 1981
Jack Fingleton, The Immortal Victor Trumper; Collins, London, 1981
Jack Fingleton, Batting From Memory; Collins, London, 1981
David Foot, Wally Hammond: The Reasons Why; Robson, London, 1996
Mike Gatting, Leading From the Front; Queen Anne Press, London, 1988
George Giffen, With Bat and Ball; Ward, Lock and Co., London, 1898
David Gower, Gower: The Autobiography; Collins Willow, London, 1992
WG Grace, WG: Cricketing Reminiscences & Personal Recollections; The Hambledon Press, London, 1980 (first published in 1899)
Gordon Greenidge, The Man in the Middle; David & Charles, London, 1980
Gideon Haigh, The Big Ship; Text Publishing, Melbourne, 2001
Neil Harvey, My World of Cricket; Hodder & Stoughton, London, 1963
Ian Healy, Hands & Heals; HarperSports, Sydney, 2000
Sir Jack Hobbs, My Life Story; The Hambledon Press, London, 1978 (first published in 1935)
Gerald Howat, Walter Hammond; Allen & Unwin, London, 1984
Len Hutton, Just My Story; Hutchinson, London, 1956
James Knight, Mark Waugh: The Biography; HarperSports, Sydney, 2002
Imran Khan, Imran, Pelham Books, London, 1983
Imran Khan, All Round View, Chatto & Windis, London, 1988
Kapil Dev, By God's Decree, Harper & Row, Sydney, 1985
Patrick Keane, Merv: The Full Story; HarperSports, Sydney, 1977
Allan Lamb, My Autobiography; Collins Willow, London, 1996
Harold Larwood, The Larwood Story; WH Allen & Co.; London, 1965
Bridget Lawrence, Masterclass: The Biography of George Headley; Polar Publishing, Leicester, 1995
Dennis Lillee, Over and Out; Methuen Australia; Sydney, 1984
Adrian McGregor, Greg Chappell; Collins, Sydney, 1985
Jack McHarg, Stan McCabe: The Man and his Cricket; Collins, Sydney, 1987
Jack McHarg, Bill O'Reilly: A Cricketing Life; Millennium, Sydney, 1990
Arthur Mailey, 10 for 66 and All That; Phoenix Sports Books, London, 1958

Further Reading

Keith Miller, Cricket Crossfire; Oldbourne Press, London, 1956
AG Moyes, Bradman; Angus & Robertson, Sydney, 1948
AG Moyes, Benaud; Angus & Robertson, Sydney, 1962
MA Noble, The Game's The Thing; Cassell & Company, Sydney, 1926
Bill O'Reilly, Tiger; Collins, Sydney, 1985
Graeme Pollock, Down the Wicket; Pelham Books, London, 1968
Mike Procter, Mike Procter and Cricket; Pelham Books, London, 1981
Simon Rae, WG Grace; Faber & Faber, London, 1998
Barry Richards, The Barry Richards Story; Angus & Robertson, Sydney, 1978
Viv Richards, Hitting Across the Line; Pan Macmillan, Sydney, 1991
John Ringwood, Ray Lindwall: Cricket Legend; Kangaroo Press, Sydney, 1995
Irving Rosenwater, Sir Donald Bradman; BT Batsford Limited, London, 1978
Peter Sharpham, Trumper: The Definitive Biography; Hodder & Stoughton; Sydney, 1985
John Snow, Cricket Rebel; Hamlyn, London, 1976
Sir Garfield Sobers, Sobers: Twenty Years at the Top; Macmillan, Melbourne 1988
Rob Steen, David Gower: A Man Out of Time; Cassell, London, 1995
EW Swanton, As I Said at the Time; A Lifetime in Cricket; Collins Willow, London, 1983
Fred Trueman, As It Was: The Memoirs of Fred Trueman; Macmillan, London, 2004
Sir Clyde Walcott, Sixty Years on the Back Foot; Victor Gollancz, London, 1999
Doug Walters, Looking For Runs; Pelham Books, London, 1971
Doug Walters, The Doug Walters Story; Rigby, Sydney 1981
Shane Warne, My Autobiography; Hodder & Stoughton, London, 2001
Wasim Akram, Wasim; Judy Piatkus (Publishers) Ltd, London, 1998
Steve Waugh, Out Of My Comfort Zone; Penguin Books, Melbourne 2005
RS Whitington, Time of the Tiger; Hutchinson, Melbourne, 1970
RS Whitington & George Hele, Bodyline Umpire; Rigby, Adelaide, 1974
RS Whitington, Keith Miller: The Golden Nugget; Rigby, Adelaide, 1981
Simon Wilde, Ranji: A Genius Rich and Strange; Kingswood Press, London, 1990
Charles Williams, Bradman; Little Brown & Company, London, 1996

Profiles and Interviews

John Arlott, Cricket: The Great Bowlers; Pelham Books, London, 1968
John Arlott, John Arlott's Book of Cricketers; Angus & Robertson, London, 1979
John Arlott & Fred Trueman, Arlott & Trueman on Cricket; BBC, London, 1977
Geoff Armstrong, ESPN's Legends of Cricket; Allen & Unwin, Sydney, 2002
Trevor Bailey, The Greatest Of My Time; Eyre & Spottiswoode, London, 1968
Richie Benaud, Willow Patterns; Hodder & Stoughton, London, 1969
Keith Butler, Howzat; Collins, Sydney, 1979
Denis Compton, Compton on Cricketers; Cassell, London, 1980
Philip Derriman, The Top 100 & The 1st XI; The Fairfax Library, Sydney, 1987
Jack Fingleton, Masters of Cricket; Pavilion Books, London, 1990
David Frith, The Fast Men; Transworld, London, 1975
David Frith (ed), Cricket Gallery; Rigby, London, 1976
David Frith, The Slow Men; Horwitz Grahame, Sydney, 1984
David Frith, By His Own Hand; ABC Books, Sydney, 1990
Sunil Gavaskar, Idols; George Allen & Unwin, London, 1984
Kenneth Gregory (ed), In Celebration of Cricket; Granada, London, 1978
David Lemmon; The Great Wicketkeepers; Stanley Paul, London, 1984
Christopher Martin-Jenkins, The Complete Who's Who of Test Cricketers; Rigby, Sydney, 1981
AG Moyes, A Century of Cricketers; Harrap, London, 1950
AG Moyes, Australian Bowlers; Angus & Robertson, Sydney, 1953
AG Moyes, Australian Batsmen; Angus & Robertson, Sydney, 1954
Patrick Murphy, The Centurions; JM Dent & Sons, London, 1986
Patrick Murphy, Declarations; Ringpress Books, Letchworth UK, 1989
Ray Robinson, On Top Down Under; Cassell Australia, Sydney, 1976
Bob Simpson, The Reasons Why; HarperSports, Sydney, 1996

Further Reading

History and Tour Books

HS Altham & EW Swanton, A History of Cricket; George Allen & Unwin, London, 1948
John Arlott, Test Match Diary; James Barrie, London, 1953
John Arlott, The Ashes 1972; Pelham, London, 1973
Geoff Armstrong, A Century of Summers; Ironbark Press, Sydney 1992
Geoff Armstrong & Mark Gately, The People's Game; Ironbark, Sydney, 1994
Geoff Armstrong & Ian Russell, Top 10s of Australian Test Cricket; ABC Books, Sydney, 2003
Warwick Armstrong, The Art of Cricket; Methuen & Co. Ltd, London, 1922
Ralph Barker & Irving Rosenwater, Test Cricket: England v Australia; Batsford Ltd, London, 1969
Peter Baxter & Peter Hayter, The Ashes: Highlights Since 1948; BBC Books, London, 1989
Richie Benaud, A Tale of Two Tests; Hodder & Stoughton, London, 1962
Scyld Berry (ed), The Observer on Cricket; Unwin Hyman, London, 1987
Henry Blofeld, The Packer Affair; Collins, London, 1978
Mihir Bose, A History of Indian Cricket; Andre Deutsch, London, 2002
The Bradman Albums (Volumes 1 & 2); Weldon, Sydney, 1987
Lionel H Brown, Victor Trumper and the 1902 Australians; Secker & Warburg, London, 1981
Geoff Boycott, In The Fast Lane; Sphere Books, London, 1981
Neville Cardus, Cardus on Cricket; Souvenir Press, London, 1977 (first published in 1949)
Neville Cardus, Cardus in the Covers; Souvenir Press, London, 1978
Neville Cardus, Play Resumed With Cardus; Souvenir Press, London, 1979
Neville Cardus, A Fourth Innings With Cardus; Souvenir Press, London, 1981
Neville Cardus, A Cardus For All Seasons; Souvenir Press, London, 1985
Greg Chappell, The 100th Summer; Garry Sparke & Associates, Melbourne, 1977
Ian Chappell, Passing Tests; Lynton Publications; Adelaide, 1973
Mike Coward, Cricket Beyond the Bazaar; Allen & Unwin, Sydney, 1990
Brian Mathew Crowley & Pat Mullins, Cradle Days of Australian Cricket; Macmillan, Sydney, 1989
Philip Derriman, The Grand Old Ground; Cassell, Sydney, 1981
Philip Derriman, True to the Blue; Richard Smart Publishing, Sydney, 1985
Jack Fingleton, Cricket Crisis; Cassell, Sydney, 1946
Jack Fingleton, Brightly Fades The Don; Collins, London, 1949
Jack Fingleton, The Ashes Crown the Year; Collins, Sydney, 1954
David Frith, England Versus Australia; Rigby, Adelaide, 1977
David Frith, Stoddy's Mission: The First Great Test Series; Allen & Unwin, Sydney, 1994
David Frith, Bodyline Autopsy; ABC Books, Sydney, 2002
Gideon Haigh, The Cricket War; Text Publishing; Melbourne, 1993
Gideon Haigh, The Summer Game; Text Publishing, Melbourne, 1997
Chris Harte, Two Tours and Pollock; Sports Marketing, Adelaide, 1988
Reg Hayter (ed), The Best of The Cricketer 1921-1981; Cassell, Lopndon, 1981
CLR James, Cricket; Allison & Busby, London, 1986
Jim Laker, A Spell From Laker; Hamlyn, London, 1979
Jim Laker, Cricket Contrasts; Stanley Paul, London, 1985
Michael Manley, A History of West Indies Cricket; Andre Deutsch, London, 1988
Ronald Mason, Warwick Armstrong's Australians; Epworth Press, London, 1971

AG Moyes, The Fight for the Ashes 1950-51; Angus & Robertson, Sydney, 1951
AG Moyes, With the West Indies in Australia 1951-52; Angus & Robertson, Sydney, 1952
AG Moyes, The Fight for the Ashes 1954-55; Angus & Robertson, Sydney, 1955
AG Moyes, Australian Cricket: A History; Angus & Robertson, Sydney, 1959
AG Moyes, With the West Indies in Australia 1960-61; Angus & Robertson, Sydney, 1961
AG Moyes, The Changing Face of Cricket; Angus & Robertson, Sydney, 1963
MA Noble, Gilligan's Men; Chapman & Hall, London, 1925
David Rayvern Allen, Cricket on the Air; BBC, London, 1985
Jack Pollard, Cricket the Australian Way; Lansdowne Press, Melbourne, 1968 (first published in 1961)
Jack Pollard, Australian Cricket: The Game and the Players; Hodder and Stoughton, Sydney, 1982
Ricky Ponting's Tour Diaries; HarperSports, Sydney, 2003-05
Ray Robinson, The Wildest Tests; Cassell, Sydney, 1979
Peter Roebuck, Ashes to Ashes; Kingswood Press, London, 1987
Sir Pelham Warner, Cricket Between Two Wars; Chatto & Windus, London, 1942
Sir Pelham Warner, Lord's 1787–1945; White Lion, London, 1946
Steve Waugh's Tour Diaries; Pan Macmillan (1993-94), HarperSports (1995-97, 1999-2002), both Sydney
RS Whitington, Simpson's Safari; William Heinemann, Melbourne, 1967
RS Whitington, Captains Outrageous?; Hutchinson, Melbourne, 1972
Simon Wilde, Caught: The Full Story of Corruption in International Cricket; Aurum Press, London 2001
Bob Willis, The Cricket Revolution: Test Cricket in the 1970s; Sidgwick & Jackson, London, 1981
Peter Wynne-Thomas, The Complete History of Cricket Tours; Hamlyn, London, 1989

Further Reading

Scorecards and Statistics

ABC Australian Cricket Almanacs (1990-1994)

Bill Frindall, The Wisden Book of Test Cricket Volume 1 1877-1970; Headline, London 2000

Bill Frindall, The Wisden Book of Test Cricket Volume 2 1970-1996; Headline, London 2000

Bill Frindall, The Wisden Book of Test Cricket Volume 3 1996-2000; Headline, London 2000

The Sydney Morning Herald Australian Cricket Almanac, 1995

Ray Webster & Allan Miller, First-Class Cricket in Australia (Volume 1, 1850-51 to 1941-42); published by Ray Webster, Glen Waverley, 1991

Ray Webster, First-Class Cricket in Australia (Volume 2, 1945-46 to 1976-77); published by Ray Webster, Glen Waverley, 1997

Wisden Cricketers' Almanack 2005; John Wisden & Co. Ltd, Alton, Hampshire 2003 (and earlier editions)

Peter Wynne-Thomas, The Rigby A-Z of Cricket Records; Rigby Publishers, London, 1983

Websites, Newspapers and Magazines

Among websites consulted were howstat.com.au, cricketarchive.com and cricinfo.com; newspapers included The Advertiser (Adelaide), The Age (Melbourne), The Australasian (Melbourne), The Australian, The Daily Telegraph (Sydney), The Referee (Sydney), The Sydney Morning Herald, The Sun-Herald (Sydney), The Times (London); also various ABC Cricket Books, Cricketer magazines, Australian Cricket magazines, Playfair Cricket Monthly magazines, Wisden Cricket Monthly magazines and NSW Cricket Association Yearbooks.

Index

A

Abbas, Zaheer, 28, 240, 241, 297, 307
ABC Cricket Book, 313, 314
Adams, Jimmy, 111
Adams, Paul, 25
Adelaide Oval, 40, 96, 152, 176, 251, 253
Afridi, Shahid, 44, 211, 213
Ahmed, Imitiaz, 274
Ahmed, Mushtaq, 25
Akhtar, Shoaib, 43, 160, 213, 276
Akram, Wasim, 25, 28, 37, 43, 54, 61, 84, 96–8, 130, 134, 140, 159, 185, 228, 236, 257, 259, 263, 265, 266
Alam, Intikhab, 29, 240, 241
Alderman, Terry, 69, 263
All Round View, 199
Allen, David, 130
Allen, Gubby, 60, 93, 209
Allott, Paul, 257
Altham, HS, 40, 64, 105, 108, 146, 150, 174, 268, 289
Amarnath, Mohinder, 84
Ambrose, Curtly, 25, 34, 40, 78, 111, 135, 139–41, 153, 185, 263, 265, 278
Ames, Les, 42, 92, 121, 152, 209–10, 288
Amiss, Dennis, 89
Anwar, Saeed, 28, 38
The Appeal of Cricket, 270
Archer, Ron, 143, 165
Archie: A Biography of AC MacLaren, 145
Argus, 108
Arlott, John, 50, 133, 170, 171, 175, 249
Armstrong, Lance, 27
Armstrong, Warwick, 40, 71, 147, 196, 197, 198, 225, 227, 266
The Art of Cricket, 16
As It Was, 292
The Ashes 1972, 50, 249
Atherton, Mike, 110, 140, 257, 265, 279
Australasian, 109, 272
Australian Cricket Yearbook 1971, 248
Australian Summer, 60
Azharuddin, Mohammad, 37, 244

B

Bacher, Ali, 171, 192
Bailey, Trevor, 122, 128, 132, 144, 168, 177, 270
Bairstow, David, 74
Bannerman, Charles, 216, 225
Bannister, Alex, 192
Baptiste, Eldine, 201
Bardsley, Warren, 40, 71, 196, 243
Bari, Wasim, 179, 240–2
Barker, Ralph, 290
Barlow, Eddie, 45, 277, 301
Barnes, Sydney, 40–1, 73, 128, 143, 147, 177, 200, 217, 226, 252, 276, 288, 301, 303
Barrington, Ken, 61, 222–4, 237, 264, 307, 309
Bedi, Bishan, 179, 205–8, 234
Bedser, Alec, 60, 61, 131, 157, 159, 168, 176–8, 274
Benaud, John, 240
Benaud, Richie, 46, 51, 95, 122, 123, 128, 129, 130, 133, 138, 143, 161, 165–7, 218, 222, 225, 232, 233, 234, 269, 270, 275, 287
Benjamin, Winston, 30
Berry, Scyld, 85
Bevan, Michael, 255
Bird, 'Dickie', 228, 229
Bishop, Ian, 25, 139
Blackham, Jack, 108–9, 219, 271
Bland, Colin, 222
Blofeld, Henry, 297
Blythe, Colin, 128
Bodyline Umpire, 114
Bonnor, George, 271
Boon, David, 36, 127, 140, 153, 255, 285
Border, Allan, 34, 36, 55, 57, 79, 80, 89, 96, 125–7, 134, 155, 244, 255, 263, 265, 307

Index

Bosanquet, Bernard, 312
Bose, Mihir, 164, 293
Botham, Ian, 42, 54, 57, 68–70, 84, 97, 120, 138, 156,
185, 190, 202, 203, 265, 298, 306
Boucher, Mark, 256, 304
Bowes, Bill, 293
Boyce, Keith, 139, 228
Boycott, Geoff, 24, 60, 68, 76, 86, 89, 191, 202-4, 231
Boyle, Harry, 63, 273
Brabourne Stadium, 293
Bradman, Sir Don, 16-18, 22, 24, 31, 33, 34, 37, 41, 42,
43, 44, 45, 47, 59, 60, 61, 66, 71, 73, 79, 85, 88, 90, 92, 93, 102,
104, 118, 122, 130, 136, 143, 151, 153, 154, 156, 158, 160, 167, 171,
176, 178, 186, 187, 188, 191, 196, 204, 209, 210, 216, 225, 234, 238,
239, 243, 244, 260, 282, 283, 293, 294, 295, 303, 307, 310, 311
Brearley, Mike, 74, 199
Brearley, Walter, 147
Briggs, Johnny, 80, 105, 128, 219, 235-6
Bright, Ray, 172
Broad, Chris, 191
Brown, Bill, 209
Burge, Peter, 207, 228
Burke, Jim, 128, 142, 232
Burn, Kenny, 109
Butcher, Mark, 255
Butler, Keith, 51

C

Calthorpe, Frederick, 102
Cameron, 'Jock', 189
Campbell, Sherwin, 111
Cardus, Neville, 17, 33, 40, 41, 60, 64, 72, 103, 106, 115, 137,
145, 150, 151, 157, 290, 310
Carr, Arthur, 196
Carter, Hanson, 304
The Centurions, 115
A Century of Cricketers, 40, 108, 221
Chandrasekhar, Bhagwat, 179, 180, 205-8, 234

Chapman, Percy, 147, 187
Chappell, Greg, 18, 55, 57, 68, 76, 87-9, 104, 125, 127, 134, 171,
172, 202, 206, 250, 307, 313
Chappell, Ian, 87, 193, 203, 206, 240, 248, 250, 313, 314
Chappell, Trevor, 87
Chester, Frank, 152
Chifley, Ben, 189
Clarke, Sylvester, 29, 47, 84, 139
Coldwell, Len, 168
Collins, Herbert, 73, 227
Complete Who's Who of Test Cricketers, 235
Compton, Denis, 93, 119, 120, 123, 156-8, 159, 160, 161, 169,
177, 237, 260, 268, 283
Compton on Cricketers Past and Present, 157
Connolly, Alan, 248
Constantine, Learie, 104
Cotter, Tibby, 32
Coulthard, George, 271, 272
Cowdrey, Colin, 24, 60, 75, 87, 142, 185, 204, 269
Cowper, Bob, 207
Cozier, Tony, 285
Crafter, Tony, 184
Craig, Ian, 128, 142, 143, 165, 166, 217
Cricket Crossfire, 176
Cricket Rebel, 250
The Cricket Revolution, 199, 241
Cricket: the Australian Way, 313
Cricket Typhoon, 217
Cricketer, The, 131, 206, 260, 285, 287, 296
Cricketers' Annual, 235, 291
Croft, Colin, 29, 52, 139, 228, 264
Cronje, Hansie, 255
Crowe, Jeff, 70
Crowe, Martin, 36, 89, 258
Cullinan, Daryll, 262
Daily Mail, 147, 150

D

Daniel, Wayne, 84, 139, 200
Darling, Joe, 43, 164, 266, 298

Darling, Len, 60, 283
David Gower: A Man Out of Time, 268
Davidson, Alan, 23, 128–30, 159, 166, 200, 217, 232, 237, 269, 275
Davis, JC, 271
Deane, Sid, 109
Declarations, 186, 203
DeFreitas, Phillip, 25
DeSilva, Arvinda, 308, 309
Dev, Kapil, 29, 54, 58, 84, 99–101, 138, 140, 179, 180, 181, 190, 208, 242, 263, 306
Dexter, Ted, 130, 218, 268
Dillon, Mervyn, 140
D'Oliveira, Basil, 250
Donald, Allan, 135, 278, 297
Doug Walters Benefit Year Book, 315
Down, Michael, 145, 226
Downton, Paul, 179
Dravid, Rahul, 39, 86, 193–5, 211, 213, 309
Duckworth, George, 188, 209, 210
Duff, Reggie, 71, 227
Dujon, Jeffrey, 30, 43, 179, 304

E

Edgbaston, 68, 135, 170, 201, 223, 238, 263, 269, 299, 315
Emburey, John, 184, 185
Engineer, Farokh, 180, 304
Evans, Godfrey, 43, 74, 75, 131–3, 158, 177, 179, 210, 216

F

Fairfax, Alan, 151
Fames, Ken, 160
Farewell to Cricket, 294
Faulkner, Aubrey, 147, 277, 278, 279, 312
Favell, Les, 233
Federer, Roger, 27
Ferris, Jack, 62, 221, 266
Fifteen Paces, 129, 217
The Fight for the Ashes 1954-55, 158
Fingleton, Jack, 60, 115, 161, 171, 189, 282
Flavell, Jack, 168
Fleetwood-Smith, Chuck, 65, 90, 283, 312
Fletcher, Keith, 190
Flintoff, Andrew, 259, 298–300
Flower, Andy, 42, 256, 304–6, 308
Flower, Grant, 305
Foster, Frank, 40, 288
Foster, Reg, 138, 265, 267, 271
Fowler, Graeme, 201
Fraser, Angus, 25
Fred: Portrait of a Fast Bowler, 170
Fredericks, Roy, 237
Freeman, Eric, 171
Frith, David, 268
Fry, CB, 21, 72, 73, 106, 145, 163, 191, 226, 266, 289

G

Gabba, the, 57, 69, 129, 244, 255, 286
The Game's The Thing, 64, 73
Gambhir, Gautam, 307
Ganguly, Sourav, 211
Garner, Joel, 29, 34, 51, 84, 126, 139, 199–201, 228, 229, 230, 263, 268
Gatting, Mike, 26, 254, 264
Gavaskar, Sunil, 16, 35, 38, 39, 55, 65, 76, 84–6, 89, 101, 179, 180, 204, 205, 230, 249, 307, 309
George Giffen Stand, 45
Gibbs, Lance, 22, 88, 206, 228, 230, 250, 315
Giffen, Geoff, 80
Giffen, George, 63, 109, 163, 219, 227, 251, 253, 266
Gilchrist, Adam, 42–4, 110, 124, 153, 193, 211, 212, 243, 251, 256, 299, 300, 304
Gillespie, Jason, 26, 78, 99, 111, 112, 153, 212, 228
Gilligan's Men, 115
Gilmour, Gary, 172, 239
Gleeson, Johnny, 202
Goddard, Trevor, 277, 301
Gomes, Larry, 35, 230, 287
Gooch, Graham, 86, 87, 231, 263–5

Index

Goodwin, Murray, 304
Gower, David, 69, 195, 201, 268
Grace, WG, 19–21, 24, 31, 55, 62, 63, 65, 73, 88, 105, 106, 108, 109, 136, 137, 145, 152, 162, 174, 220, 236, 271, 272, 288, 303
Graham, Harry, 216
Graveney, Tom, 131, 157, 168, 249
The Great Wicketkeepers, 242
The Greatest of My Time, 270
Greenidge, Gordon, 79, 86, 172, 238, 287, 303
Gregory, Dave, 225, 272
Gregory, Jack, 32, 118, 151, 160, 217, 260, 297, 312
Gregory, Syd, 109
Greig, Tony, 138, 229, 249, 250, 296
Griffith, Charlie, 22, 139, 200, 208, 231, 234, 237, 250, 268
Grimmett, Clarrie, 32, 41, 90, 102, 143, 161, 177, 261, 262, 284, 310, 311, 312
Grout, Wally, 166, 179, 304
Gunn, Goerge, 122
Gupte, Subash, 205, 312

H

Hadlee, Barry, 56
Hadlee, Dayle, 56
Hadlee, Richard, 25, 34, 41, 54, 56–8, 84, 89, 99, 127, 140, 159, 184, 190, 203, 230, 263
Hadlee, Walter, 56
Haigh, Schofield, 288
Hair, Darrell, 80
Hall, Wes, 22, 50, 139, 159, 200, 208, 222, 223, 231, 233, 234, 237, 250, 268, 285, 297
Hameed, Yasir, 194
Hammond, Wally, 16, 59–61, 90, 103, 121, 146, 151, 157, 158, 186, 210, 237, 260, 262, 303
Harris, Lord, 271
Harry, Jack, 109
Hartigan, Roger, 253
Harvey, Mervyn, 216
Harvey, Neil, 16, 24, 43, 89, 129, 142, 165, 166, 177, 216–18, 232, 314

Hassett, Lindsay, 92, 165, 176
Hayden, Matthew, 79, 136, 211, 243–5, 251, 303
Haynes, Desmond, 38, 52, 79, 287, 302, 303
Hayward, Tom, 162, 164
Hazare, Vijay, 292–4
Headingley, 24, 35, 69, 153, 160, 250, 258, 277, 315
Headley, George, 16, 102–4, 121, 306
Healy, Ian, 42, 43, 96, 110, 111, 254–6
Hele, George, 33, 91, 114, 282
Hemmings, Eddie, 100
Hendren, Patsy, 189, 260
Hick, Graeme, 139
Higgs, Ken, 250
Hill, Clem, 40, 71, 73, 138, 226, 227, 251–3, 260, 291, 298
Hirst, George, 137, 145, 147, 298
A History of Cricket, 40, 64, 146
A History of Indian Cricket, 293
A History of West Indies Cricket, 34, 93
Hobbs, Sir John Berry (Jack), 16, 31–3, 40, 61, 65, 67, 71, 73, 88, 103, 114, 115, 136, 137, 146, 150, 151, 203, 244, 260, 277, 303, 310, 312
Hogg, Rodney, 54, 84, 184
Holder, Vanburn, 228
Holding, Michael, 34, 51, 54, 75, 84, 88, 99, 139, 180, 189, 199, 200, 201, 203, 228–31, 263, 265, 268, 296
Holford, David, 24
Hollies, Eric, 18, 189
Holmes, Percy, 203
Hookes, David, 229
Hooper, Carl, 138
Horan, Tom, 108, 220
Hordern, Herbert, 32, 71
Houghton, David, 101, 304
Hughes, Kim, 52, 88, 96, 206, 315
Hughes, Merv, 25, 26, 255, 285
Hunte, Conrad, 237, 276
Hunter, Joe, 235
Hussey, Mike, 112, 307
Hutton, Sir Len, 61, 65–7, 92, 119, 120, 133, 144, 150, 156, 157, 158, 159, 160, 177, 178, 203, 210, 216, 232, 260, 268, 269, 270, 274, 292, 303, 309

325

The 100 Greatest Cricketers

I

Illingworth, Ray, 74, 203, 204, 248, 249, 250
Ins and Outs, 218
Inzamam-ul-Haq, 28, 279, 307, 308
Iqbal, Asif, 28, 179, 240, 241
Iredale, Frank, 71, 163
Irvine, Lee, 46

J

Jackson, Archie, 16, 102, 216, 225, 282
Jackson, Les, 168
Jackson, Stanley, 145, 147, 220, 298
Jacobs, Ridley, 241
James, CLR, 238, 274
Jardine, Douglas, 187, 282
Jayasuriya, Sanath, 308, 309
Jayawardene, Mahela, 307, 309
Jenner, Terry, 249
Jessop, Gilbert, 137, 145, 147, 164, 266, 268, 291
Johnson, Ian, 128, 161, 165
Johnson, Mitchell, 308
Johnston, Bill, 66, 119, 123, 165
Johnston, Fred, 216
Jones, Dean, 96, 127, 140
Jones, Ernie, 146, 164, 291
Jones, Jeff, 75
Jones, Sammy, 63
Jones, Simon, 259, 299
Julien, Bernard, 139, 228
Just My Story, 177

K

Kallicharran, Alvin, 285, 287
Kallis, Jacques, 138, 277–9, 307
Kanhai, Rohan, 23, 89, 104, 237–9, 315
Keegan, Kevin, 68
Kellaway, Charlie, 40, 71
Kensington Oval, 123
Khan, Imran, 28–30, 34, 37, 51, 54, 84, 98, 139, 159, 185,190, 199, 241, 257, 287
Khan, Majid, 28, 171, 240, 241
Khan, Younis, 307
Kilner, Roy, 152
King, Collis, 200
Kippax, Alan, 118, 187, 282, 310
Kirmani, Syed, 101, 179–81, 242, 306
Kline, Lindsay, 128, 129
Knott, Alan, 43, 74–6, 133, 179, 240, 241, 242, 306
Kortright, Charles, 288
Kumble, Anil, 25, 206, 312

L

Laker, Jim, 131, 142–4, 167, 176, 207, 217, 269
Lal, Madan, 101
Lamb, Allan, 97, 201, 265
Langer, Justin, 43, 136, 243, 244, 251, 299
Langley, Gil, 165
Lara, Brian, 16, 18, 37, 39, 77–9, 104, 110, 111, 126, 186, 251, 277, 278, 279, 303
Larter, David, 168
Larwood, Harold, 34, 50, 159, 160, 187–9, 210, 228, 282, 284, 291, 295
Lawry, Bill, 89, 171, 207, 223, 234, 243
Lawson, Geoff, 54, 139
Laxman, VVS, 39, 194, 211
le Roux, Garth, 54
Lee, Brett, 155, 160, 257, 299
Lee, Philip, 59
Leeds, 35, 65, 66, 75, 143
Lees, Warren, 56, 180
Lemmon, David, 179, 180, 242
Lewis, Chris, 97
Lewis, Tony, 206
Leyland, Maurice, 91
Lillee, Dennis, 24, 27, 28, 34, 45, 47, 50–2, 54, 57, 62, 69,75, 84, 87, 128, 134, 159, 161, 172, 173, 184, 202, 228, 229, 230, 237, 240, 242, 248, 250, 255, 263, 285, 290, 296, 297, 313

Index

Lilley, 'Dick', 209, 252, 291
Lillywhite, James, 62
Lindsay, Denis, 42, 179, 304
Lindwall, Jack, 160
Lindwall, Ray, 50, 60, 66, 67, 94, 101, 122, 123, 124, 128, 143, 156, 157, 159–61, 165, 216, 228, 249, 293, 294
Lloyd, Andy, 35
Lloyd, Clive, 55, 89, 95, 238, 285–7
Lock, Tony, 142, 143, 173
Lockwood, Bill, 106, 145, 288–91
Lohmann, George, 80, 105–7, 128, 236, 288, 289, 291
Looking for Runs, 190, 206
Lord's, 58, 63, 65, 68, 72, 86, 88, 101, 103, 105, 111, 119, 120, 121, 123, 133, 135, 138, 147, 151, 158, 162, 174, 175, 181, 196, 204, 205, 209, 211, 226, 239, 243, 249, 250, 258, 261, 263, 268, 269, 274, 291, 308, 311
Lord's 1787-1945, 236
Lyttleton, Alfred, 209, 273

M

McAlister, Peter, 253
Macartney, Charlie, 89, 171, 173, 196–8, 210, 225, 227
McCabe, Stan, 16, 43, 90, 160, 225, 261, 282–4
McCormick, Ernie, 90, 312
McCosker, Rick, 202
McDermott, Craig, 25, 26, 54, 84, 255
McDonald, Colin, 128, 142, 143, 218
McDonald, Ted, 32, 64, 151, 160, 260, 312
McDonnell, Percy, 174
Macgill, Stuart, 25, 78
McGrath, Glenn, 26, 44, 78, 110–12, 155, 159, 166, 193, 212, 228, 255
McHarg, Jack, 283
Mackay, Ken, 130, 143
McKenzie, Graham, 128, 130, 173, 237, 248, 297, 303
McKibbin, Tom, 219, 267
MacLaren, Archie, 41, 72, 73, 137, 145–7, 164, 220, 221, 226, 269, 287, 298

Maddocks, Len, 143
Mahmood, Fazal, 217, 259, 274–6, 294
Mailey, Arthur, 32, 150, 151, 196, 197, 221, 227, 254, 260, 310–12, 315
Malcolm, Devon, 25, 58
Malik, Salim, 28
Mallett, Ashley, 191
The Man in the Middle, 86
Manchester Guardian, 115, 151, 220, 274
Manjrekar, Sanjay, 37, 292
Mankad, Vinoo, 274
Manley, Michael, 34, 93
Marsh, Geoff, 126
Marsh, Rod, 42, 43, 75, 87, 134, 153, 179, 240, 241, 242, 255, 295, 304, 313
Marshall, Malcolm, 25, 28, 29, 34–6, 84, 85, 126, 139, 159, 180, 185, 199, 200, 228, 229, 257, 263, 264, 265, 268, 295, 296, 297
Martin, Ray, 37
Martin-Jenkins, Christopher, 201, 235, 264, 265, 295
Martindale, Manny, 104
Martyn, Damien, 136
Marylebone Cricket Club (MCC), 63, 147, 162, 174, 275
Mason, Ronald, 151
Massie, Bob, 240
Masters of Cricket, 115
Matthews, 'Jimmy', 266
May, Peter, 130, 157, 168, 268–70
MCG, 24, 51, 52, 63, 80, 87, 96, 112, 125, 127, 174, 184, 186, 207, 216, 235, 253, 269, 273
Meckiff, Ian, 80, 128
Melbourne Cricket Ground see MCG
Merchant, Vijay, 292, 293, 294
Miandad, Javed, 28, 55, 89, 184–6, 241, 308, 307
Milburn, Colin, 240
Miller, Keith, 60, 66, 67, 94, 99, 101, 118–20, 122, 123, 124, 128, 138, 143, 156, 160, 161, 165, 176, 217, 227, 228, 232, 293, 294, 306
Minnett, Roy, 40
Mitchell, Bruce, 260, 301
Mohammad, Hanif, 240, 274, 276, 303

The 100 Greatest Cricketers

Mohammad, Yousuf, 307
Mohammad, Khan, 274
Mohammad, Mushtaq, 28, 240, 241
Mohammad, Sadiq, 240, 241
Mohammed, Gul, 293
Mold, Arthur, 288
Morris, Arthur, 43, 133, 143, 177, 198, 216, 243, 303
Morrison, Danny, 25
Moss, Alan, 168
Moyes, AG 'Johnnie', 23, 40, 42, 62, 66, 71, 90, 95, 108, 118, 132, 146, 157, 158, 221, 227, 232, 234, 237, 238, 253, 271, 293
Muralitharan, Muttiah, 25, 27, 80–1, 143, 193, 206, 207, 257, 308
Murdoch, Billy, 71, 79, 109, 175, 225, 271–3, 288
Murphy, Patrick, 115, 186, 203
Murray, Deryck, 179
Murray, John, 179
Mushtaq, Saqlain, 25, 43, 98, 213, 257
My World of Cricket, 129

N

Nash, Malcolm, 24
Nawaz, Sarfraz, 240, 241
Nazar, Mudassar, 29, 307
1997 Ashes Diary, 153
Noble, Montague Alfred (Monty), 32, 64, 71, 115, 138, 147, 211, 225–7, 253, 266, 267, 287, 298
Nourse, AW 'Dave', 260
Nourse, Dudley, 16, 260–2

O

Observer, The, 85, 210, 218
Old Trafford, 54, 65, 69, 72, 92, 130, 135, 142, 146, 147, 155, 157, 163, 168, 187, 226, 232, 235, 252, 261, 265, 268, 269, 278, 288, 290, 291, 292
Oldfield, Bert, 114, 179, 189, 210, 304
Olonga, Henry, 304
On Top Down Under, 108
O'Neill, Norm, 216, 218
O'Reilly, Bill 'Tiger', 25, 60, 65, 90–2, 114, 142, 150, 160, 207, 210, 221, 225, 261, 262, 283, 310, 312
Oval, The see The Oval

P

Packer, Kerry, 180
Parks, Jim, 74
Pascoe, Len, 84
Patel, Dipak, 25
Patel, Jasu, 129
Patterson, Patrick, 25, 139, 185, 265
Peebles, Jack, 150
Peel, Bobby, 105, 128, 137, 236, 289
Peterson, Robin, 79
Phadkar, Dattu, 292
Phillips, Wayne, 181
Pietersen, Kevin, 307
Pilling, Richard, 108, 209, 236
Pollard, Jack, 313
Pollock, Graeme, 16, 45–7, 104, 171, 172, 222, 237, 262, 307
Pollock, Shaun, 138, 277
Ponsford, Bill, 16, 187, 216, 282, 283, 284
Ponting, Ricky, 16, 37, 39, 42, 43, 127, 136, 153–5, 193, 211, 243, 244, 279, 299, 308, 307, 313
Prasanna, Erepalli, 179, 205, 208
Price, John, 168
Procter, Mike, 51, 172, 190–2, 248, 315
Pyke, Dr Frank, 50

Q

Qadir, Abdul, 25, 30, 37, 268, 312

R

Rae, Simon, 63
Raja, Wasim, 242
Ramadhin, Sonny, 66, 121, 269

Index

Randall, Derek, 201
Ranji: A Genius Rich and Strange, 162
Ranjitsinhji, Kumar Shri, 40, 145, 162-4, 217, 288
Ransford, Vernon, 71
Razzaq, Abdul, 236
The Reasons Why, 169
The Referee, 271
Remembering Bradman, 17
Rhodes, Jonty, 279
Rhodes, Wilfred, 40, 106, 137-8, 147, 168, 227, 267, 291, 298
Richards, Barry, 18, 46, 86, 171-3, 190, 262
Richards, Sir Viv, 30, 34, 43, 44, 52, 53-5, 79, 89, 97, 100, 102, 104, 155, 171, 172, 200, 238, 287, 297, 307, 313
Richardson, Peter, 168
Richardson, Richie, 25, 79, 285, 287
Richardson, Tom, 106, 217, 288-91
Richardson, Victor, 87, 210, 282
Ring, Doug, 165
Roberts, Andy, 29, 51, 75, 84, 88, 99, 102, 139, 180, 199, 228-31, 238, 242, 263, 265, 296
Robinson, Ray, 108, 223
Rosenwater, Irving, 290
Rowe, Lawrence, 287
Rumsey, Fred, 168
Rundigger, 223
Ryder, Jack, 284

S

Saggers, Ron, 216
Samaraweera, Thilan, 307
Sangakkara, Kumar, 256, 304, 307-309
Saunders, Jack, 252
SCG, 42, 77, 87, 110, 120, 136, 146, 160, 161, 172, 196, 206, 217, 223, 225, 232, 236, 249, 271, 272, 312, 314
Schwarz, Reggie, 312
Sehwag, Virender, 86, 211-13, 300, 313
Shackleton, Derek, 168
Sharjah, 96, 98
Sharma, Chetan, 186
Shastri, Ravi, 37, 101

Shaw, Alfred, 19, 62, 108, 174, 219, 220
Sheahan, Paul, 240
Sheppard, Rev David, 119
Sherwell, Percy, 209
Shrewsbury, Arthur, 145, 162, 174-5, 220, 235, 236, 288
Sidhu, Navjot, 38
Simpson, Bob, 89, 126, 128, 169, 223, 224, 225, 232-4, 243, 299, 300
Sinfield, Reg, 189
Singh, Harbhajan, 25
Smith, Collie, 168
Smith, Graeme, 301-303
Smith, Ian, 179, 241
Smith, Robin, 265
Snow, John, 51, 54, 84, 168, 222, 237, 248-50, 315
Sobers, Garry, 22-4, 45, 55, 70, 75, 77, 79, 85, 104, 129, 138, 165, 171, 192, 200, 204, 205, 207, 208, 218, 222, 230, 237, 250, 276, 277, 285, 306, 307
Solkar, Eknath, 204
Solomon, Joe, 130
South Australian Register, 253
Southerton, James, 62
Spofforth, Fred (the 'Demon'), 40, 51, 62-4, 105, 106, 108, 175, 217, 219, 225, 271, 273
Sporting Times, 63
Sportstar, The, 299
Stackpole, Keith, 249
Statham, Brian, 67, 123, 128, 132, 160, 168, 169, 176, 222, 228, 237, 297
Steen, Rob, 268
Stephenson, Franklyn, 47
Stevenson, Mike, 287
Stewart, Alec, 43, 265
Stoddart, Andrew, 226, 236, 266
Strauss, Andrew, 251, 300
Strudwick, Harold, 304
Strudwick, Herbert, 209
Styris, Scott, 308
Surti, Rusi, 207
Sutcliffe, Herbert, 16, 33, 61, 90, 104, 113-15, 151, 203, 244, 260, 303, 312
Swanton, EW, 93, 115, 262
Sydney Cricket Ground see SCG
Sydney Morning Herald, 72, 138, 267, 284

The 100 Greatest Cricketers

T

Tallon, Don, 132
Tate, Fred, 147, 252
Tate, Maurice, 176
Tayfield, Hugh, 312
Taylor, Bob, 74, 241, 304
Taylor, Herbie, 211, 262, 301, 303
Taylor, Mark, 127, 135, 243
Tendulkar, Sachin, 16, 26, 37–9, 86, 124, 193, 194, 211, 257, 279, 313, 307, 303
Test Cricket: England v Australia, 290
Test Match Diary, 133
The Oval, 17, 19, 21, 30, 35, 63, 65, 66, 69, 75, 76, 87, 88, 92, 105, 106, 115, 137, 138, 140, 152, 154, 157, 160, 203, 206, 209, 227, 229, 244, 245, 250, 258, 260, 266, 271, 272, 273, 274, 275, 276, 285, 300, 301, 307, 311
Thicknesse, John, 222
Thomson, Ian, 168
Thomson, Jeff, 45, 51, 54, 84, 99, 127, 128, 202, 228, 229, 250, 263, 295–7, 313
Time of the Tiger, 312
Times, The, 19, 268
Toohey, Peter, 229
Top 10s of Australian Test Cricket, 89
Toshack, Ernie, 60, 216
Treanor, Jack, 232
Trent Bridge, 21, 24, 46, 76, 94, 122, 133, 135, 157, 168, 176, 202, 211, 260, 283, 300
Trescothick, Marcus, 265, 300
Trott, Harry, 266, 290
Trueman, Fred, 23, 67, 123, 128, 131, 144, 157, 159, 160, 168–70, 176, 222, 228, 237, 249, 292, 294
Trumble, Hugh, 51, 80, 115, 226, 227, 235, 266–7, 291
Trumper, Victor, 18, 21, 40, 66, 71–3, 122, 137, 138, 146, 150, 156, 171, 175, 217, 225, 226, 227, 252, 260, 271, 272, 277, 291, 301
Turner, Alan, 250, 297
Turner, Charlie ('the Terror'), 62, 128, 219–21, 225, 266
Turner, Glenn, 56, 307

Tyson, Frank, 34, 50, 67, 129, 132, 160, 168, 170, 176, 178, 217, 295

U

Umrigar, Polly, 292
Underwood, Derek, 75, 206, 248, 312

V

Valentine, Alf, 66, 121
Valentine, Bryan, 152
Varma, Amit, 213
Vaughan, Michael, 300
Vengsarkar, Dilip, 86
Venkataraghavan, Srinivasaraghavan, 179, 205, 208
Verity, Hedley, 209, 293
Vettori, Daniel, 25
Viswanath, Gundappa, 84, 205
Voce, Bill, 160, 187, 210, 228, 284
Vogler, Ernie, 312

W

WACA, the, 50, 87, 110, 140, 184, 244
Wade, Herbie, 283
Walcott, Sir Clyde, 16, 24, 94, 104, 121–4, 157, 205, 276
Walker, Max, 202
Wall, Tim, 90, 151, 282
Walsh, Courtney, 25, 78, 84, 111, 139, 140, 153, 185, 263, 265, 278, 297
Walters, Doug, 16, 89, 190, 191, 198, 206, 216, 313–15
Wardle, Johnny, 200
Warne, Shane, 25–7, 39, 44, 73, 77, 78, 81, 92, 111, 135, 138, 166, 193, 195, 206, 207, 212, 228, 254, 255, 264, 279, 299, 308
Warner, Sir Pelham, 147, 175, 197, 227, 236, 260, 267, 288
Warwick Armstrong's Australians, 151
Wass, Tom, 175
Watson, Chester, 222, 223

Index

Waugh, Mark, 89, 134, 140, 195
Waugh, Steve, 16, 37, 41, 42, 43, 44, 59, 77, 81, 89, 104, 111, 127, 134–6, 140, 153, 154, 155, 186, 193, 195, 198, 213, 234, 243, 244, 245, 255, 256, 258, 279, 287, 305, 307, 314
Weekes, Everton, 93, 104, 120, 121–4, 157, 276
Wessels, Kepler, 96
Whitington, RS, 45, 114, 203, 217, 234, 312
Whitney, Mike, 127
Wilde, Simon, 162
The Wildest Tests, 223
Wilkins, Phil, 296
Willis, Bob, 53, 84, 199, 241, 295
Willow Patterns, 234
Wood, Harry, 209
Woodcock, John, 19, 268
Woodfull, Bill, 66, 91, 187, 188, 189
Wooldridge, Ian, 150
Woolley, Frank, 18, 150–2, 260, 312
Worrell, Sir Frank, 28, 93–5, 104, 123, 124, 139, 157, 166, 168, 170, 287
Wright, Doug, 66
Wyatt, Bob, 189
Yardley, Norman, 261

Y

Younis, Waqar, 25, 28, 37, 43, 68, 97, 99, 134, 185, 228, 257–9, 263